JACK

The Amityville

FROST

JINHO KO

5

Jack Frost

The Amityville

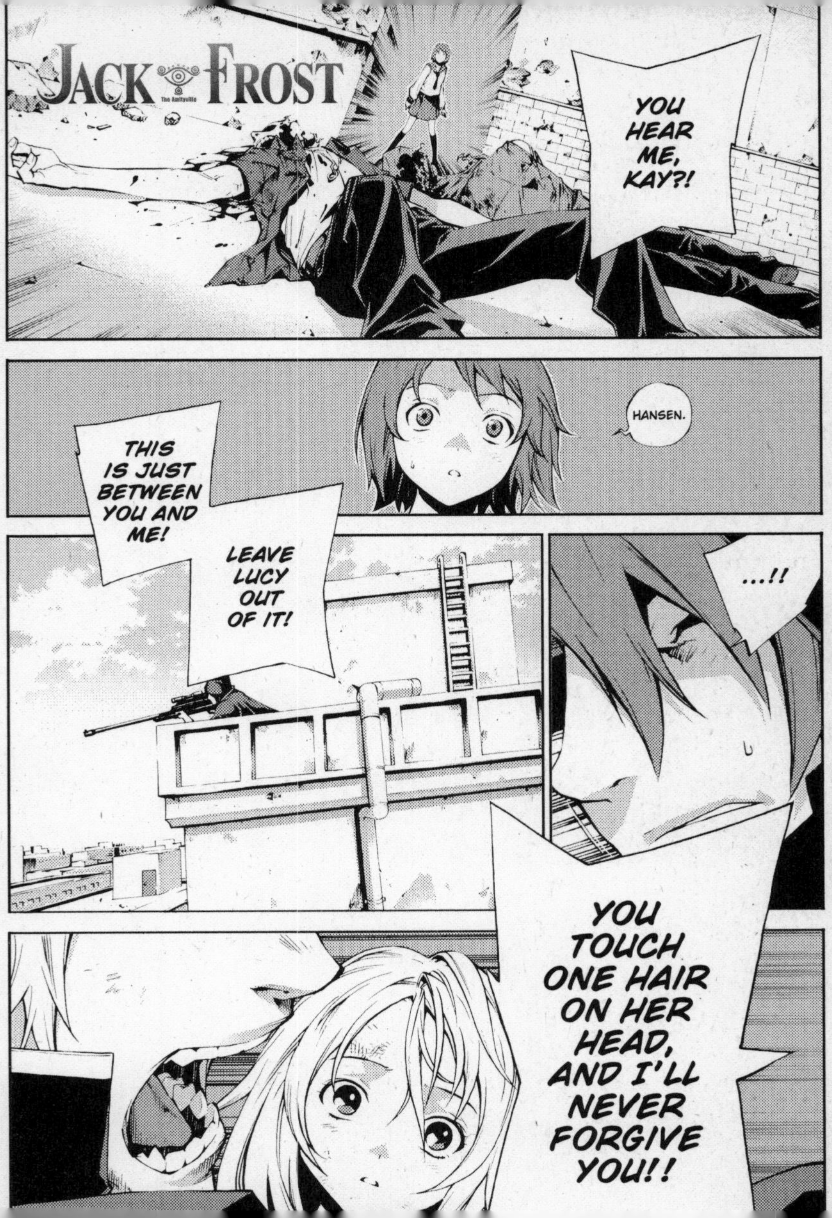
JACK FROST
The Amityville
YOU HEAR ME, KAY?!
HANSEN.
THIS IS JUST BETWEEN YOU AND ME!
LEAVE LUCY OUT OF IT!
...!!
YOU TOUCH ONE HAIR ON HER HEAD, AND I'LL NEVER FORGIVE YOU!!

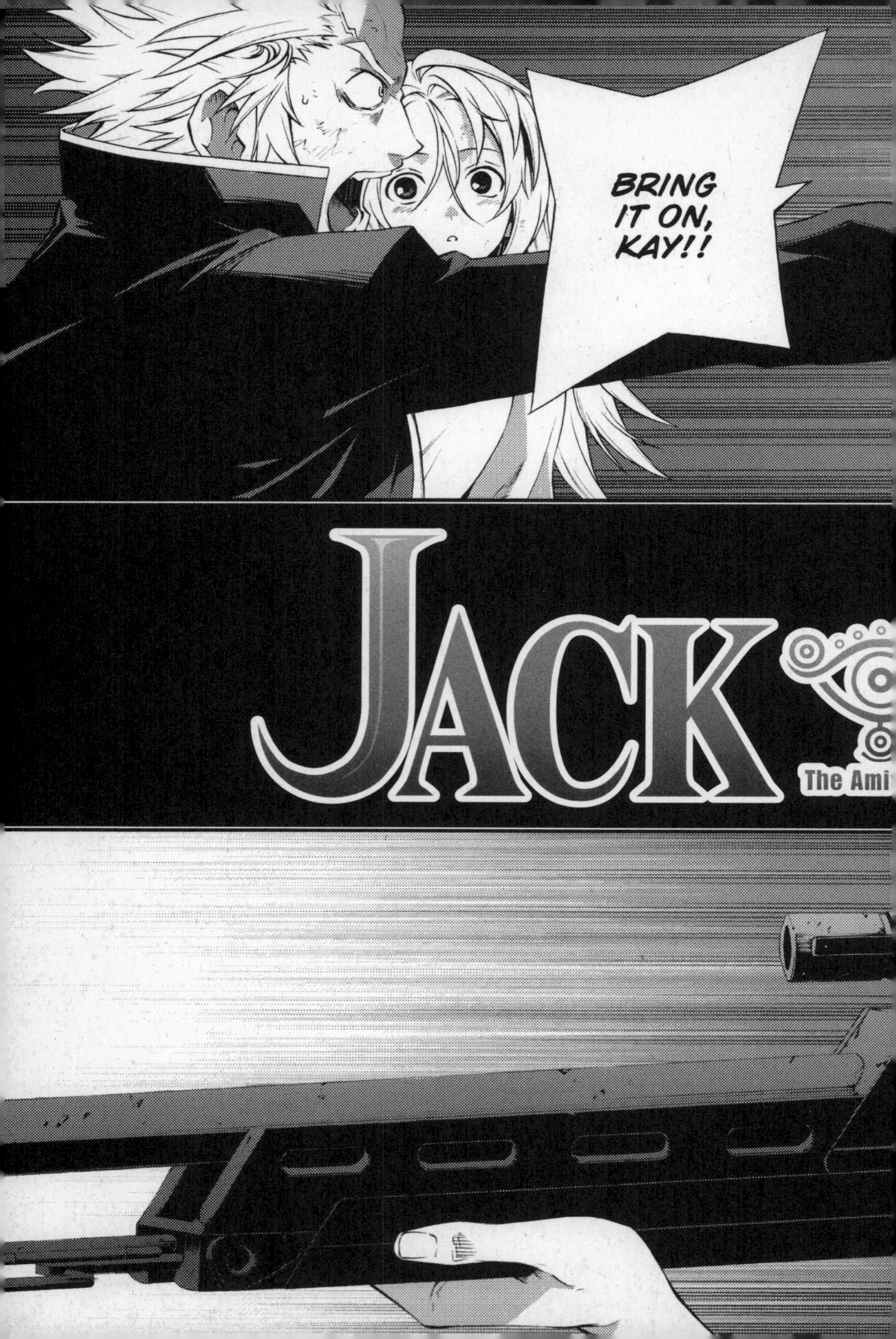
BRING IT ON, KAY!!
JACK
The Ami

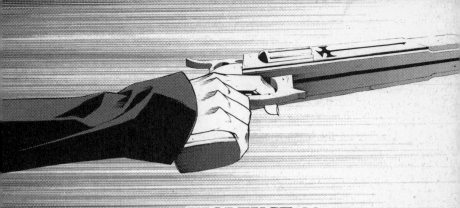

VIOLENCE 30.
DER FREISCHÜTZ – PART V

FROST

TCH...!

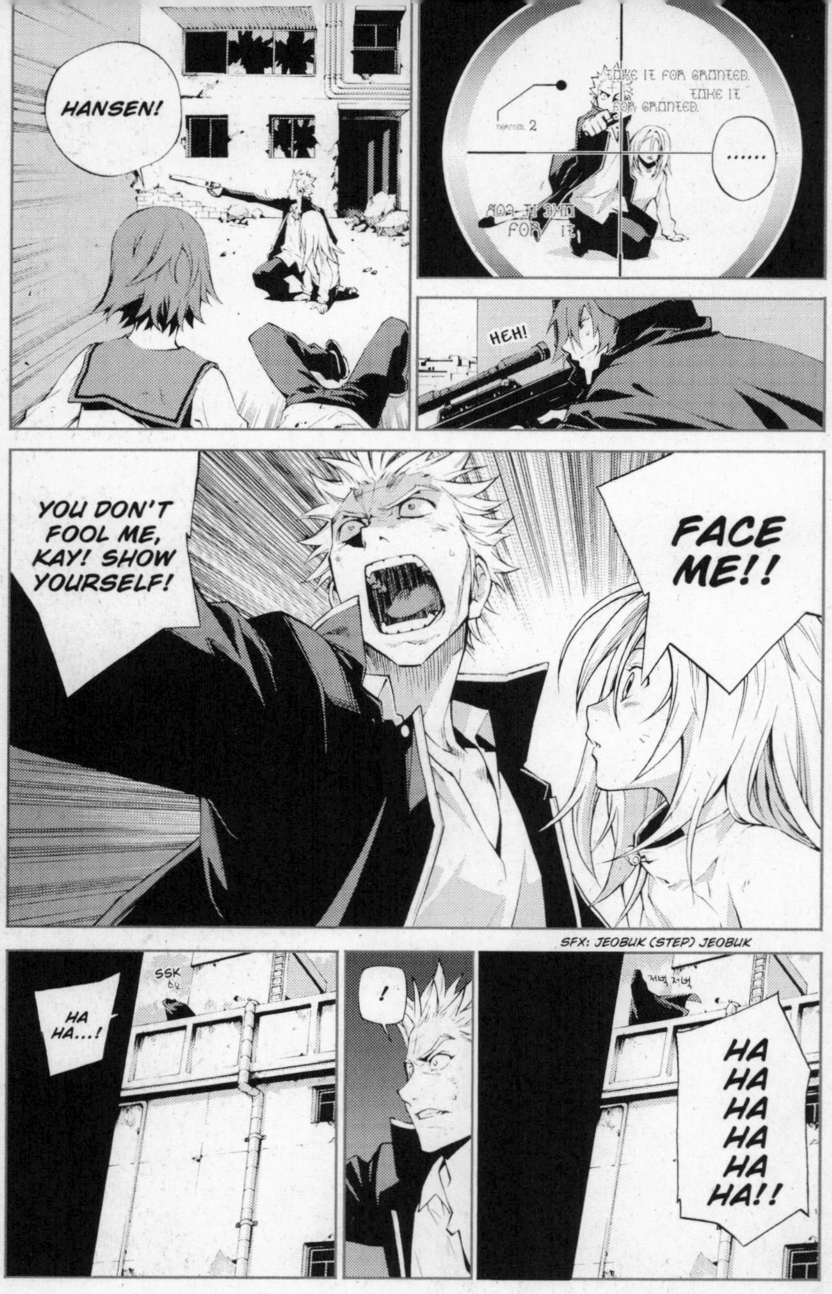
HANSEN!
TAKE IT FOR GRANTED.
TAKE IT FOR GRANTED.
......
HEH!
YOU DON'T FOOL ME, KAY! SHOW YOURSELF!
FACE ME!!
SFX: JEOBUK (STEP) JEOBUK
SSK
HA HA...!
!
HA HA HA HA HA HA!!

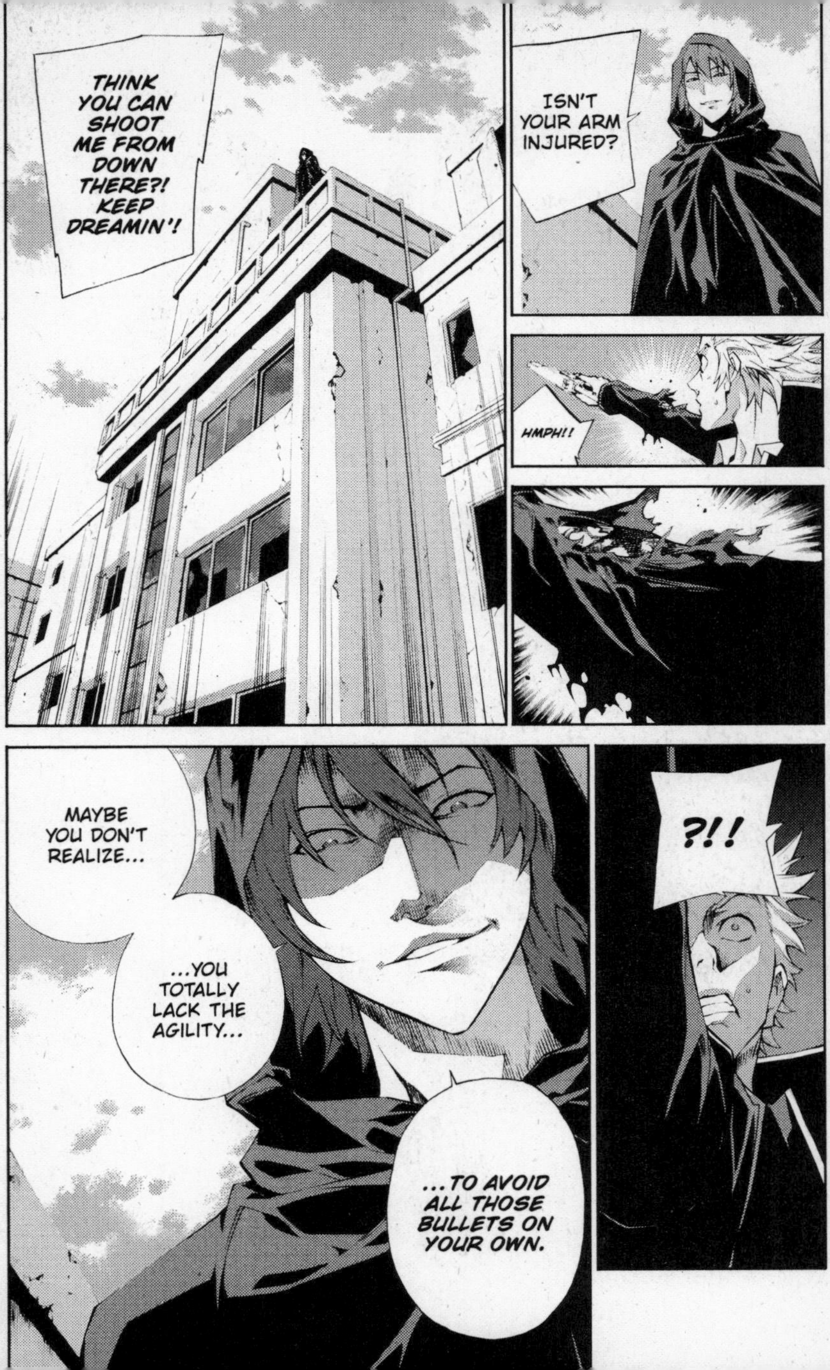
THINK YOU CAN SHOOT ME FROM DOWN THERE?! KEEP DREAMIN'!
ISN'T YOUR ARM INJURED?
HMPH!!
MAYBE YOU DON'T REALIZE...
...YOU TOTALLY LACK THE AGILITY...
...TO AVOID ALL THOSE BULLETS ON YOUR OWN.
?!!

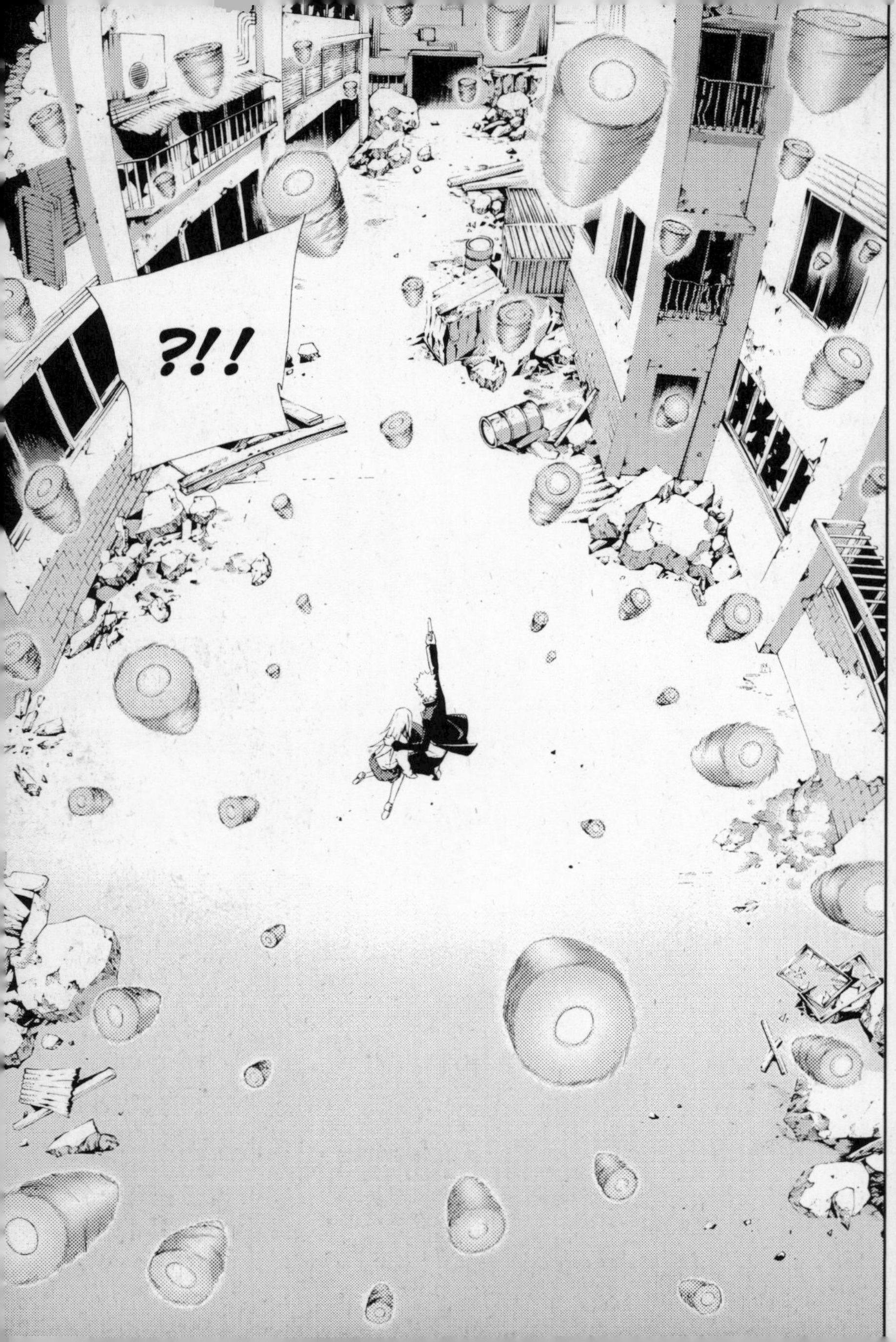
?!!

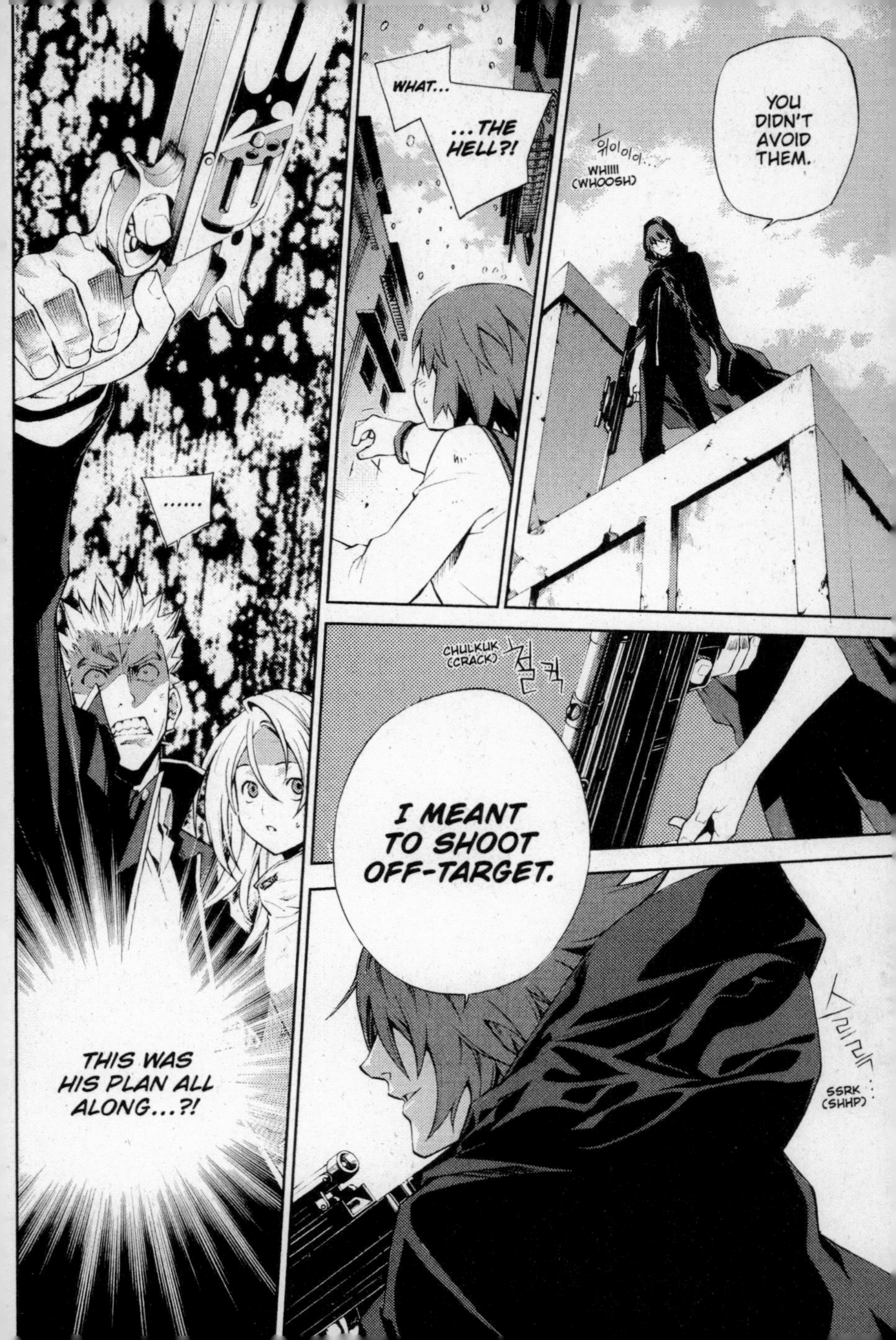

......
THIS WAS HIS PLAN ALL ALONG...?!
WHAT...
...THE HELL?!
WHIIII (WHOOSH)
YOU DIDN'T AVOID THEM.
CHULKUK (CRACK)
I MEANT TO SHOOT OFF-TARGET.
SSRK (SHHP)

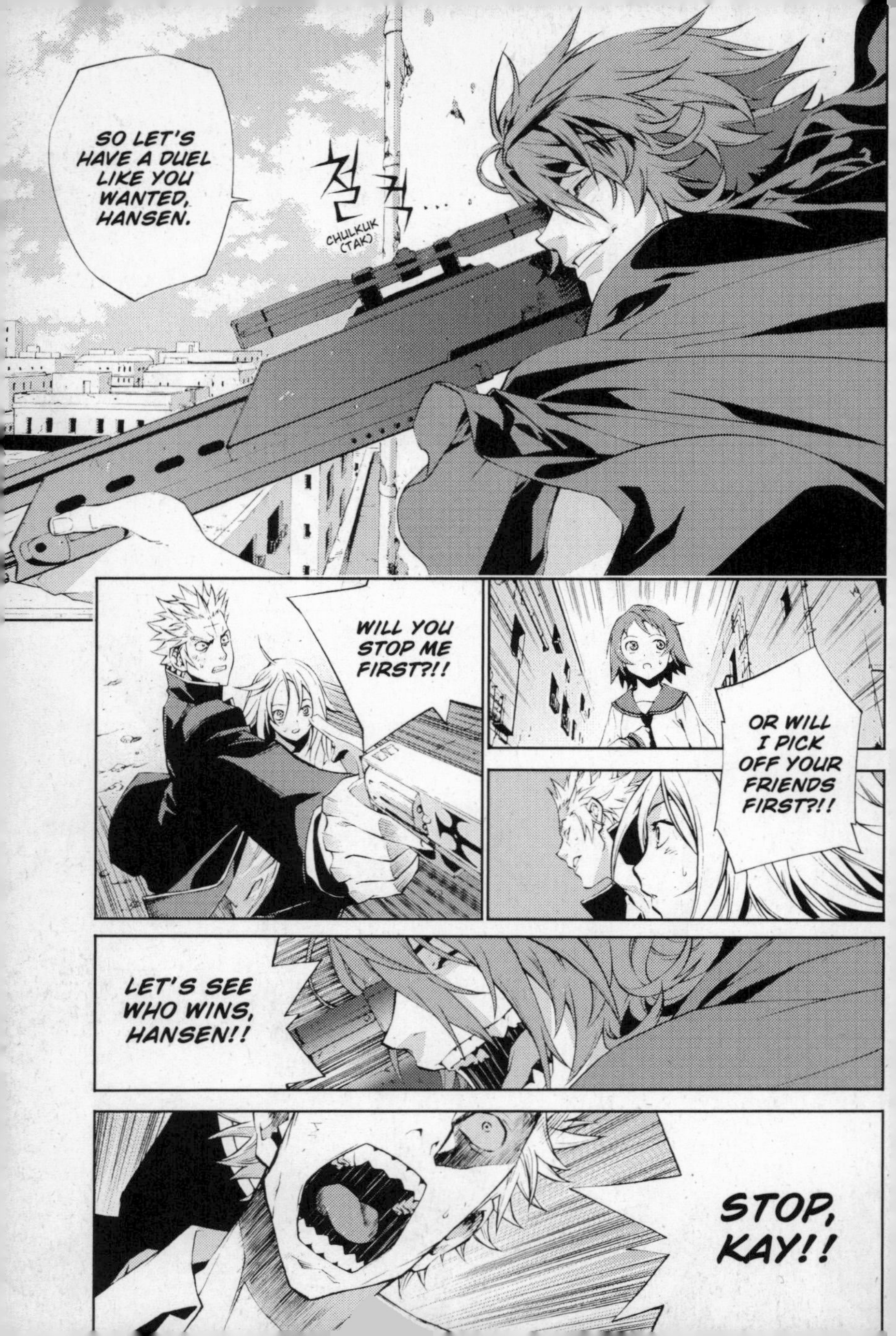
SO LET'S HAVE A DUEL LIKE YOU WANTED, HANSEN.
철컥...
CHULKUK (TAK)
WILL YOU STOP ME FIRST?!!
OR WILL I PICK OFF YOUR FRIENDS FIRST?!!
LET'S SEE WHO WINS, HANSEN!!
STOP, KAY!!

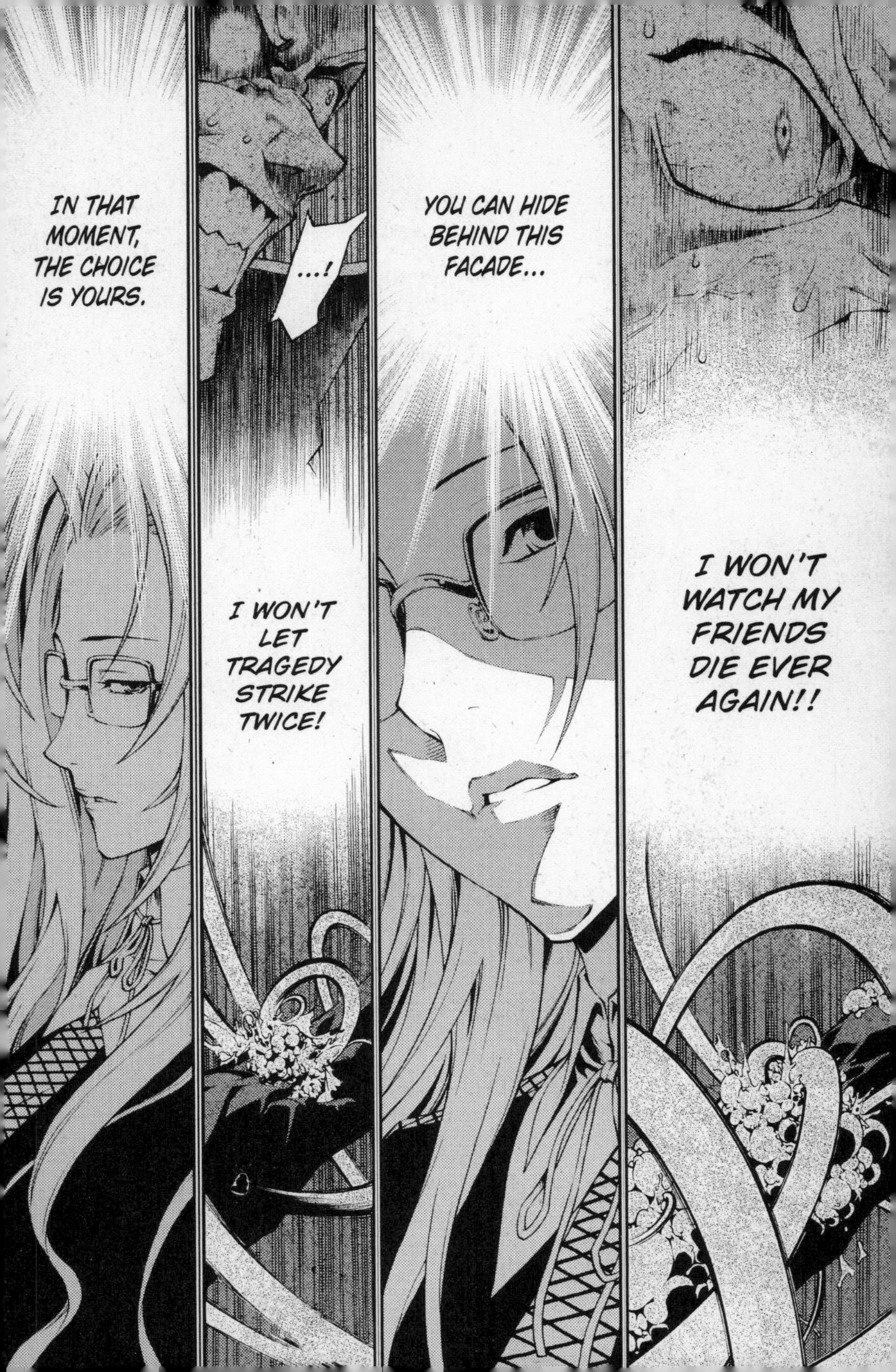
IN THAT MOMENT, THE CHOICE IS YOURS.
...!
I WON'T LET TRAGEDY STRIKE TWICE!
YOU CAN HIDE BEHIND THIS FACADE...
I WON'T WATCH MY FRIENDS DIE EVER AGAIN!!

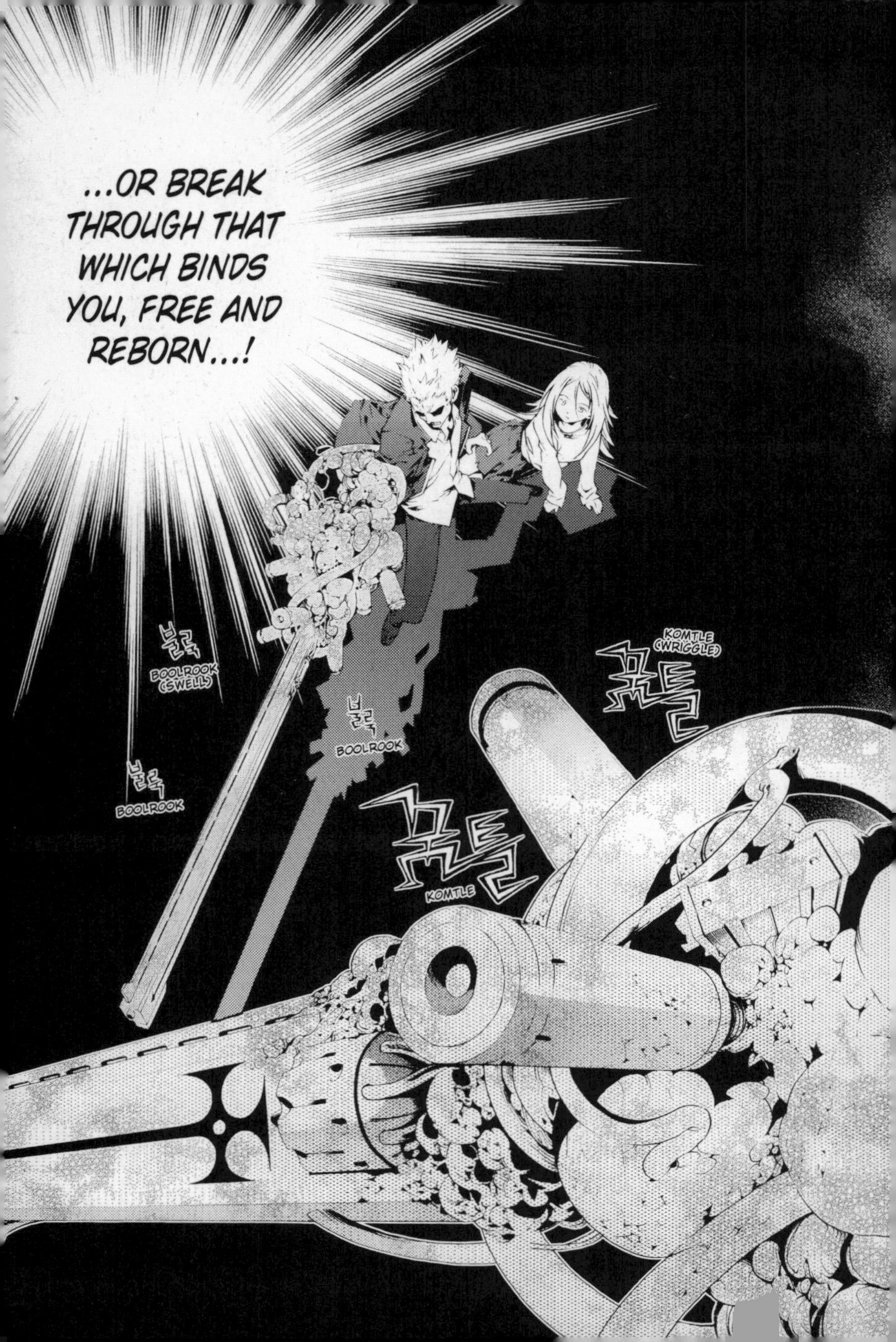
...OR BREAK THROUGH THAT WHICH BINDS YOU, FREE AND REBORN...!
블룩
BOOLROOK (SWELL)
블룩
BOOLROOK
블룩
BOOLROOK
꼼틀
KOMTLE (WRIGGLE)
꼼틀
KOMTLE

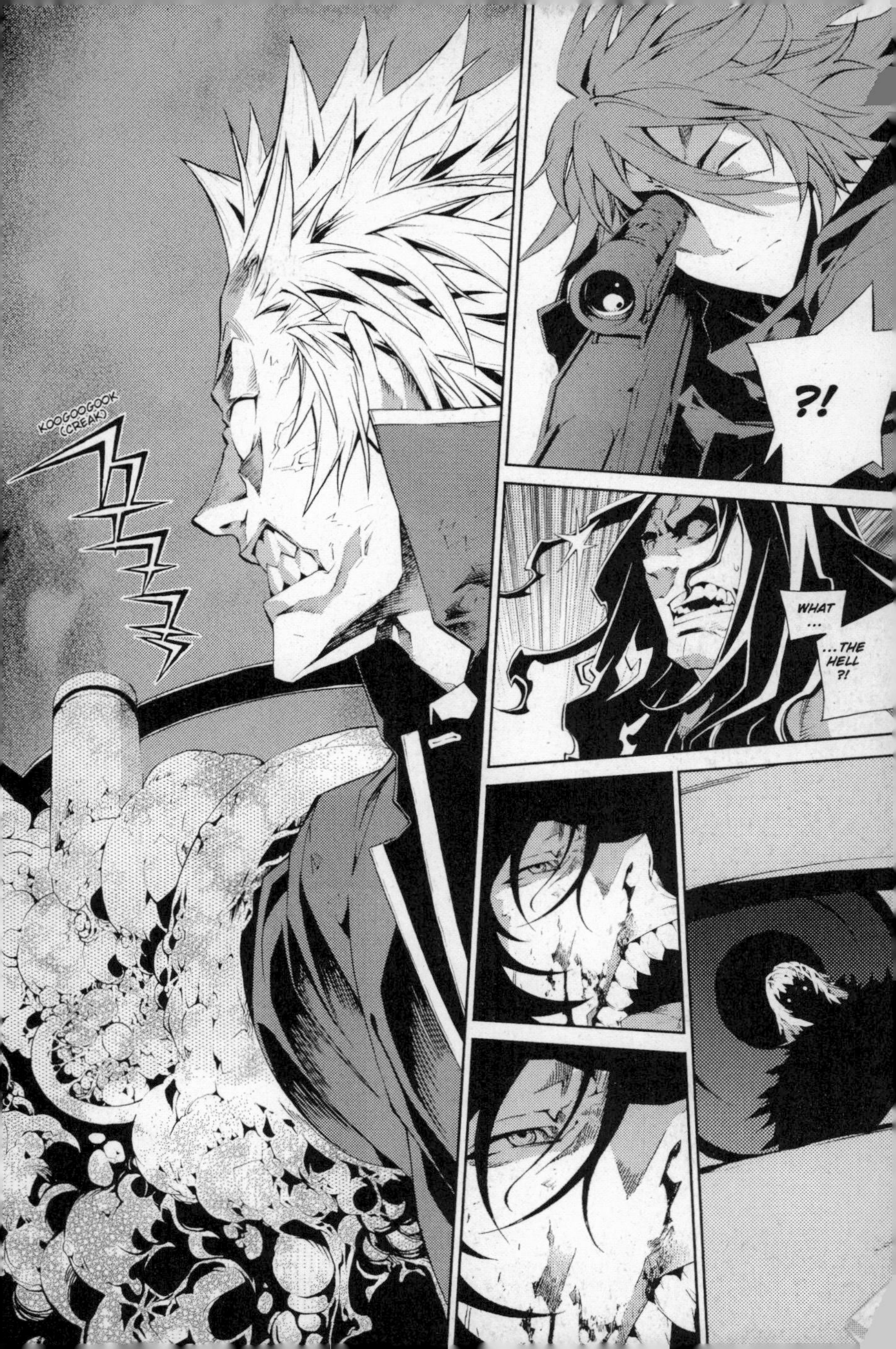
KOOGOOGOOK (CREAK)
?!
WHAT ...
...THE HELL ?!

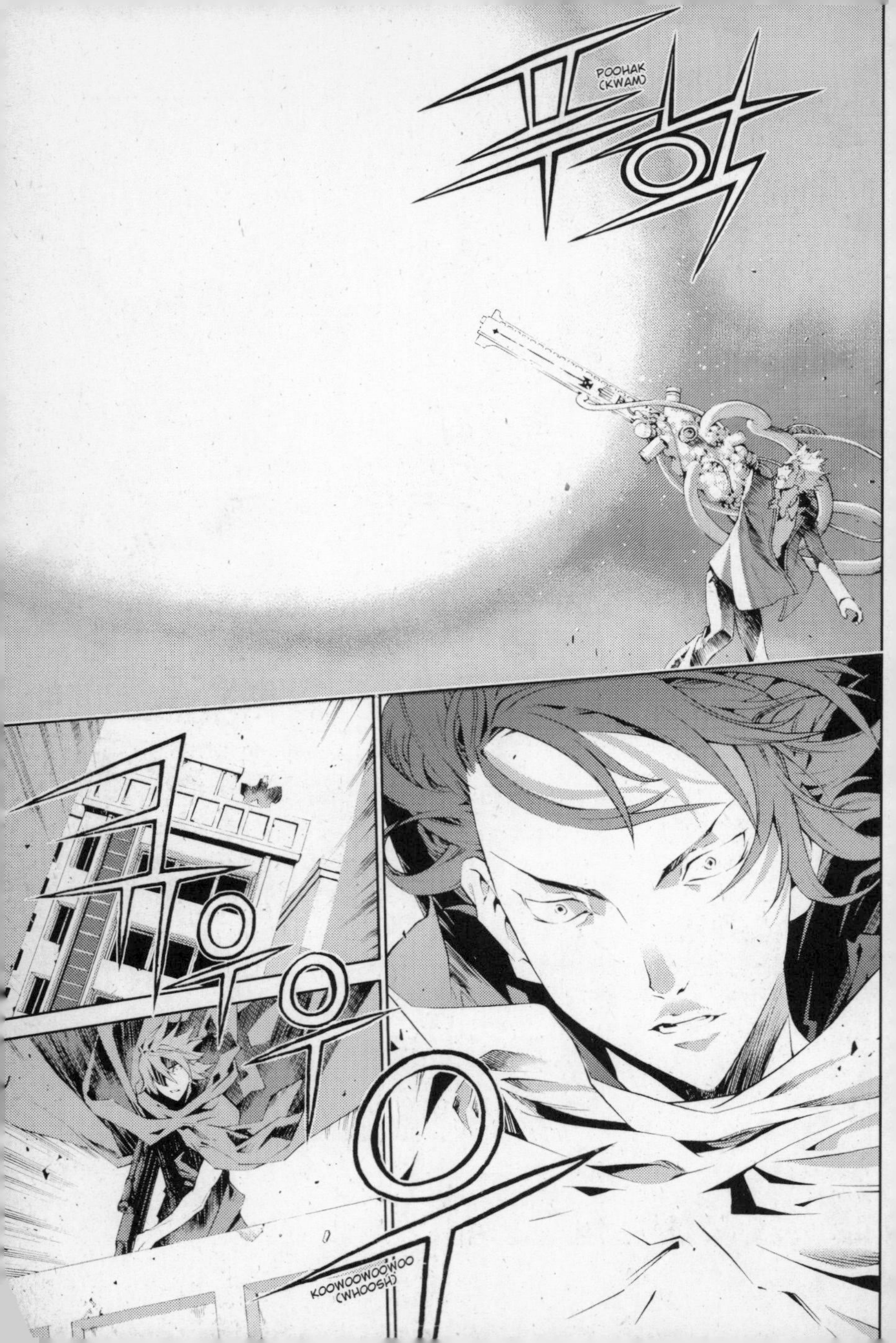

파학
POOHAK
(KWAM)
KOOWOOWOOWOO
(WHOOSH)

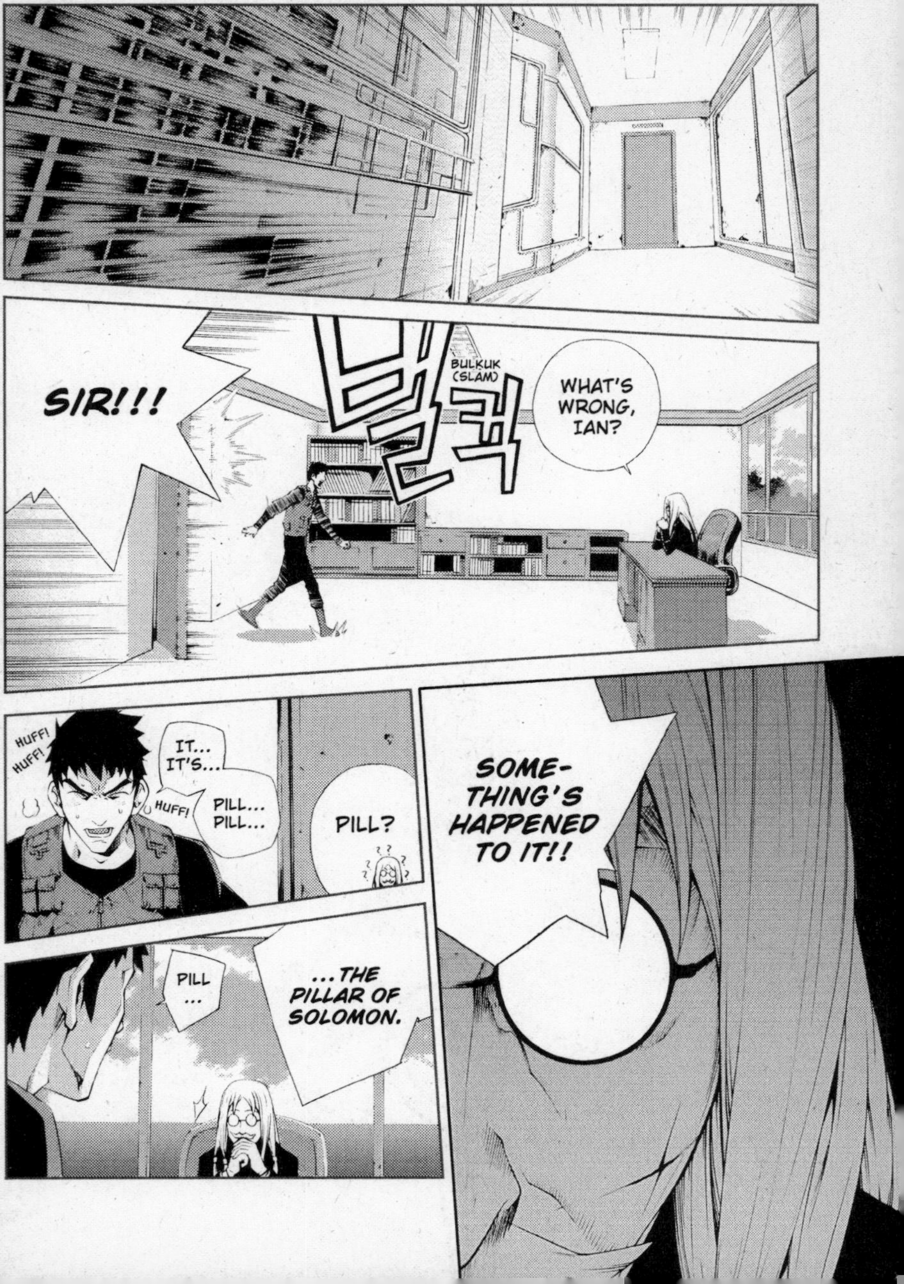
SIR!!!
벌컥
BULKUK (SLAM)
WHAT'S WRONG, IAN?
HUFF! HUFF!
IT... IT'S...
HUFF!
PILL... PILL...
PILL?
? ? ? ?
PILL ...
...THE PILLAR OF SOLOMON.
SOME-THING'S HAPPENED TO IT!!

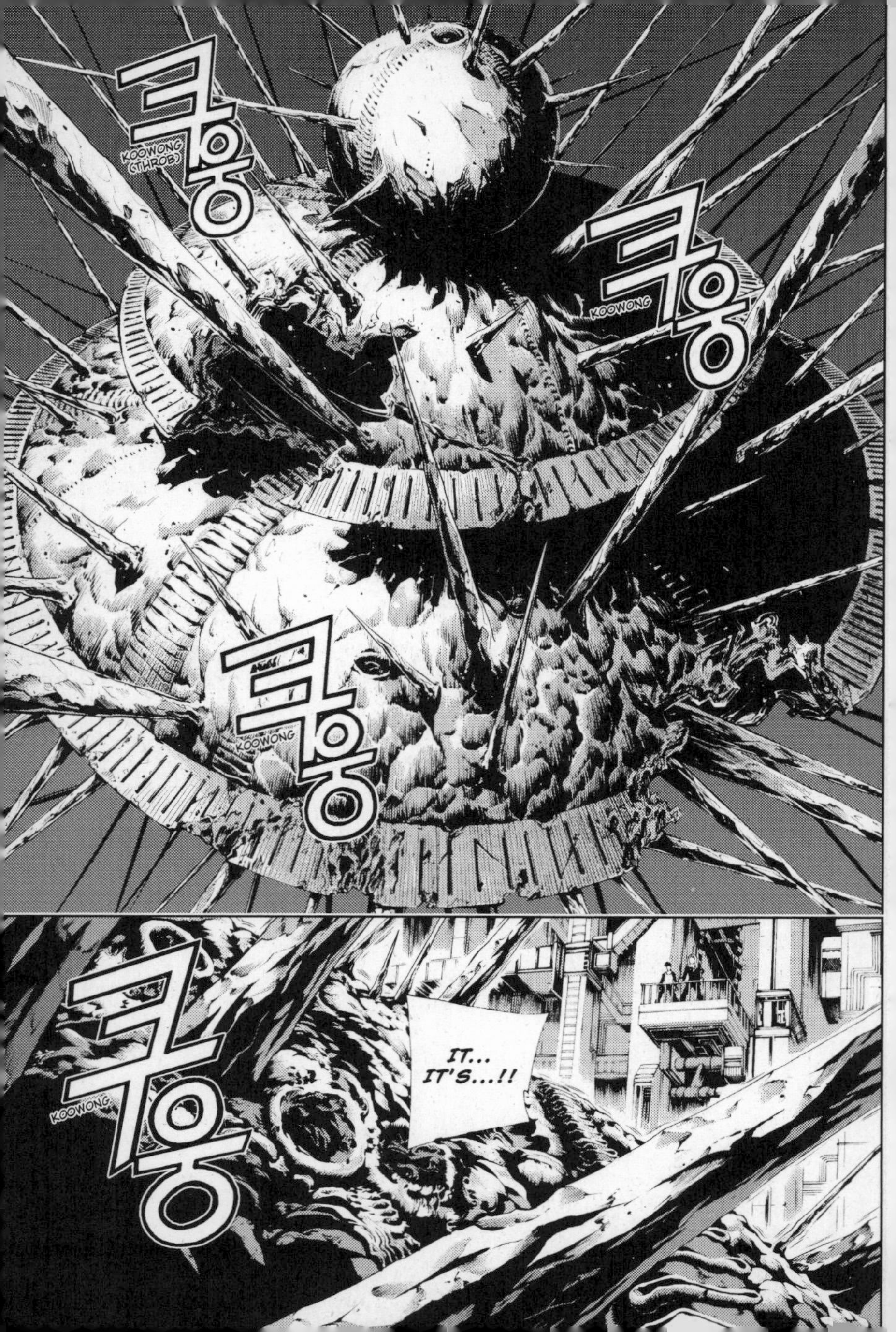
KOOWONG (THROB)
KOOWONG
KOOWONG
KOOWONG
IT... IT'S...!!

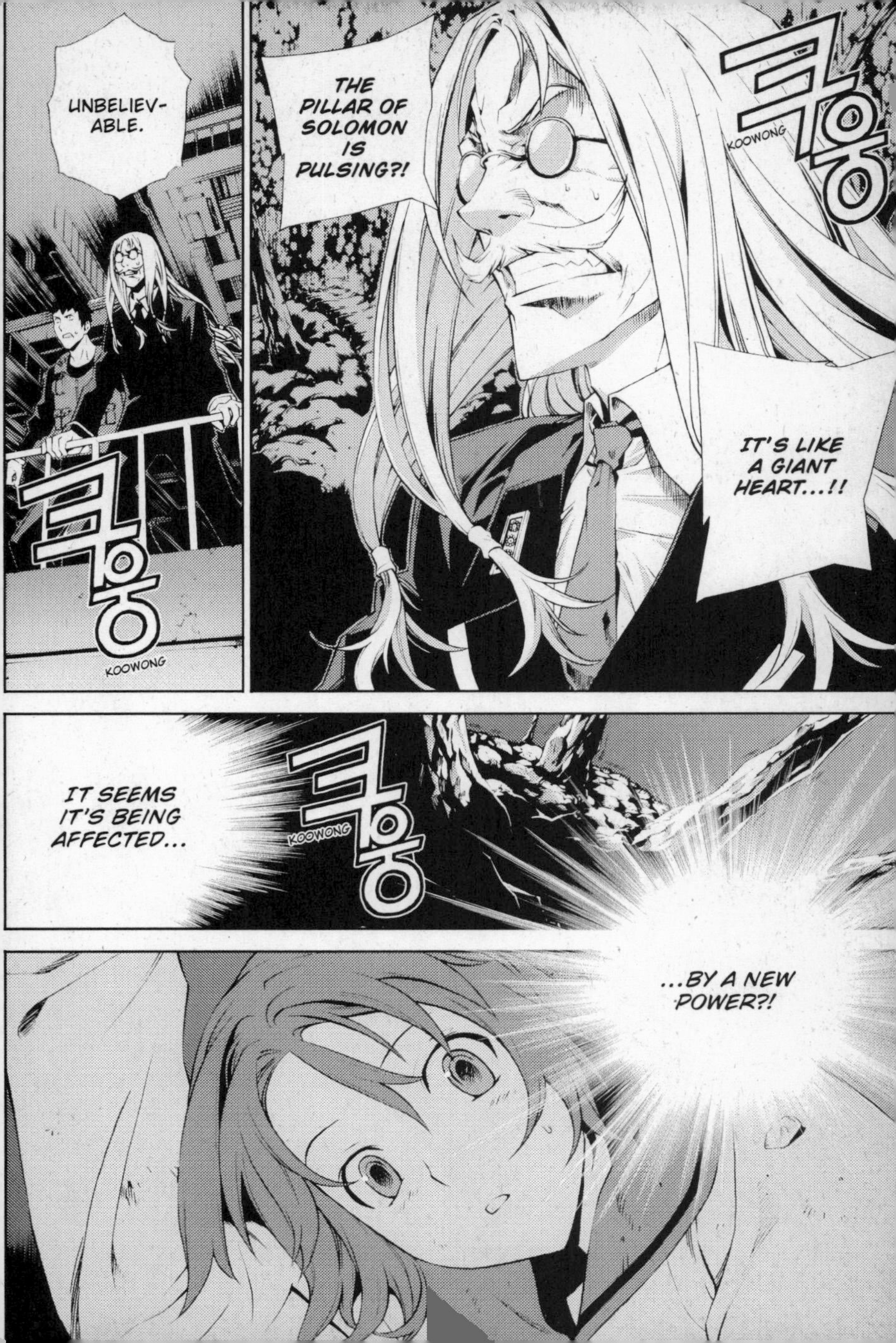
UNBELIEV-
ABLE.
크웅
KOOWONG
THE PILLAR OF SOLOMON IS PULSING?!
크웅
KOOWONG
IT'S LIKE A GIANT HEART...!!
IT SEEMS IT'S BEING AFFECTED...
크웅
KOOWONG
...BY A NEW POWER?!

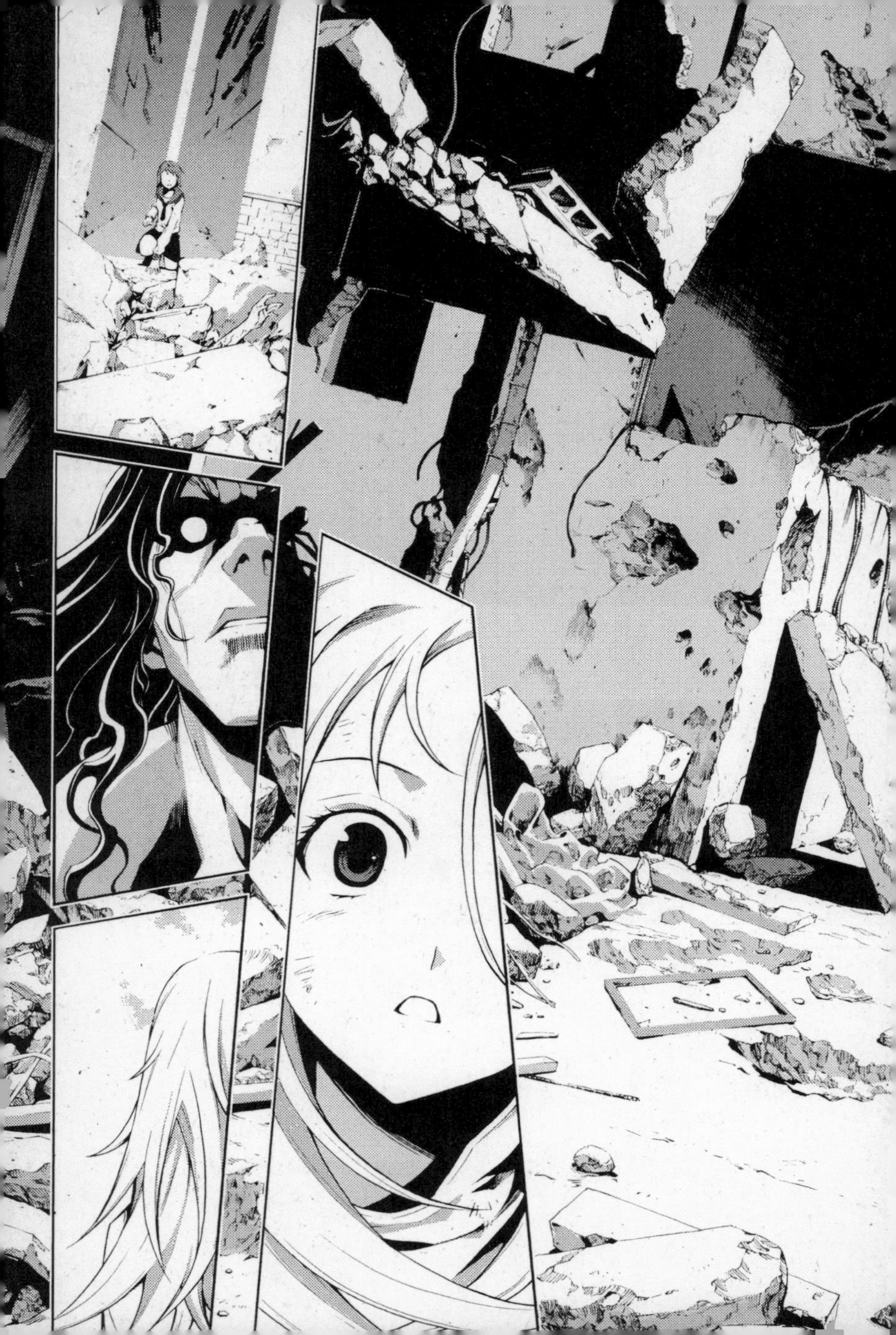

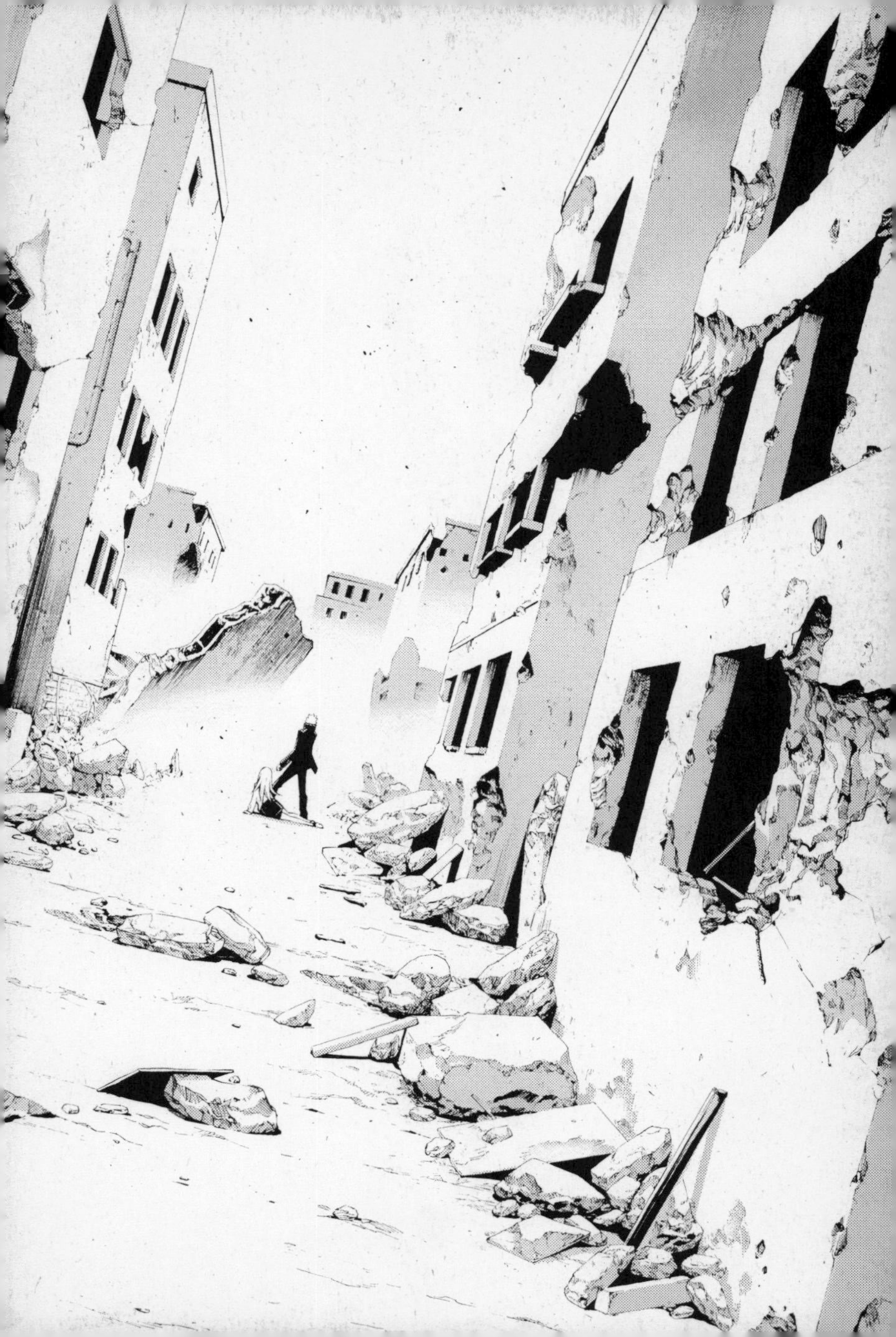

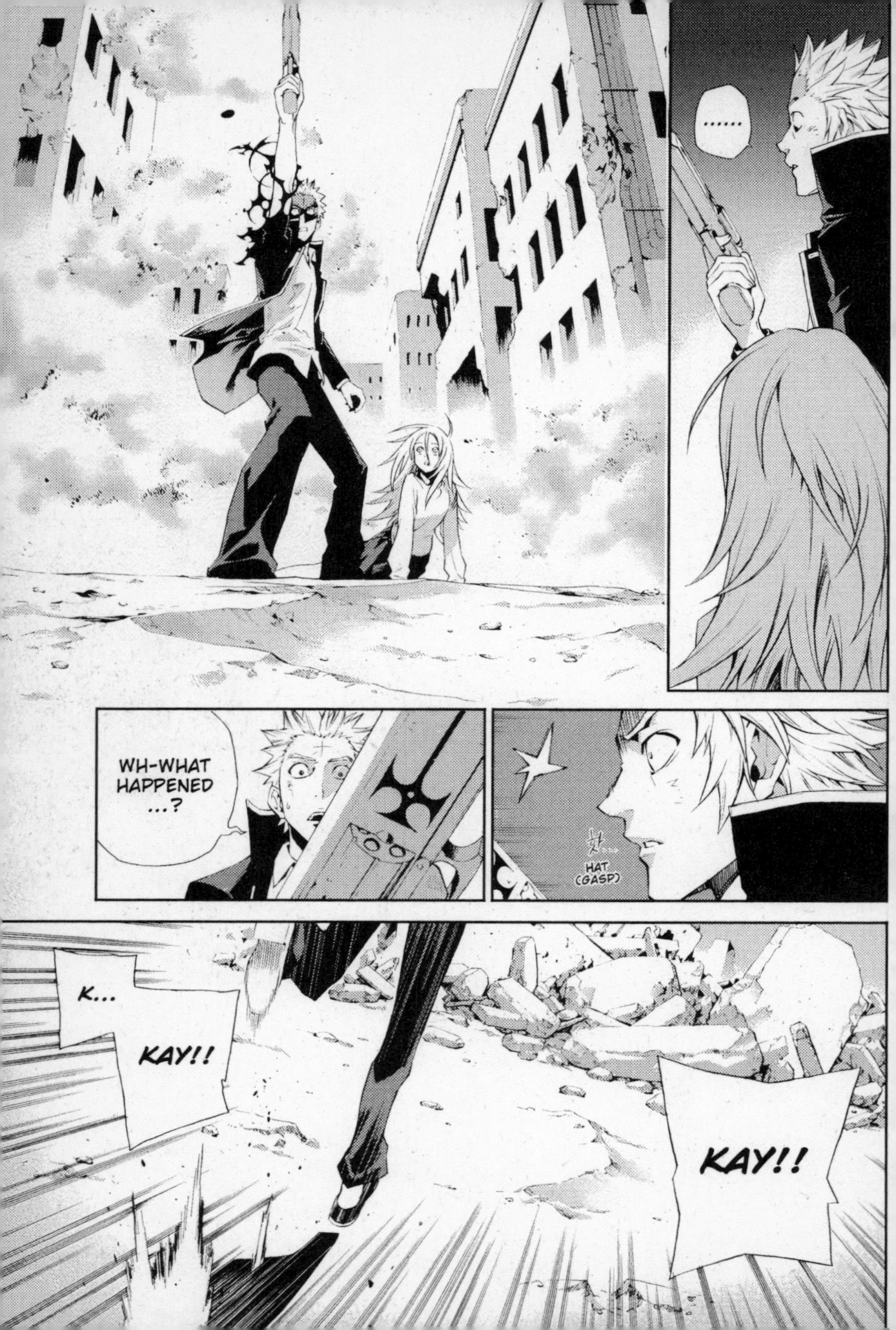
......
WH-WHAT HAPPENED ...?
핫
HAT (GASP)
K...
KAY!!
KAY!!

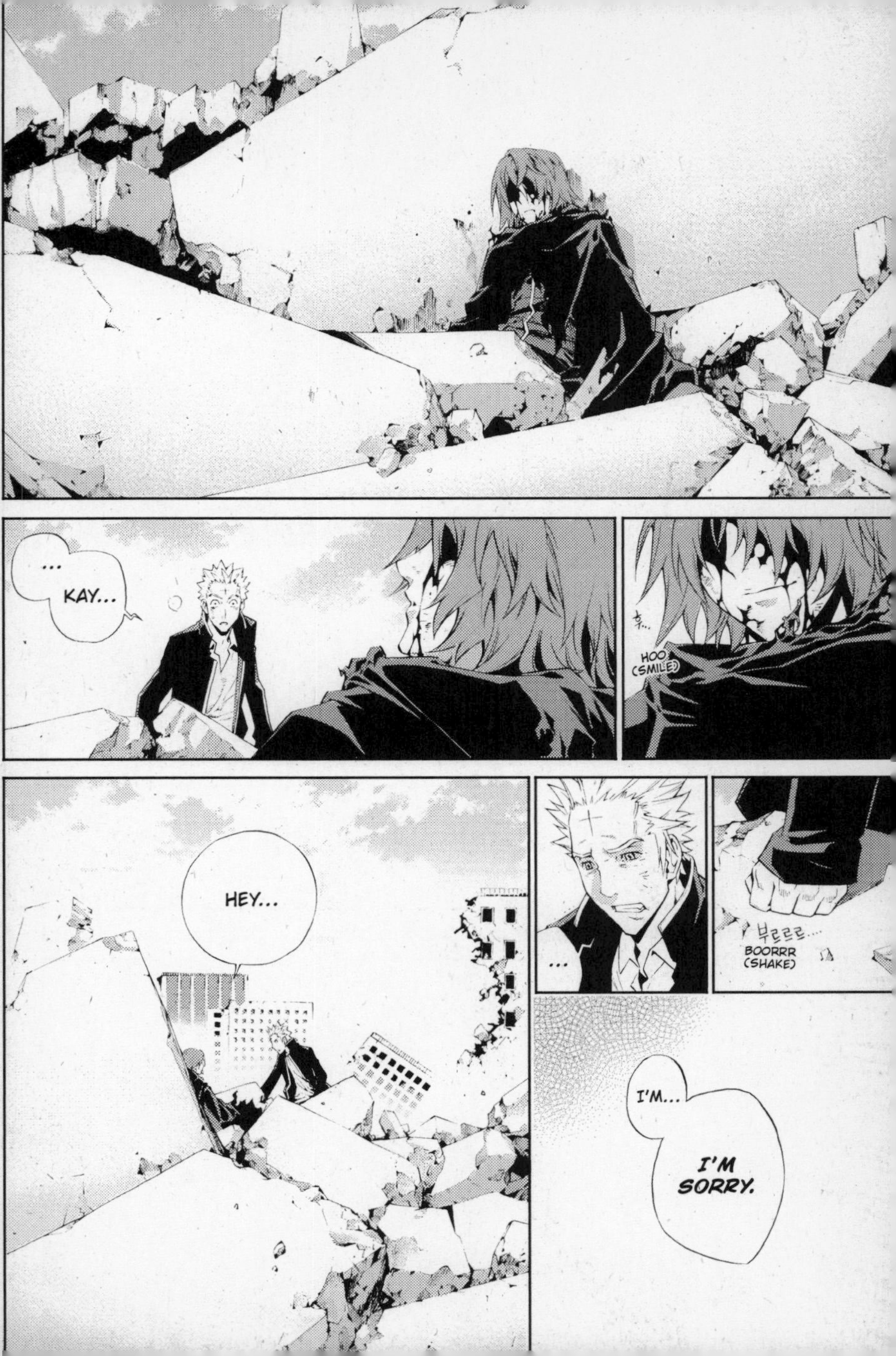
... KAY...
후...
HOO (SMILE)
HEY...
...
부르르르....
BOORRR (SHAKE)
I'M...
I'M SORRY.

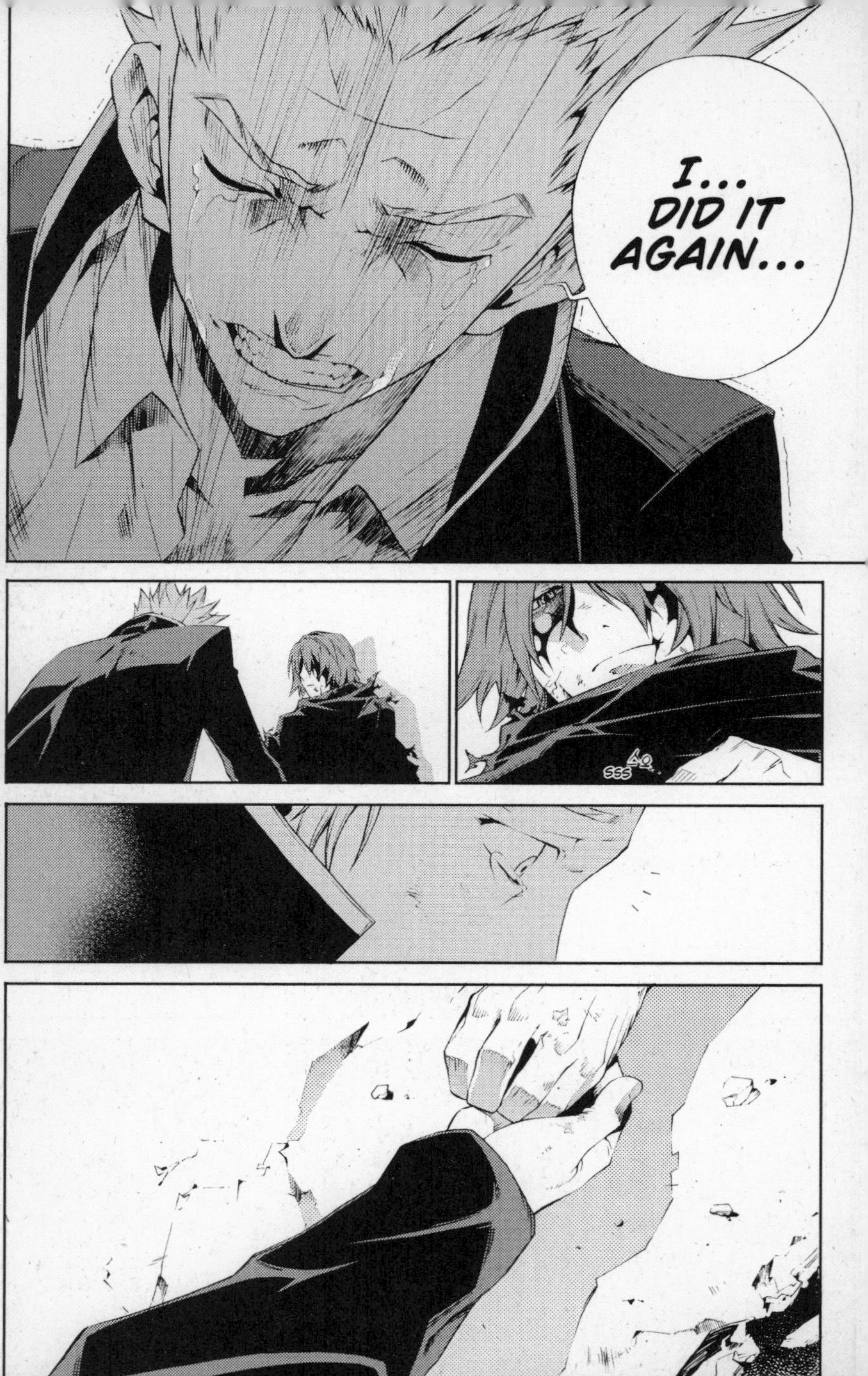
I... DID IT AGAIN...
SSS

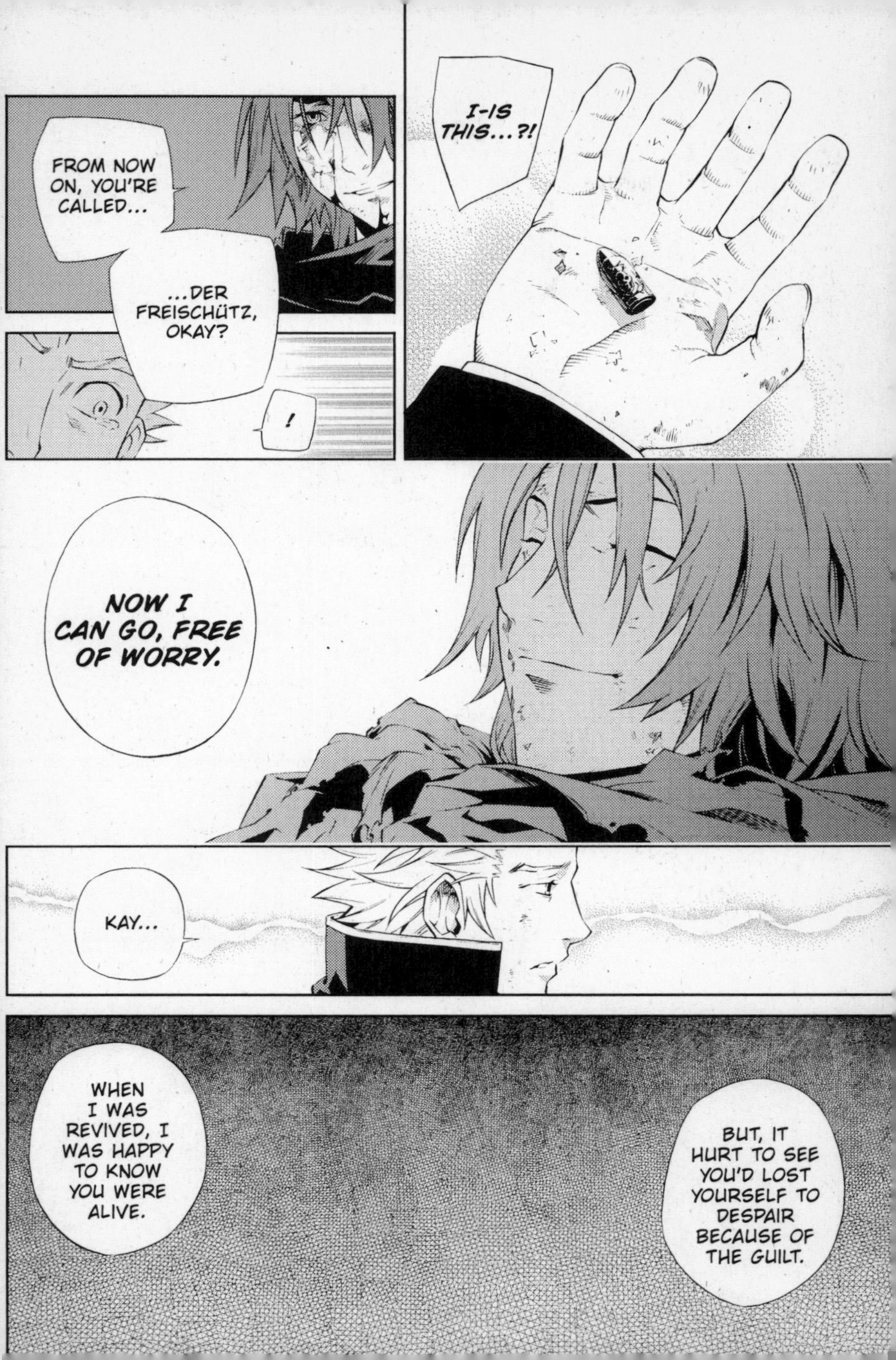
FROM NOW ON, YOU'RE CALLED...
...DER FREISCHÜTZ, OKAY?
!
I-IS THIS...?!
NOW I CAN GO, FREE OF WORRY.
KAY...
WHEN I WAS REVIVED, I WAS HAPPY TO KNOW YOU WERE ALIVE.
BUT, IT HURT TO SEE YOU'D LOST YOURSELF TO DESPAIR BECAUSE OF THE GUILT.

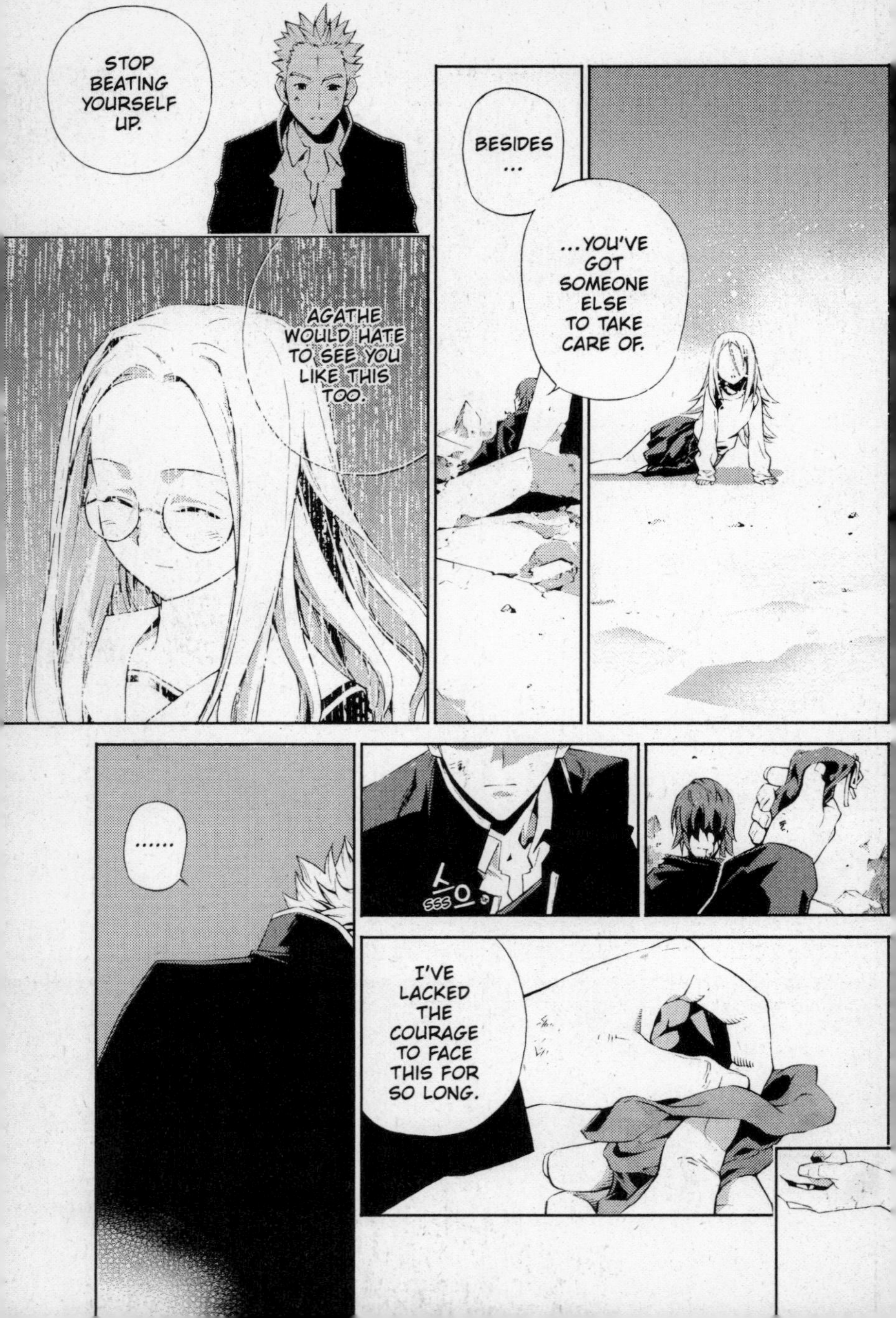
STOP BEATING YOURSELF UP.
AGATHE WOULD HATE TO SEE YOU LIKE THIS TOO.
BESIDES...
...YOU'VE GOT SOMEONE ELSE TO TAKE CARE OF.
......
SSS
I'VE LACKED THE COURAGE TO FACE THIS FOR SO LONG.

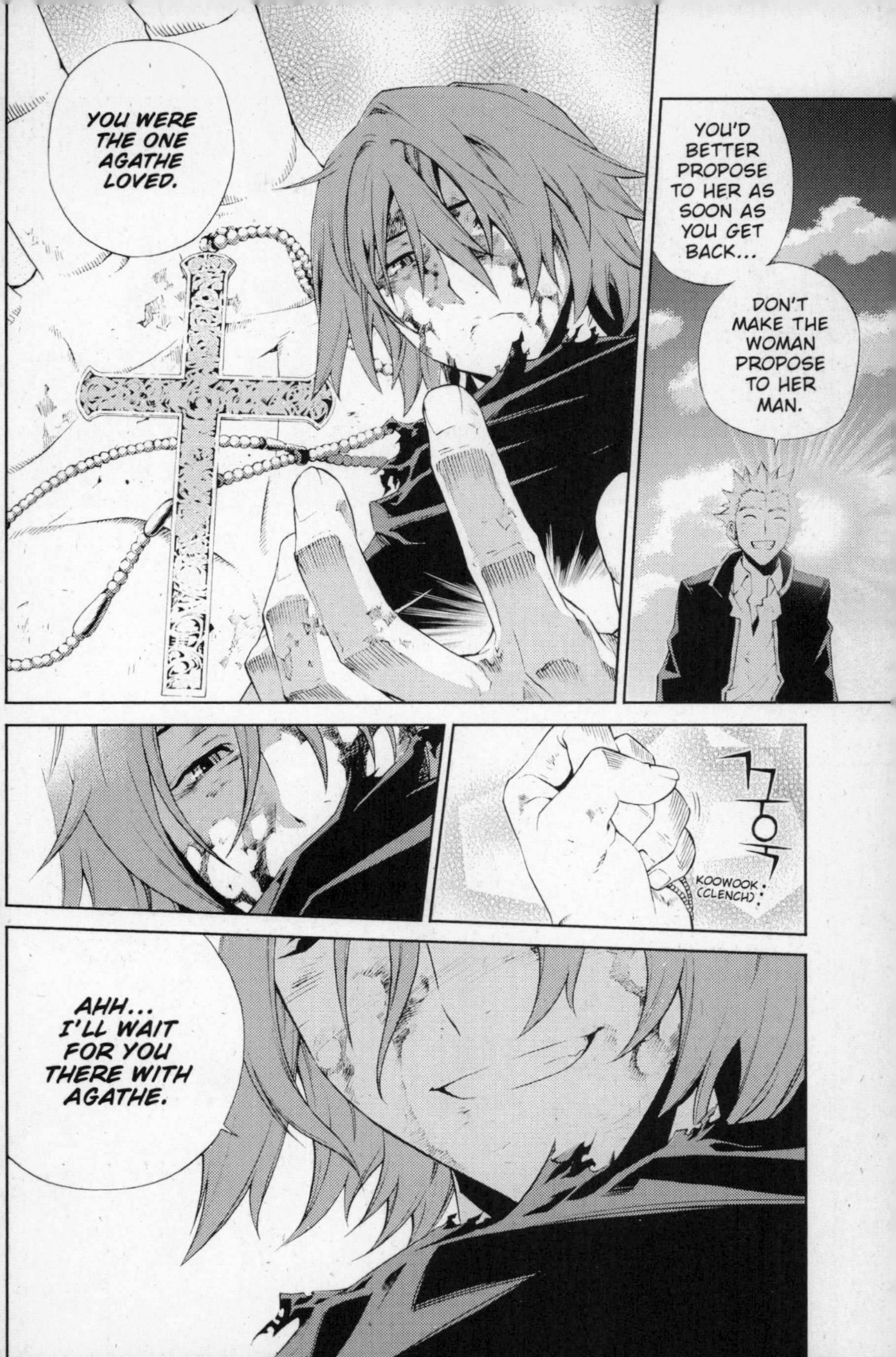
YOU WERE THE ONE AGATHE LOVED.
YOU'D BETTER PROPOSE TO HER AS SOON AS YOU GET BACK...
DON'T MAKE THE WOMAN PROPOSE TO HER MAN.
KOOWOOK (CLENCH)
AHH... I'LL WAIT FOR YOU THERE WITH AGATHE.

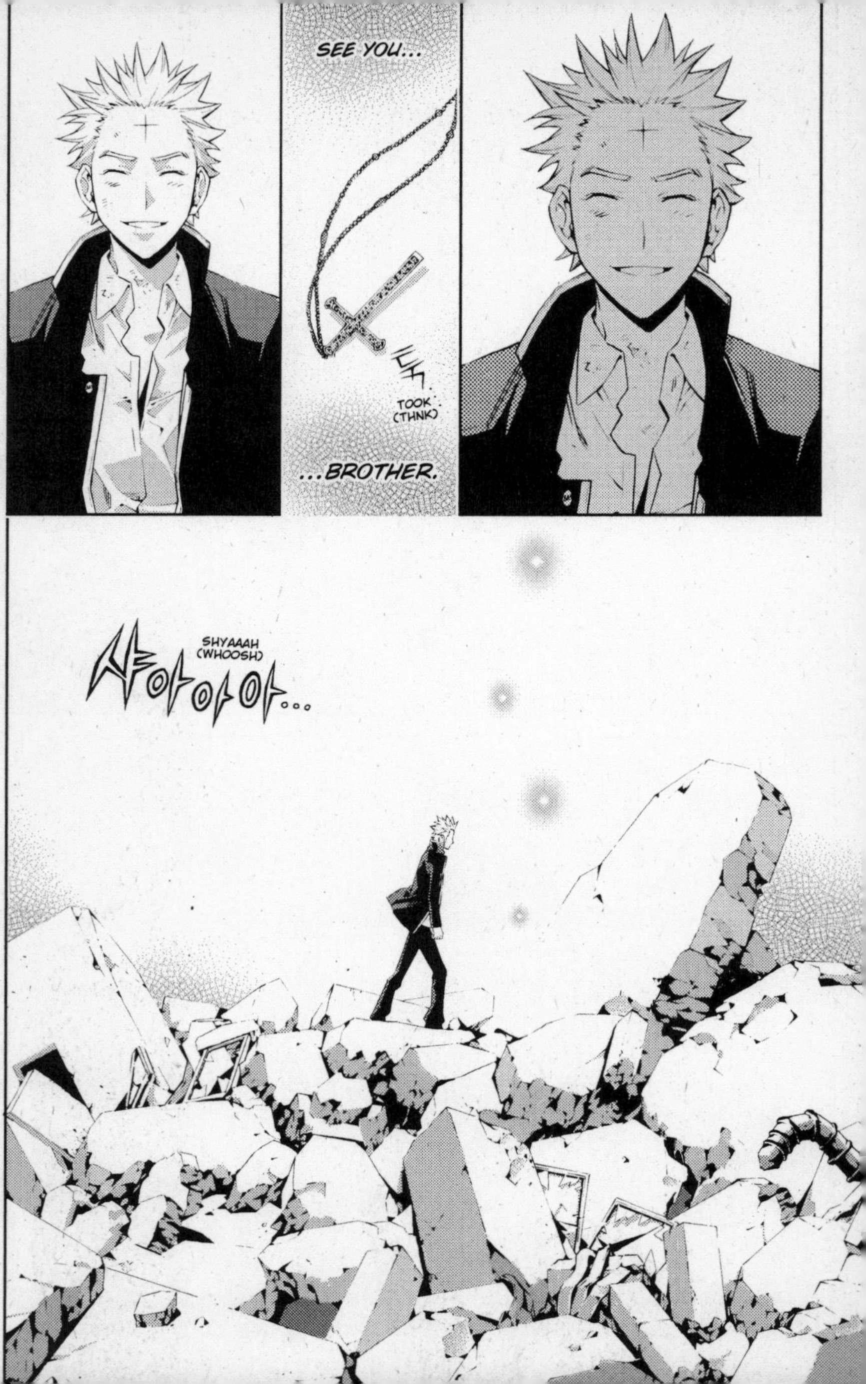
SEE YOU...
TOOK (THNK)
...BROTHER.
SHYAAAH (WHOOSH)

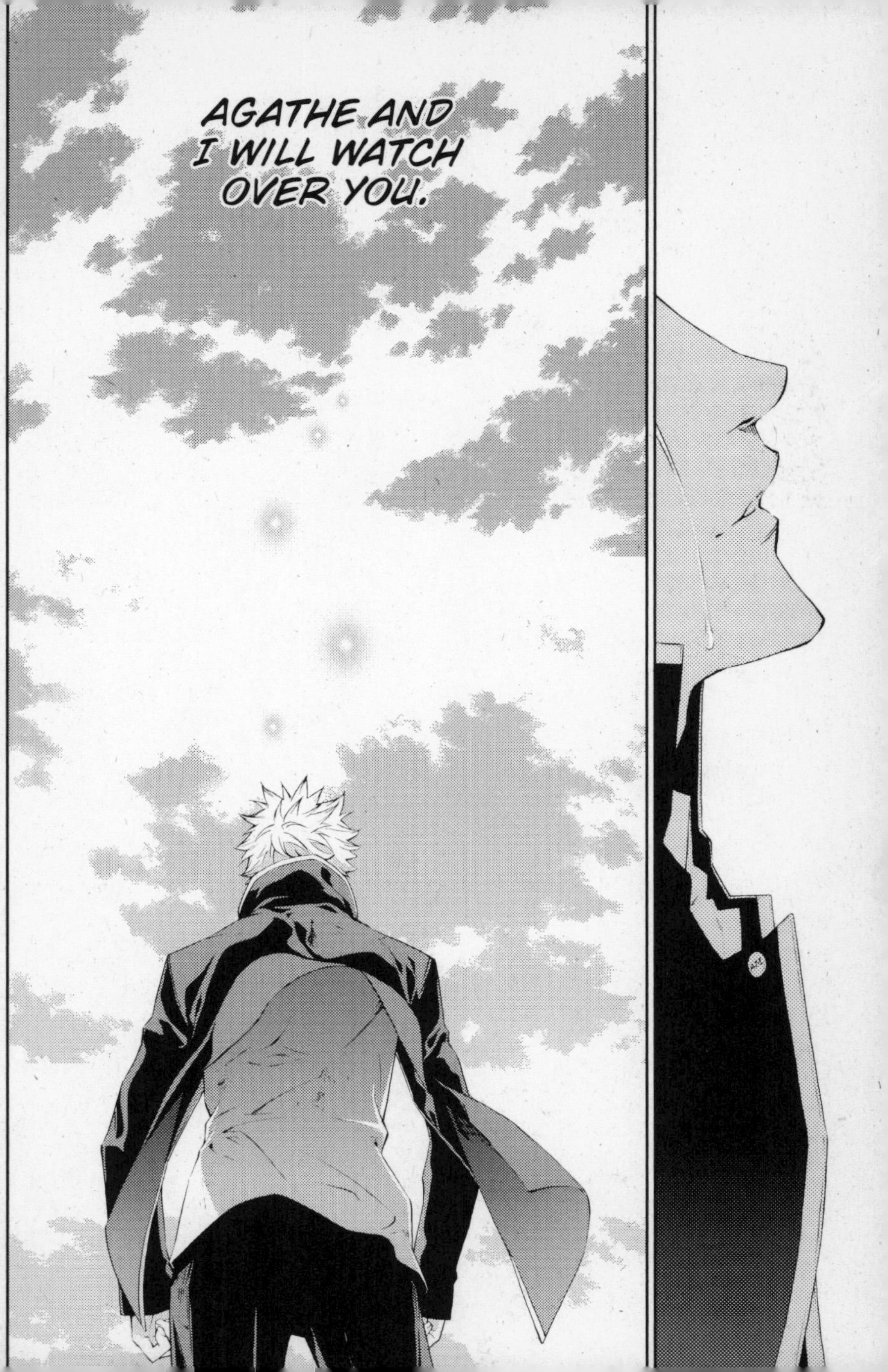
AGATHE AND
I WILL WATCH
OVER YOU.

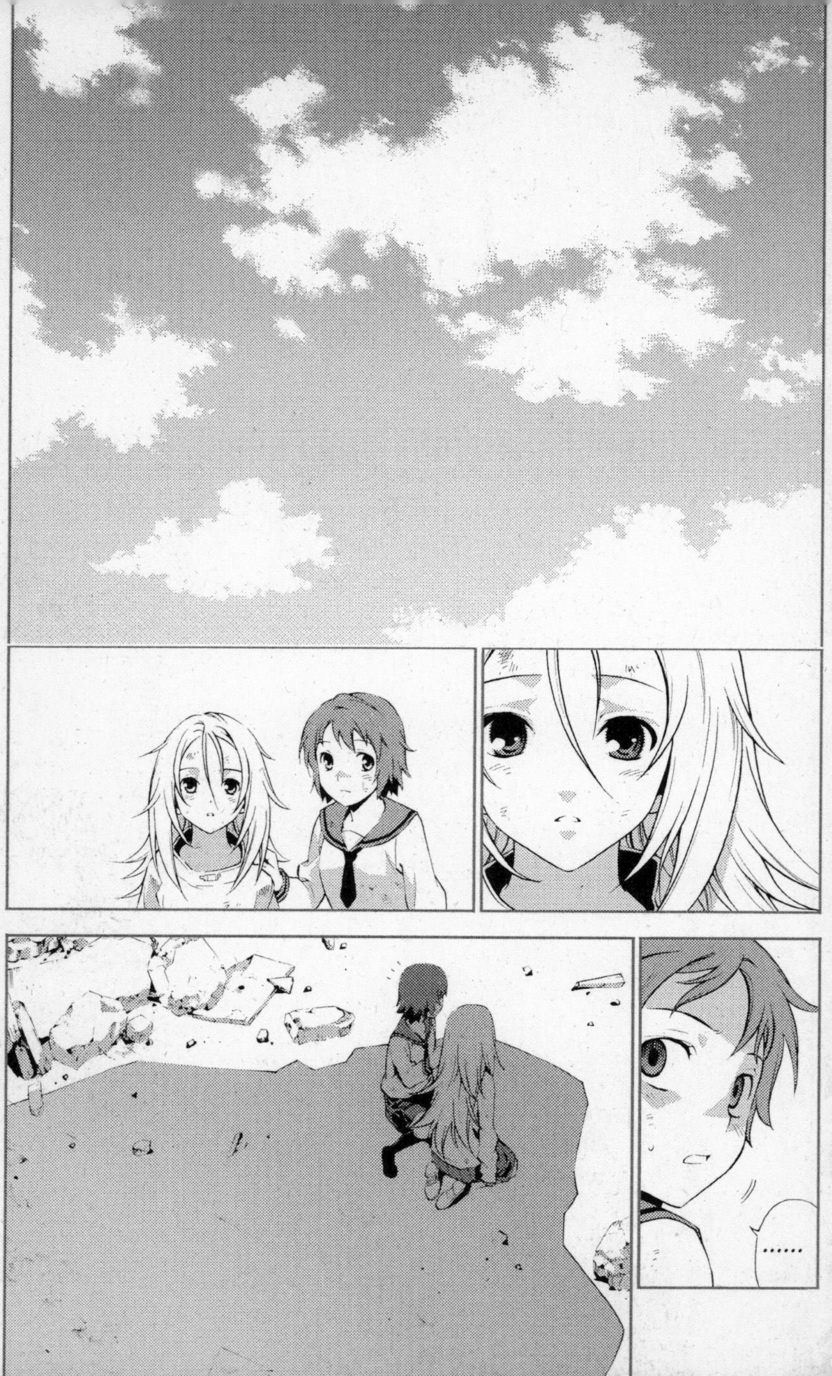
……

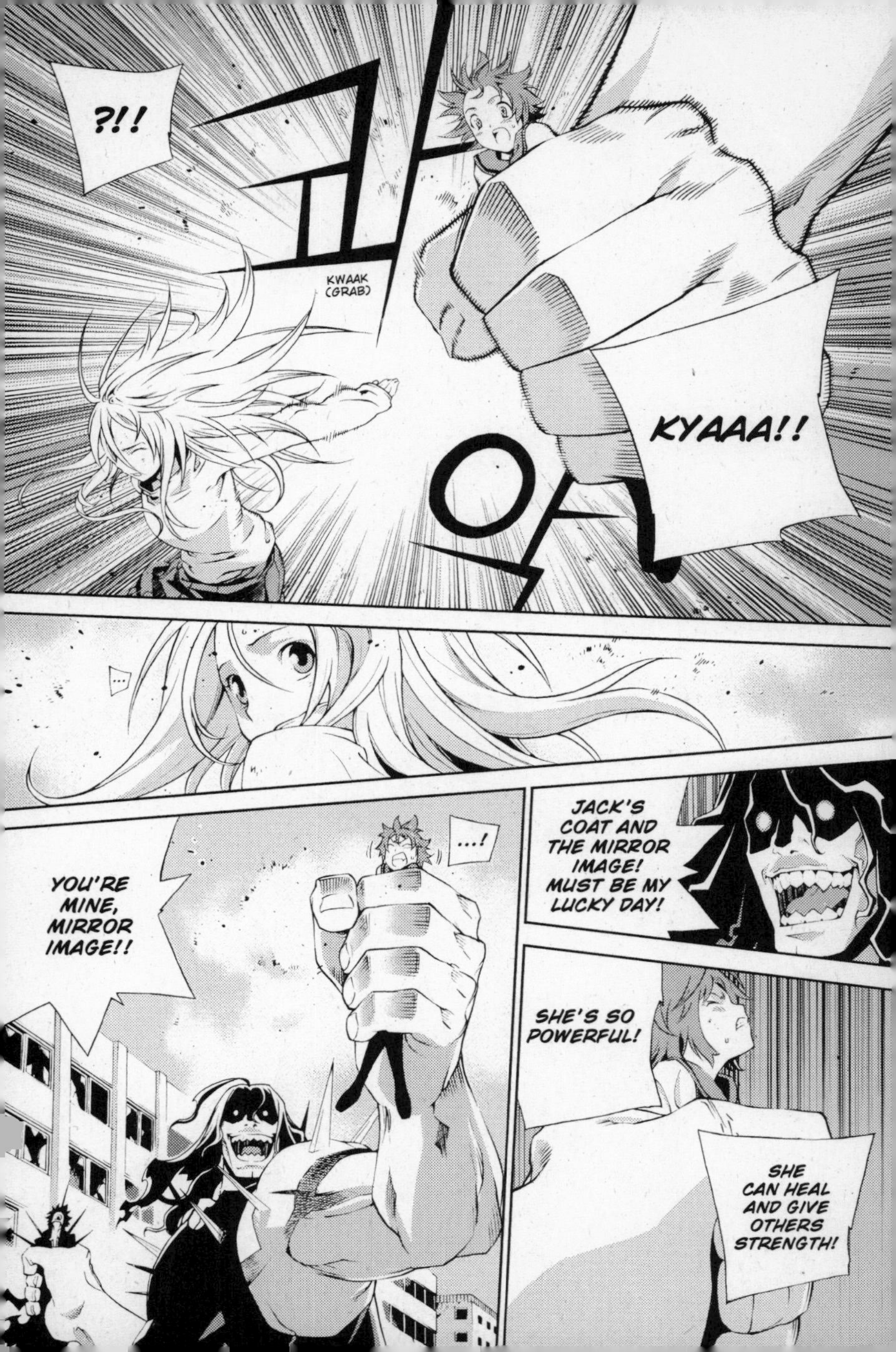
?!!
KWAAK
(GRAB)
KYAAA!!
...
YOU'RE MINE, MIRROR IMAGE!!
...!
JACK'S COAT AND THE MIRROR IMAGE! MUST BE MY LUCKY DAY!
SHE'S SO POWERFUL!
SHE CAN HEAL AND GIVE OTHERS STRENGTH!

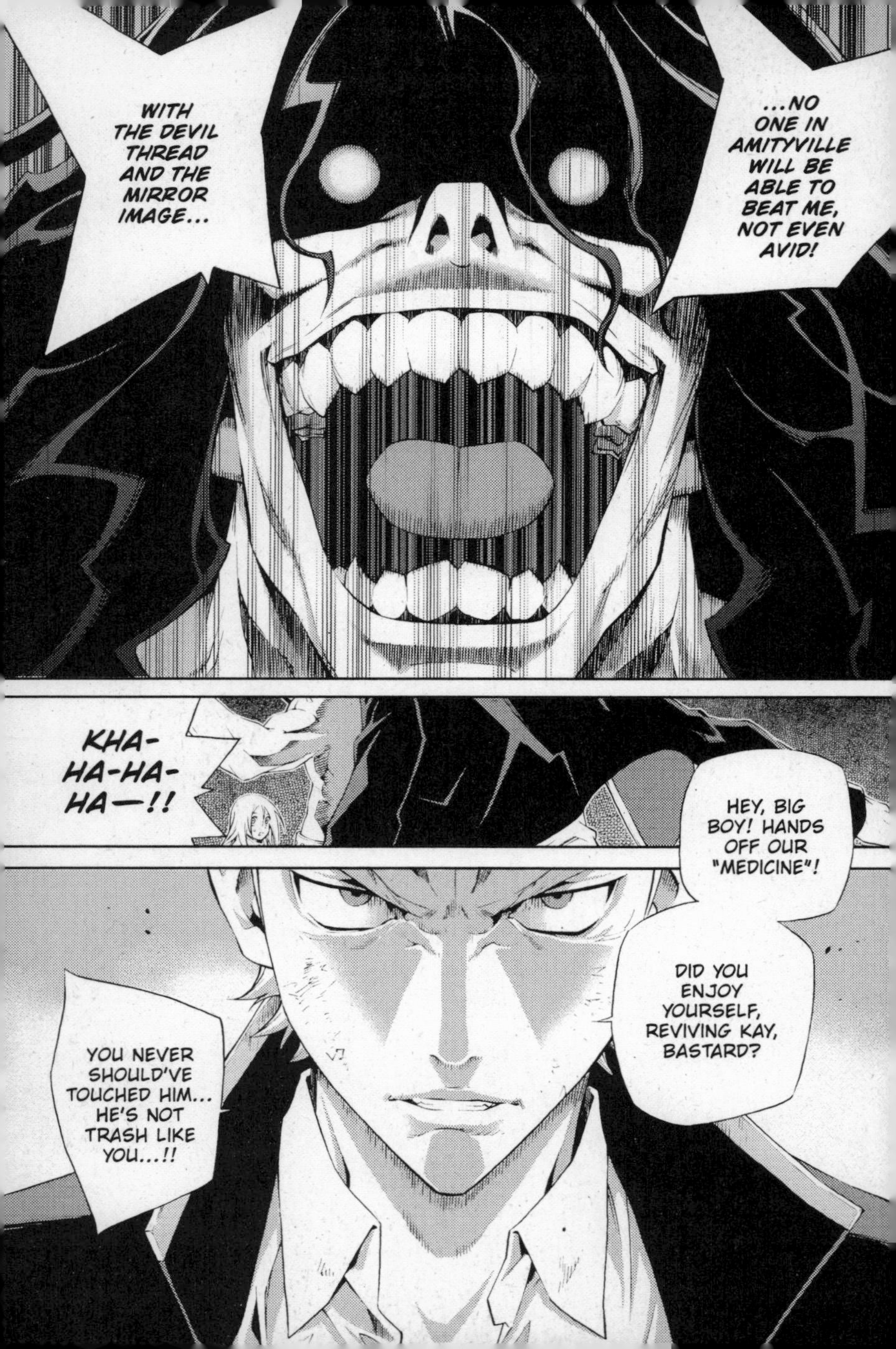
WITH THE DEVIL THREAD AND THE MIRROR IMAGE...
...NO ONE IN AMITYVILLE WILL BE ABLE TO BEAT ME, NOT EVEN AVID!
KHA-HA-HA-HA—!!
HEY, BIG BOY! HANDS OFF OUR "MEDICINE"!
YOU NEVER SHOULD'VE TOUCHED HIM... HE'S NOT TRASH LIKE YOU...!!
DID YOU ENJOY YOURSELF, REVIVING KAY, BASTARD?

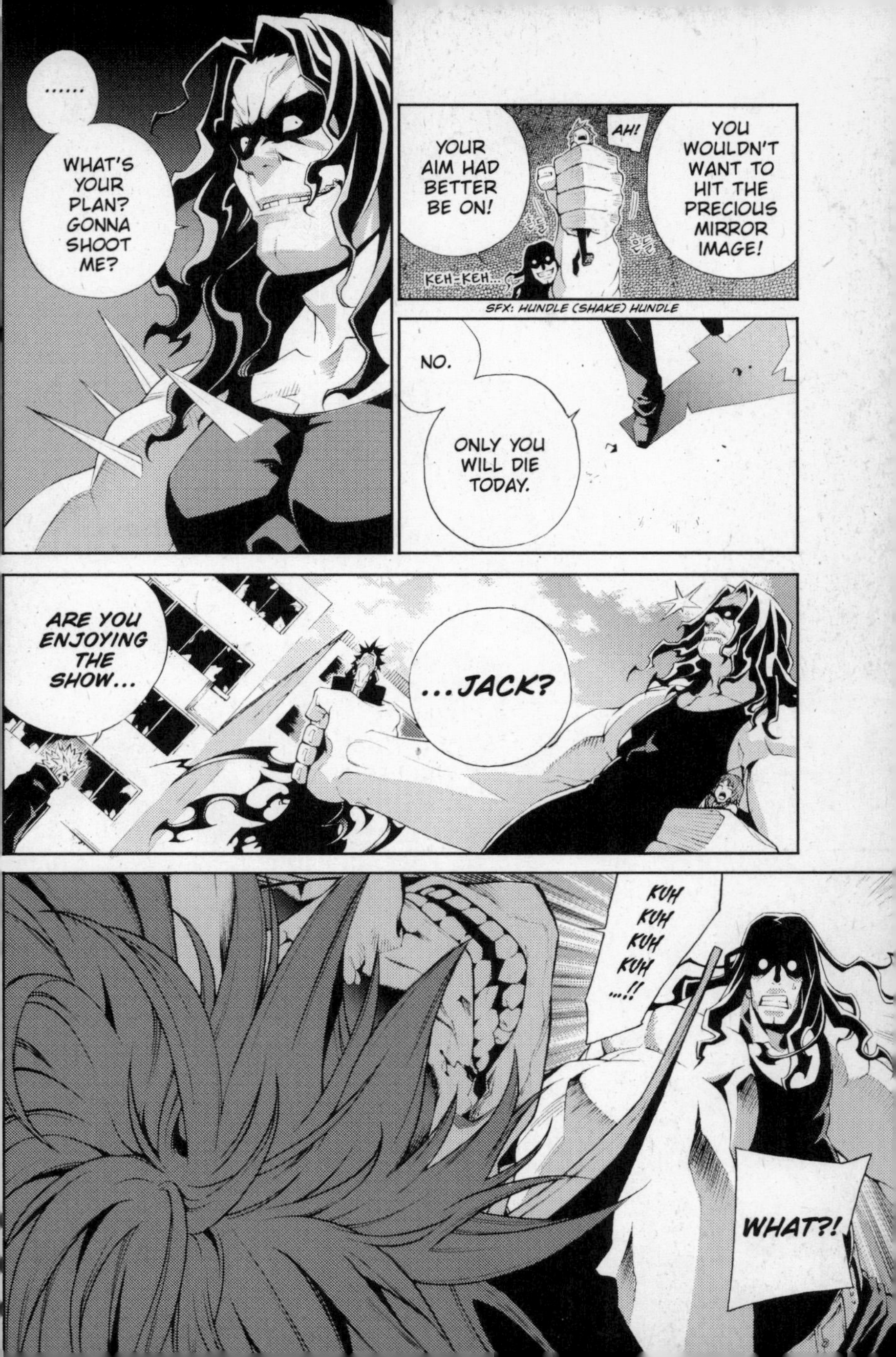
......
WHAT'S YOUR PLAN? GONNA SHOOT ME?
YOUR AIM HAD BETTER BE ON!
AH!
YOU WOULDN'T WANT TO HIT THE PRECIOUS MIRROR IMAGE!
KEH-KEH...
SFX: HUNDLE (SHAKE) HUNDLE
NO.
ONLY YOU WILL DIE TODAY.
ARE YOU ENJOYING THE SHOW...
...JACK?
KUH KUH KUH KUH ...!!
WHAT?!

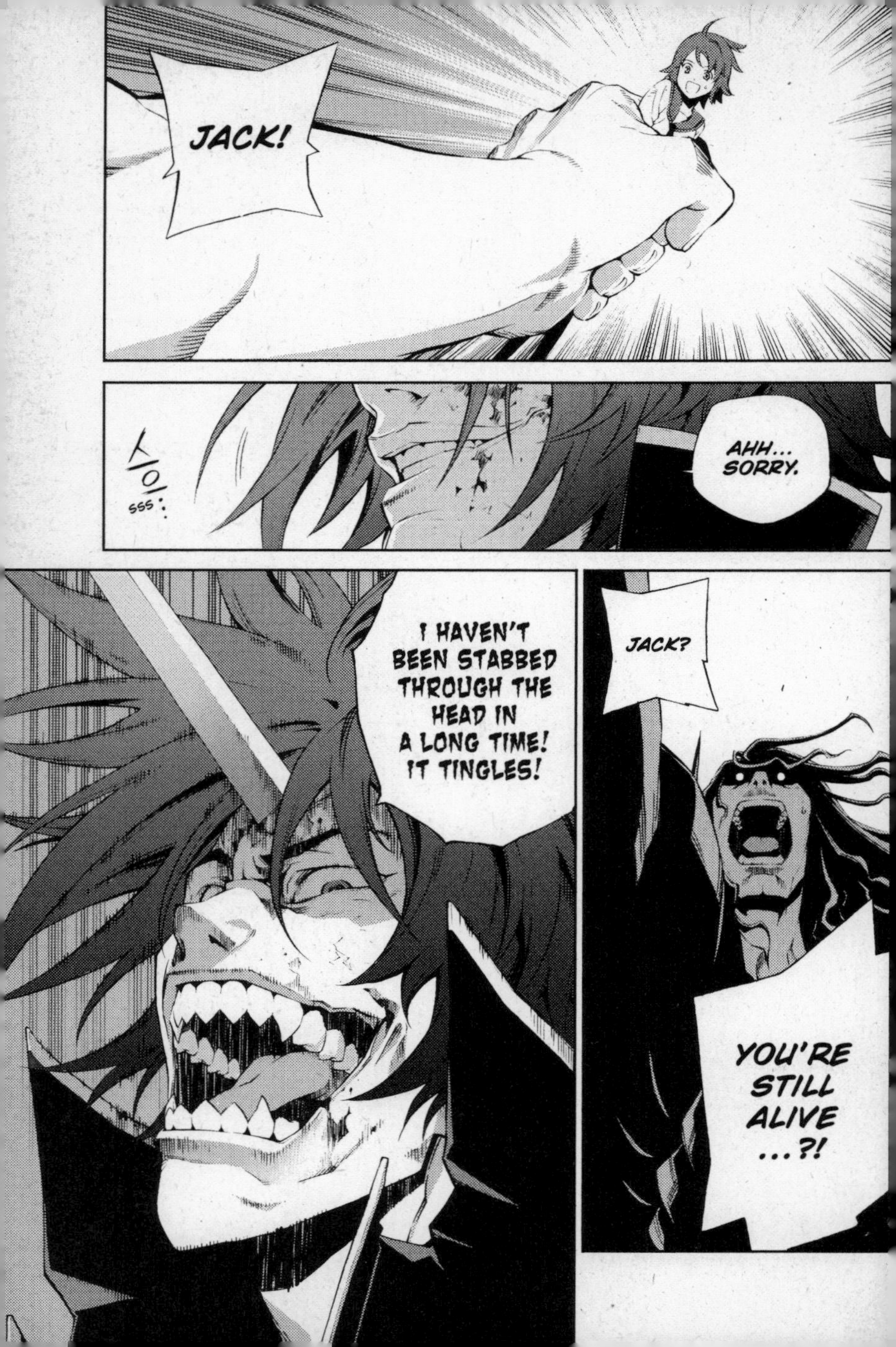
JACK!
SSS
AHH... SORRY.
I HAVEN'T BEEN STABBED THROUGH THE HEAD IN A LONG TIME! IT TINGLES!
JACK?
YOU'RE STILL ALIVE ...?!

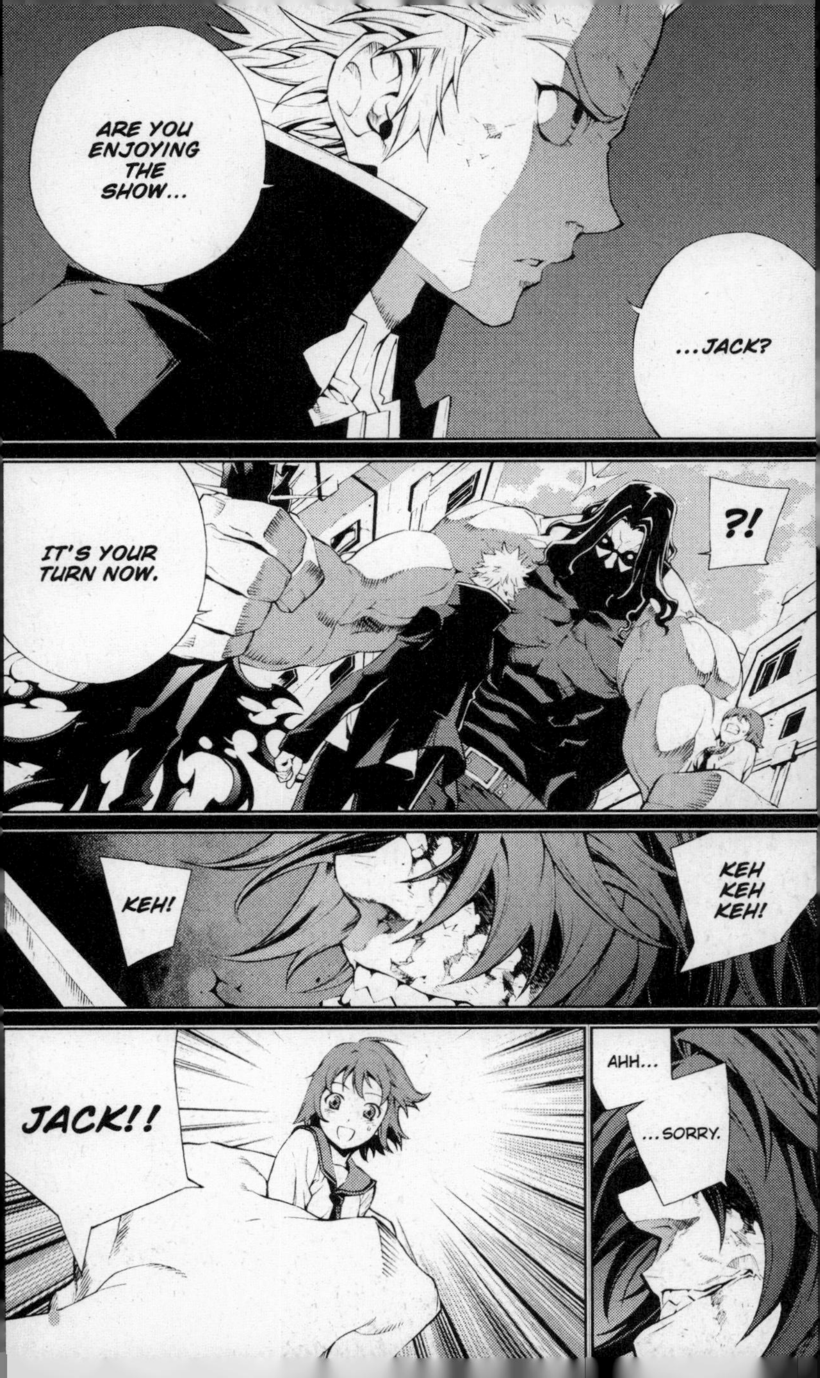
ARE YOU ENJOYING THE SHOW...
...JACK?
IT'S YOUR TURN NOW.
?!
KEH!
KEH KEH KEH!
JACK!!
AHH...
...SORRY.

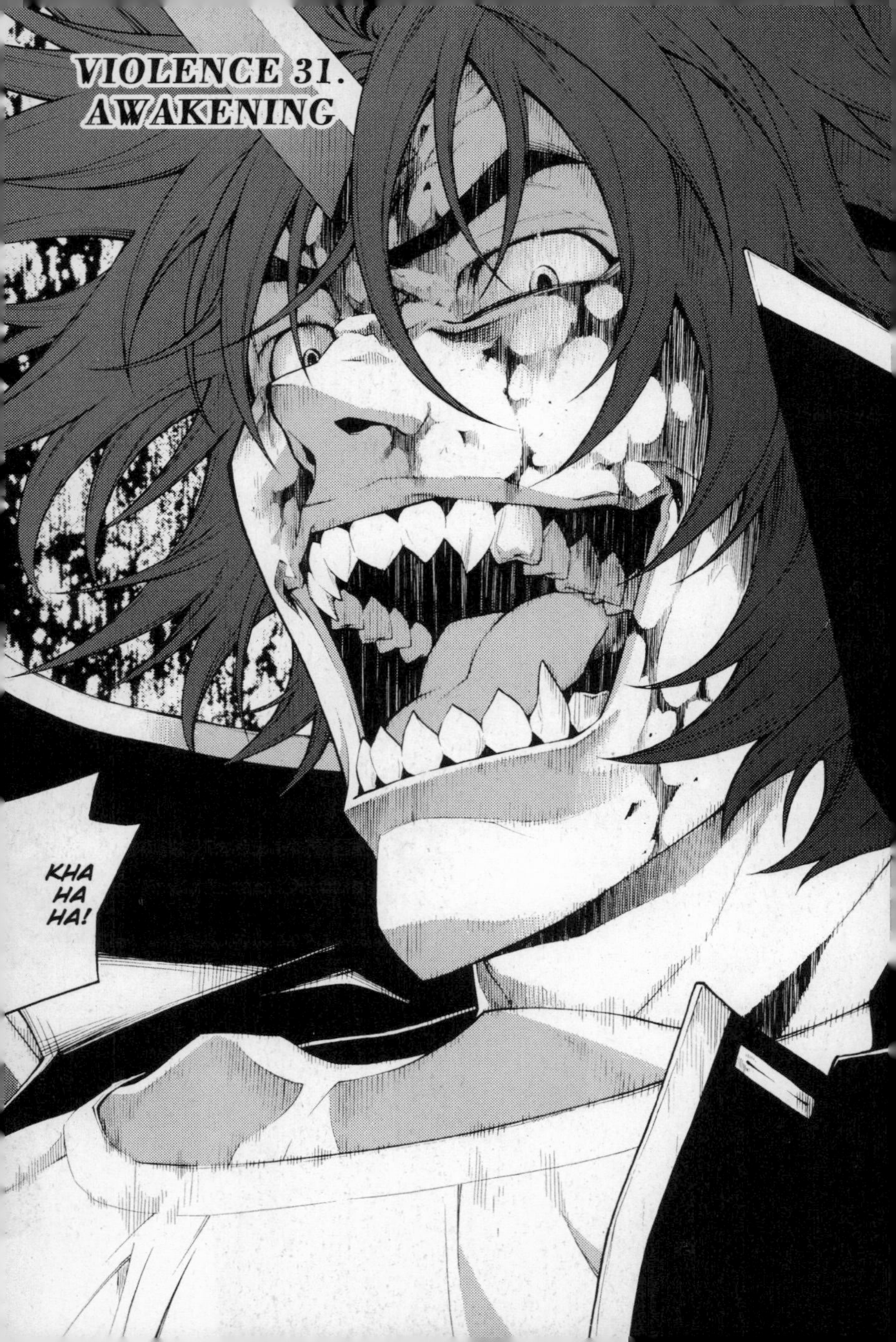
VIOLENCE 31.
AWAKENING
KHA HA HA!

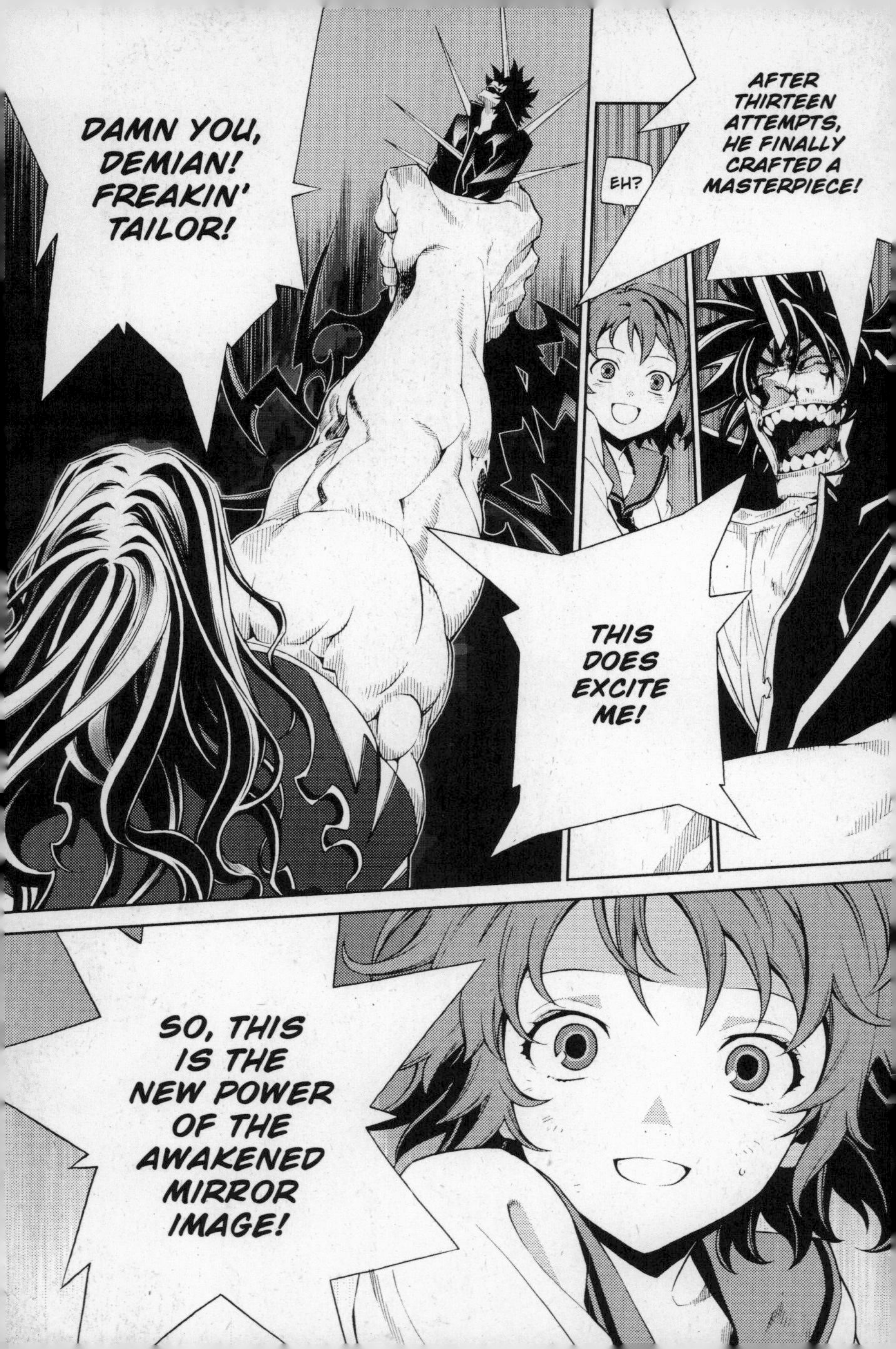
DAMN YOU, DEMIAN! FREAKIN' TAILOR!
EH?
AFTER THIRTEEN ATTEMPTS, HE FINALLY CRAFTED A MASTERPIECE!
THIS DOES EXCITE ME!
SO, THIS IS THE NEW POWER OF THE AWAKENED MIRROR IMAGE!

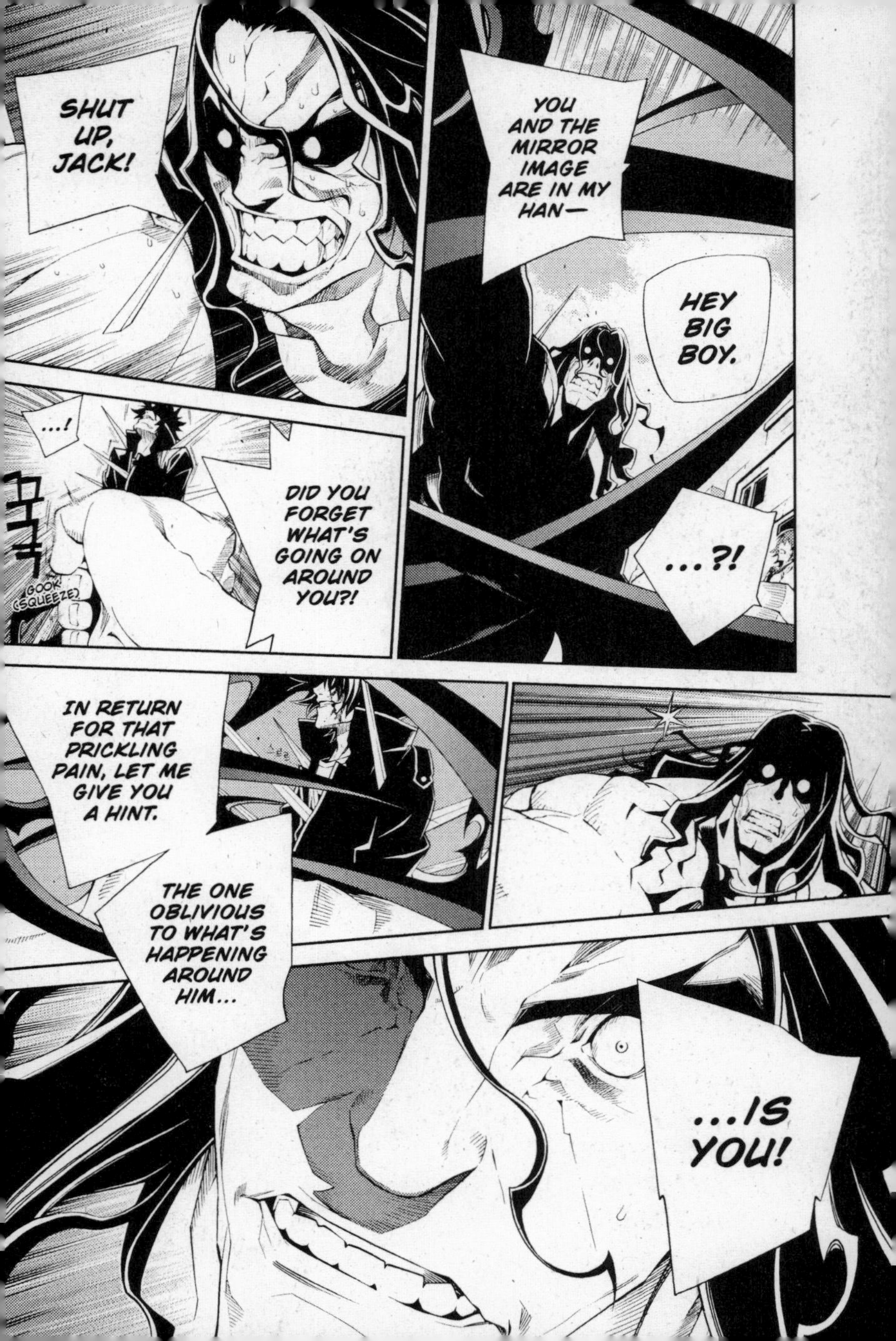
SHUT UP, JACK!
...!
GOOK (SQUEEZE)
DID YOU FORGET WHAT'S GOING ON AROUND YOU?!
YOU AND THE MIRROR IMAGE ARE IN MY HAN—
HEY BIG BOY.
...?!
IN RETURN FOR THAT PRICKLING PAIN, LET ME GIVE YOU A HINT.
THE ONE OBLIVIOUS TO WHAT'S HAPPENING AROUND HIM...
...IS YOU!

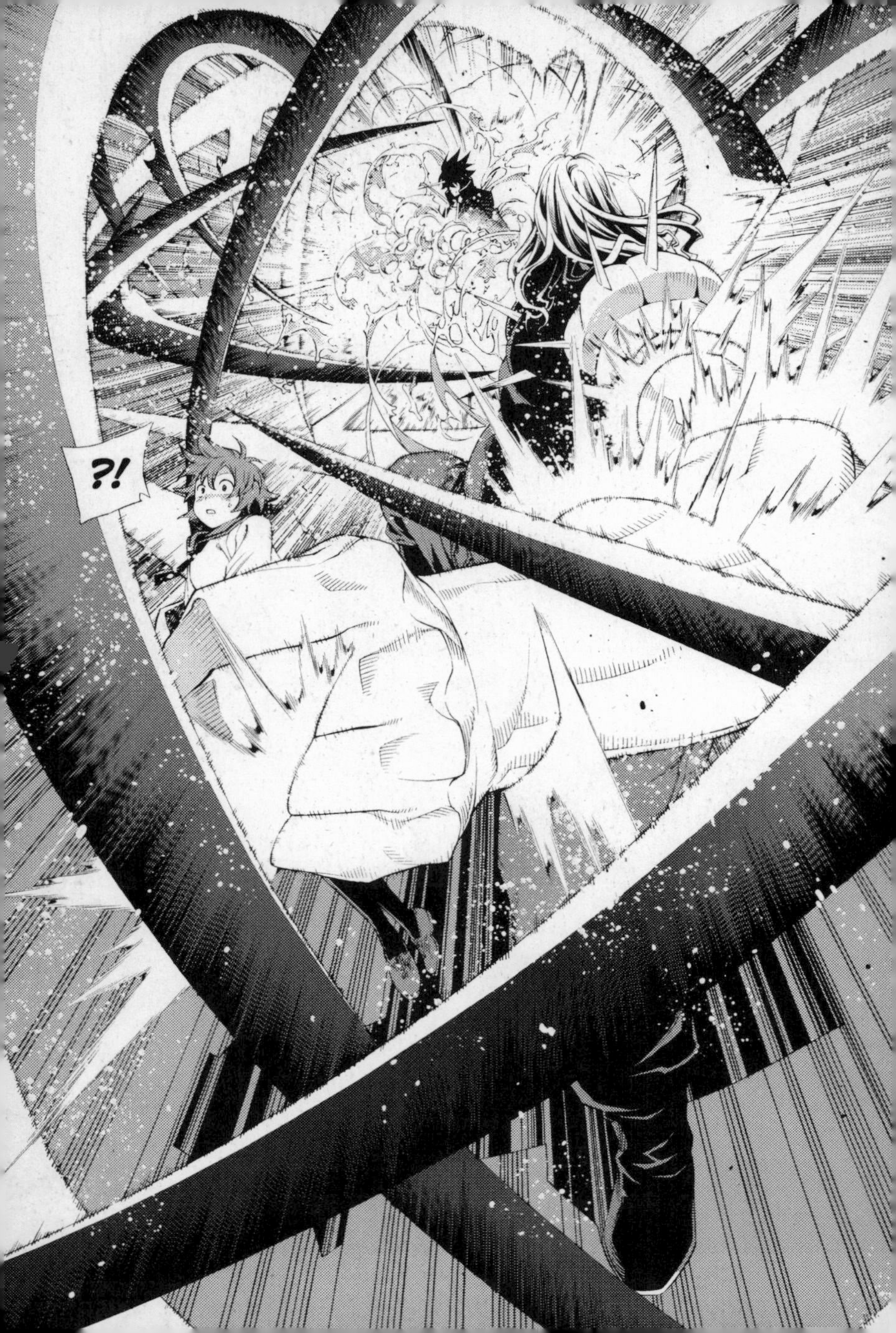
?!

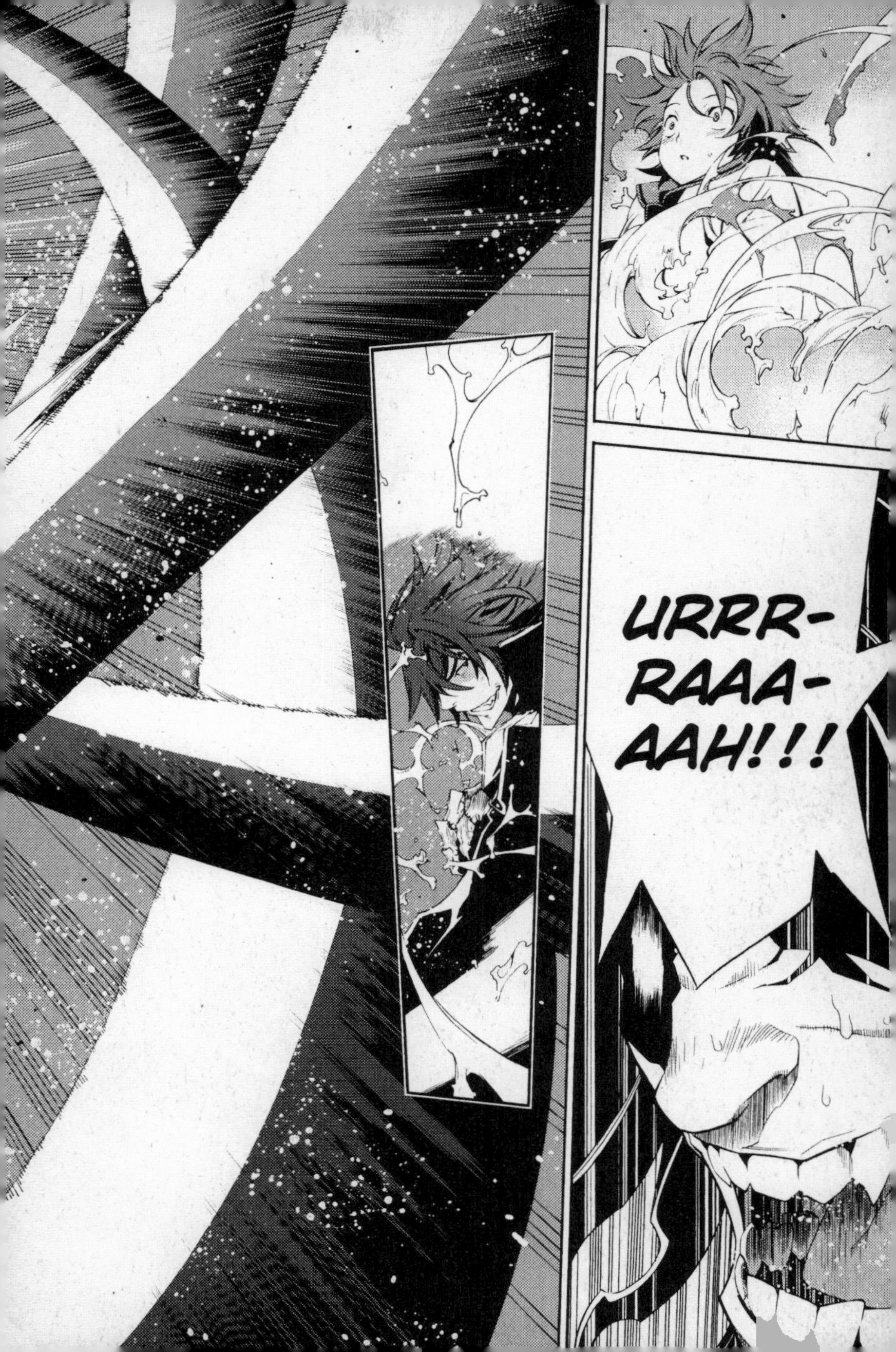
URRR-
RAAA-
AAH!!!

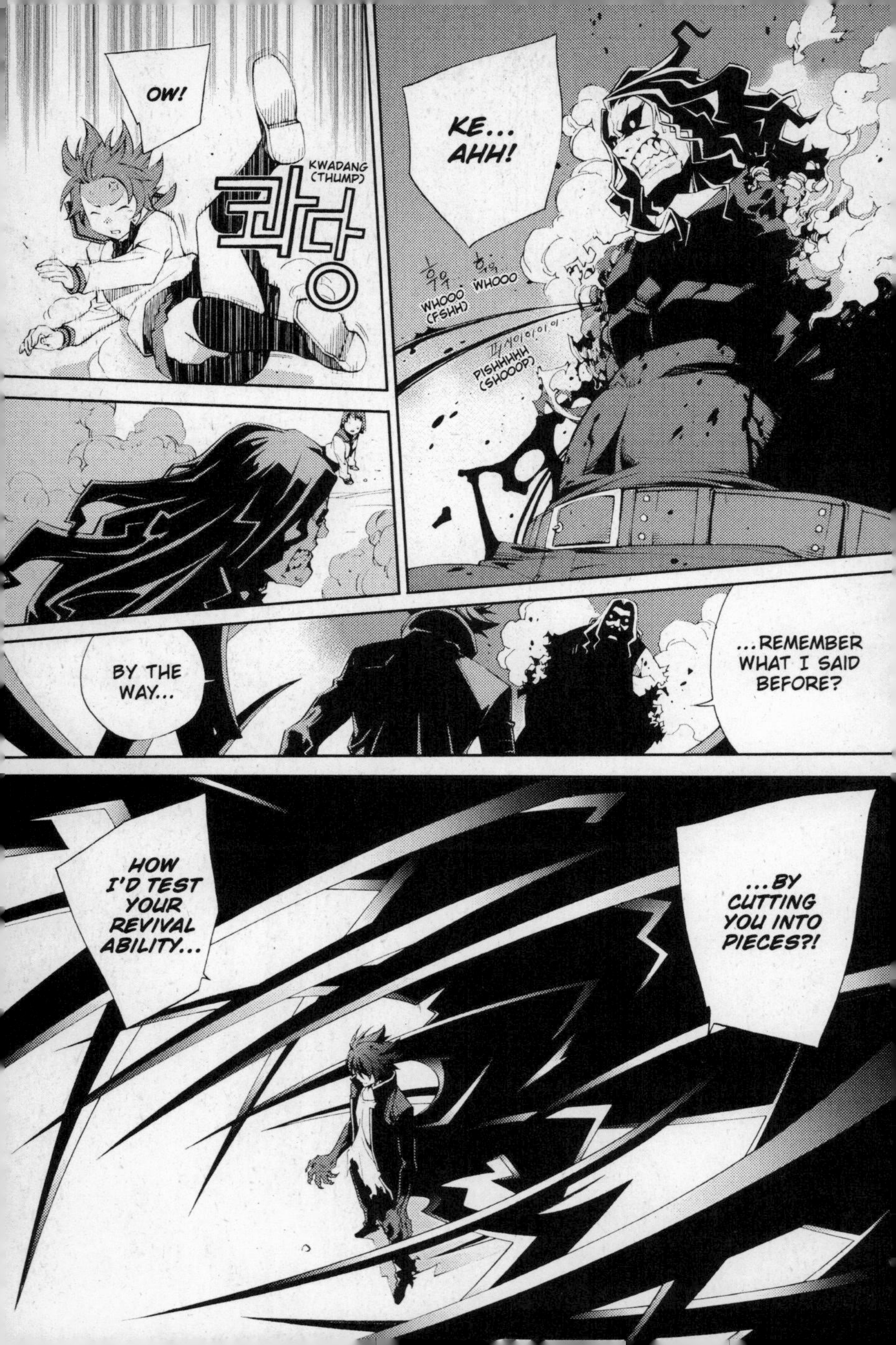
OW!
KWADANG (THUMP)
콰당
KE... AHH!
후우
WHOOO (FSHH)
후우
WHOOO
피시이이이이
PISHHHHH (SHOOOP)
BY THE WAY...
...REMEMBER WHAT I SAID BEFORE?
HOW I'D TEST YOUR REVIVAL ABILITY...
...BY CUTTING YOU INTO PIECES?!

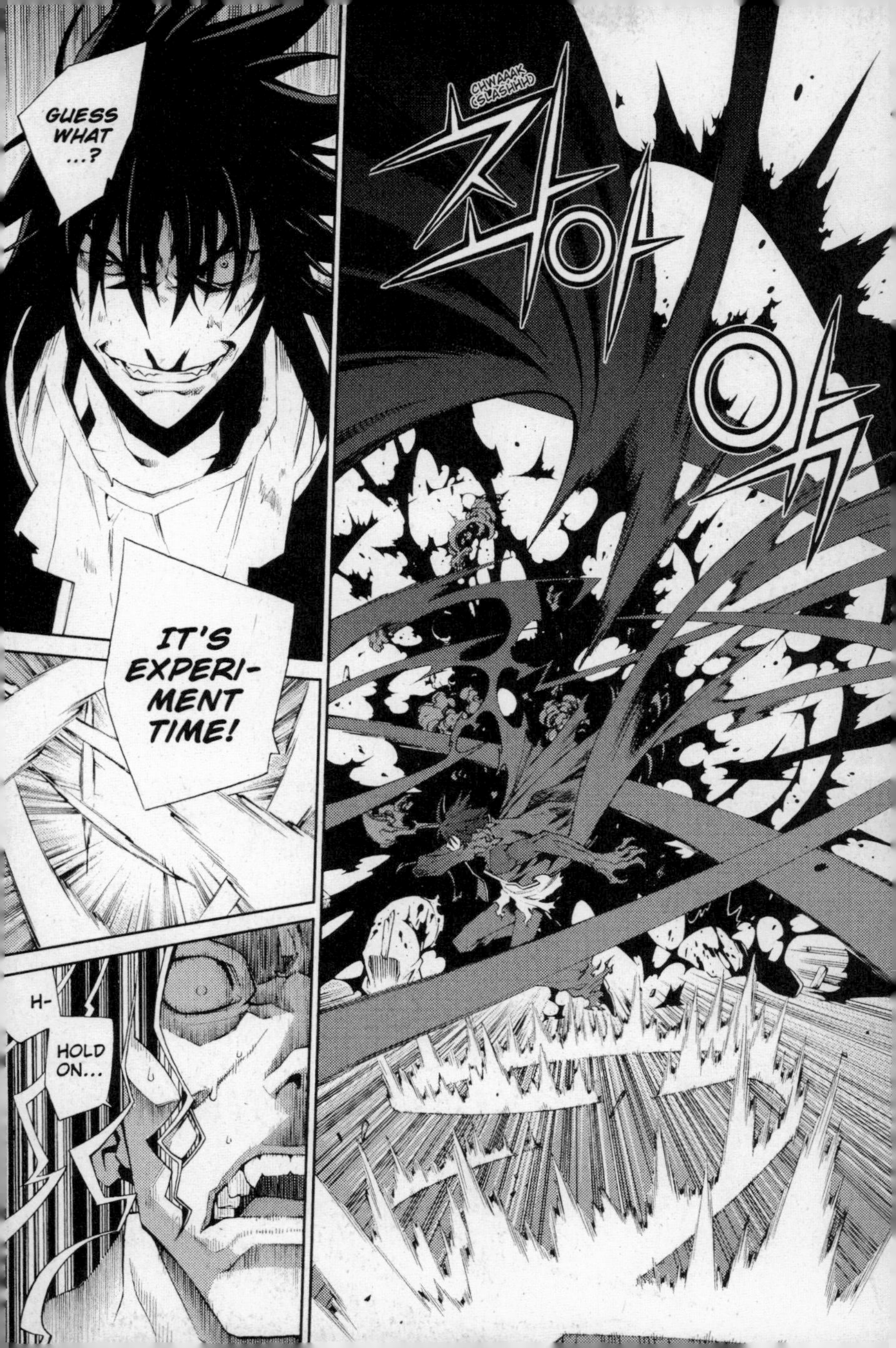
GUESS WHAT ...?
IT'S EXPERI-MENT TIME!
H-
HOLD ON...
CHWAAAK (SLASHHH)

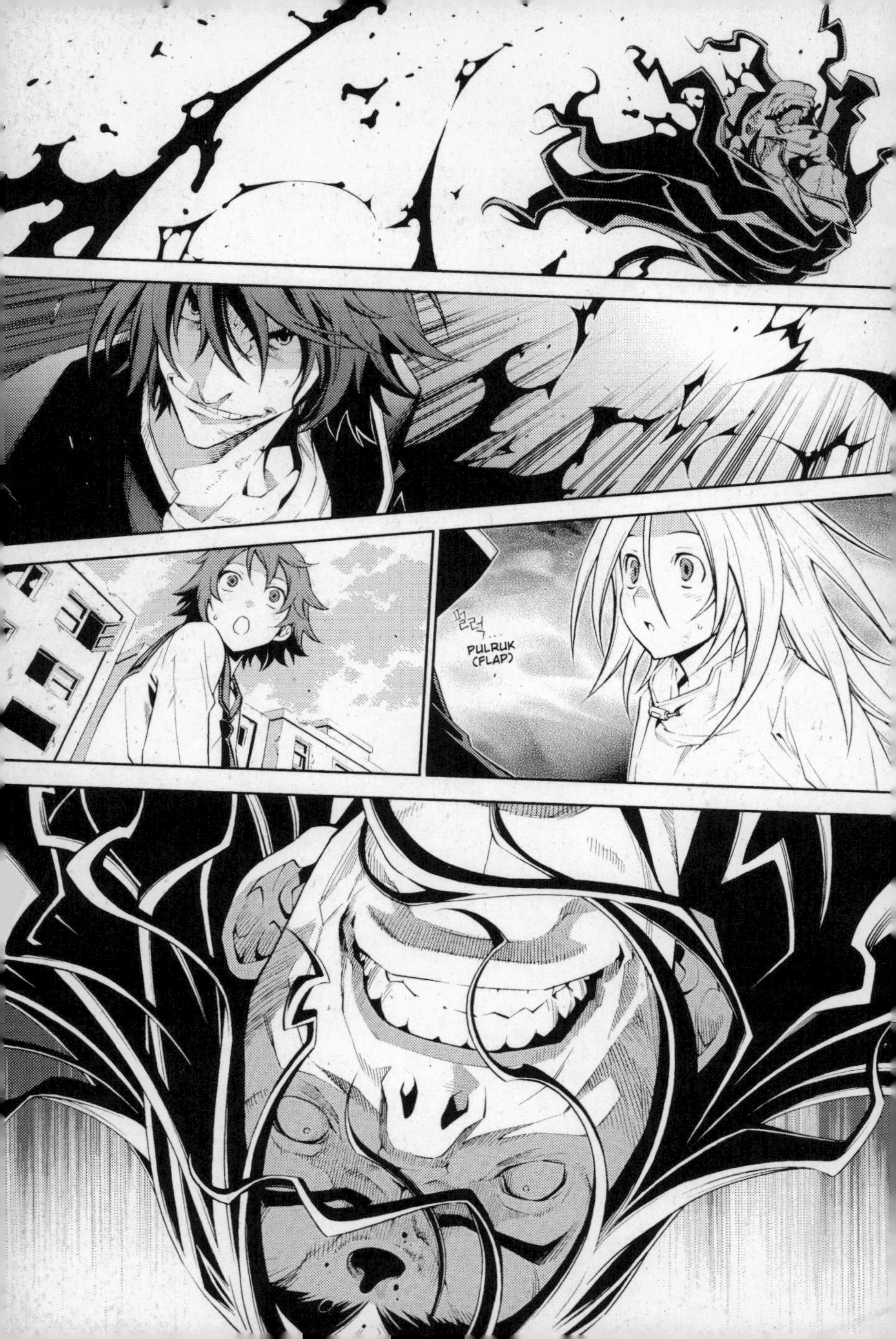
펄럭…
PULRUK (FLAP)

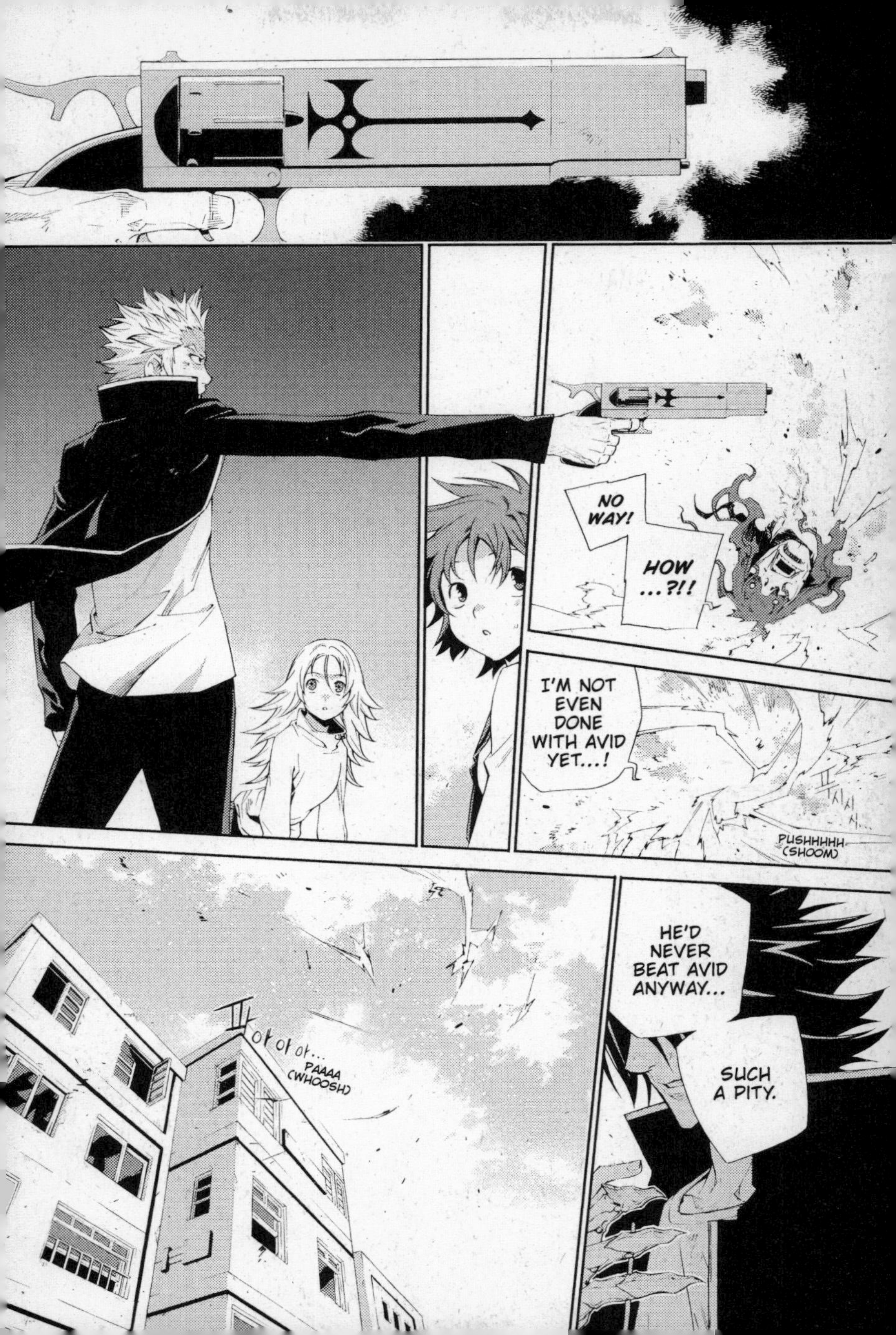
NO WAY!
HOW ...?!!
I'M NOT EVEN DONE WITH AVID YET...!
프시시시...
PUSHHHHH (SHOOM)
파아아아...
PAAAA (WHOOSH)
HE'D NEVER BEAT AVID ANYWAY...
SUCH A PITY.

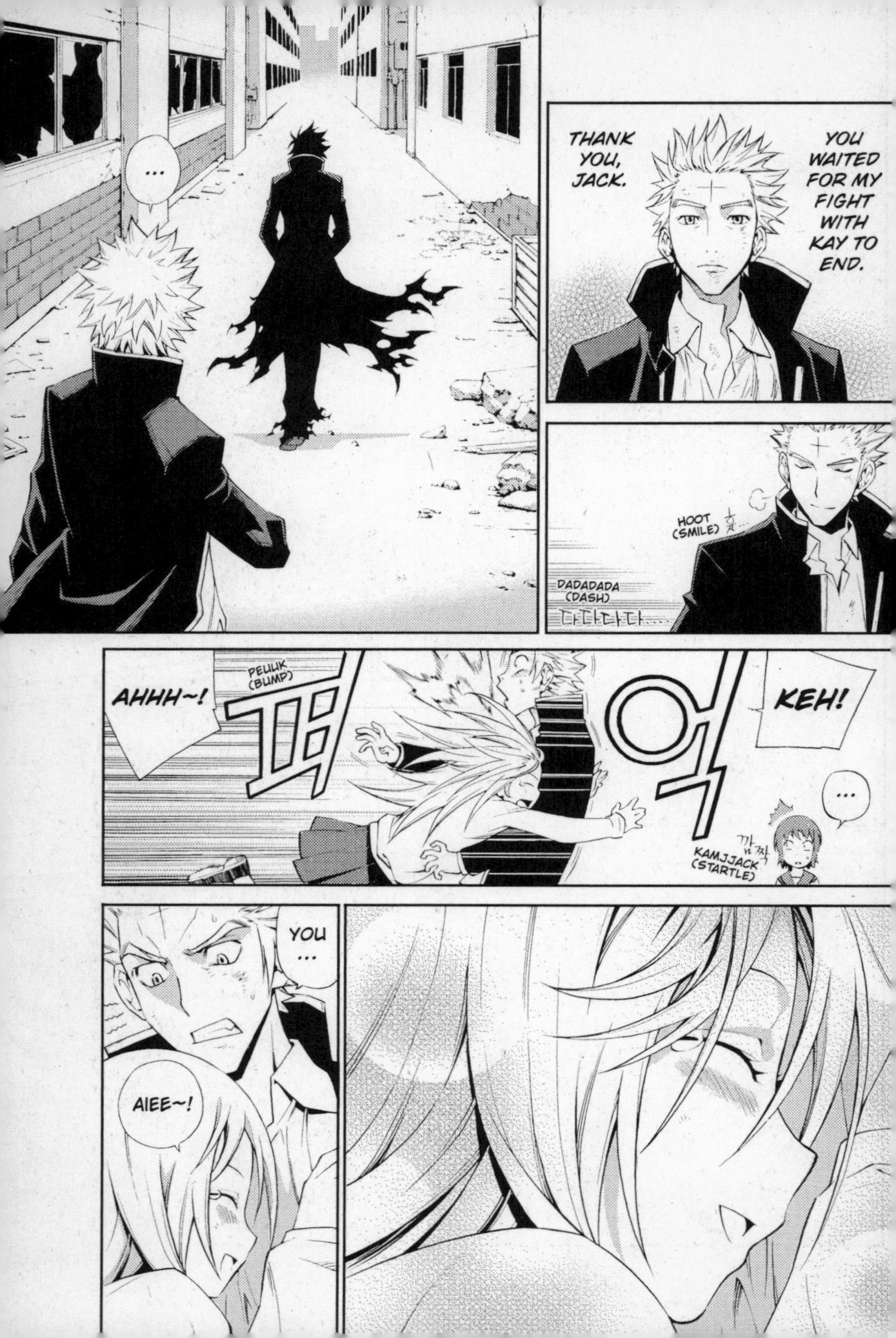
...
THANK YOU, JACK.
YOU WAITED FOR MY FIGHT WITH KAY TO END.
HOOT (SMILE) 훗
DADADADA (DASH)
다다다다...
AHHH~!
PEULK (BUMP)
퍽
억
KEH!
...
깜짝
KAMJJACK (STARTLE)
YOU ...
AIEE~!

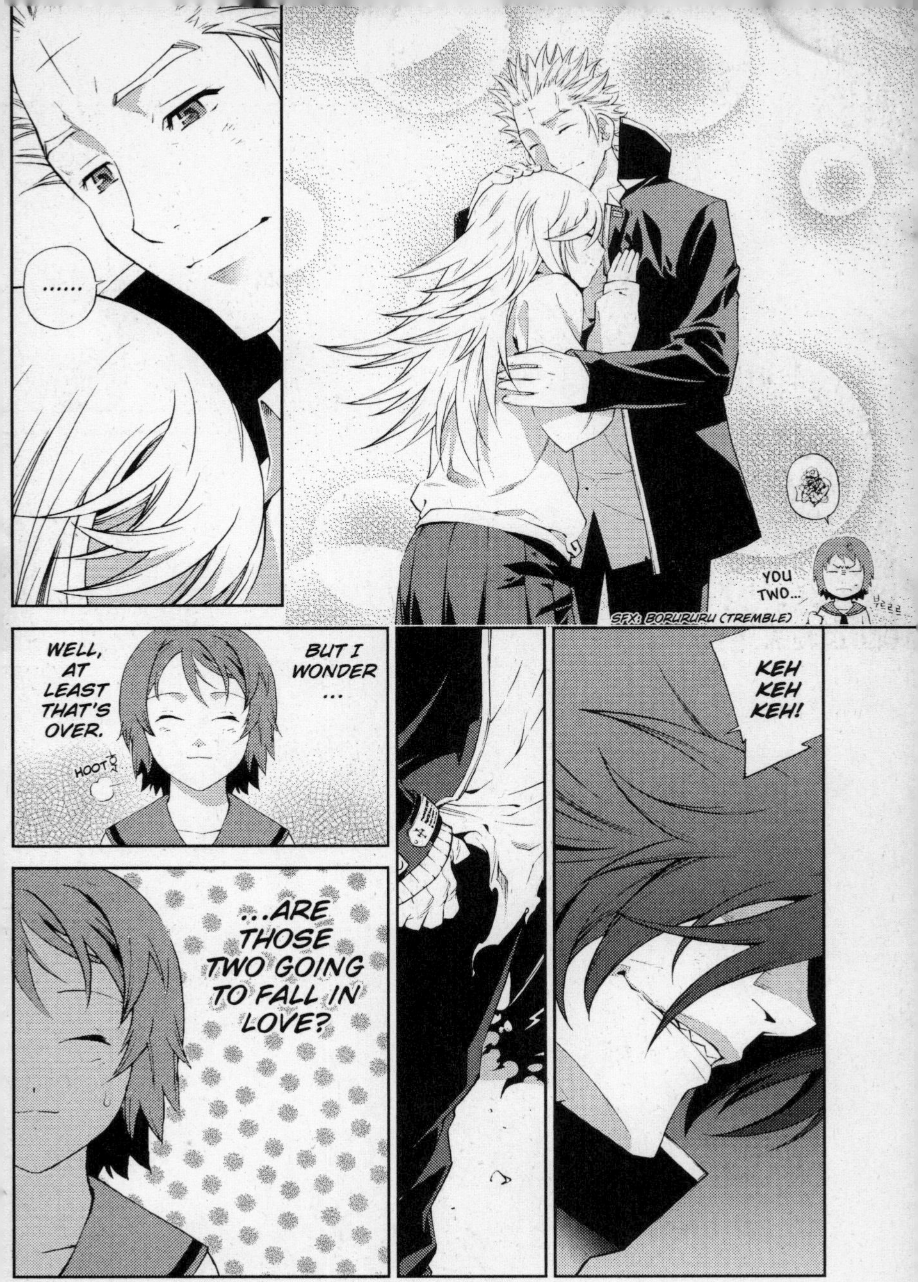
......
YOU TWO...
SFX: BORURURU (TREMBLE)
WELL, AT LEAST THAT'S OVER.
HOOT
BUT I WONDER ...
...ARE THOSE TWO GOING TO FALL IN LOVE?
KEH KEH KEH!

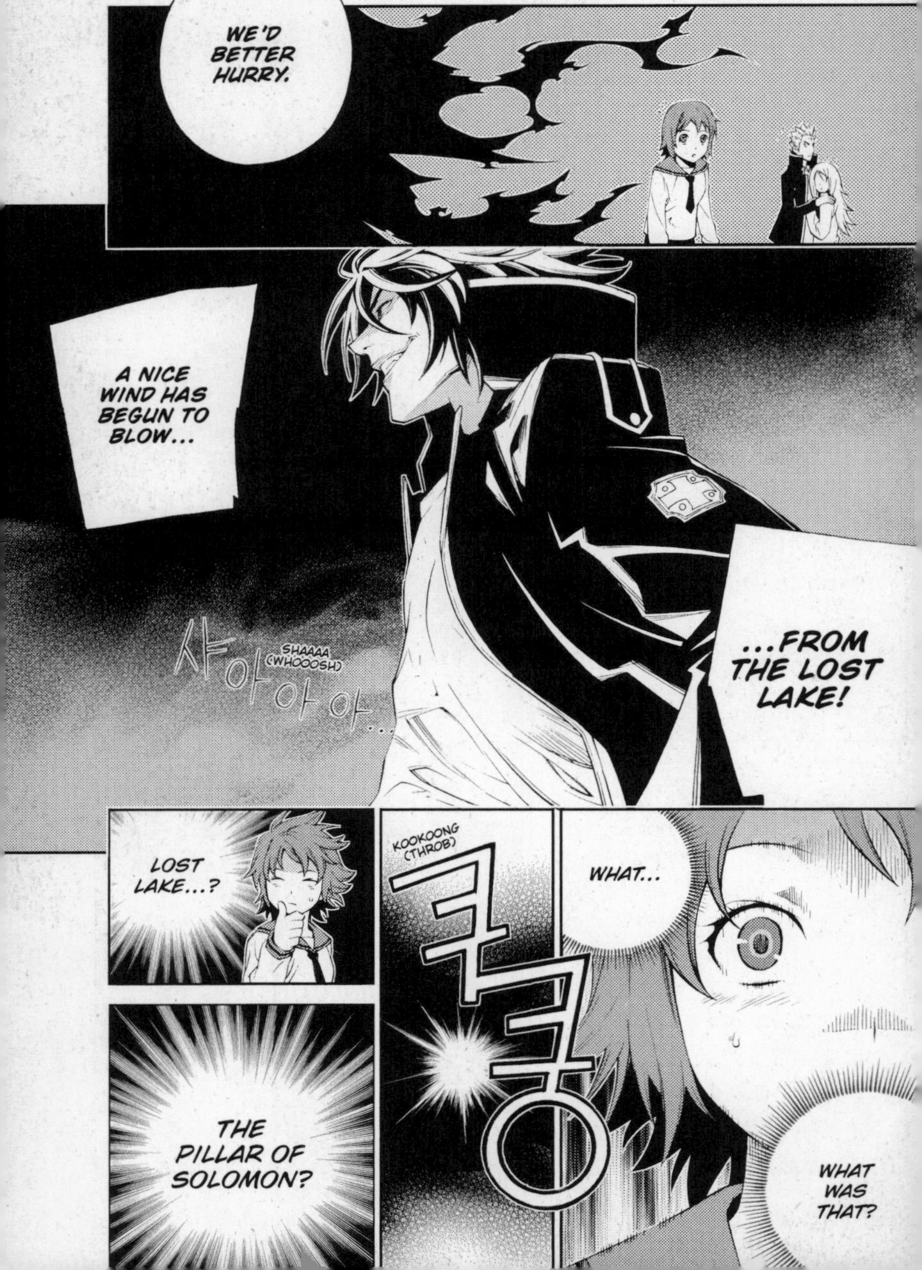
WE'D BETTER HURRY.
A NICE WIND HAS BEGUN TO BLOW...
샤아아아...
SHAAAA (WHOOOSH)
...FROM THE LOST LAKE!
LOST LAKE...?
THE PILLAR OF SOLOMON?
쿠쿵
KOOKOONG (THROB)
WHAT...
WHAT WAS THAT?

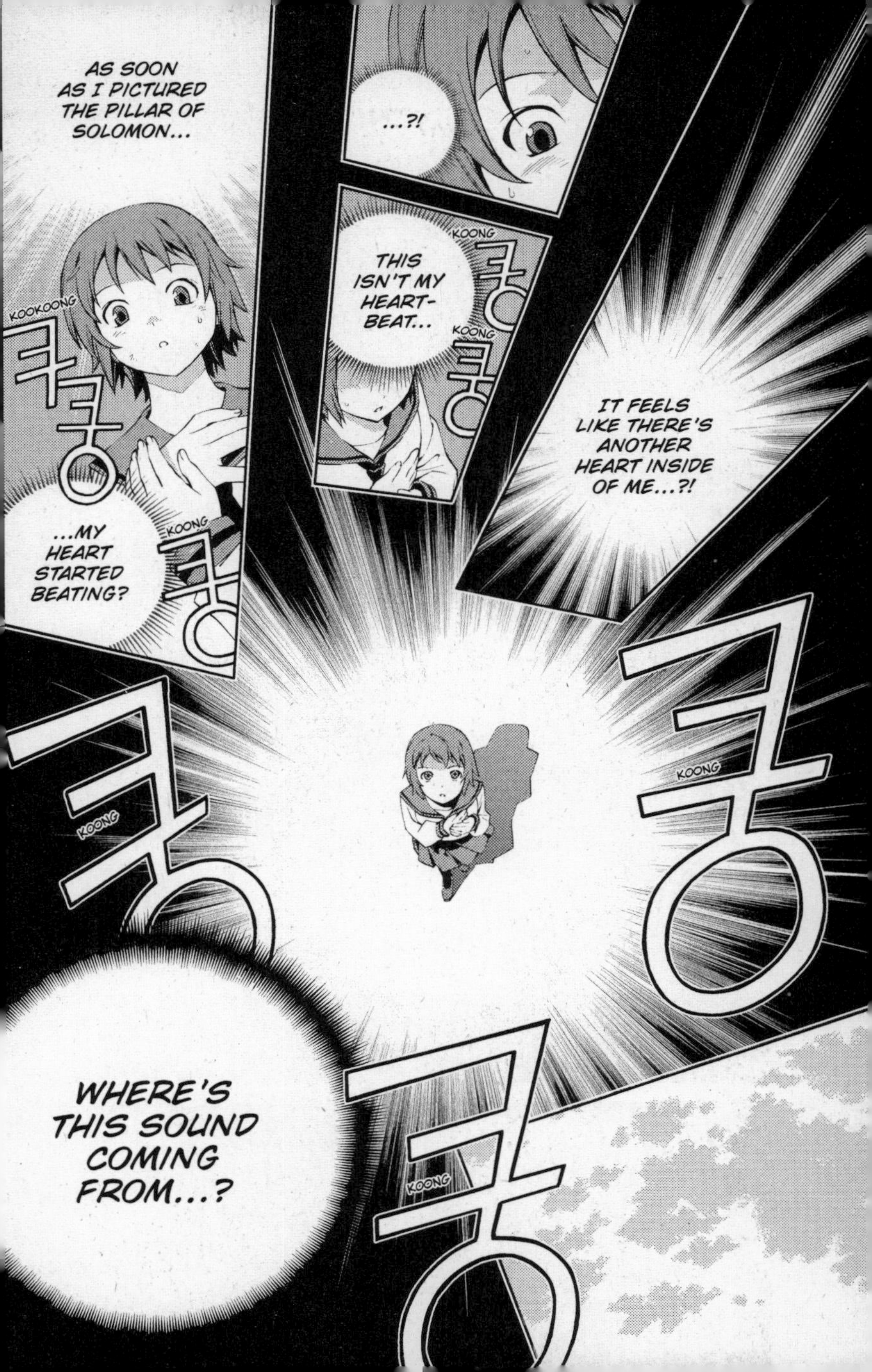
AS SOON AS I PICTURED THE PILLAR OF SOLOMON...
KOOKOONG
쿠쿵
...MY HEART STARTED BEATING?
KOONG
쿵
...?!
KOONG
쿵
THIS ISN'T MY HEART-BEAT...
KOONG
쿵
IT FEELS LIKE THERE'S ANOTHER HEART INSIDE OF ME...?!
KOONG
쿵
KOONG
쿵
KOONG
쿵
WHERE'S THIS SOUND COMING FROM...?

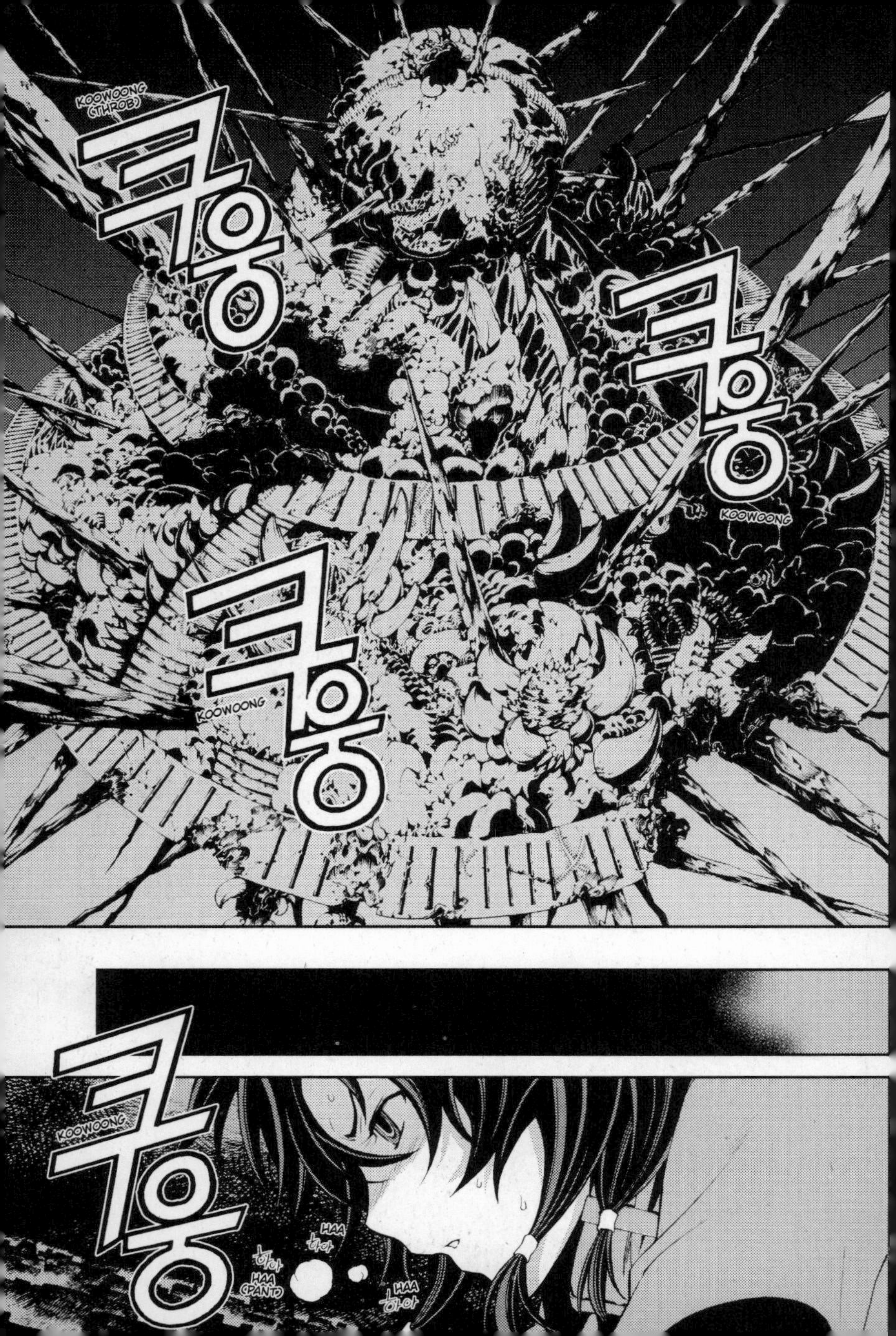
KOOWOONG (THROB)
쿠웅
쿠웅
KOOWOONG
쿠웅
KOOWOONG
쿠웅
KOOWOONG
HAA
하아
하아
HAA (PANT)
HAA
하아

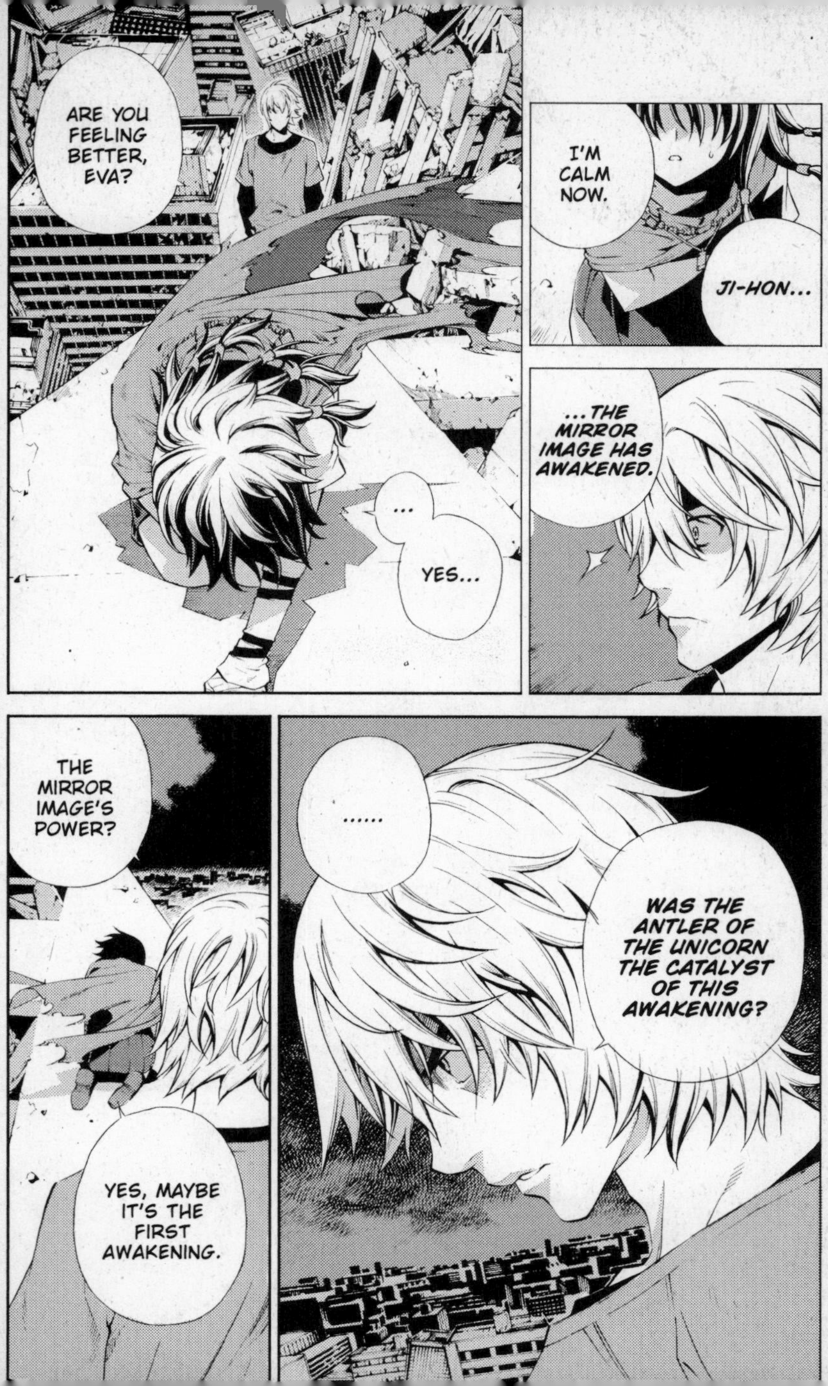
ARE YOU FEELING BETTER, EVA?
...
YES...
I'M CALM NOW.
JI-HON...
...THE MIRROR IMAGE HAS AWAKENED.
THE MIRROR IMAGE'S POWER?
YES, MAYBE IT'S THE FIRST AWAKENING.
......
WAS THE ANTLER OF THE UNICORN THE CATALYST OF THIS AWAKENING?

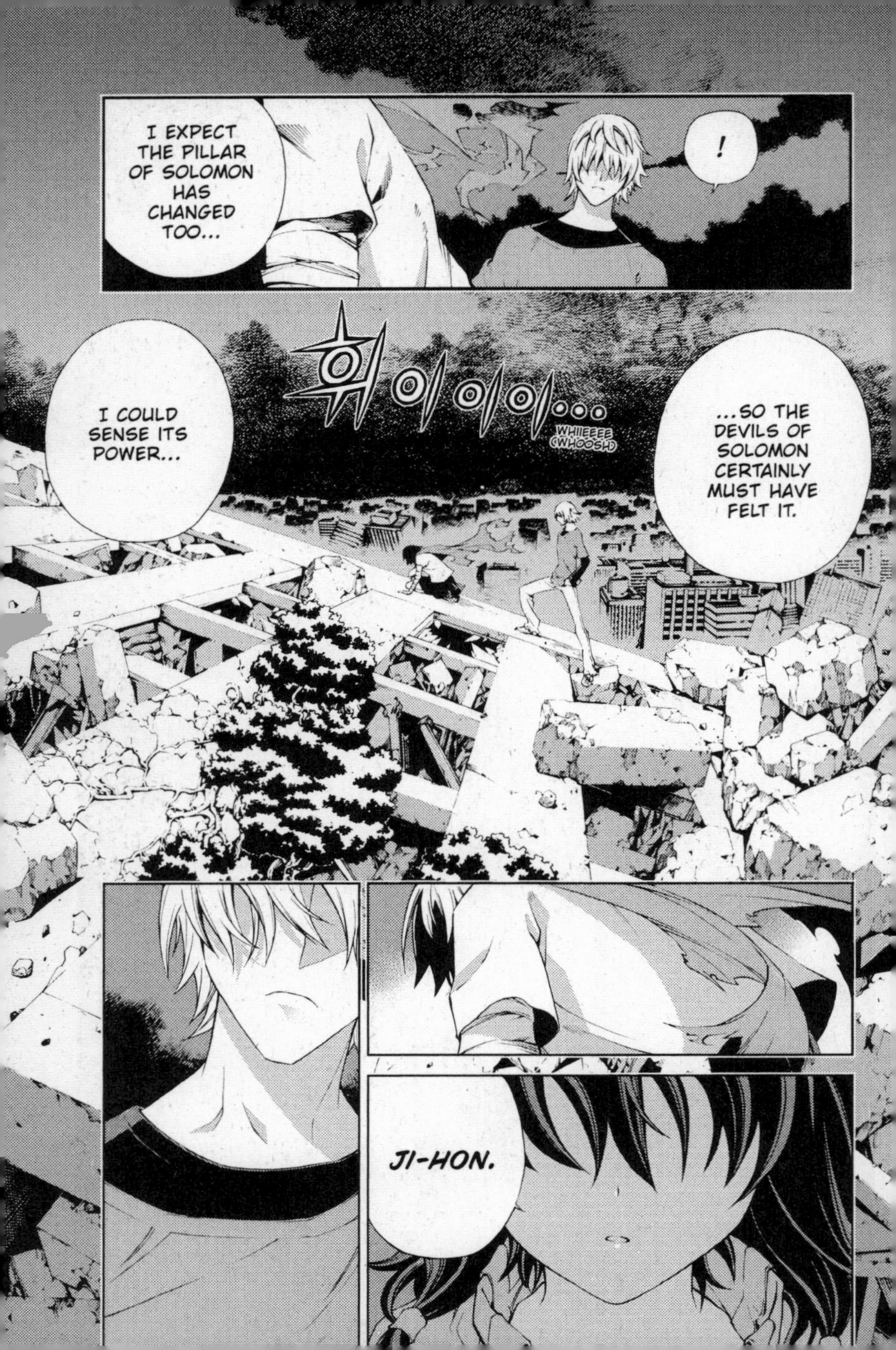
I EXPECT THE PILLAR OF SOLOMON HAS CHANGED TOO...
!
I COULD SENSE ITS POWER...
화이이이이...
WHIIEEEE (WHOOSH)
...SO THE DEVILS OF SOLOMON CERTAINLY MUST HAVE FELT IT.
JI-HON.

YOU HAVEN'T FORGOT-TEN...

...OUR PROMISE, HAVE YOU?

YOU SAID THAT IF I CHANGED...

...YOU'D KILL ME.

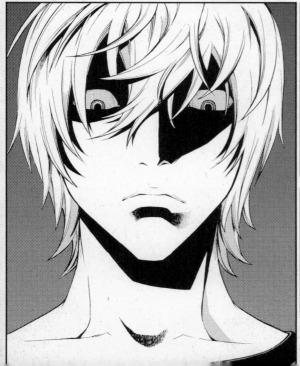

sss

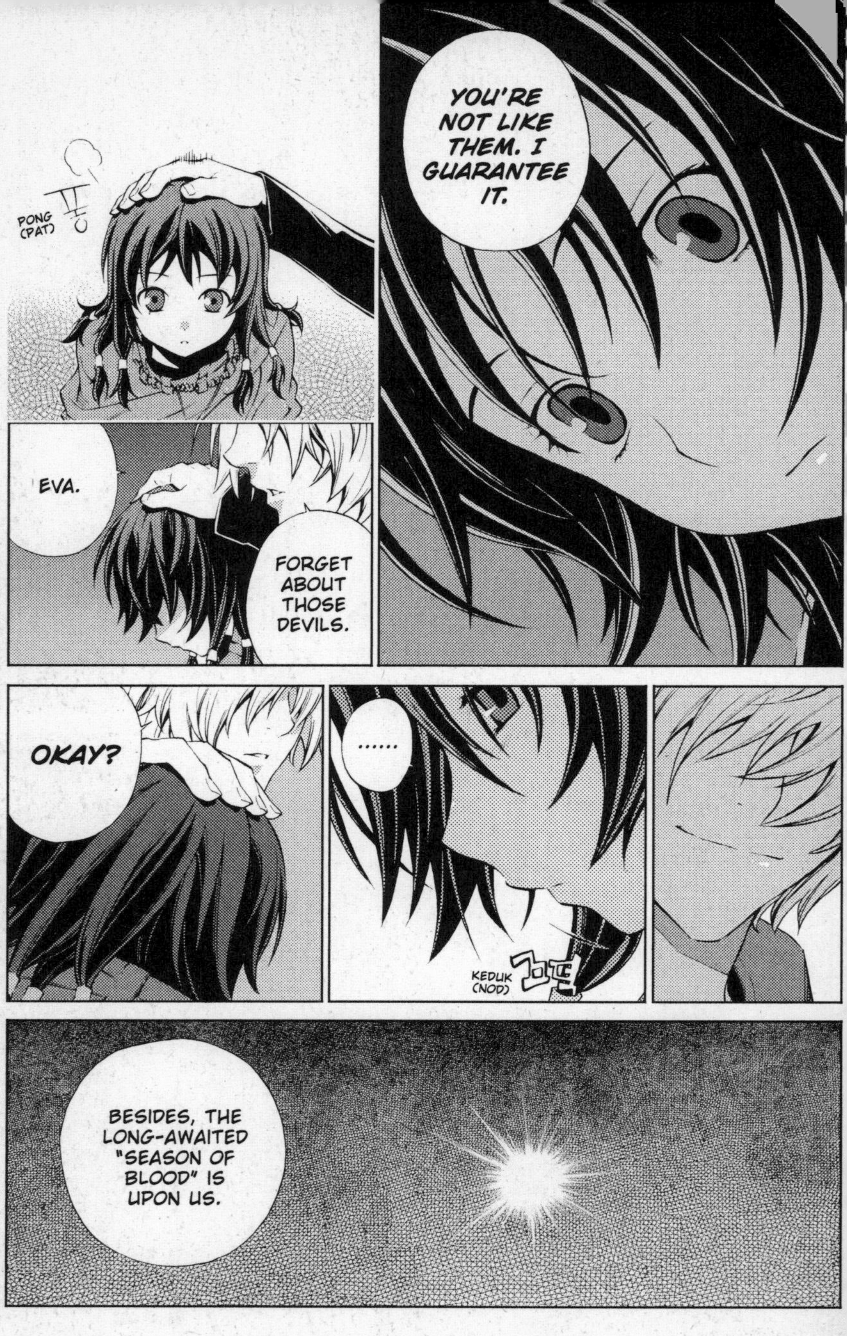
PONG (PAT)
EVA.
FORGET ABOUT THOSE DEVILS.
YOU'RE NOT LIKE THEM. I GUARANTEE IT.
OKAY?
......
KEDUK (NOD)
BESIDES, THE LONG-AWAITED "SEASON OF BLOOD" IS UPON US.

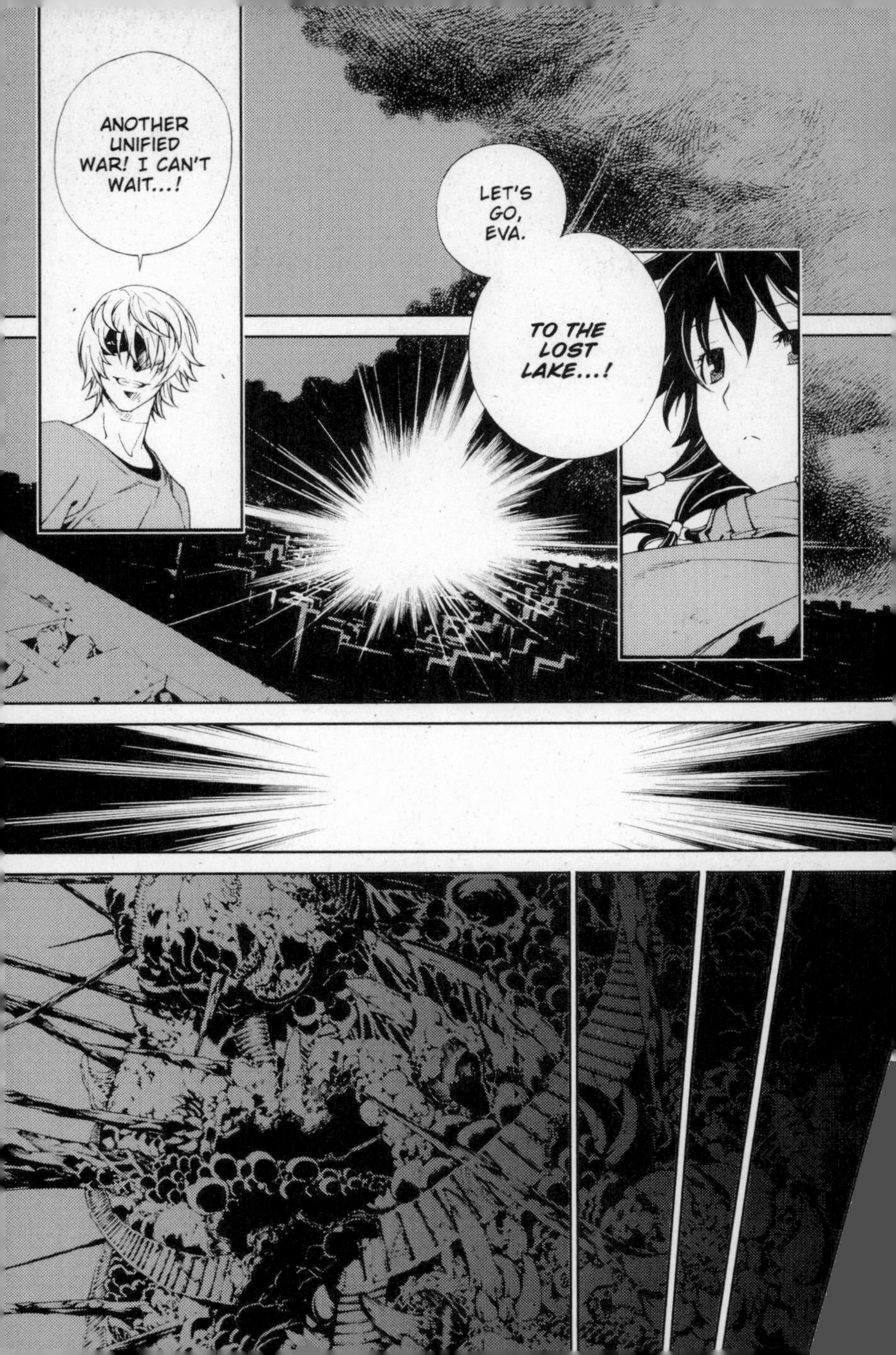
ANOTHER UNIFIED WAR! I CAN'T WAIT...!
LET'S GO, EVA.
TO THE LOST LAKE...!

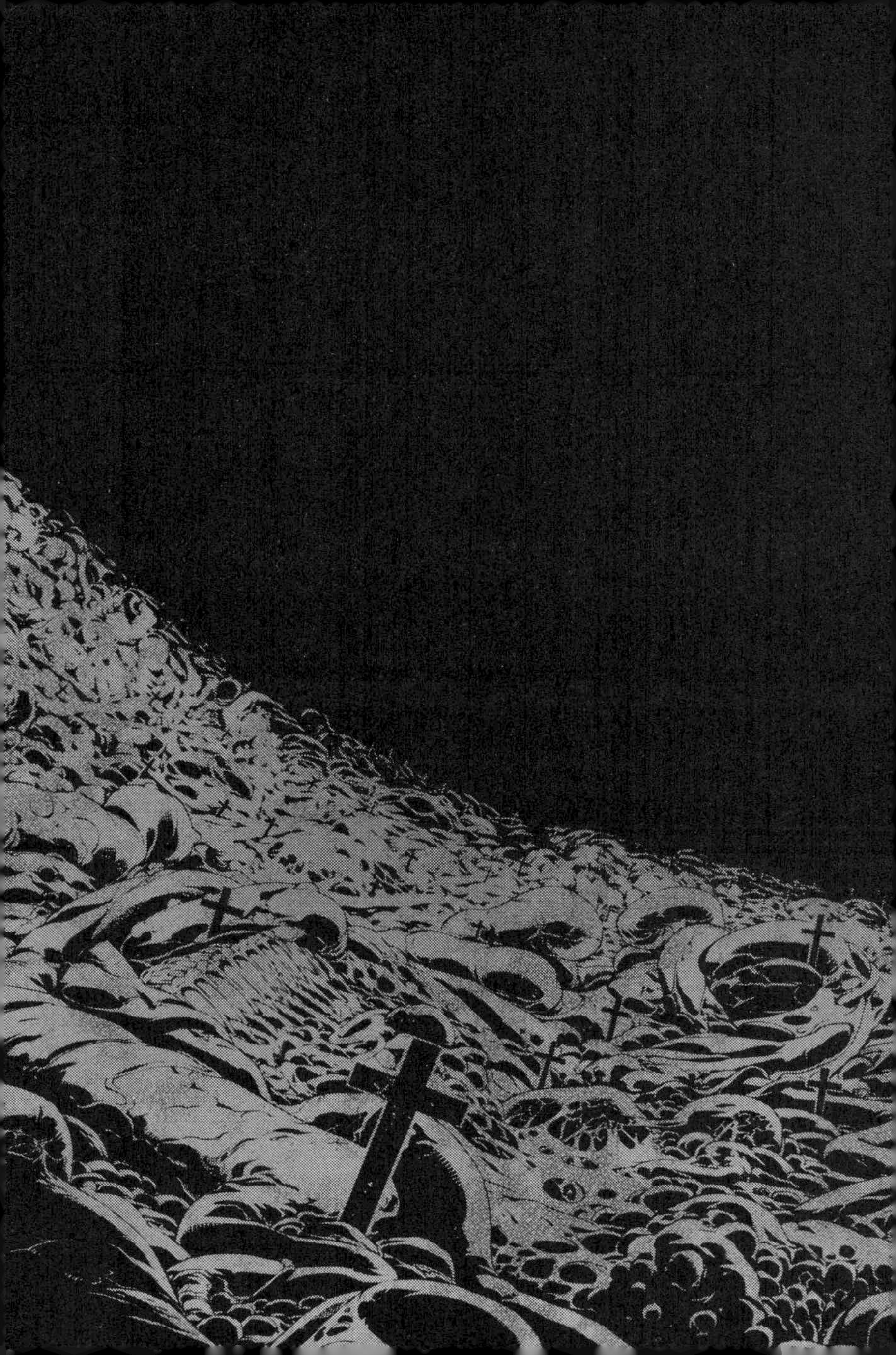

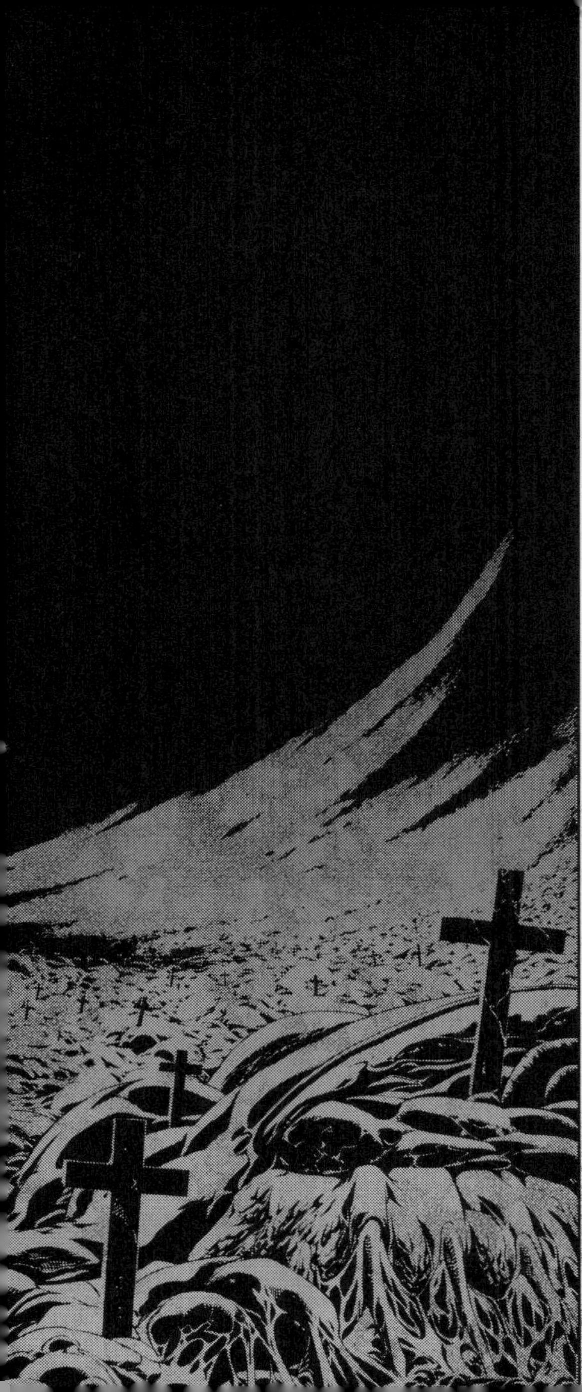
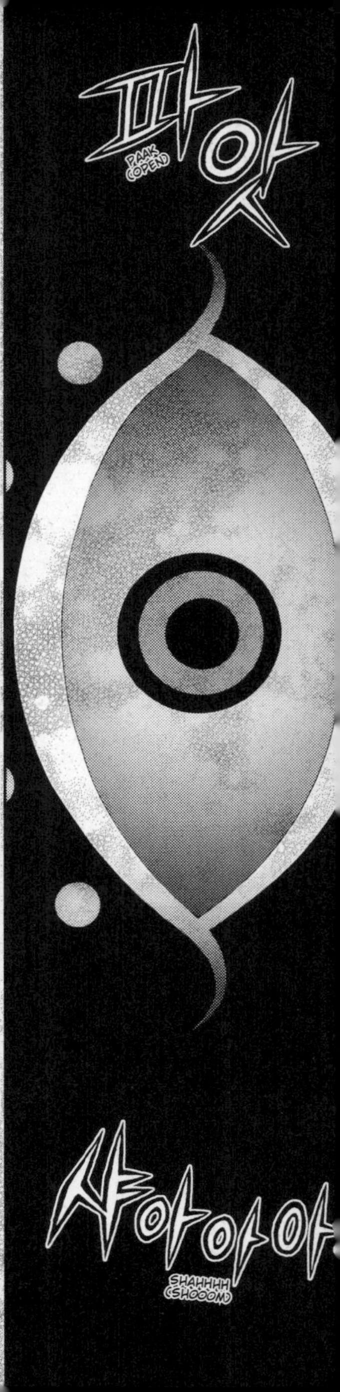
파앗
PAAK (OPEN)
샤아아아
SHAHHHH (SHOOOM)

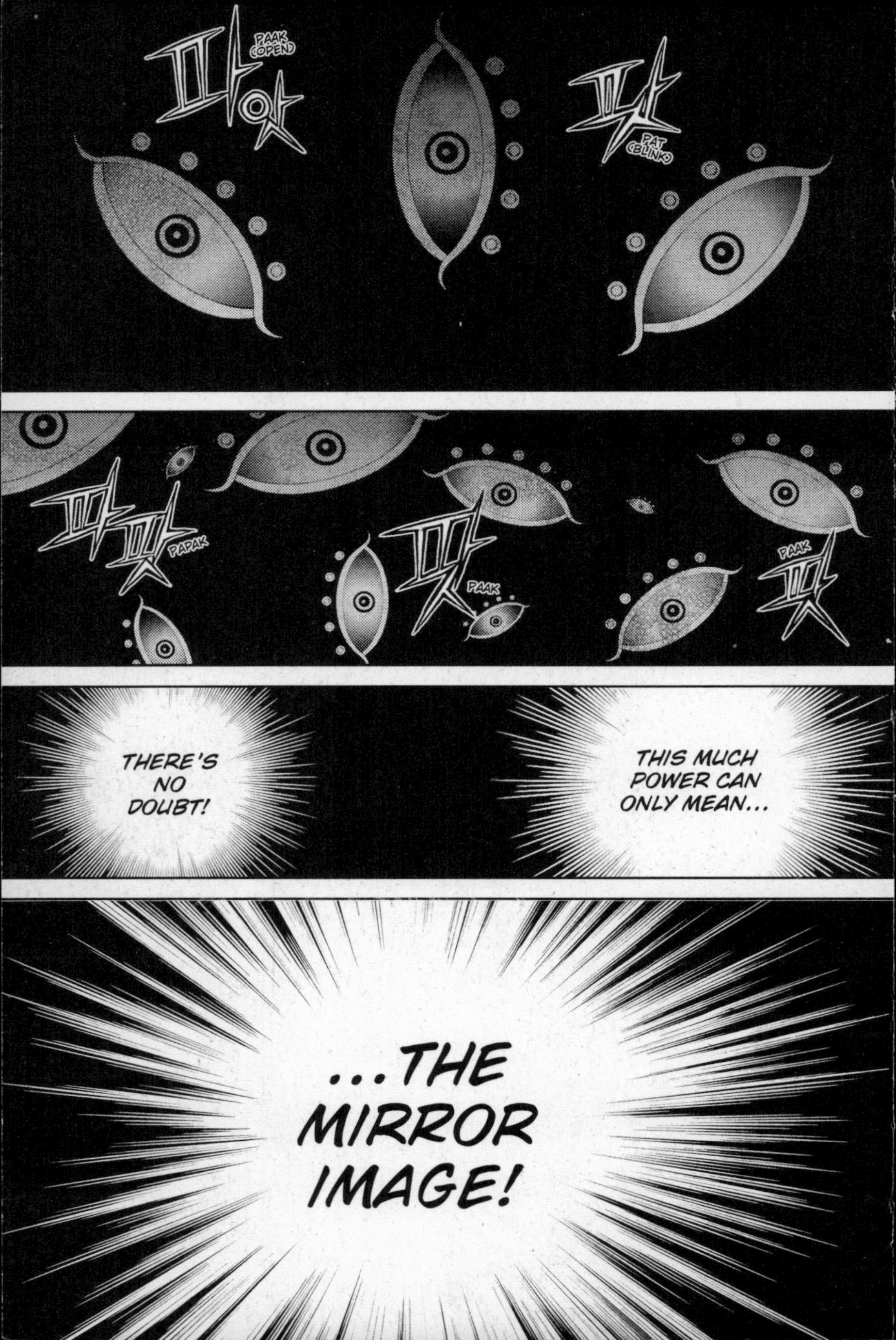
PAAK (OPEN)
PAT (BLINK)
PAPAK
PAAK
PAAK
THERE'S NO DOUBT!
THIS MUCH POWER CAN ONLY MEAN...
...THE MIRROR IMAGE!

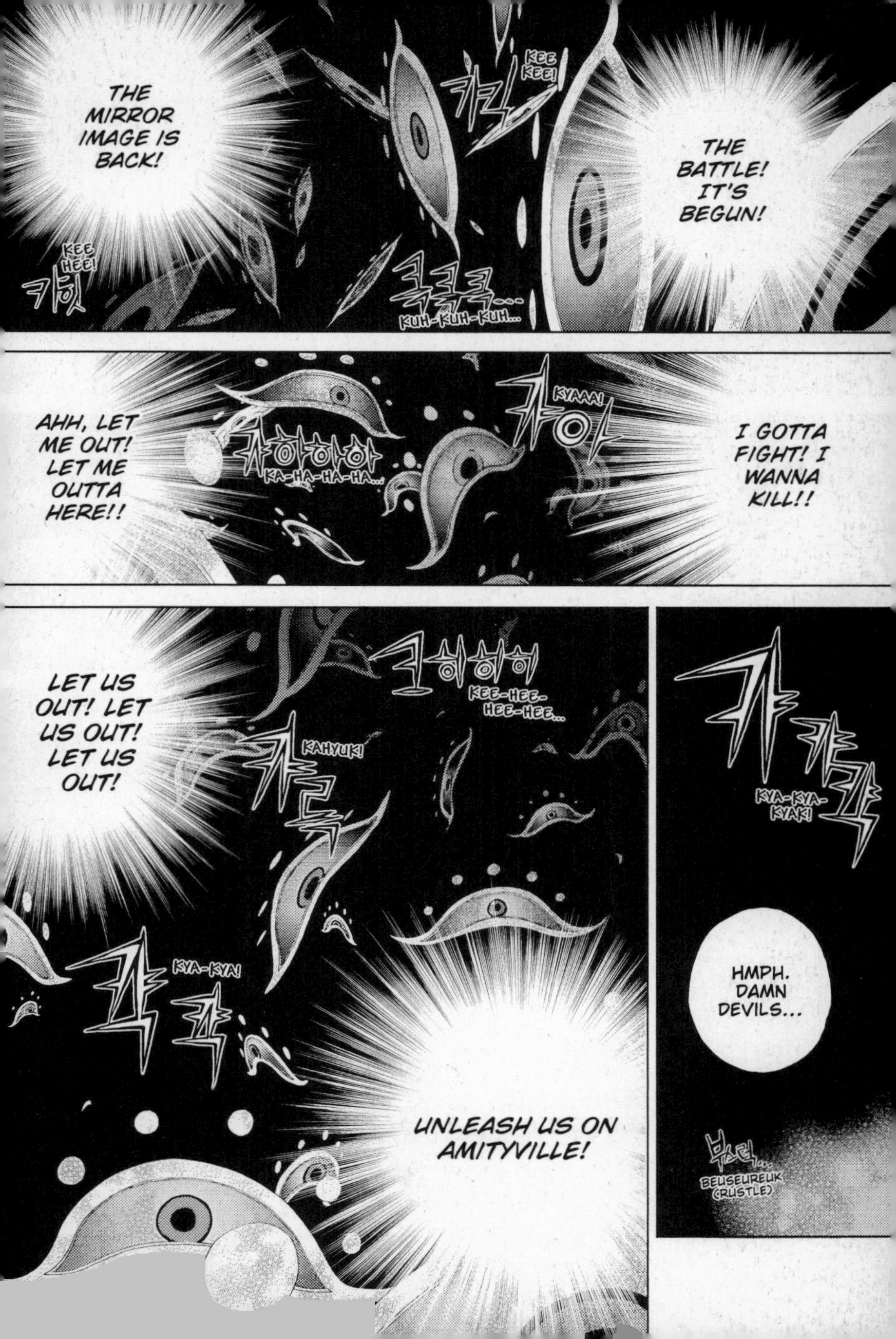
THE MIRROR IMAGE IS BACK!
KEE KEE!
THE BATTLE! IT'S BEGUN!
KEE HEE!
KUH-KUH-KUH...
AHH, LET ME OUT! LET ME OUTTA HERE!!
KA-HA-HA-HA...
KYAAA!
I GOTTA FIGHT! I WANNA KILL!!
LET US OUT! LET US OUT! LET US OUT!
KEE-HEE-HEE-HEE...
KAHYUK!
KYA-KYA!
UNLEASH US ON AMITYVILLE!
KYA-KYA-KYAK!
HMPH. DAMN DEVILS...
BEUSEUREUK (RUSTLE)

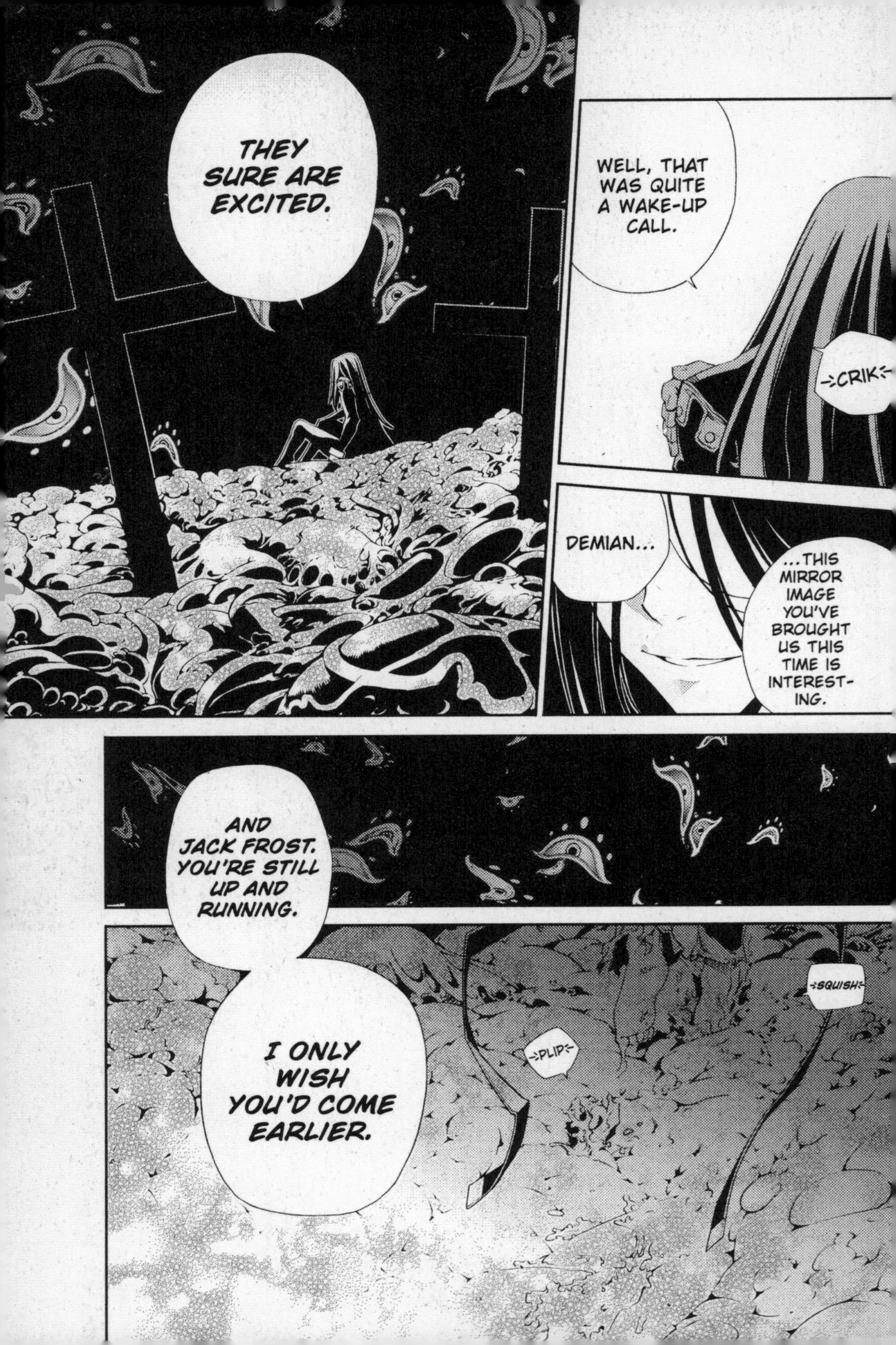
THEY SURE ARE EXCITED.
WELL, THAT WAS QUITE A WAKE-UP CALL.
CRIK
DEMIAN...
...THIS MIRROR IMAGE YOU'VE BROUGHT US THIS TIME IS INTEREST-ING.
AND JACK FROST. YOU'RE STILL UP AND RUNNING.
I ONLY WISH YOU'D COME EARLIER.
PLIP
SQUISH

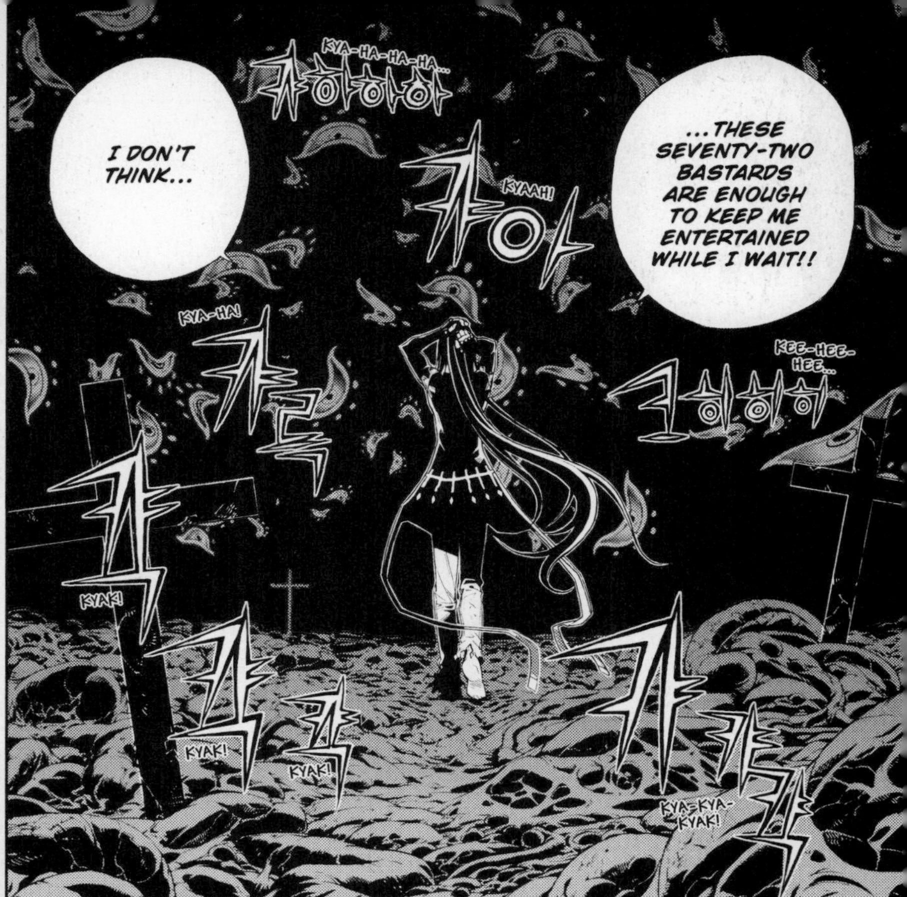
KYA-HA-HA-HA...
I DON'T THINK...
KYAAH!
...THESE SEVENTY-TWO BASTARDS ARE ENOUGH TO KEEP ME ENTERTAINED WHILE I WAIT!!
KYA-HA!
KEE-HEE-HEE...
KYAK!
KYAK!
KYAK!
KYA-KYA-KYAK!
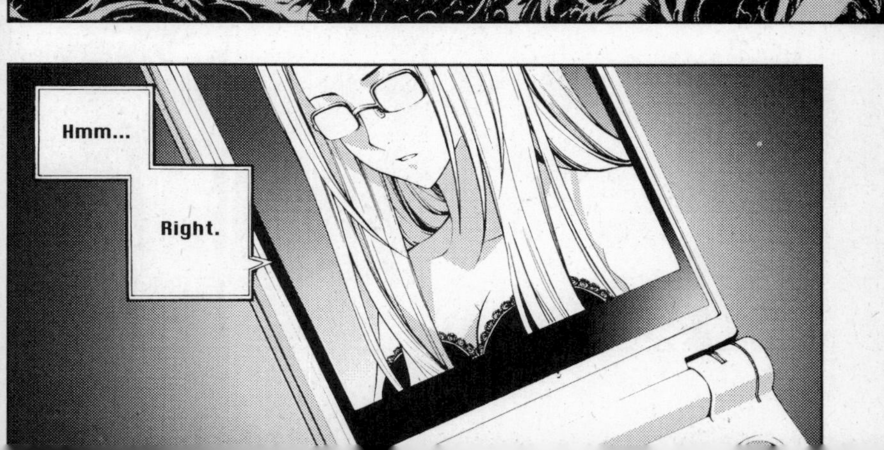
Hmm...
Right.

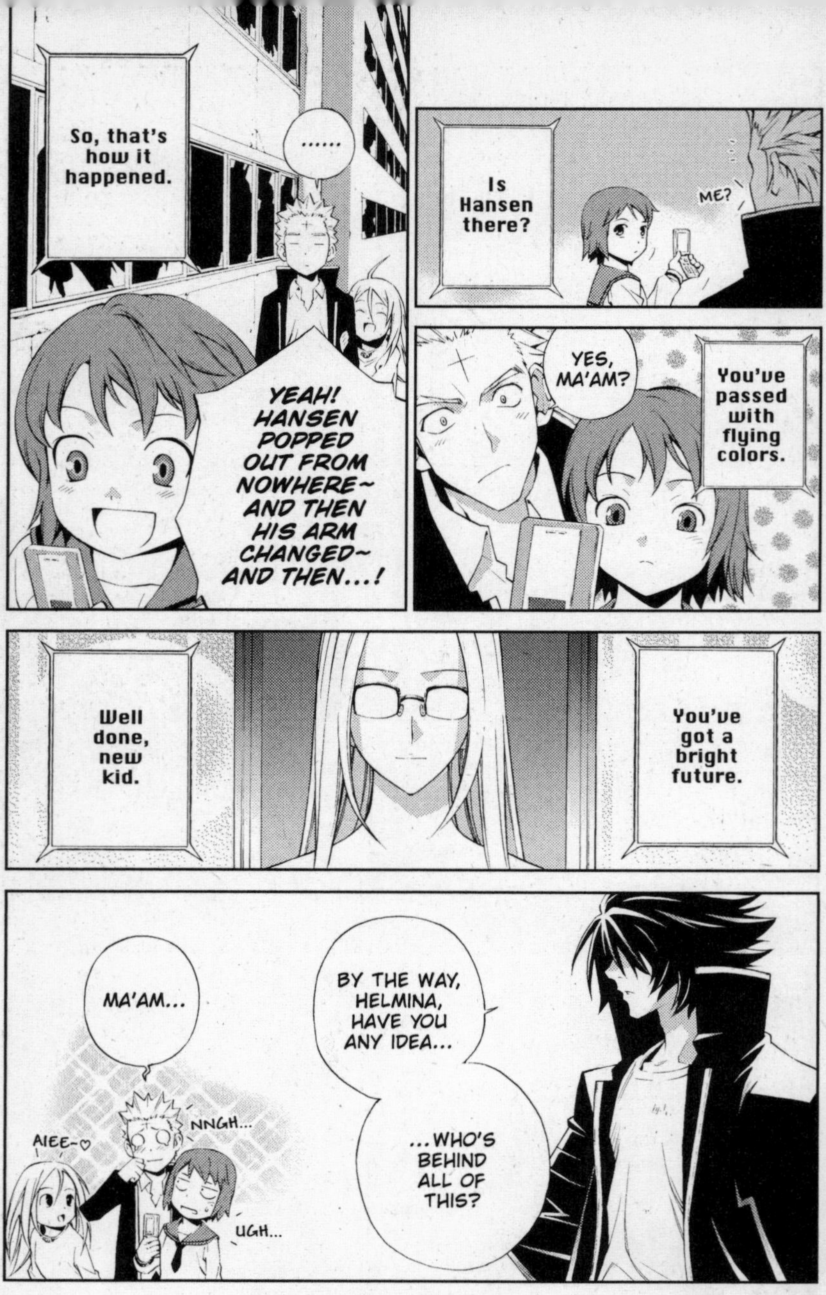
So, that's how it happened.
......
YEAH! HANSEN POPPED OUT FROM NOWHERE~ AND THEN HIS ARM CHANGED~ AND THEN...!
Is Hansen there?
ME?
YES, MA'AM?
You've passed with flying colors.
Well done, new kid.
You've got a bright future.
MA'AM...
AIEE-♡
NNGH...
UGH...
BY THE WAY, HELMINA, HAVE YOU ANY IDEA...
...WHO'S BEHIND ALL OF THIS?

WHAT DO YOU MEAN?

THAT GUY'S ALREADY DEAD.

If it were just a matter of reanimating a body, Dr. Sod could do it.

But not just anyone can revive a soul in Amityville.

ACK!

ARE YOU SAYING SOME OTHER BASTARD REVIVED KAY?!

WHO THE HELL WAS IT?!

WHO THE HELL...

...DID A THING LIKE THAT TO KAY?!!

......

I can think of only one with such poor taste.

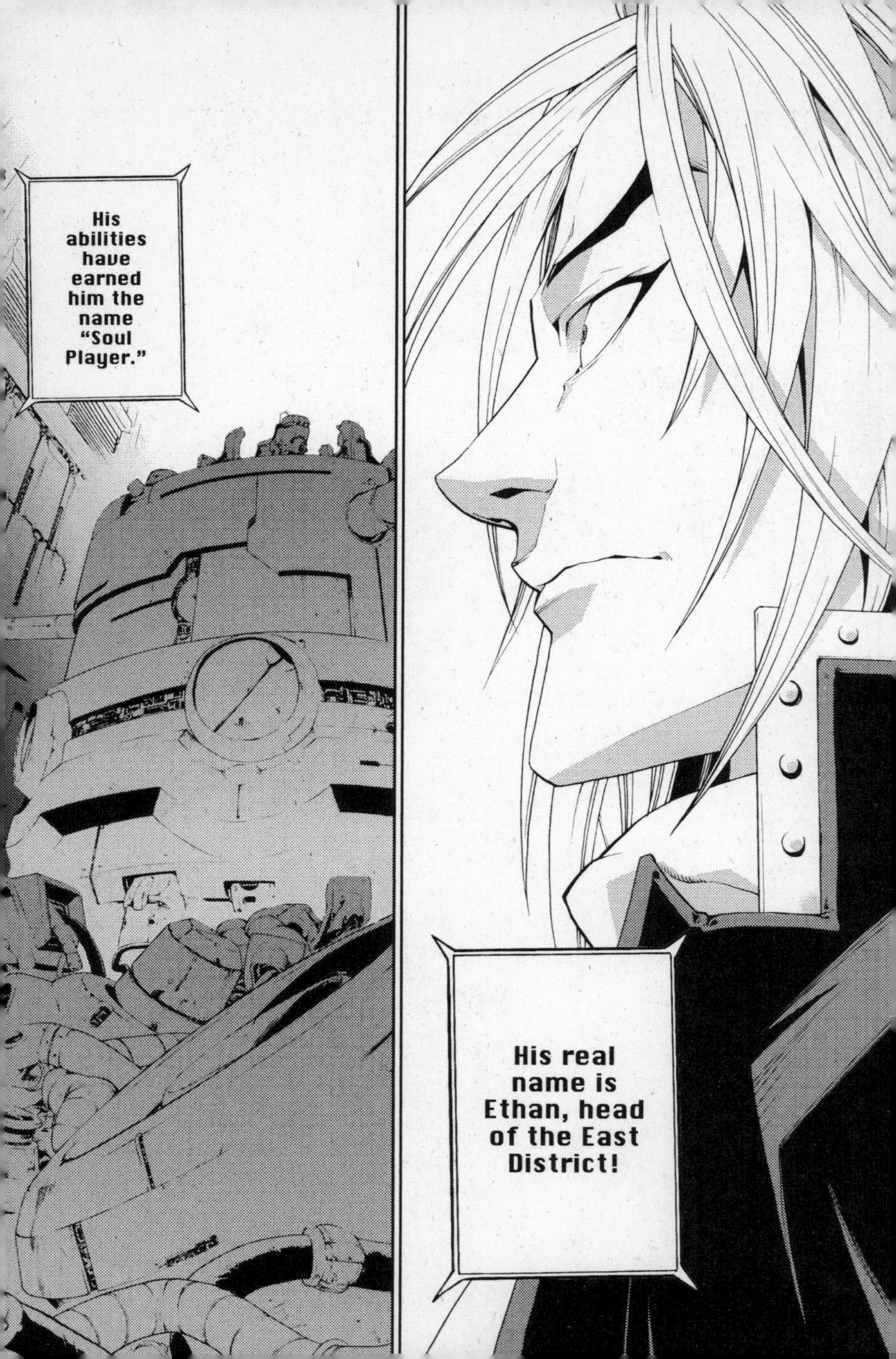
His abilities have earned him the name "Soul Player."
His real name is Ethan, head of the East District!

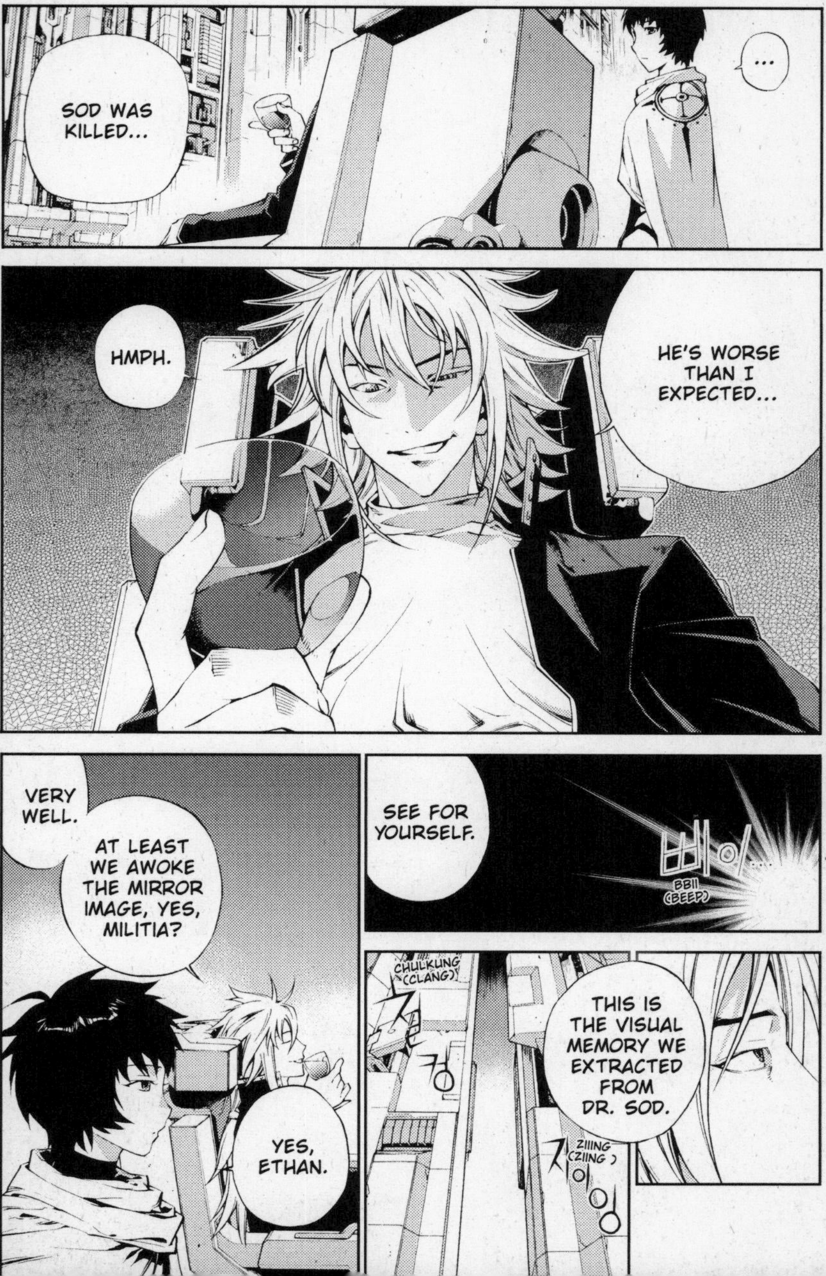
SOD WAS KILLED...
...
HMPH.
HE'S WORSE THAN I EXPECTED...
VERY WELL.
AT LEAST WE AWOKE THE MIRROR IMAGE, YES, MILITIA?
YES, ETHAN.
SEE FOR YOURSELF.
삐이...
BBII (BEEP)
CHULKUNG (CLANG)
THIS IS THE VISUAL MEMORY WE EXTRACTED FROM DR. SOD.
ZIIING (ZIING)

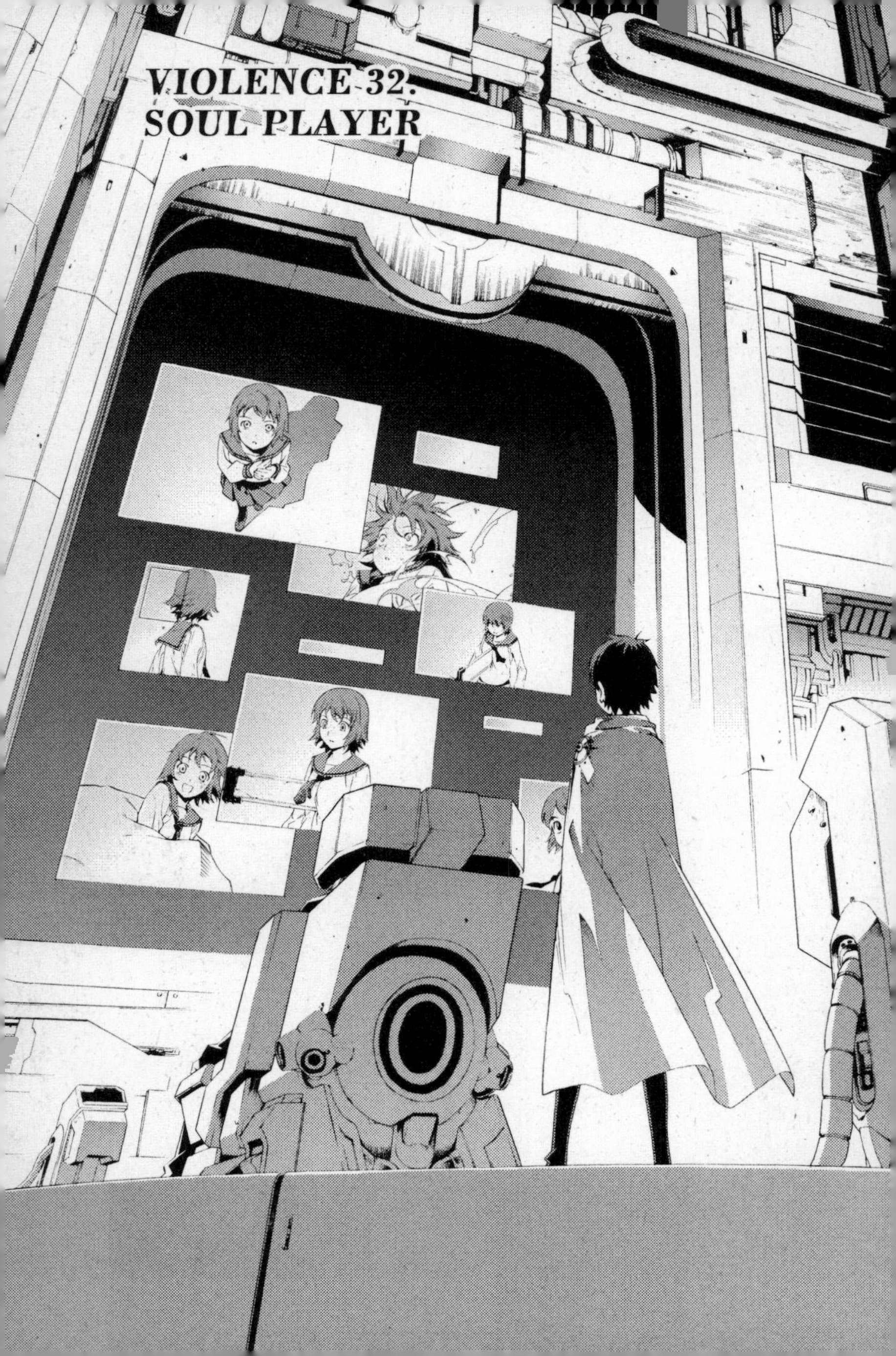
VIOLENCE 32.
SOUL PLAYER

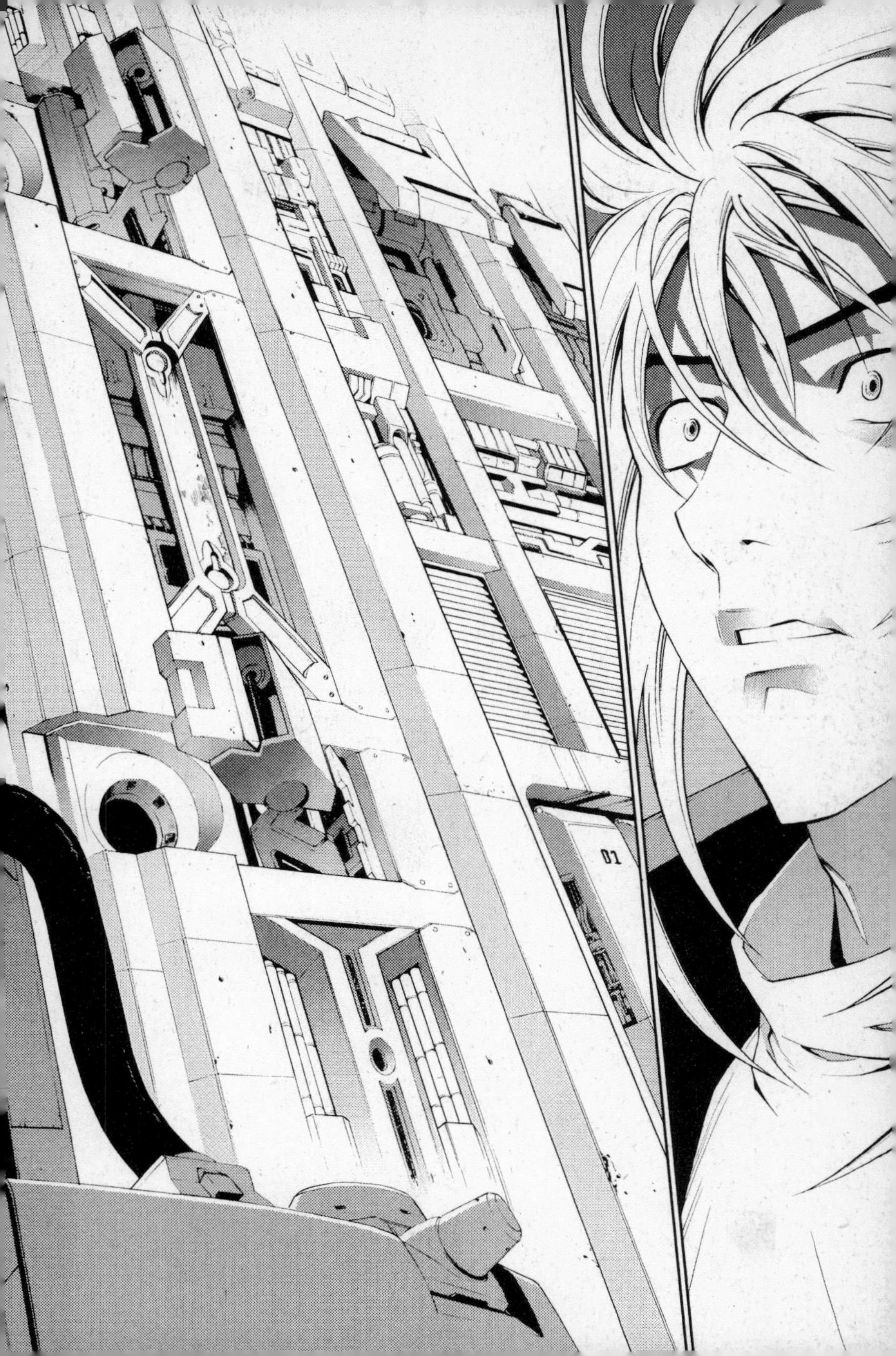
01

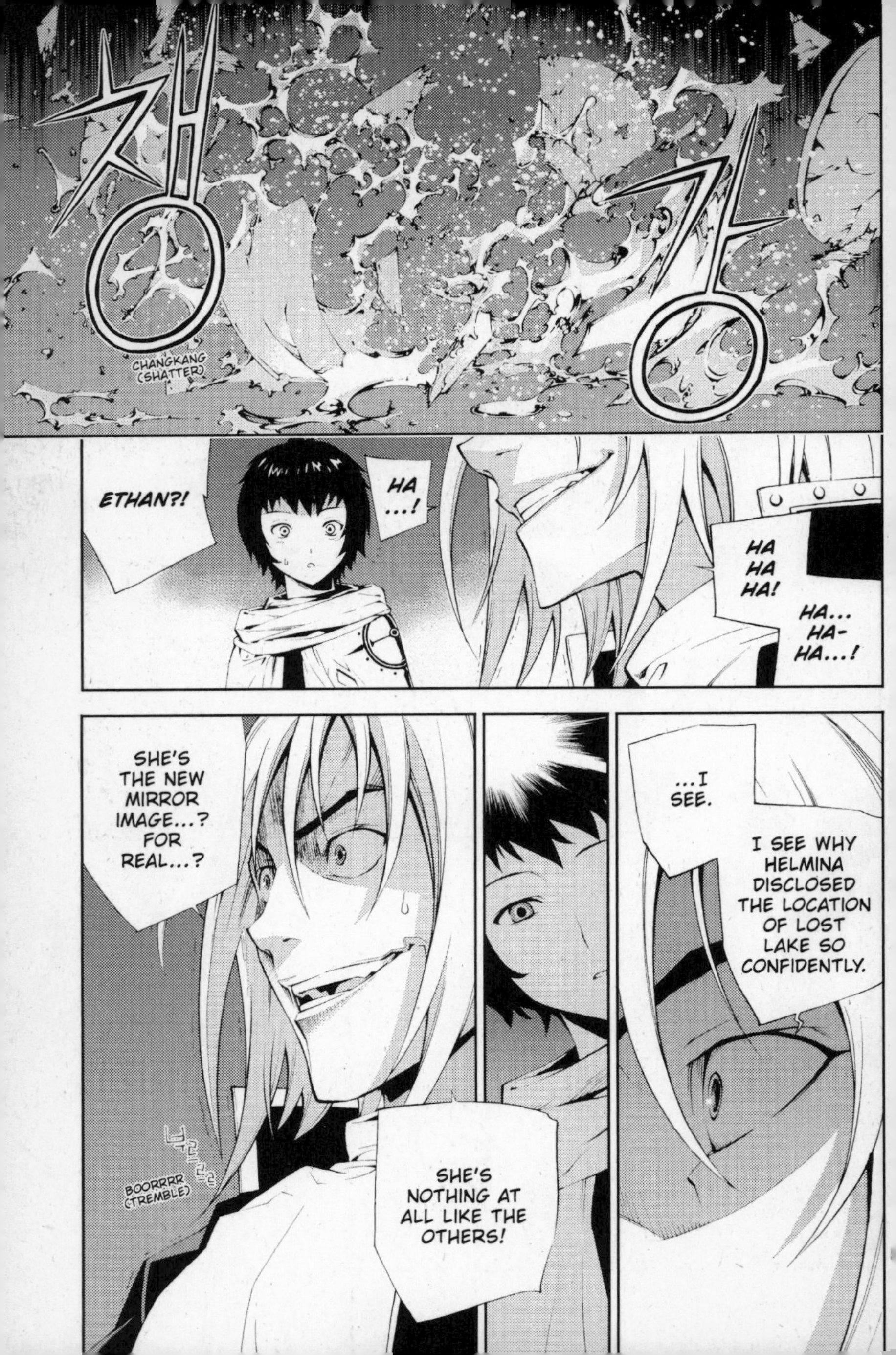
CHANGKANG (SHATTER)
ETHAN?!
HA ...!
HA HA HA!
HA... HA- HA...!
SHE'S THE NEW MIRROR IMAGE...? FOR REAL...?
BOORRRR (TREMBLE)
SHE'S NOTHING AT ALL LIKE THE OTHERS!
...I SEE.
I SEE WHY HELMINA DISCLOSED THE LOCATION OF LOST LAKE SO CONFIDENTLY.

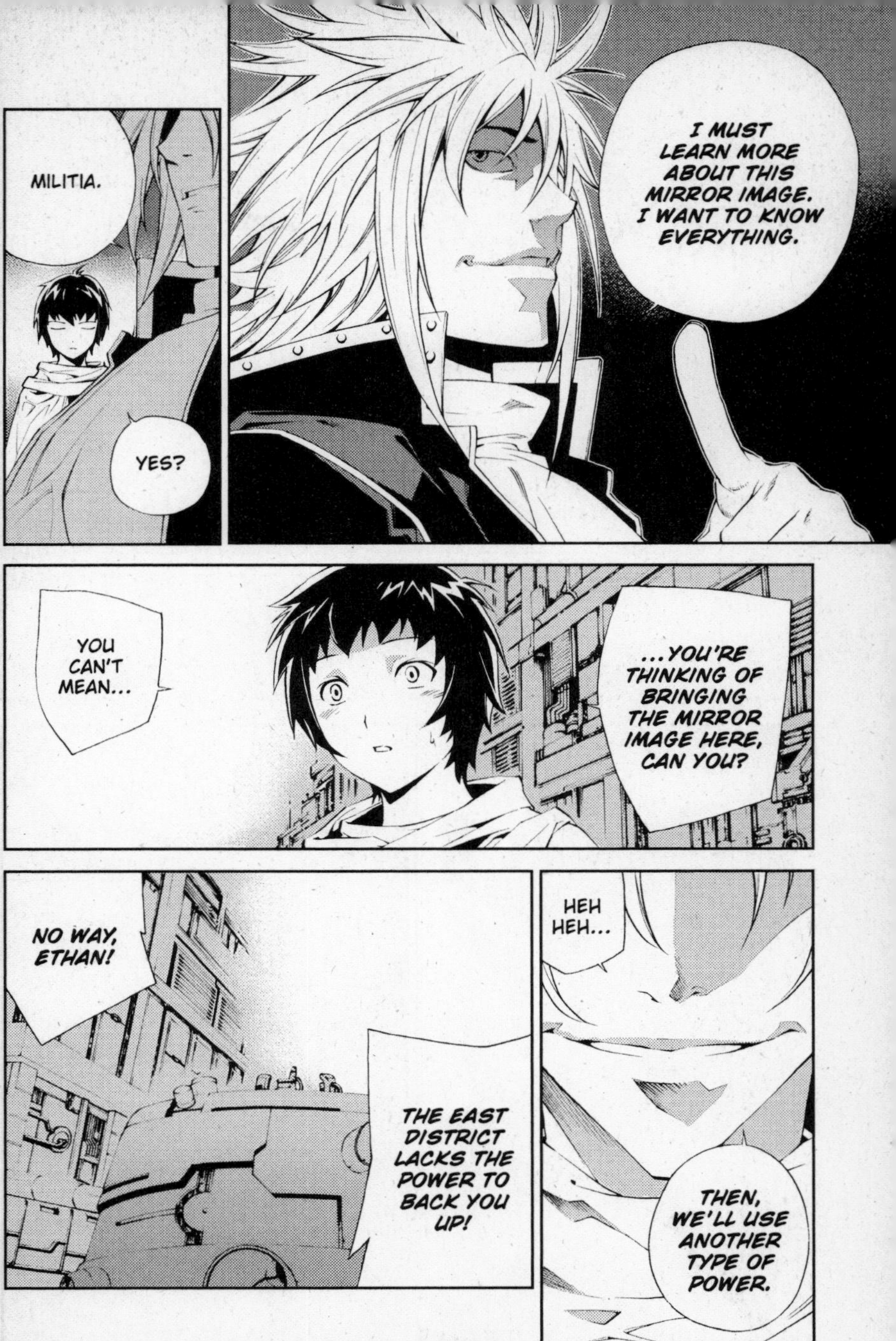
MILITIA.
YES?
I MUST LEARN MORE ABOUT THIS MIRROR IMAGE. I WANT TO KNOW EVERYTHING.
YOU CAN'T MEAN...
...YOU'RE THINKING OF BRINGING THE MIRROR IMAGE HERE, CAN YOU?
NO WAY, ETHAN!
THE EAST DISTRICT LACKS THE POWER TO BACK YOU UP!
HEH HEH...
THEN, WE'LL USE ANOTHER TYPE OF POWER.

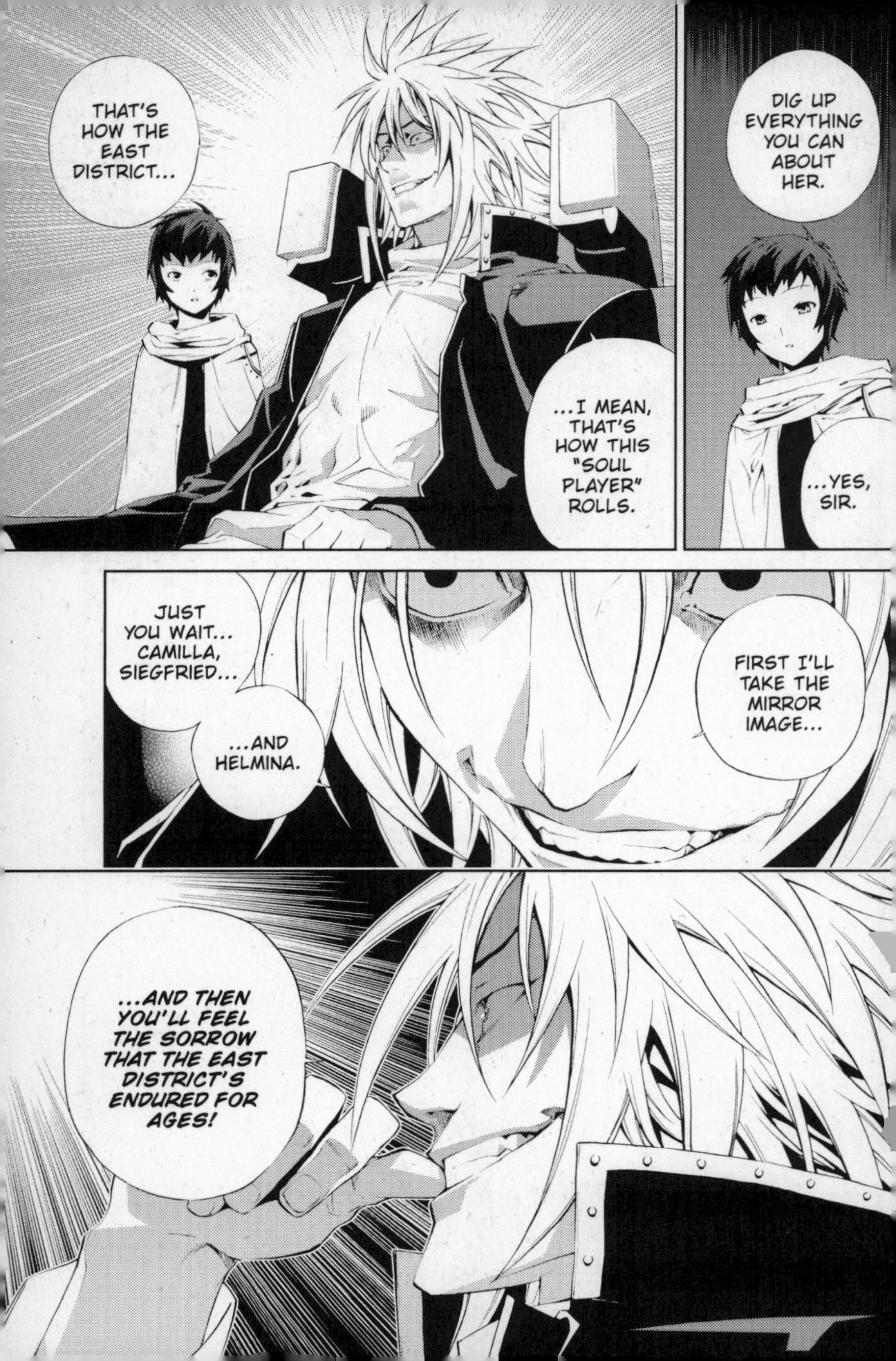
THAT'S HOW THE EAST DISTRICT...
...I MEAN, THAT'S HOW THIS "SOUL PLAYER" ROLLS.
DIG UP EVERYTHING YOU CAN ABOUT HER.
...YES, SIR.
JUST YOU WAIT... CAMILLA, SIEGFRIED...
...AND HELMINA.
FIRST I'LL TAKE THE MIRROR IMAGE...
...AND THEN YOU'LL FEEL THE SORROW THAT THE EAST DISTRICT'S ENDURED FOR AGES!

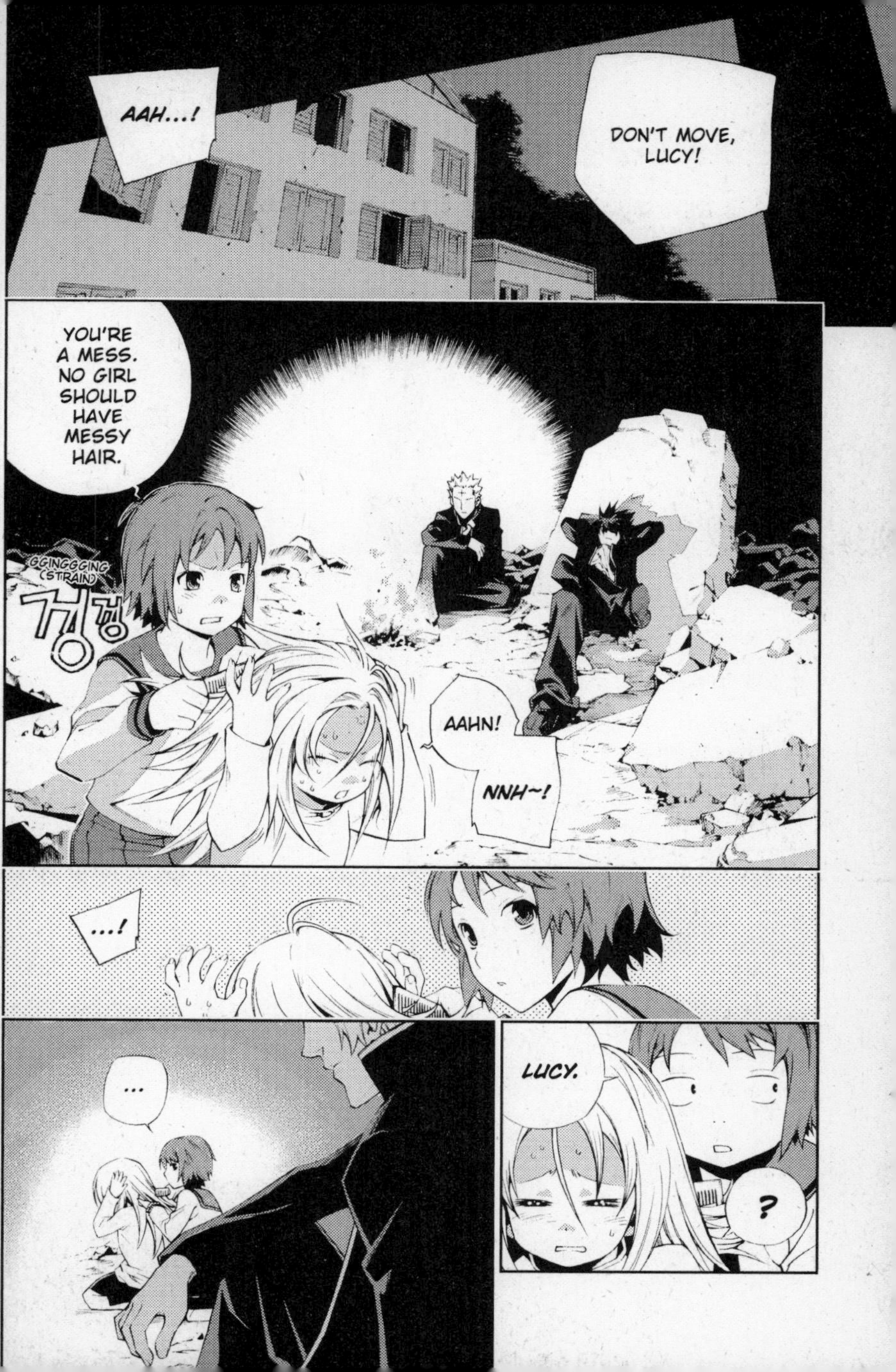
AAH...!
DON'T MOVE, LUCY!
YOU'RE A MESS. NO GIRL SHOULD HAVE MESSY HAIR.
GGINGGGING (STRAIN)
AAHN!
NNH~!
...!
...
LUCY.
?

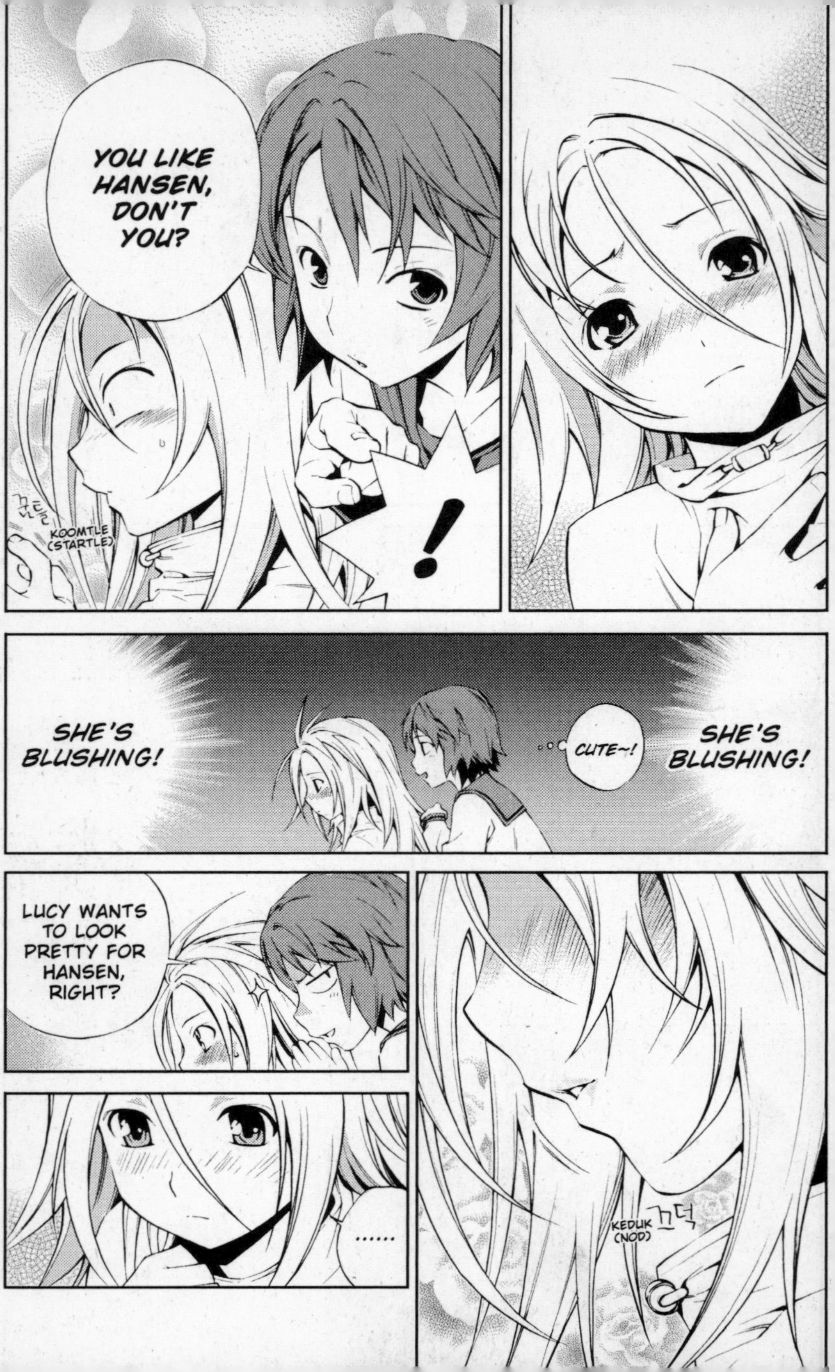
YOU LIKE HANSEN, DON'T YOU?
KOOMTLE (STARTLE)
!
SHE'S BLUSHING!
CUTE~!
SHE'S BLUSHING!
LUCY WANTS TO LOOK PRETTY FOR HANSEN, RIGHT?
......
KEDUK (NOD)
끄덕

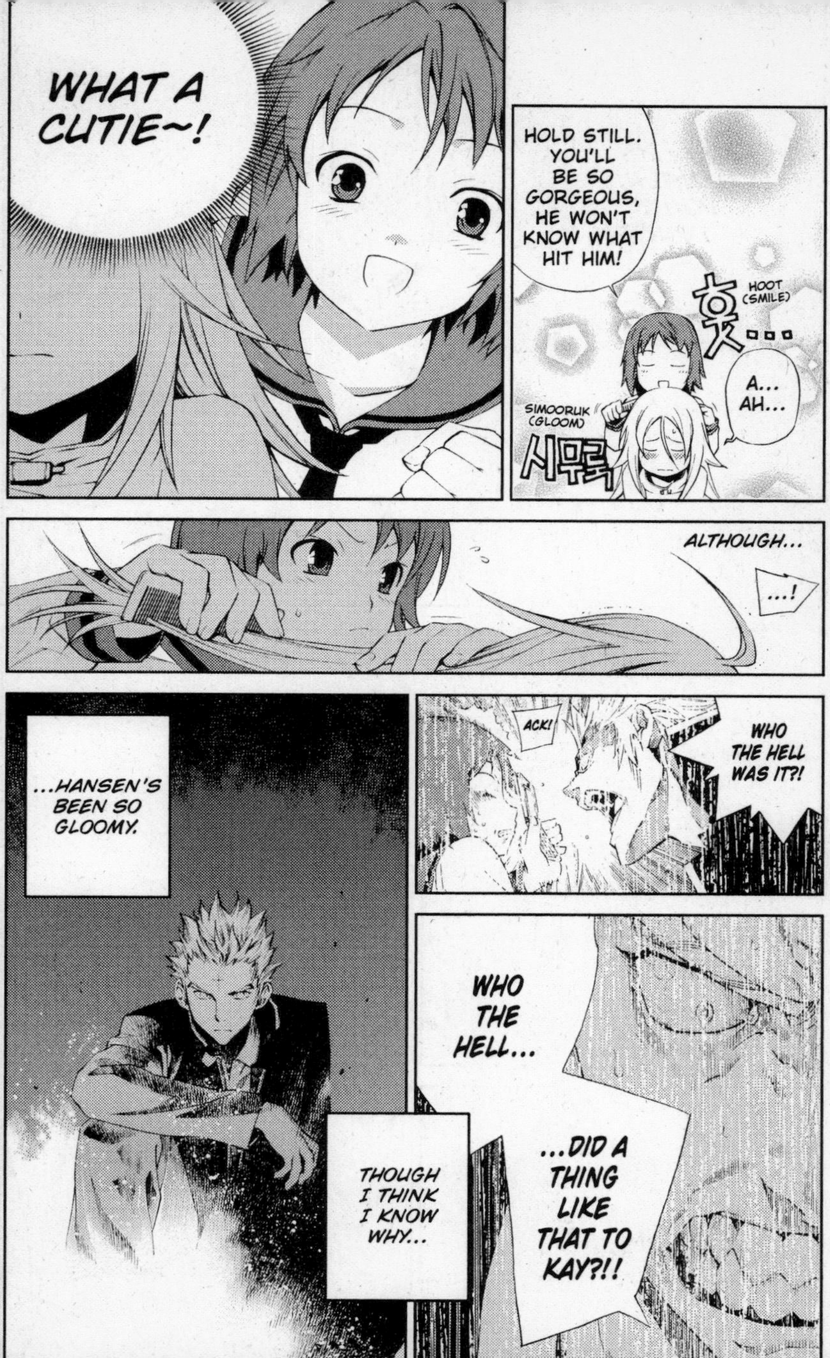
WHAT A CUTIE~!
HOLD STILL. YOU'LL BE SO GORGEOUS, HE WON'T KNOW WHAT HIT HIM!
HOOT (SMILE)
훗...
A... AH...
SIMOORUK (GLOOM)
시무룩
ALTHOUGH...
...!
...HANSEN'S BEEN SO GLOOMY.
THOUGH I THINK I KNOW WHY...
ACK!
WHO THE HELL WAS IT?!
WHO THE HELL...
...DID A THING LIKE THAT TO KAY?!!

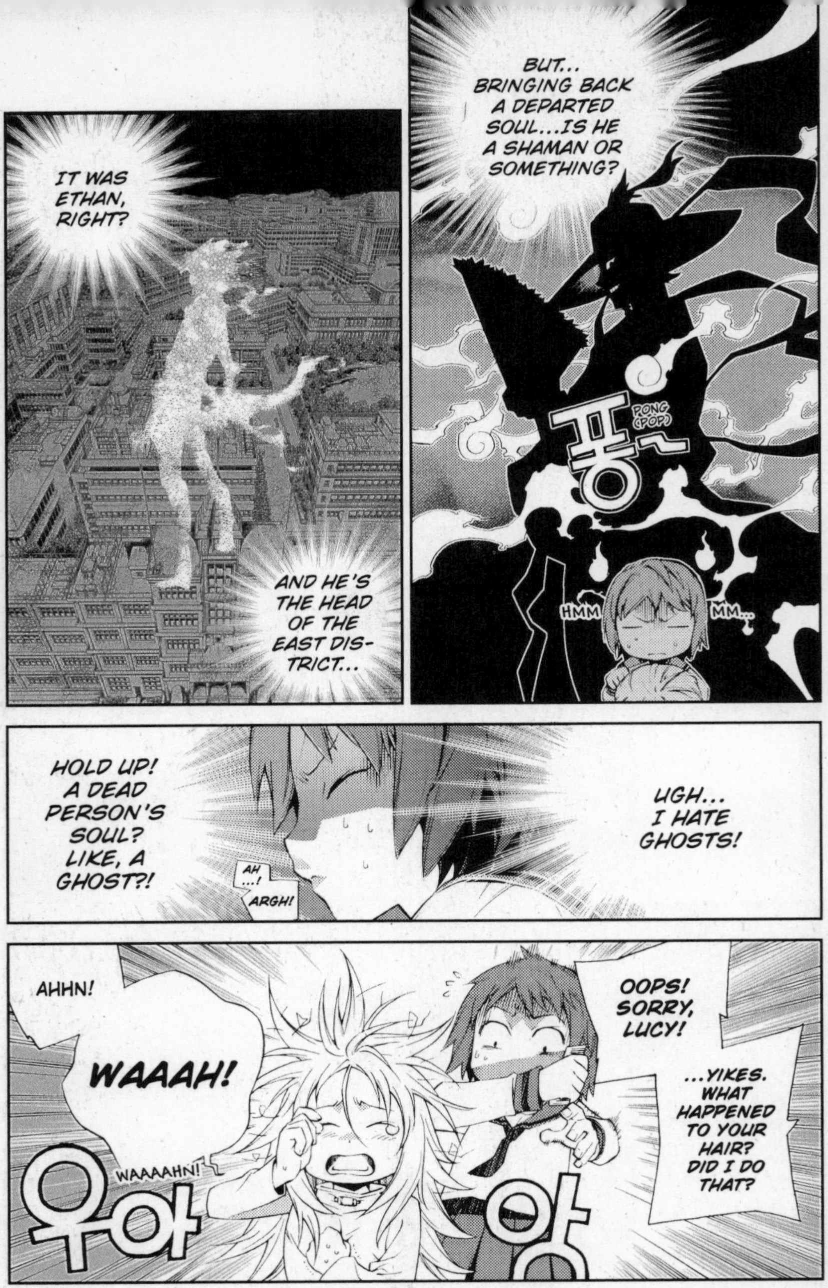
IT WAS ETHAN, RIGHT?
AND HE'S THE HEAD OF THE EAST DIS-TRICT...
BUT... BRINGING BACK A DEPARTED SOUL...IS HE A SHAMAN OR SOMETHING?
퐁~
PONG (POP)
HMM
MM...
HOLD UP! A DEAD PERSON'S SOUL? LIKE, A GHOST?!
AH ...!
ARGH!
UGH... I HATE GHOSTS!
AHHN!
WAAAH!
우아
WAAAAHN!
앙
OOPS! SORRY, LUCY!
...YIKES. WHAT HAPPENED TO YOUR HAIR? DID I DO THAT?

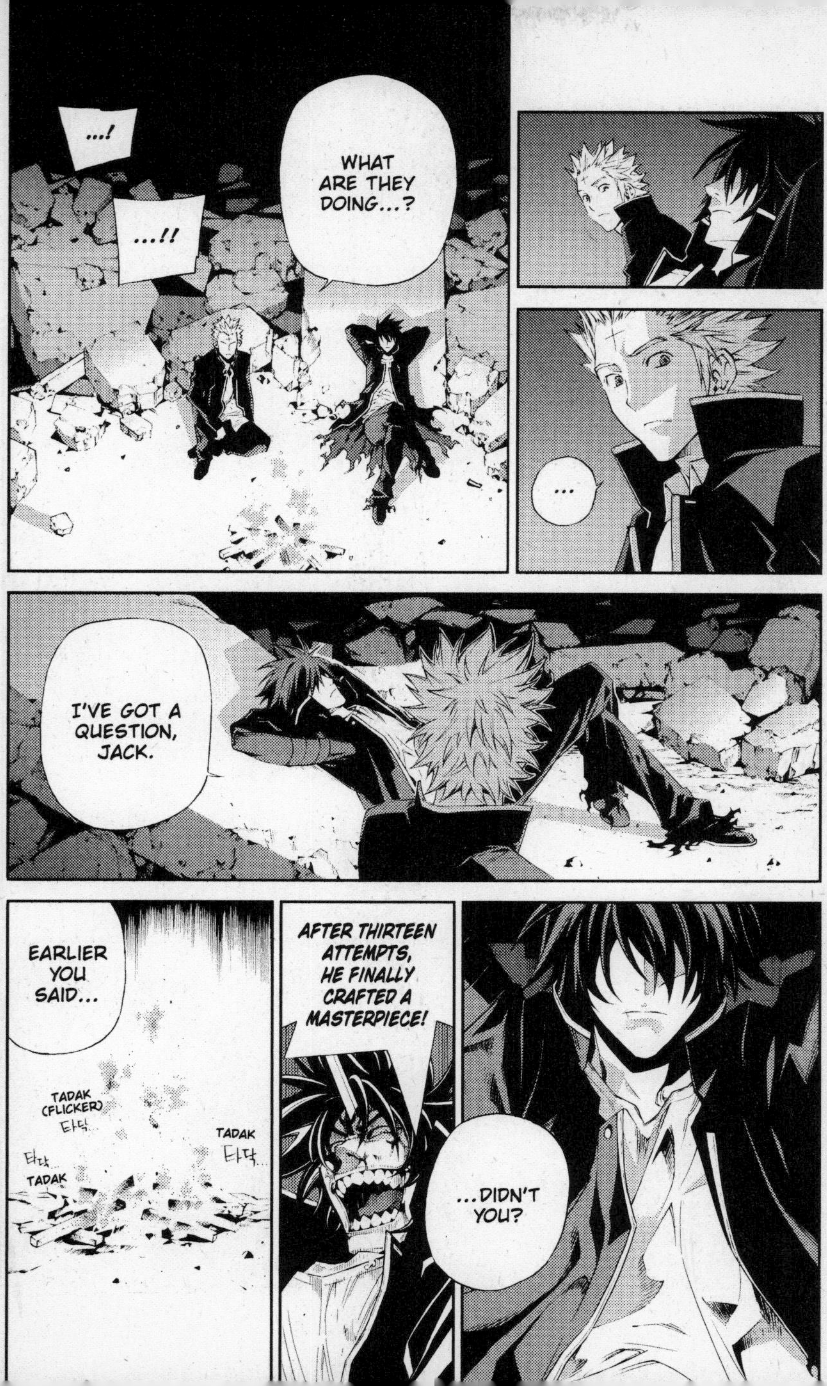
...!
...!!
WHAT ARE THEY DOING...?
...
I'VE GOT A QUESTION, JACK.
EARLIER YOU SAID...
TADAK (FLICKER)
타닥...
TADAK
타닥...
TADAK
타닥...
AFTER THIRTEEN ATTEMPTS, HE FINALLY CRAFTED A MASTERPIECE!
...DIDN'T YOU?

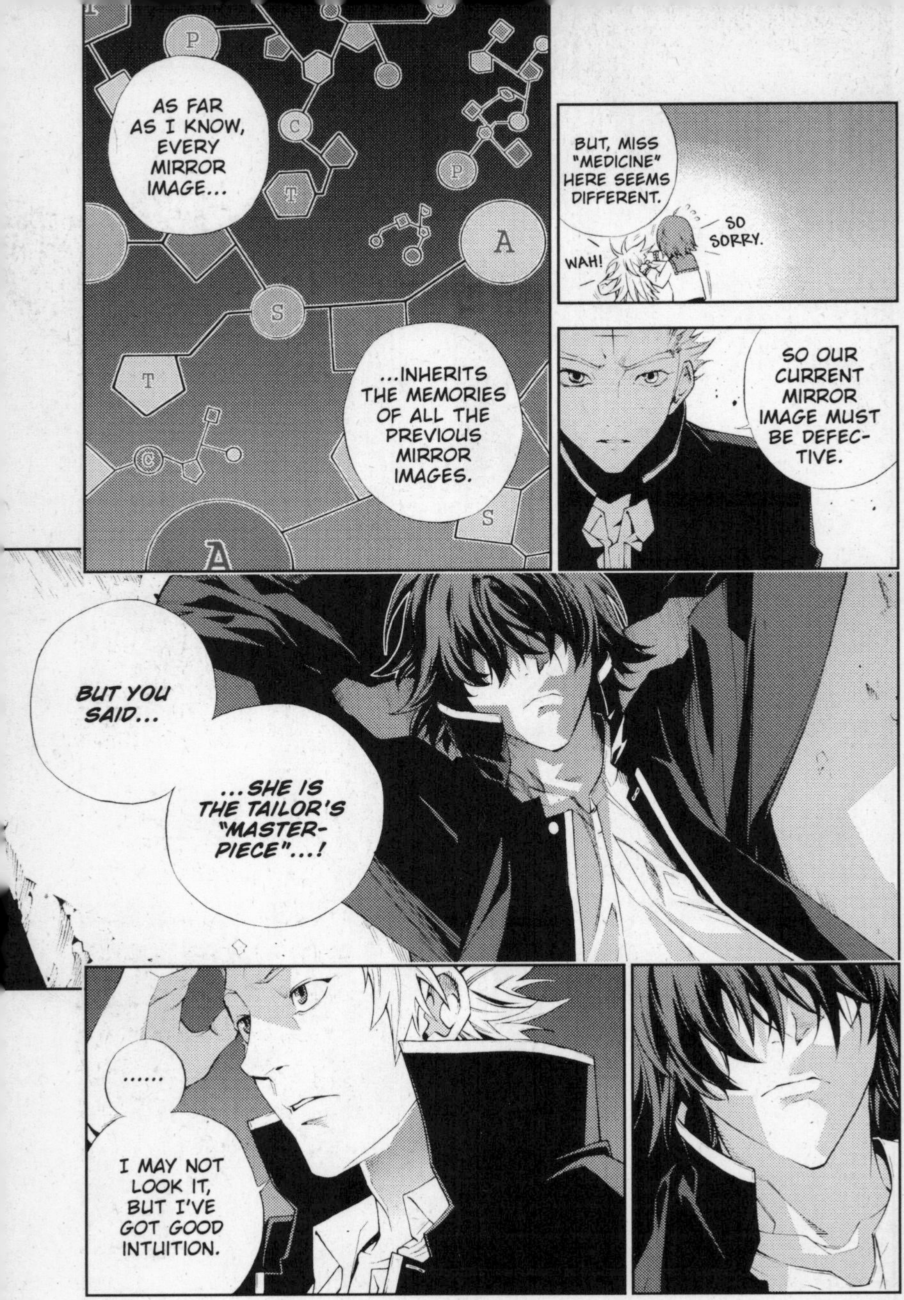
AS FAR AS I KNOW, EVERY MIRROR IMAGE...
...INHERITS THE MEMORIES OF ALL THE PREVIOUS MIRROR IMAGES.
BUT, MISS "MEDICINE" HERE SEEMS DIFFERENT.
WAH!
SO SORRY.
SO OUR CURRENT MIRROR IMAGE MUST BE DEFECTIVE.
BUT YOU SAID...
...SHE IS THE TAILOR'S "MASTERPIECE"...!
......
I MAY NOT LOOK IT, BUT I'VE GOT GOOD INTUITION.

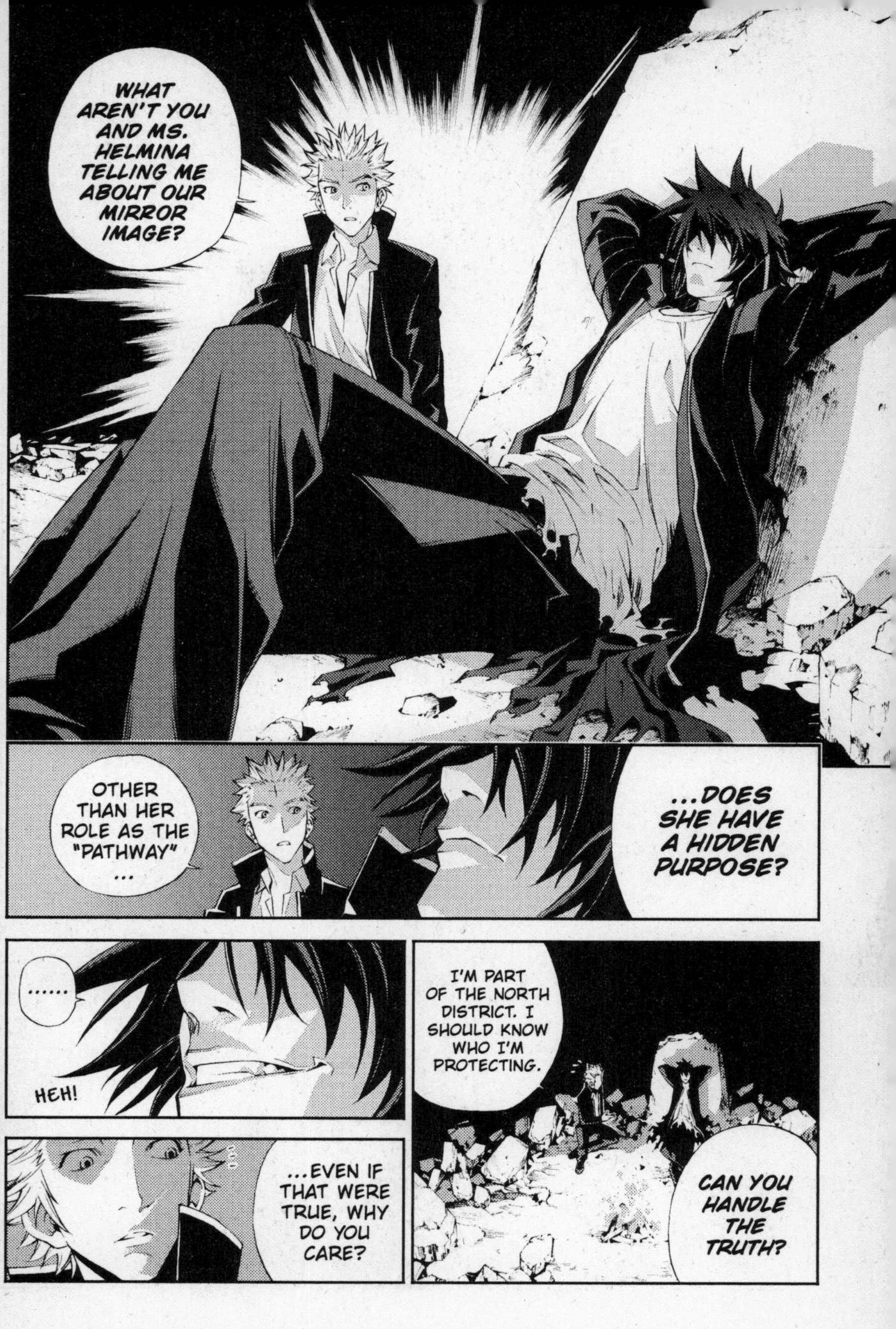

WHAT AREN'T YOU AND MS. HELMINA TELLING ME ABOUT OUR MIRROR IMAGE?
OTHER THAN HER ROLE AS THE "PATHWAY"...
...DOES SHE HAVE A HIDDEN PURPOSE?
......
HEH!
I'M PART OF THE NORTH DISTRICT. I SHOULD KNOW WHO I'M PROTECTING.
...EVEN IF THAT WERE TRUE, WHY DO YOU CARE?
CAN YOU HANDLE THE TRUTH?

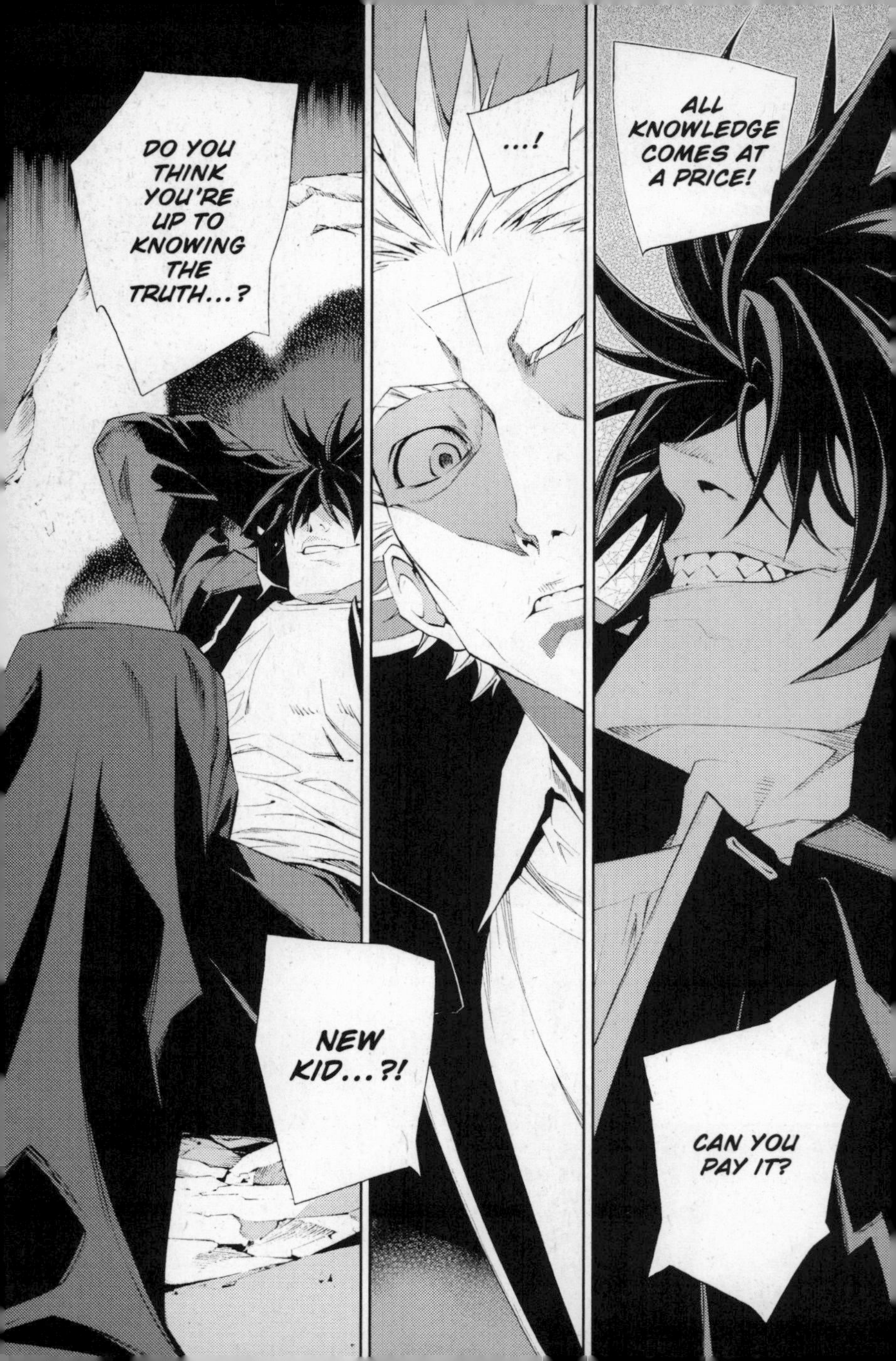
DO YOU THINK YOU'RE UP TO KNOWING THE TRUTH...?
NEW KID...?!
...!
ALL KNOWLEDGE COMES AT A PRICE!
CAN YOU PAY IT?

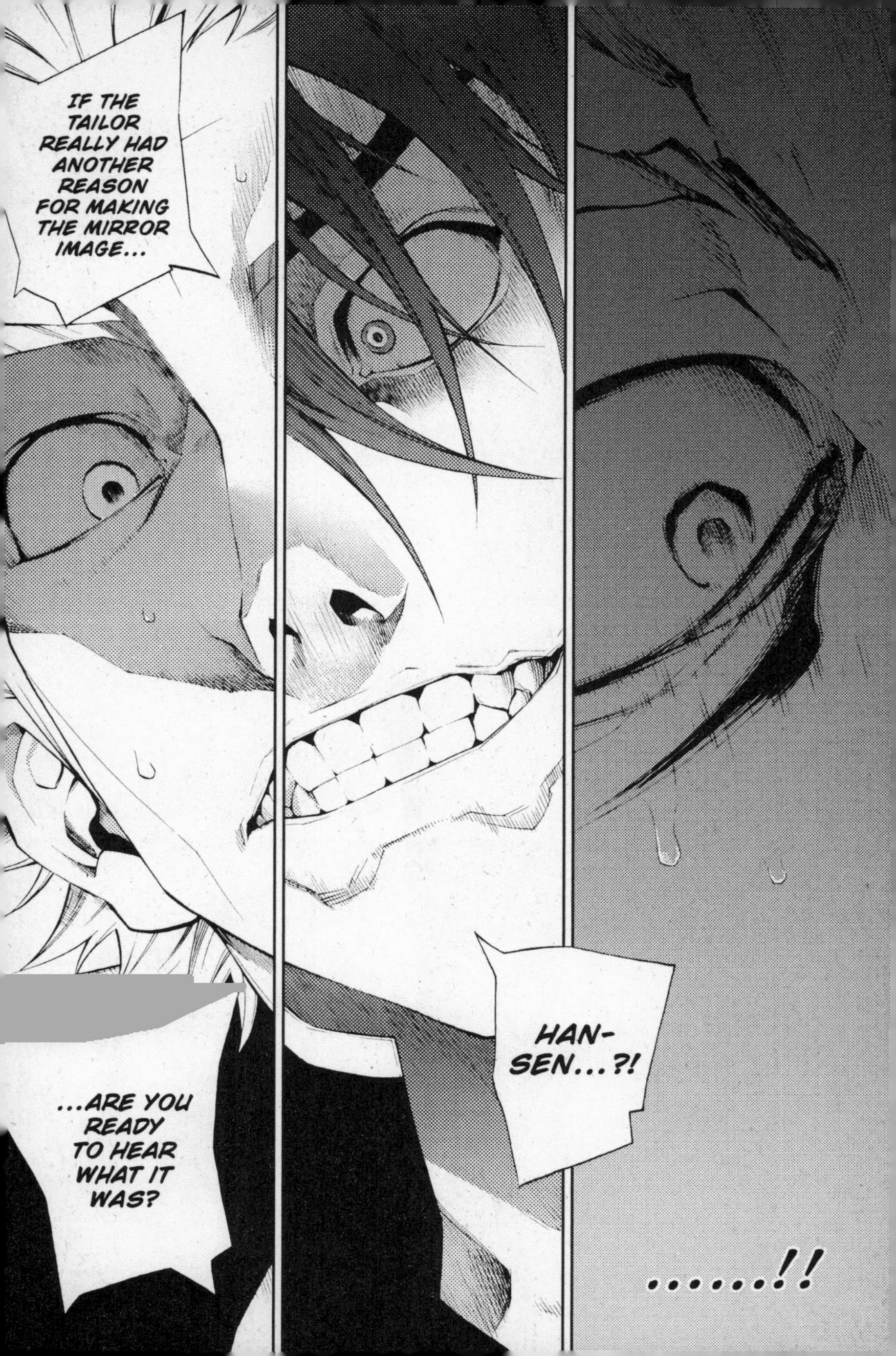
IF THE TAILOR REALLY HAD ANOTHER REASON FOR MAKING THE MIRROR IMAGE...
...ARE YOU READY TO HEAR WHAT IT WAS?
HAN-SEN...?!
......!!

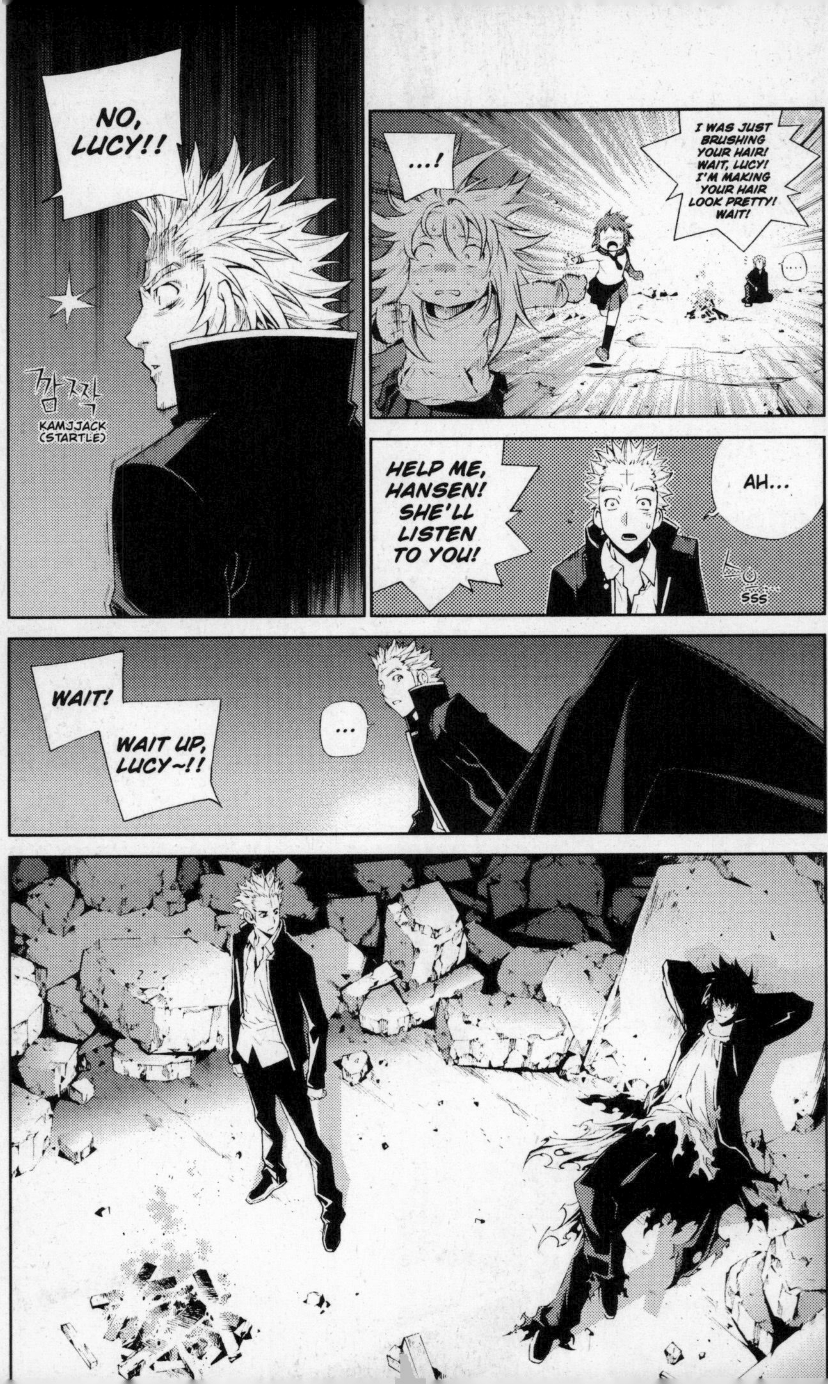
NO, LUCY!!
깜짝
KAMJJACK (STARTLE)
...!
I WAS JUST BRUSHING YOUR HAIR! WAIT, LUCY! I'M MAKING YOUR HAIR LOOK PRETTY! WAIT!
...
HELP ME, HANSEN! SHE'LL LISTEN TO YOU!
AH...
SSS
WAIT!
WAIT UP, LUCY~!!
...

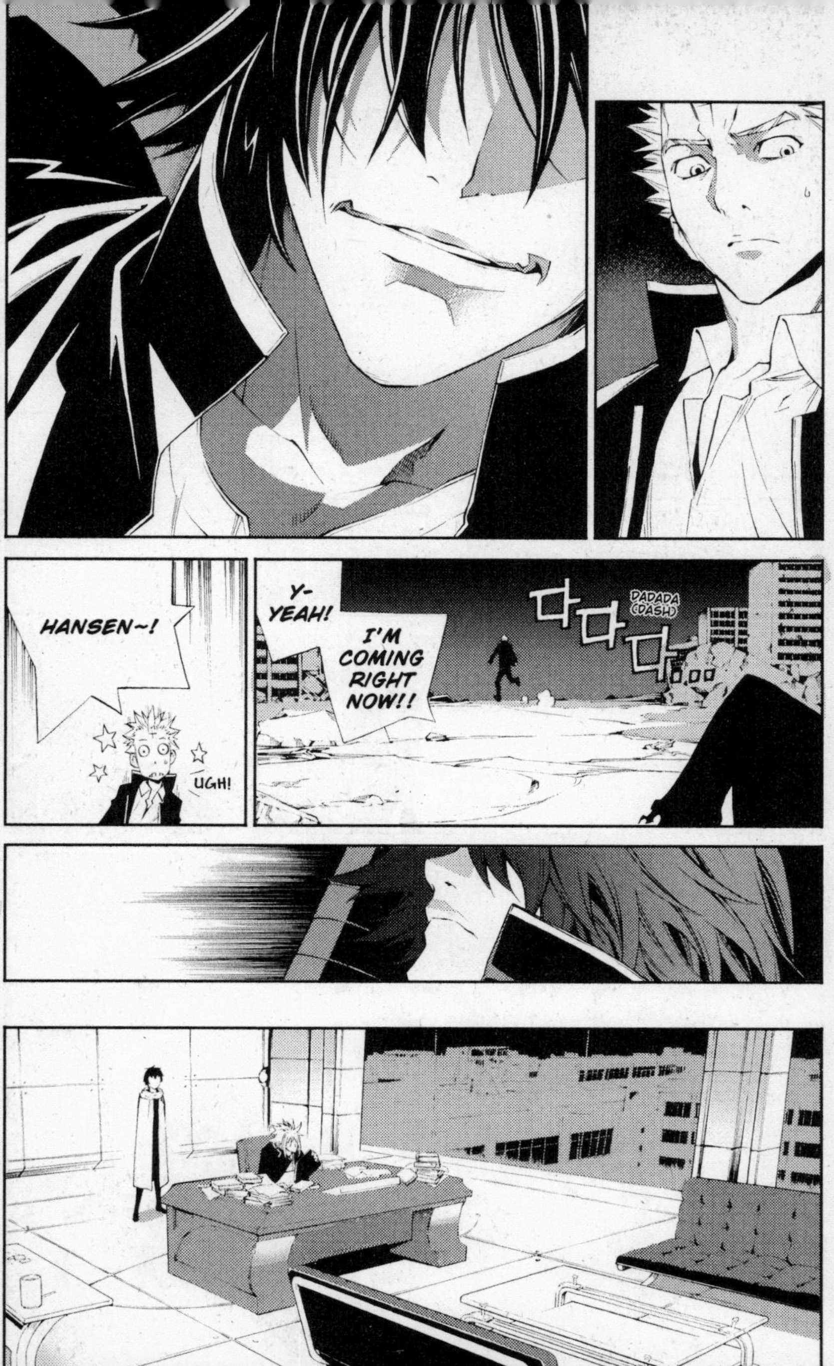
HANSEN~!
UGH!
Y-YEAH!
I'M COMING RIGHT NOW!!
DADADA (DASH)

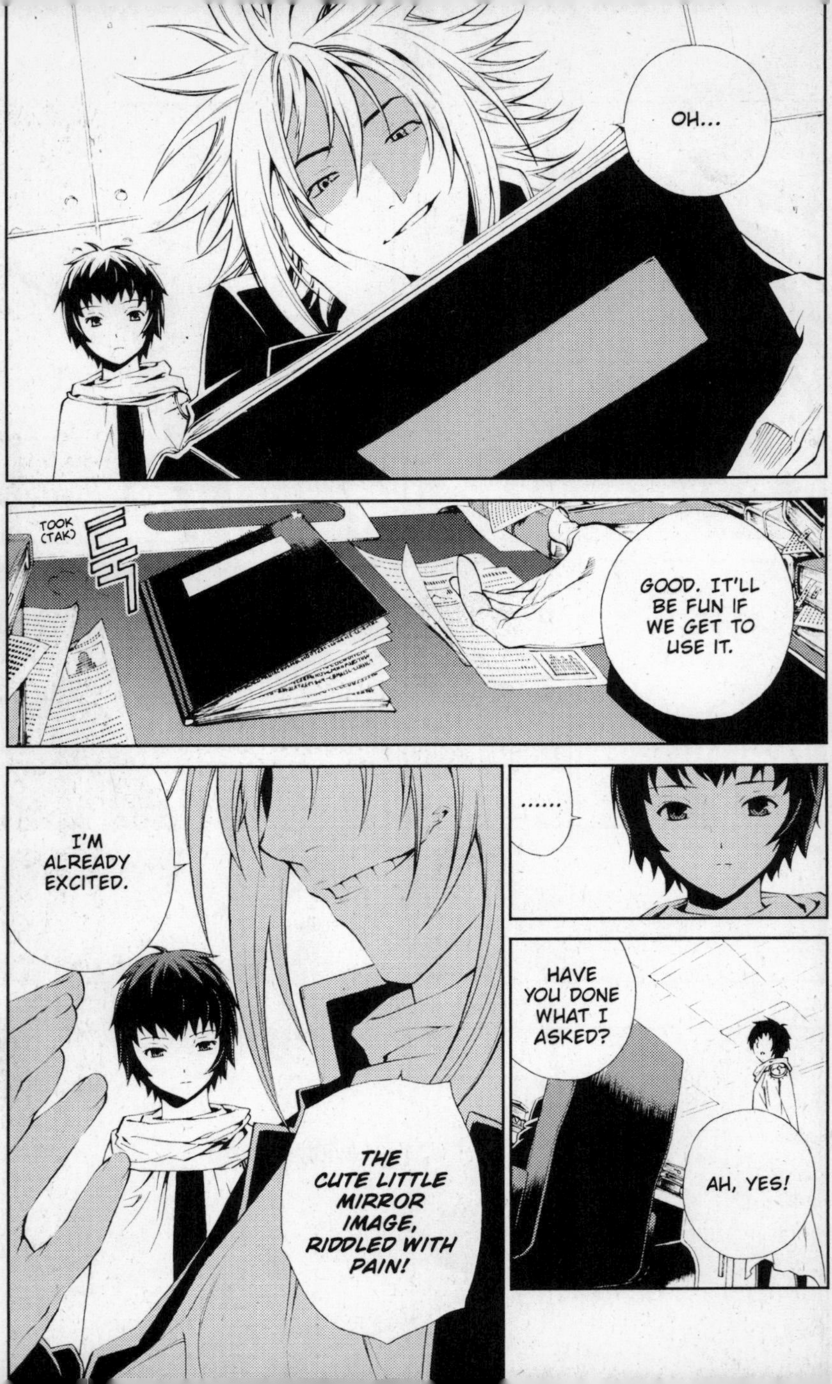
OH...
TOOK (TAK)
GOOD. IT'LL BE FUN IF WE GET TO USE IT.
I'M ALREADY EXCITED.
THE CUTE LITTLE MIRROR IMAGE, RIDDLED WITH PAIN!
......
HAVE YOU DONE WHAT I ASKED?
AH, YES!

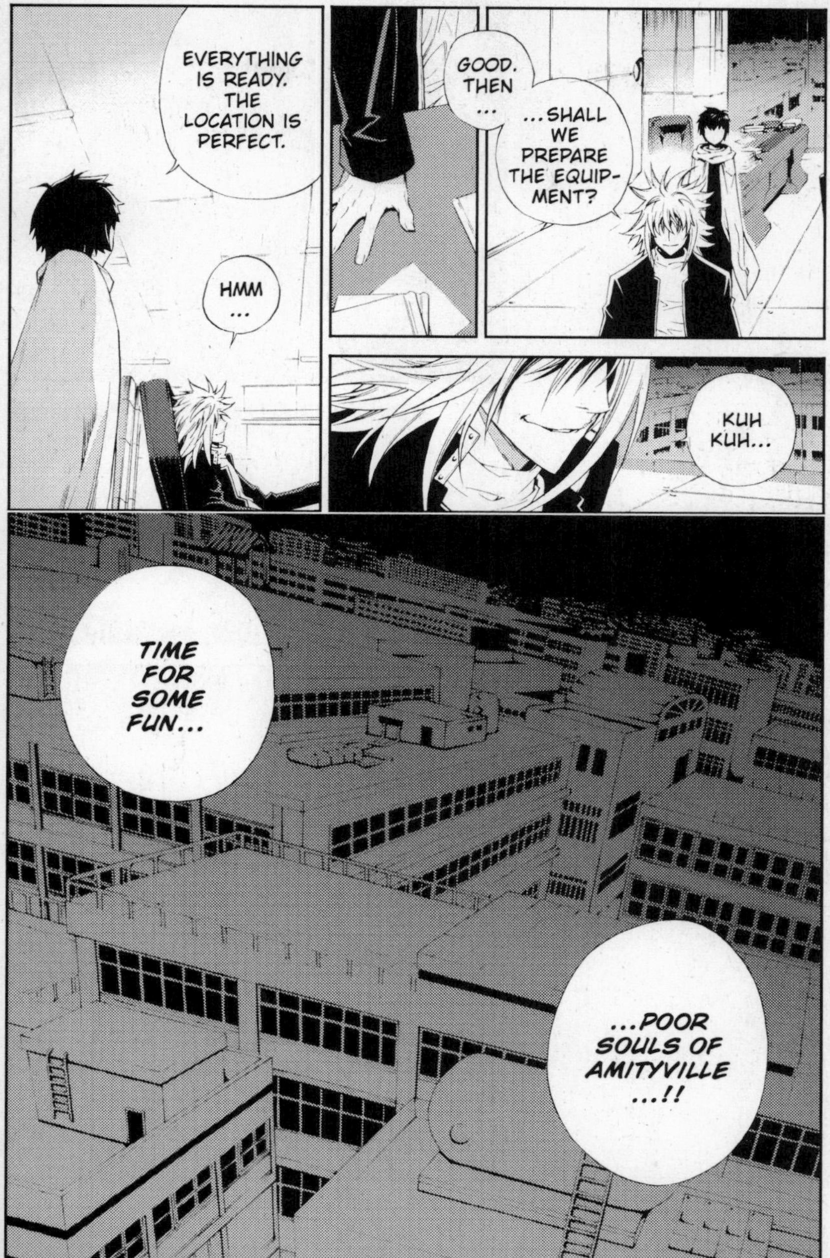
EVERYTHING IS READY. THE LOCATION IS PERFECT.
HMM ...
GOOD. THEN ...
...SHALL WE PREPARE THE EQUIP-MENT?
KUH KUH...
TIME FOR SOME FUN...
...POOR SOULS OF AMITYVILLE ...!!

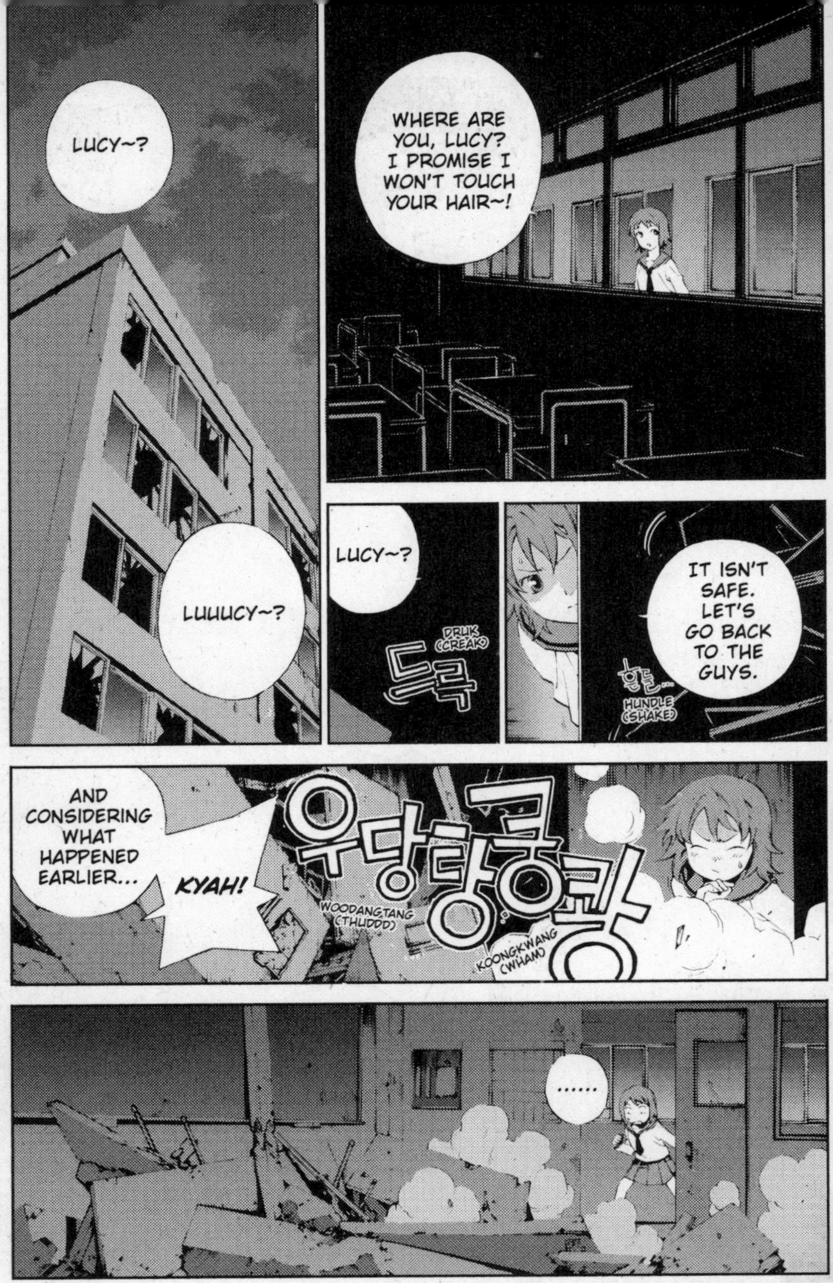
LUCY~?
LUUUCY~?
WHERE ARE YOU, LUCY? I PROMISE I WON'T TOUCH YOUR HAIR~!
LUCY~?
드륵
DRUK (CREAK)
IT ISN'T SAFE. LET'S GO BACK TO THE GUYS.
흔들...
HUNDLE (SHAKE)
AND CONSIDERING WHAT HAPPENED EARLIER...
KYAH!
우당탕
WOODANGTANG (THUDDD)
쿵쾅
KOONGKWANG (WHAM)
......

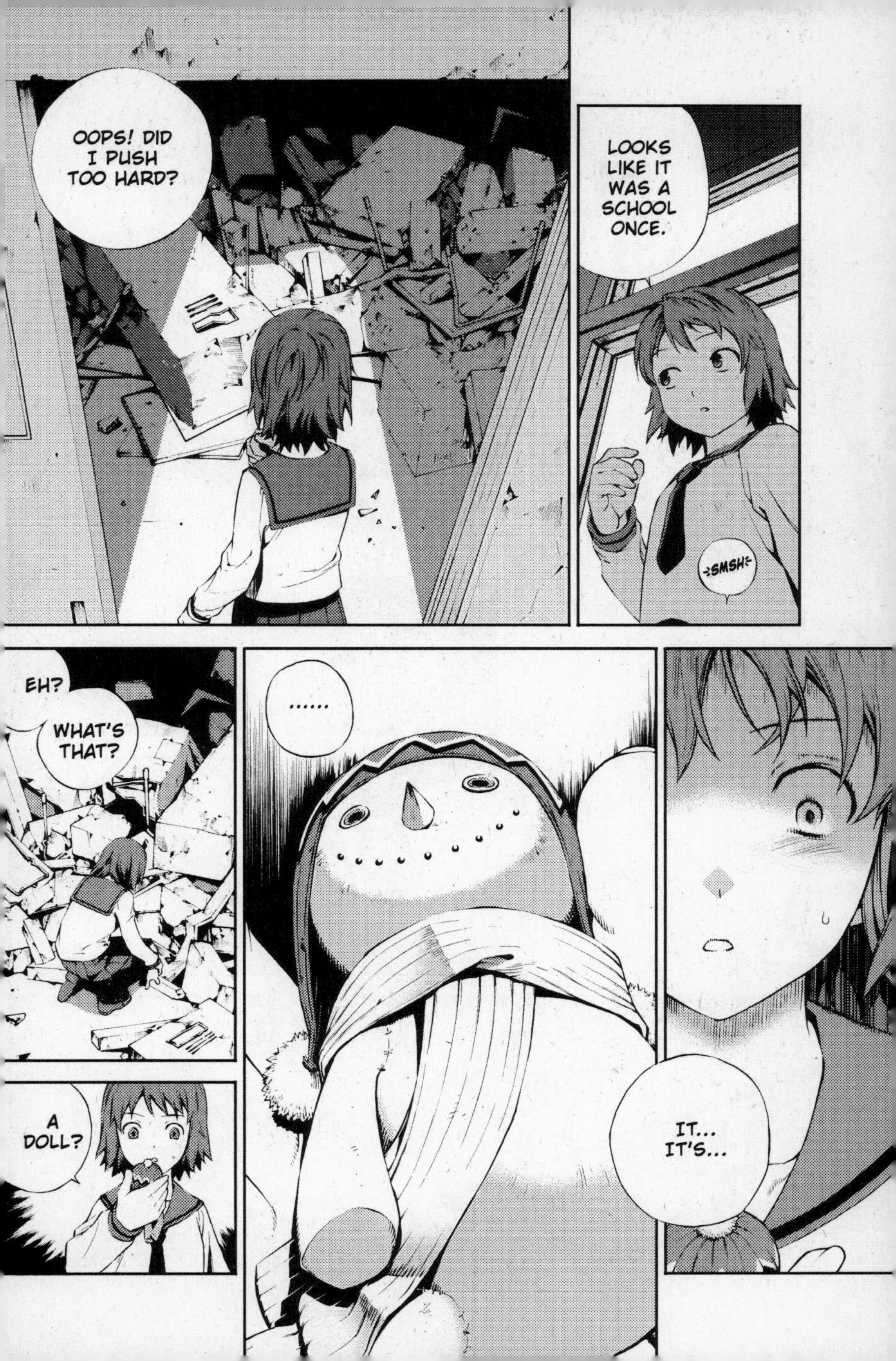
OOPS! DID I PUSH TOO HARD?
LOOKS LIKE IT WAS A SCHOOL ONCE.
SMSH
EH?
WHAT'S THAT?
A DOLL?
......
IT... IT'S...

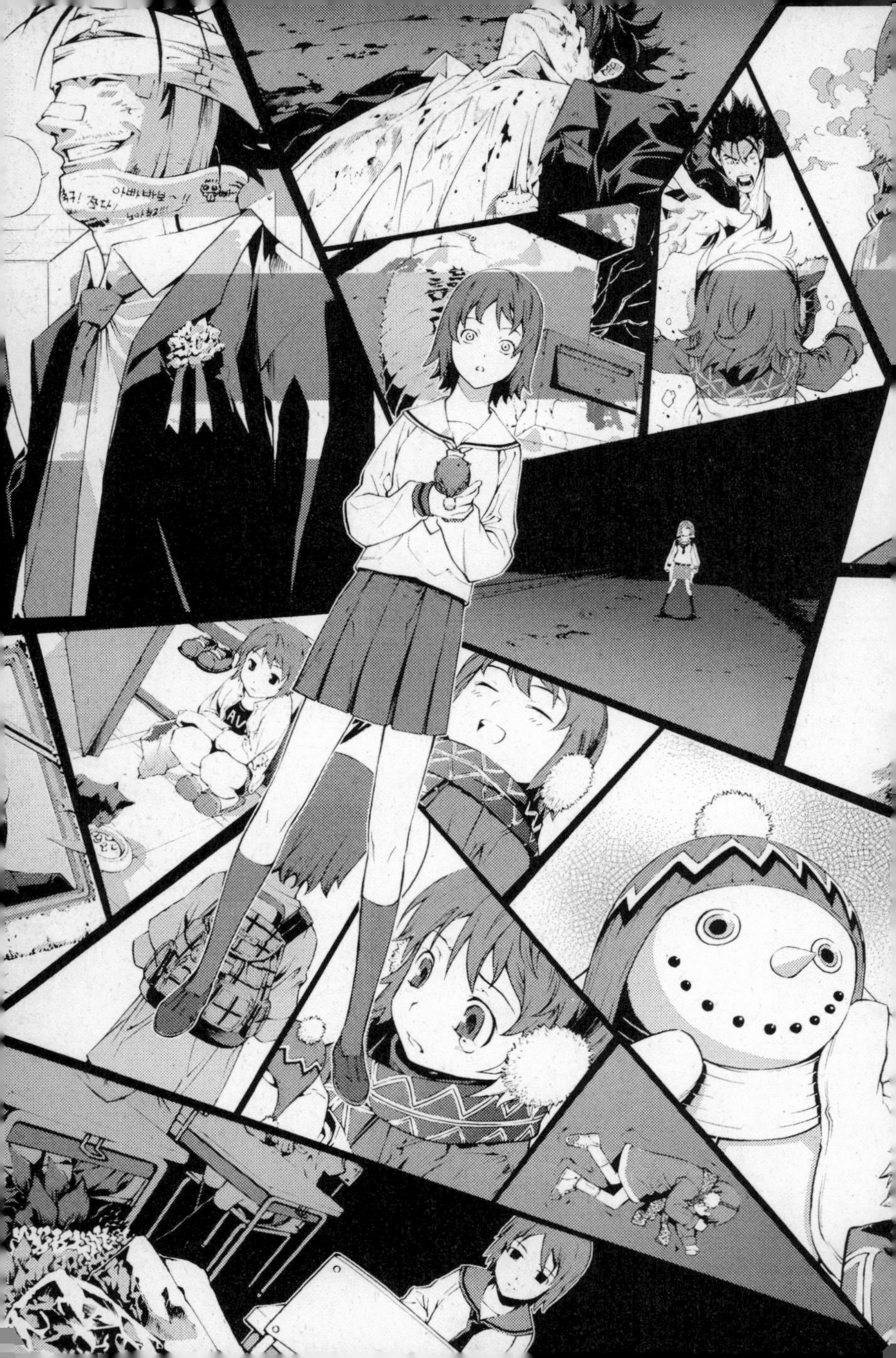
아빠바보~!!

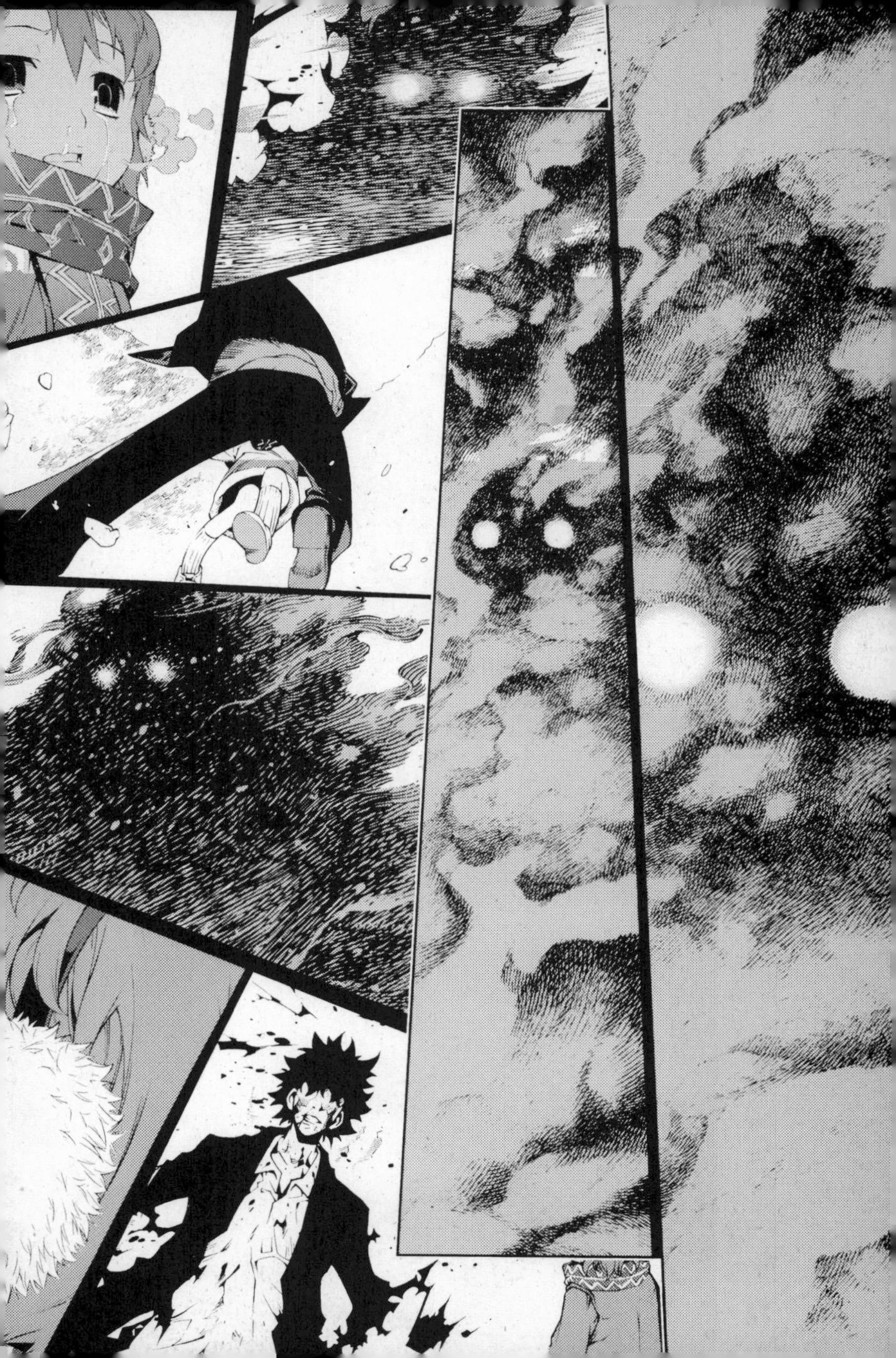

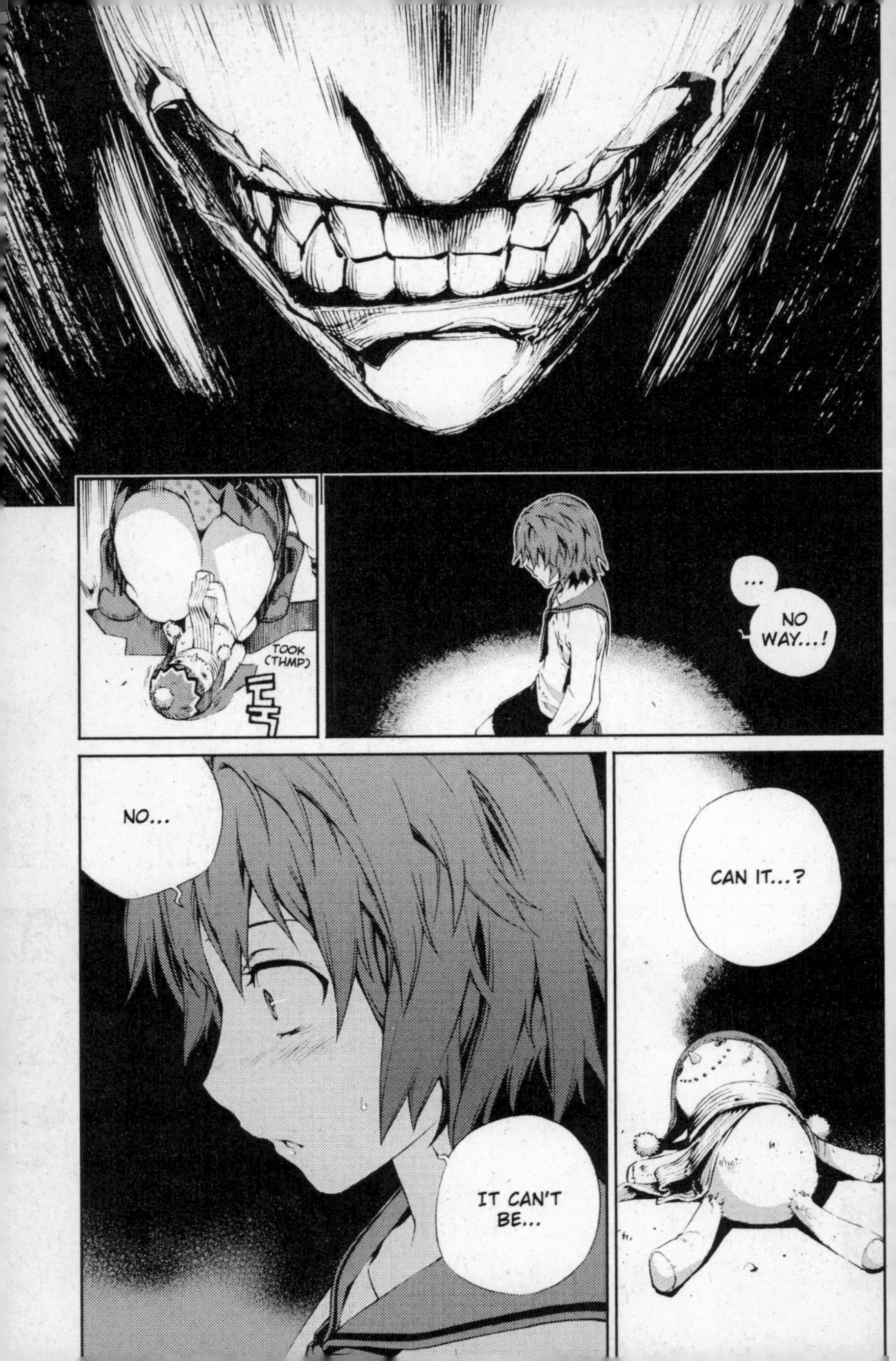
TOOK (THMP)
...
NO WAY...!
NO...
IT CAN'T BE...
CAN IT...?

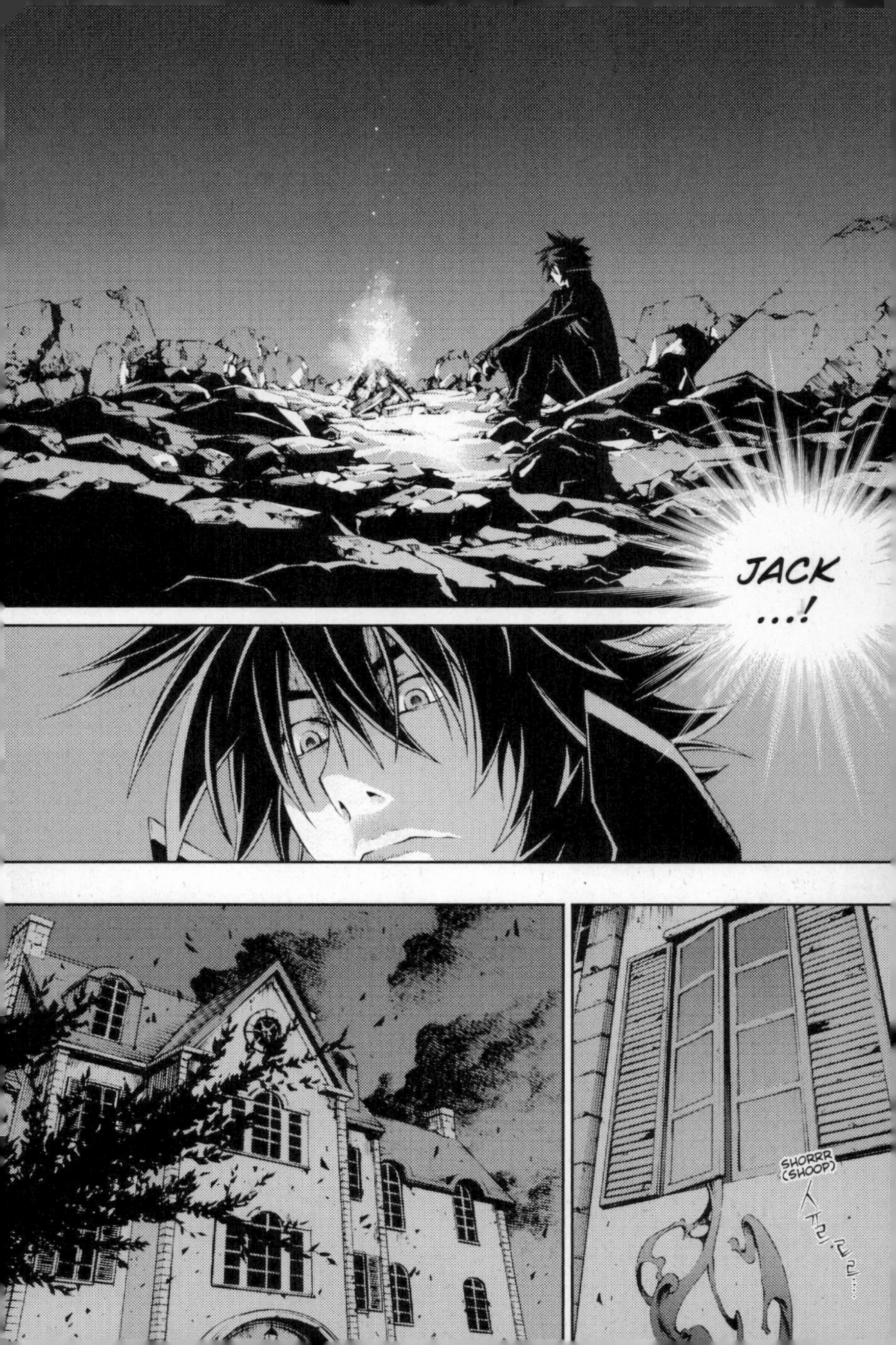
JACK
...!
SHORRR
(SHOOP)
스르르르...

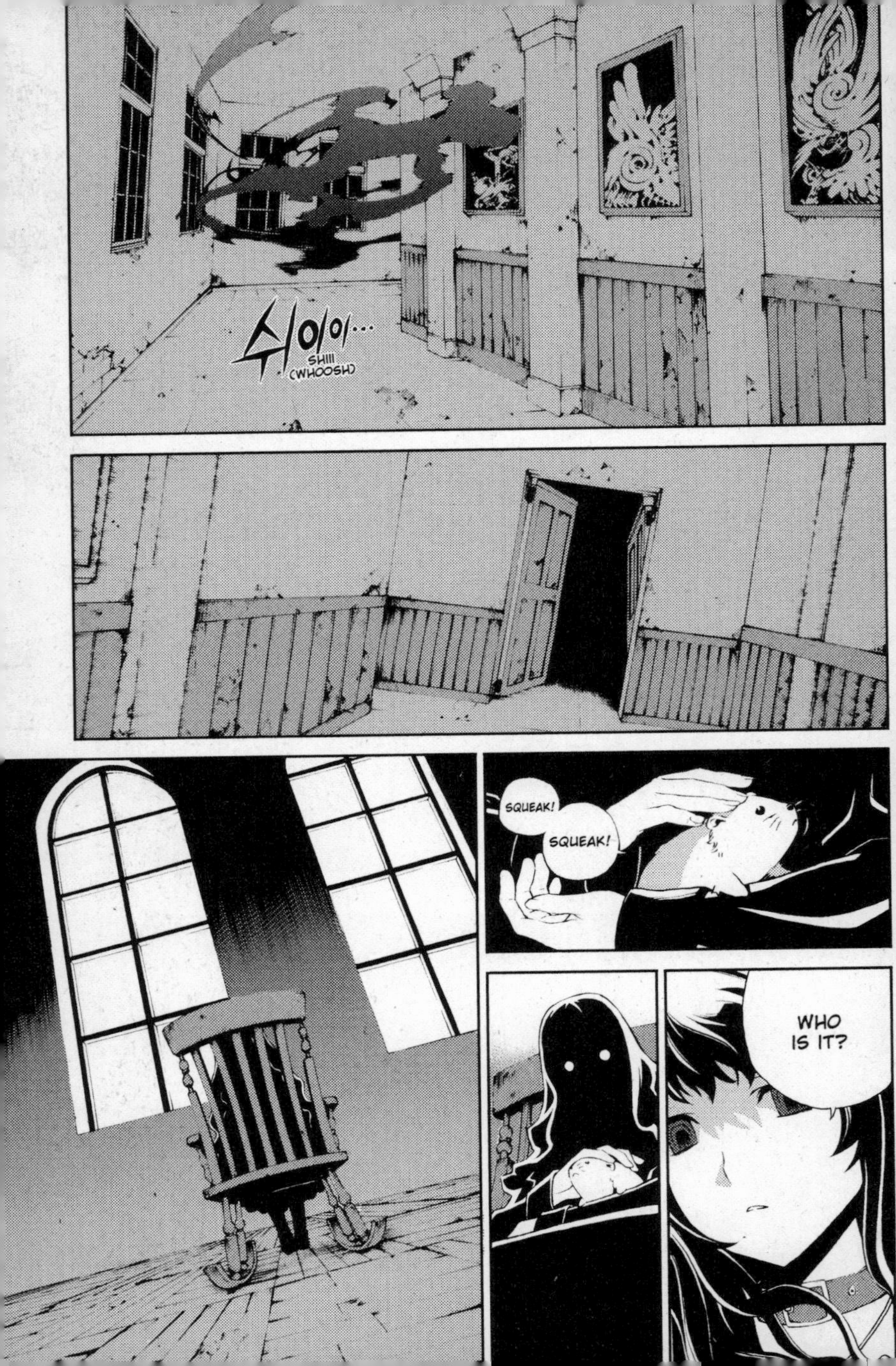
쉬이이…
SHIII
(WHOOSH)
SQUEAK!
SQUEAK!
WHO IS IT?

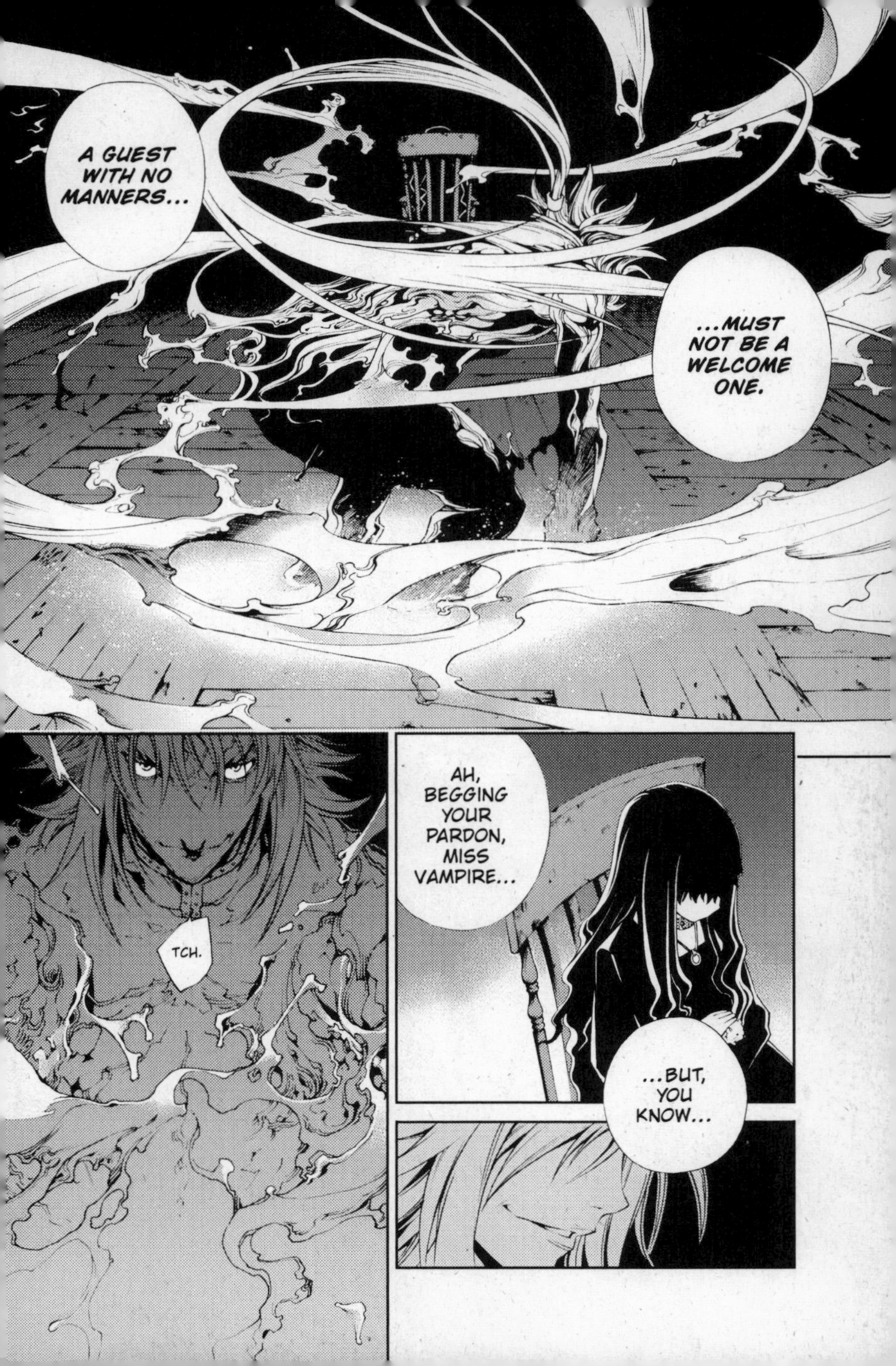
A GUEST WITH NO MANNERS...
...MUST NOT BE A WELCOME ONE.
TCH.
AH, BEGGING YOUR PARDON, MISS VAMPIRE...
...BUT, YOU KNOW...

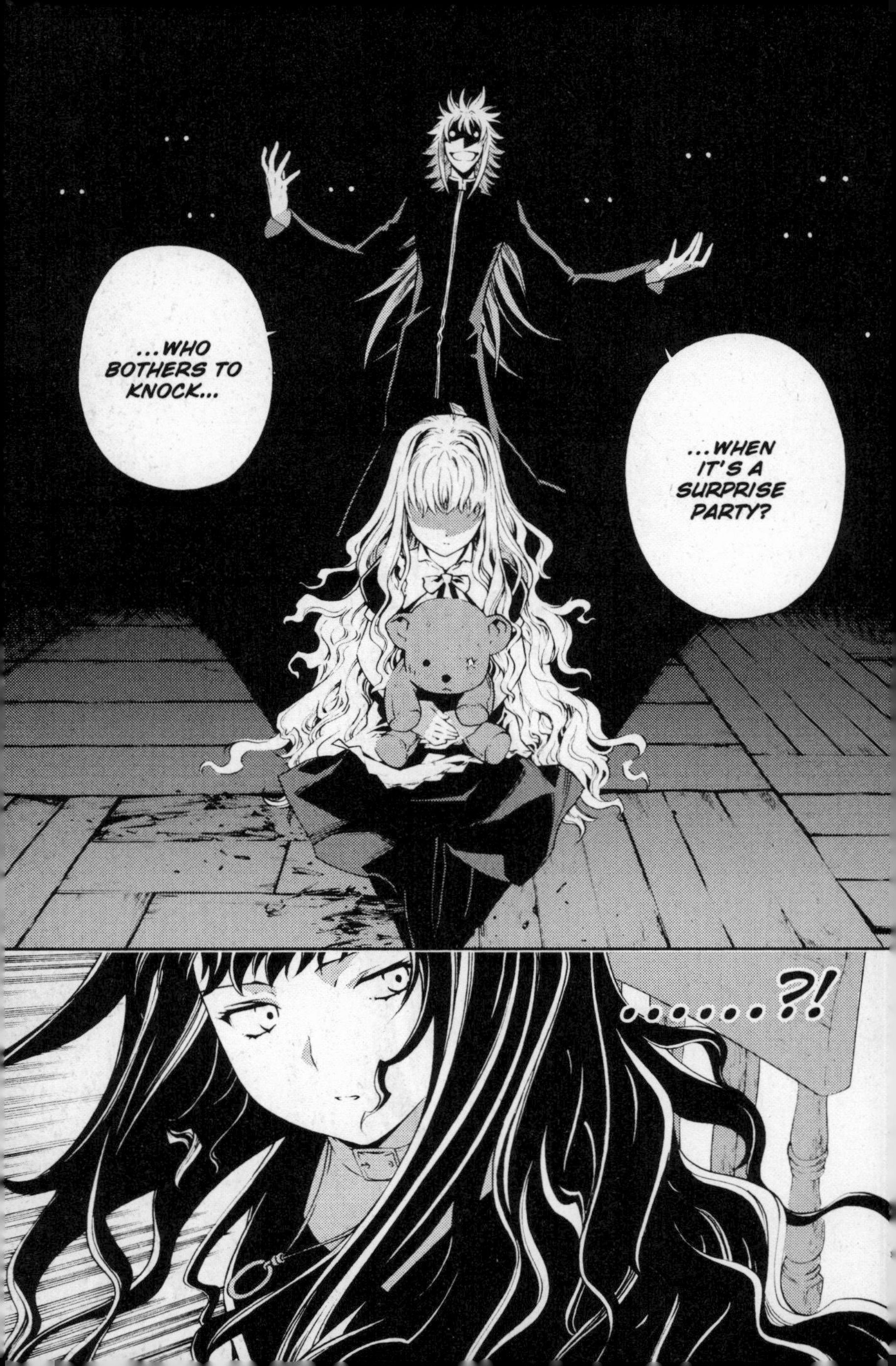
...WHO BOTHERS TO KNOCK...
...WHEN IT'S A SURPRISE PARTY?
......?!

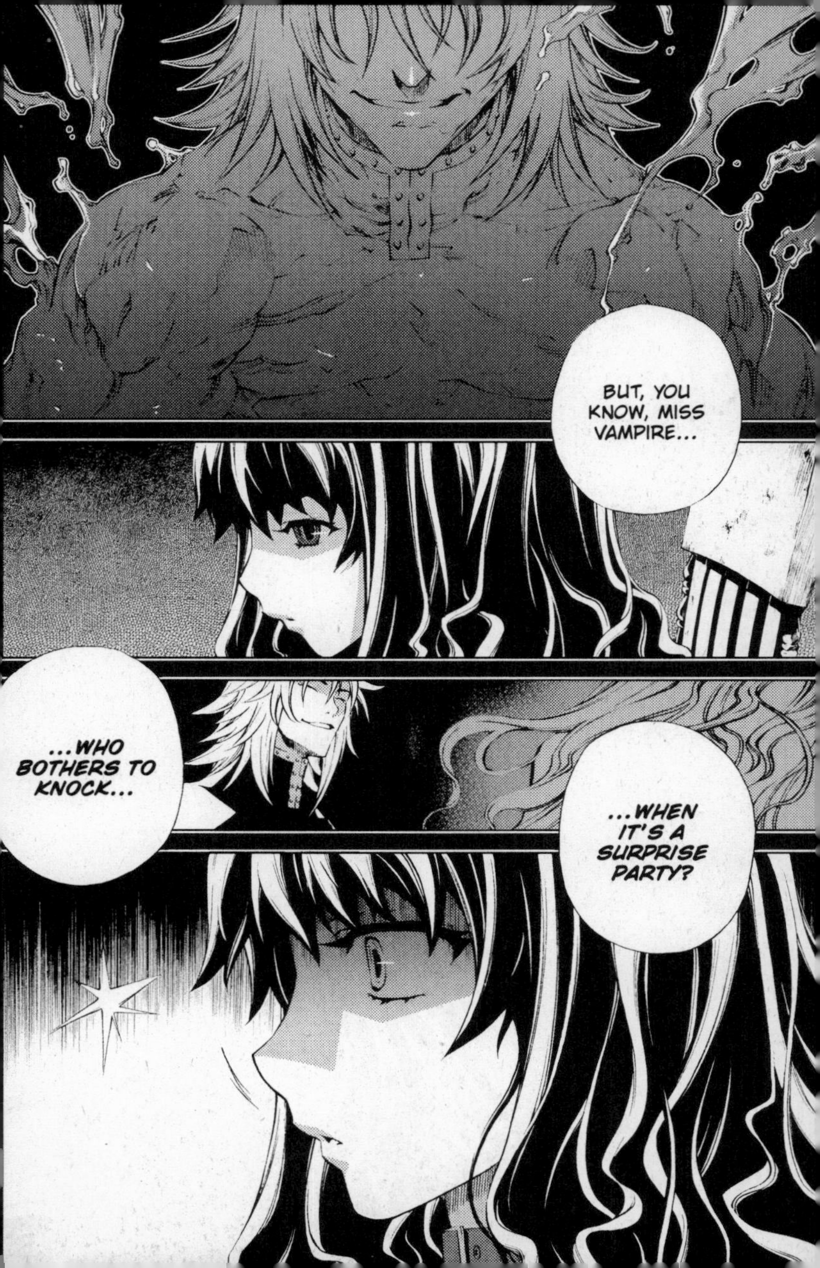
BUT, YOU KNOW, MISS VAMPIRE...
...WHO BOTHERS TO KNOCK...
...WHEN IT'S A SURPRISE PARTY?

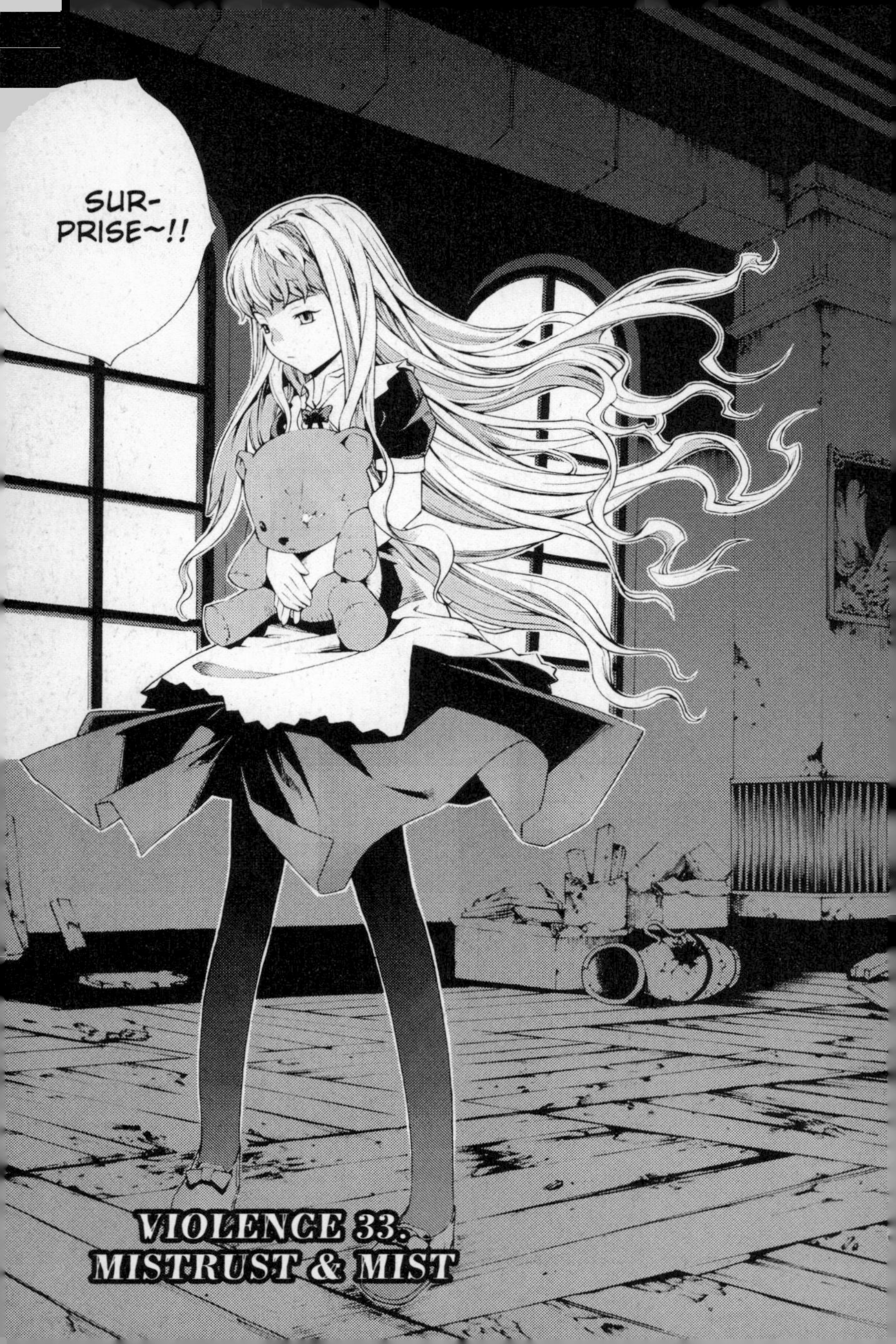
SUR-
PRISE~!!
VIOLENCE 33.
MISTRUST & MIST

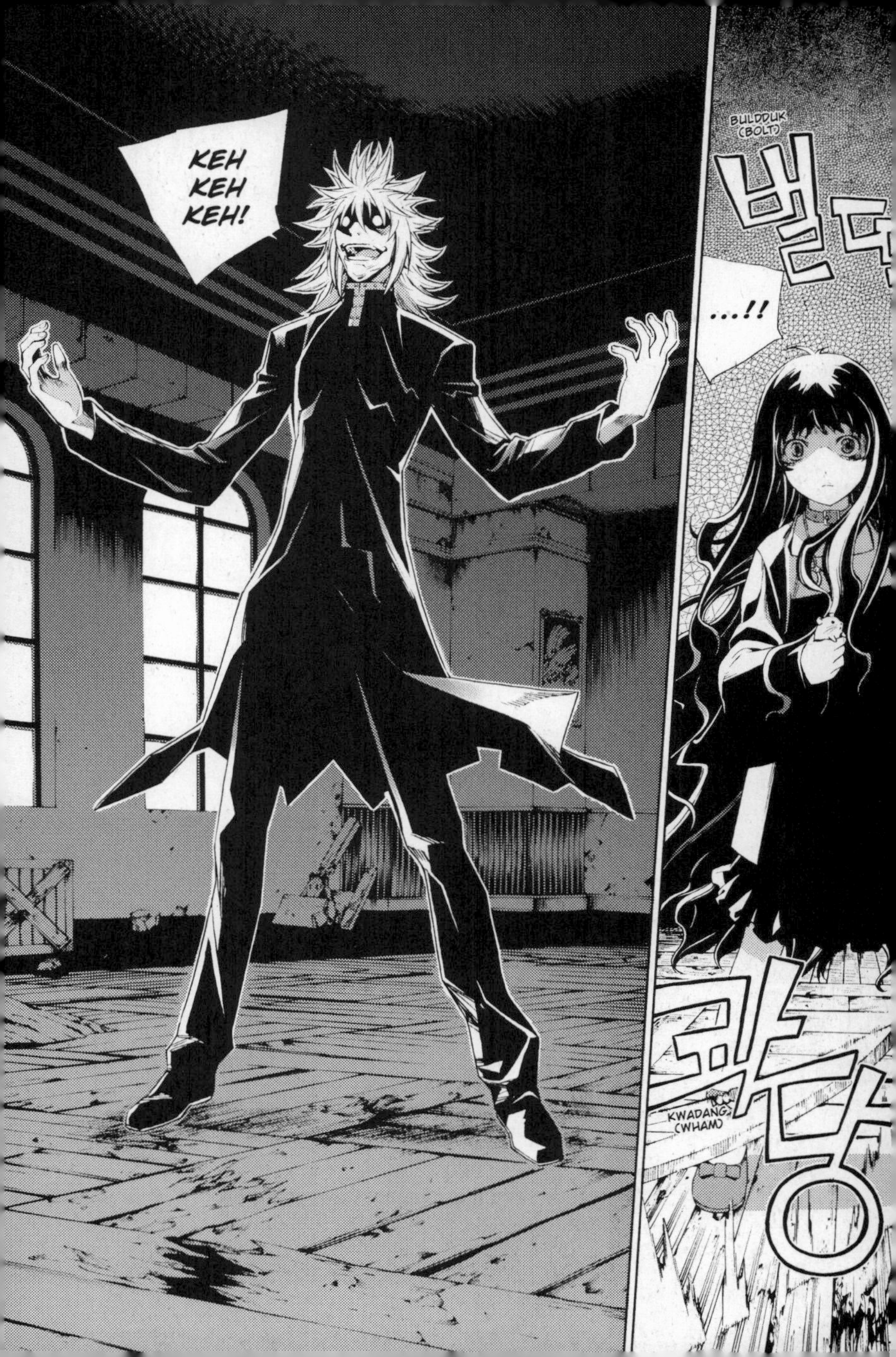
KEH KEH KEH!
BULDDUK (BOLT)
벌떡
...!!
KWADANG (WHAM)
콰당

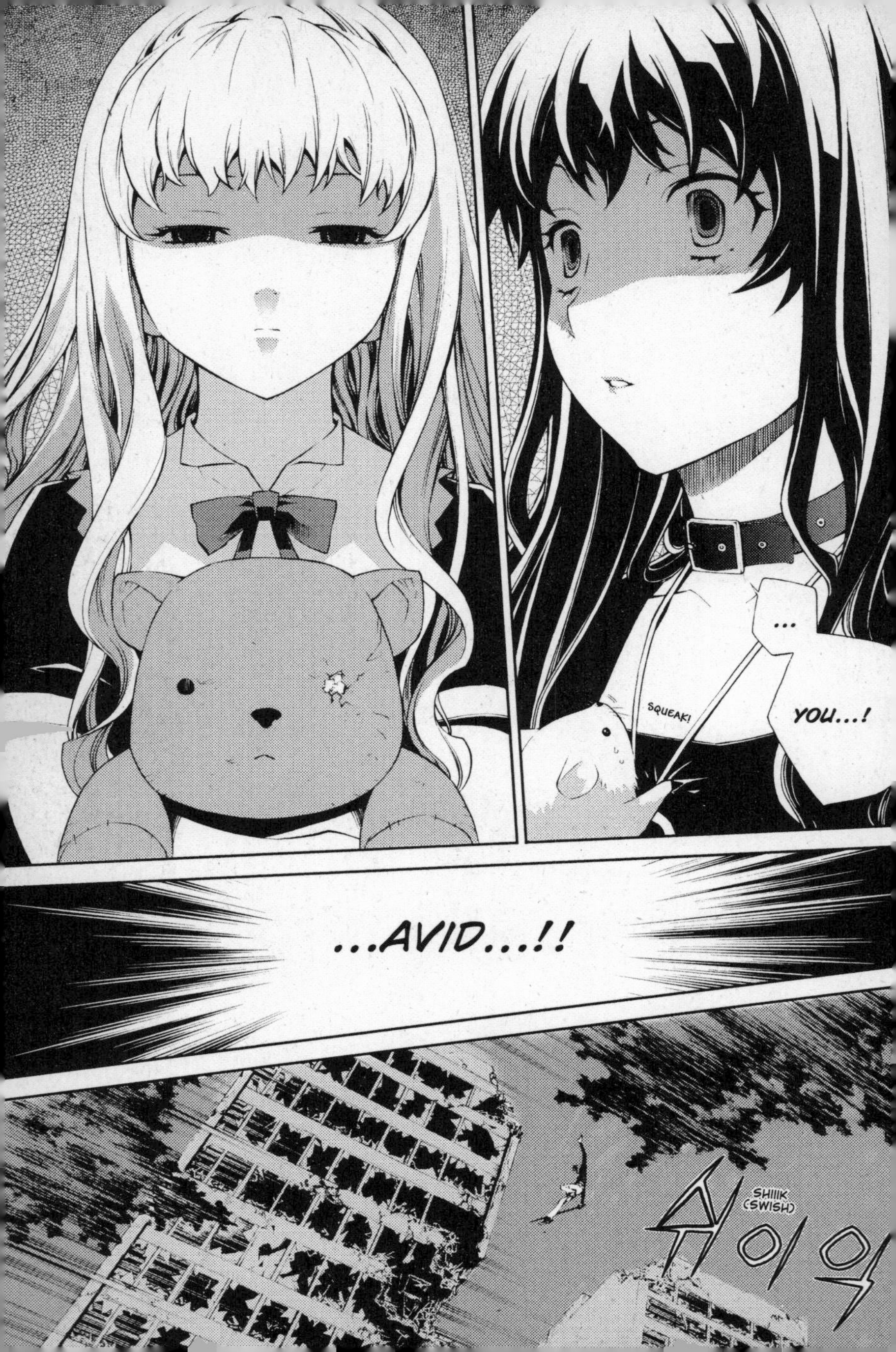
...
SQUEAK!
YOU...!
...AVID...!!
SHIIIK (SWISH)

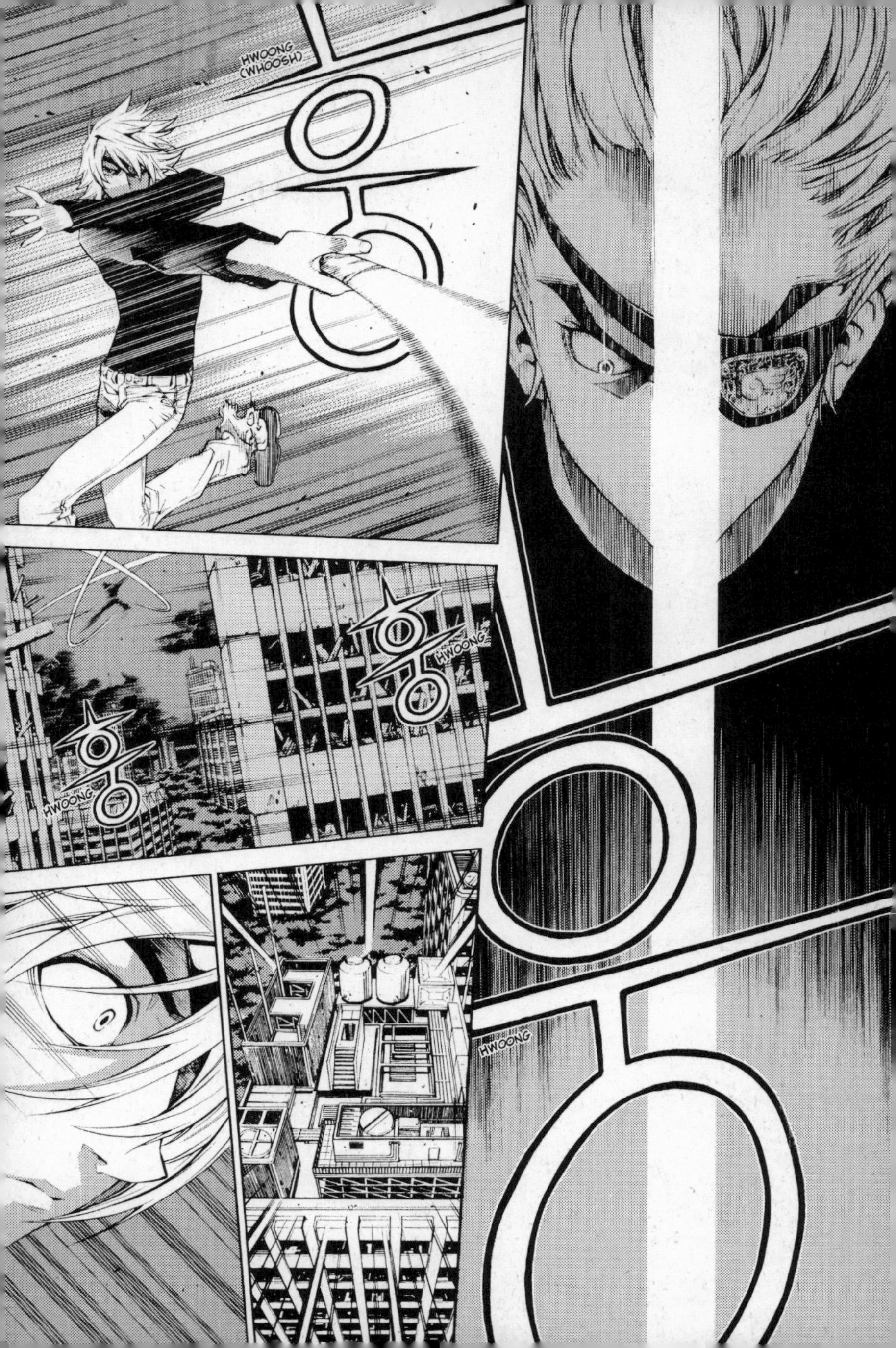
HWOONG (WHOOSH)
HWOONG
HWOONG
HWOONG

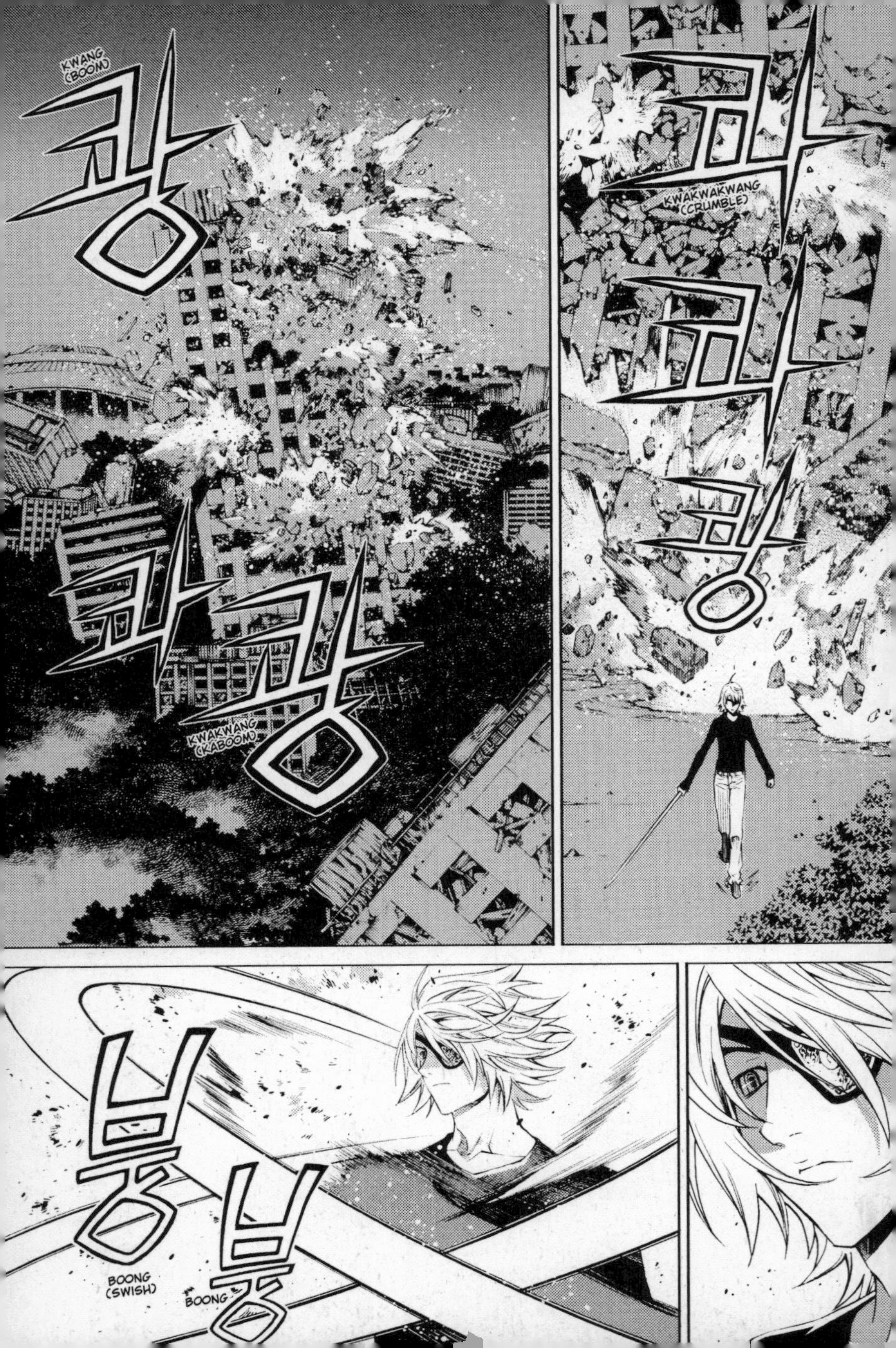

쾅
KWANG (BOOM)
콰쾅
KWAKWANG (KABOOM)
콰콰쾅
KWAKWAKWANG (CRUMBLE)
붕
BOONG (SWISH)
붕
BOONG

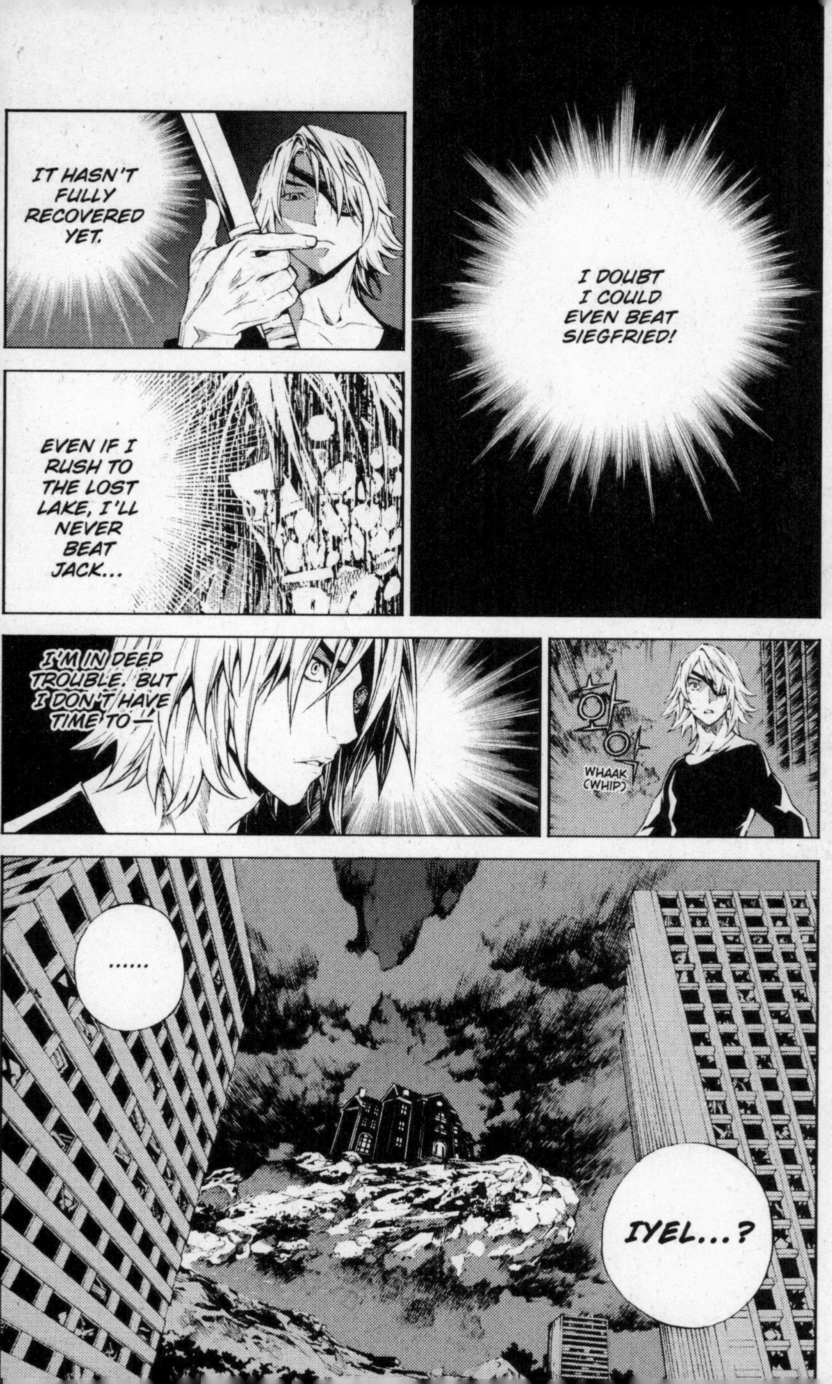
IT HASN'T FULLY RECOVERED YET.
I DOUBT I COULD EVEN BEAT SIEGFRIED!
EVEN IF I RUSH TO THE LOST LAKE, I'LL NEVER BEAT JACK...
I'M IN DEEP TROUBLE. BUT I DON'T HAVE TIME TO—
WHAAK (WHIP)
......
IYEL...?

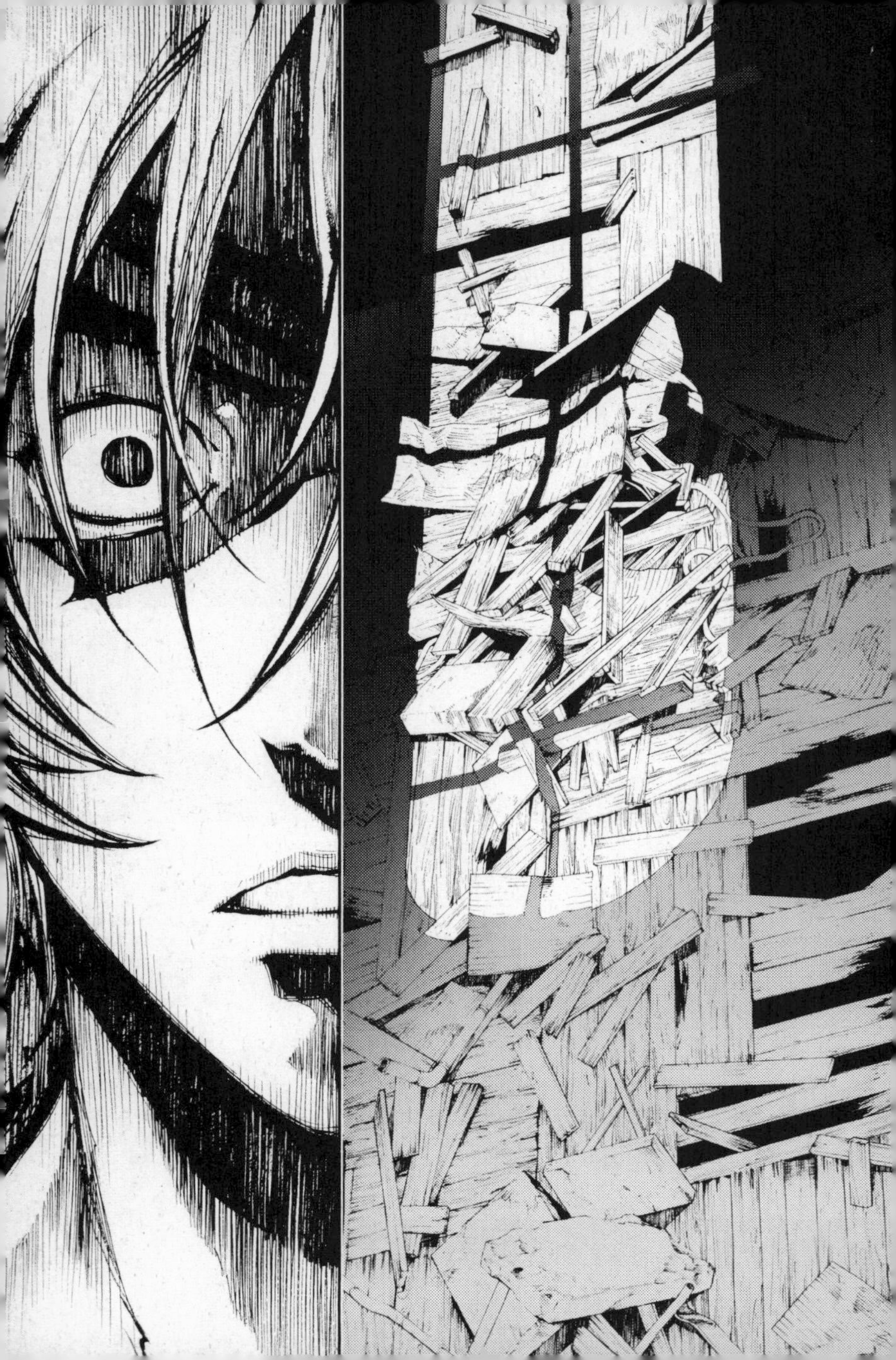

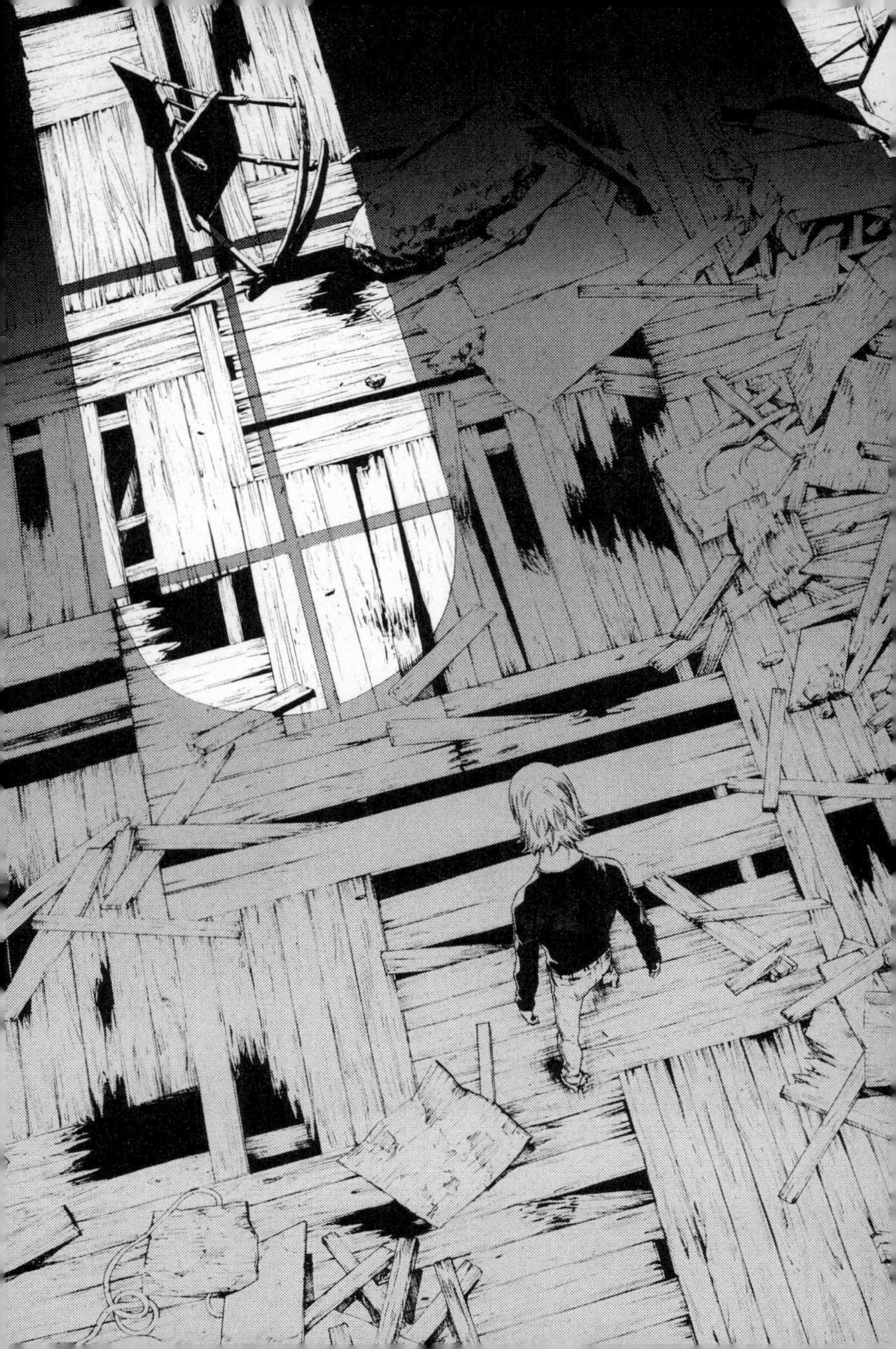

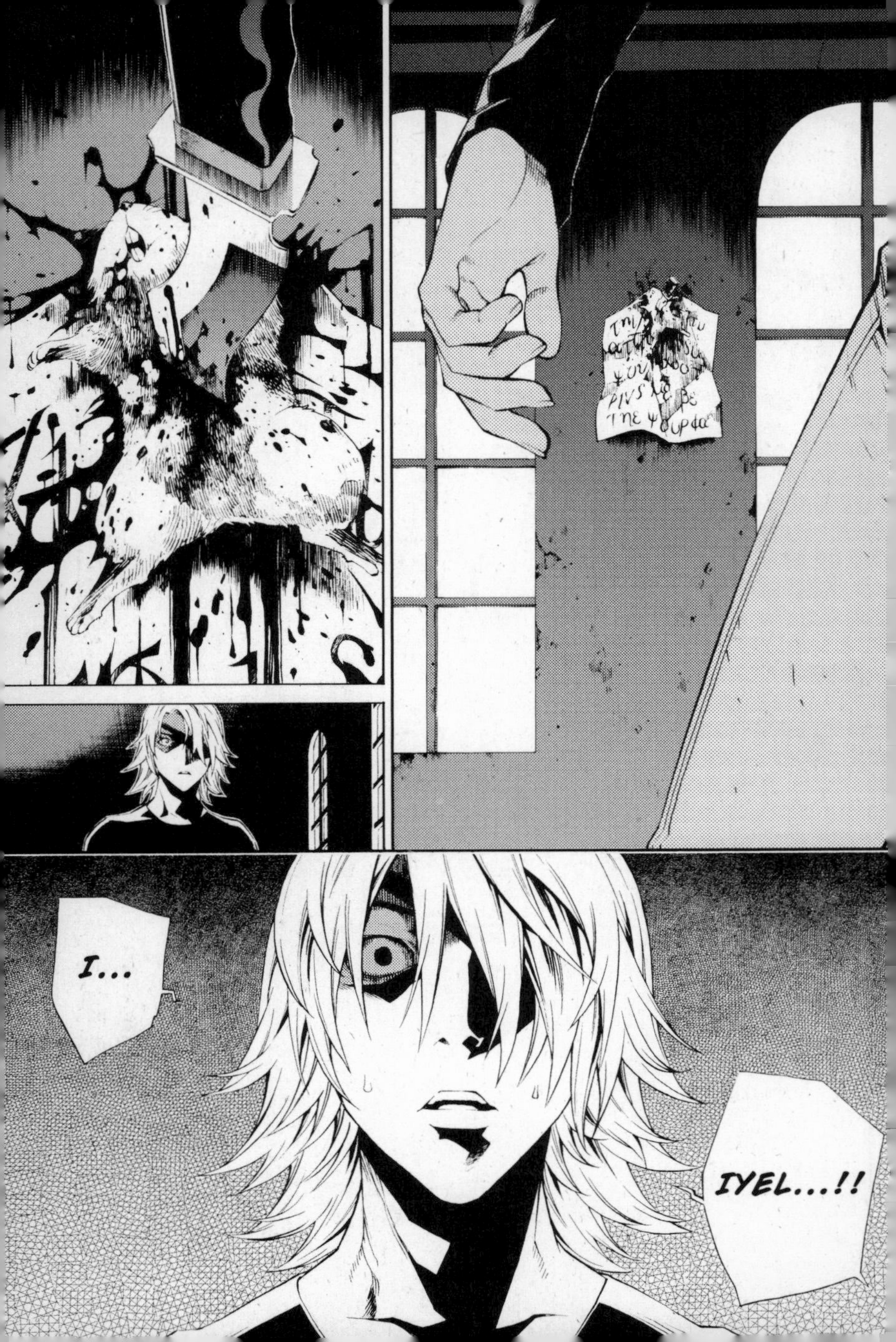
I...
IYEL...!!

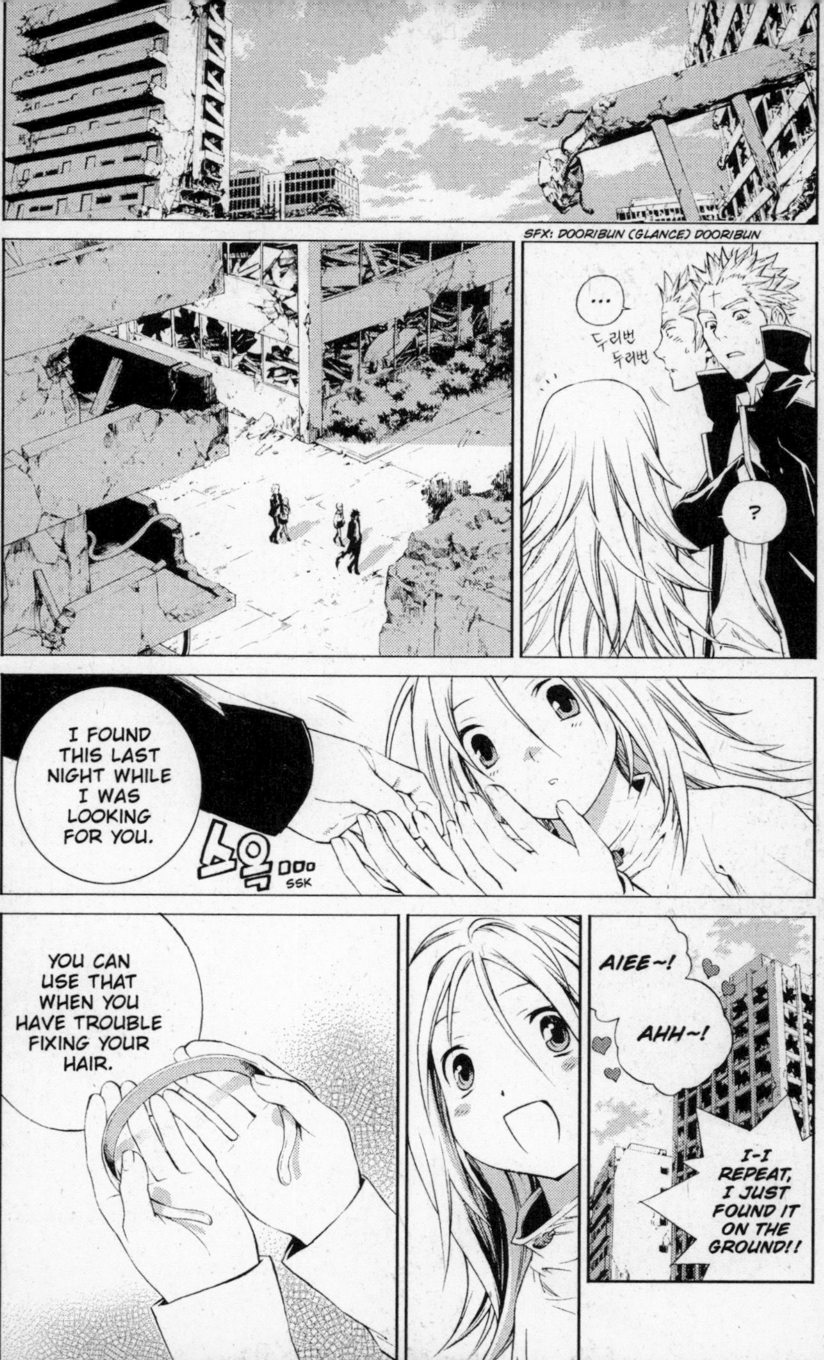
SFX: DOORIBUN (GLANCE) DOORIBUN
...
두리번
두리번
?
I FOUND THIS LAST NIGHT WHILE I WAS LOOKING FOR YOU.
스윽
SSK
YOU CAN USE THAT WHEN YOU HAVE TROUBLE FIXING YOUR HAIR.
AIEE~!
AHH~!
I-I REPEAT, I JUST FOUND IT ON THE GROUND!!

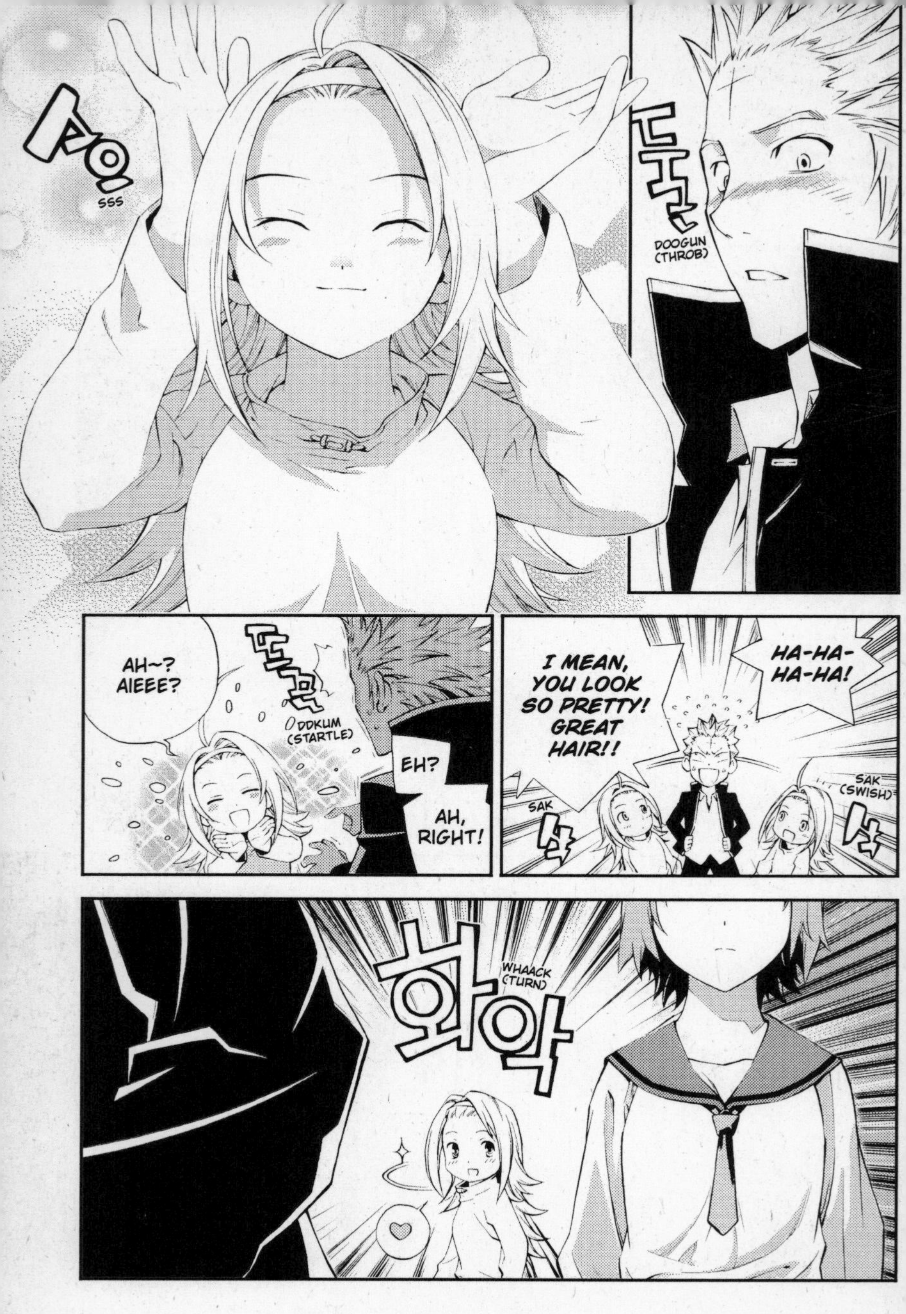
SSS
두근
DOOGUN (THROB)
AH~? AIEEE?
뜨끔
DDKUM (STARTLE)
EH?
AH, RIGHT!
I MEAN, YOU LOOK SO PRETTY! GREAT HAIR!!
HA-HA-HA-HA!
SAK
삭
SAK (SWISH)
삭
화악
WHAACK (TURN)

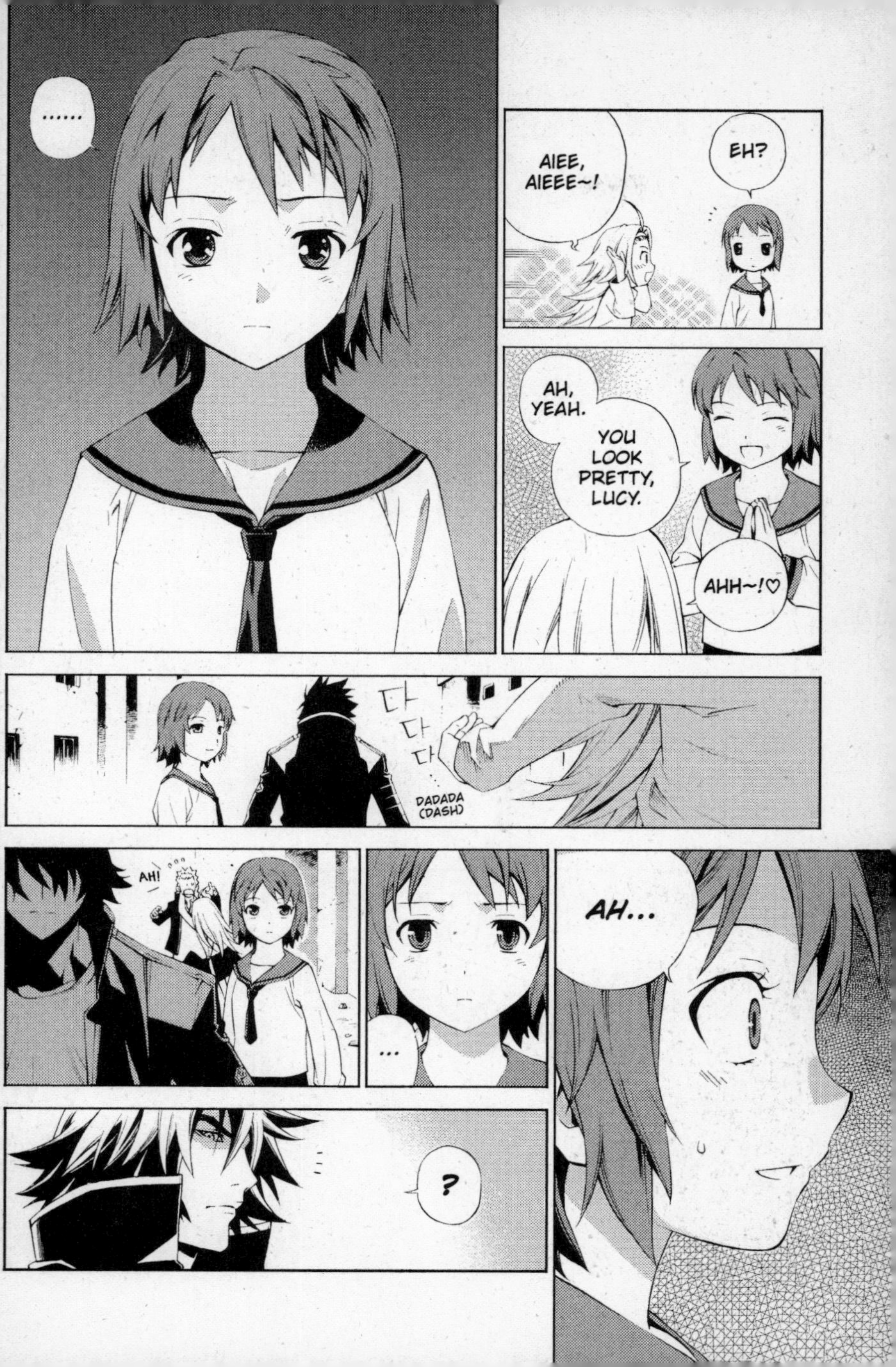
……
AIEE, AIEEE~!
EH?
AH, YEAH.
YOU LOOK PRETTY, LUCY.
AHH~!♡
다다다…
DADADA (DASH)
AH!
...
?
AH...

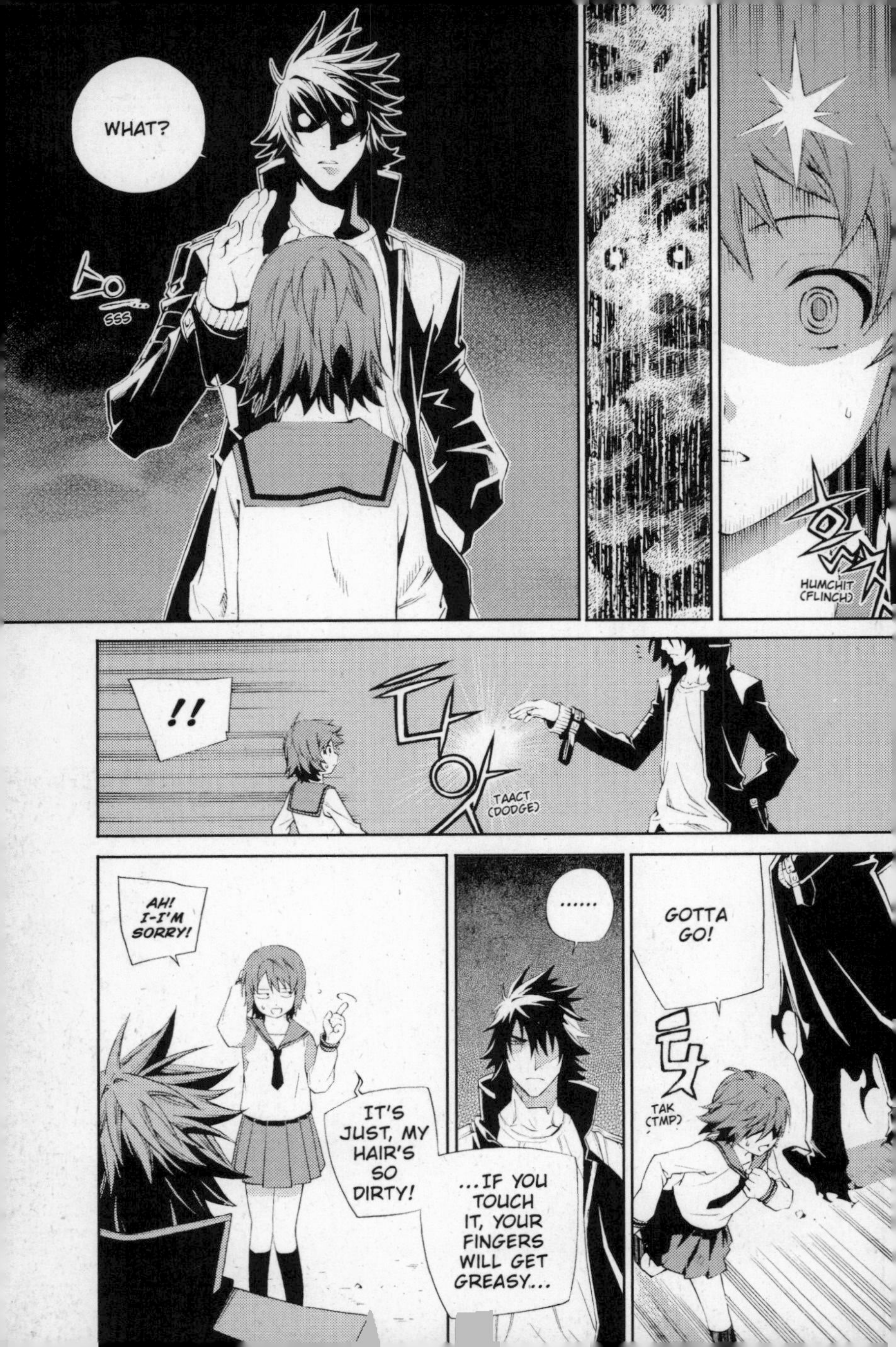
WHAT?
SSS
HUMCHIT (FLINCH)
!!
TAACT (DODGE)
AH! I-I'M SORRY!
IT'S JUST, MY HAIR'S SO DIRTY!
......
...IF YOU TOUCH IT, YOUR FINGERS WILL GET GREASY...
GOTTA GO!
TAK (TMP)

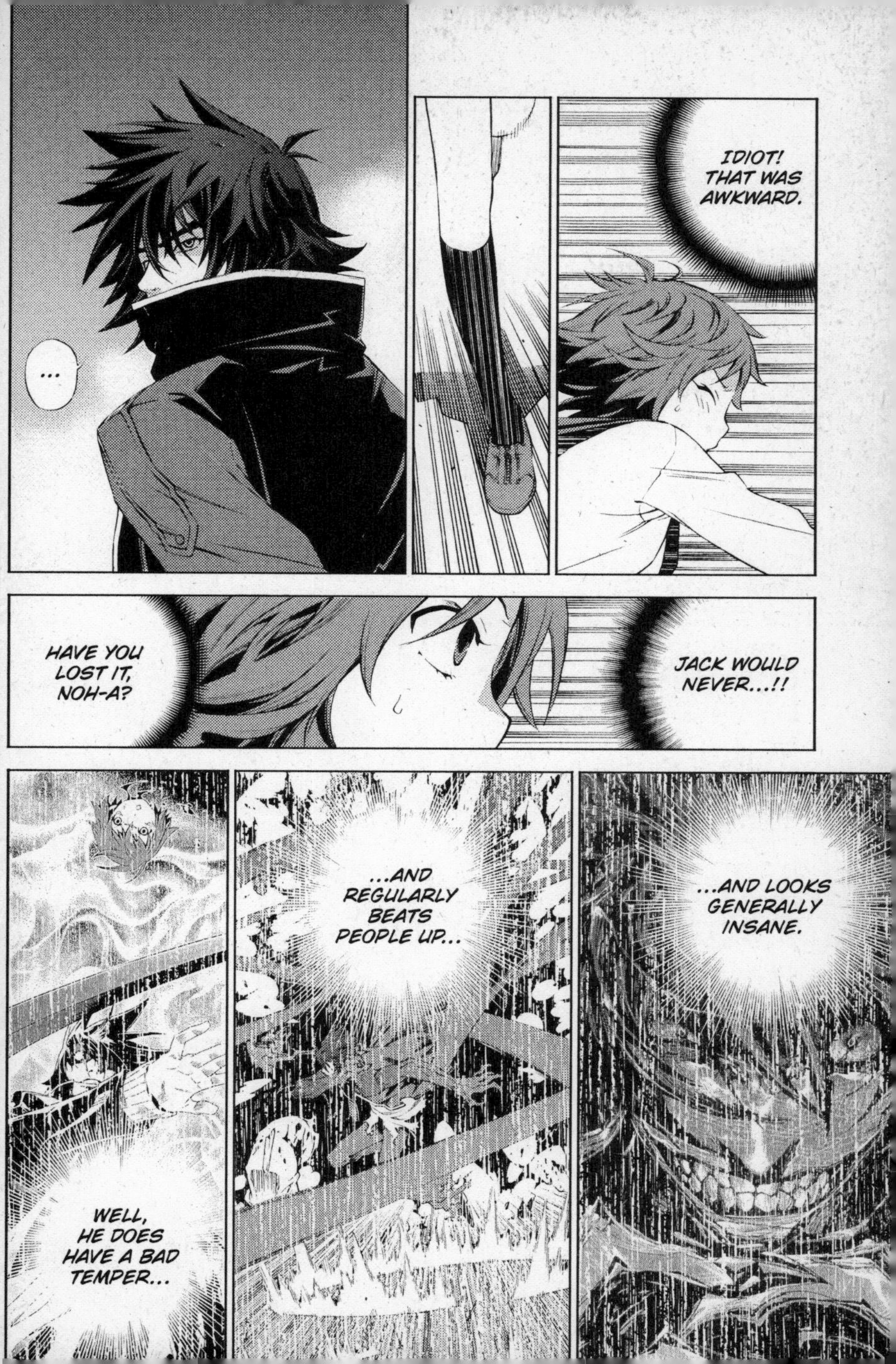
...
IDIOT! THAT WAS AWKWARD.
HAVE YOU LOST IT, NOH-A?
JACK WOULD NEVER...!!
WELL, HE DOES HAVE A BAD TEMPER...
...AND REGULARLY BEATS PEOPLE UP...
...AND LOOKS GENERALLY INSANE.

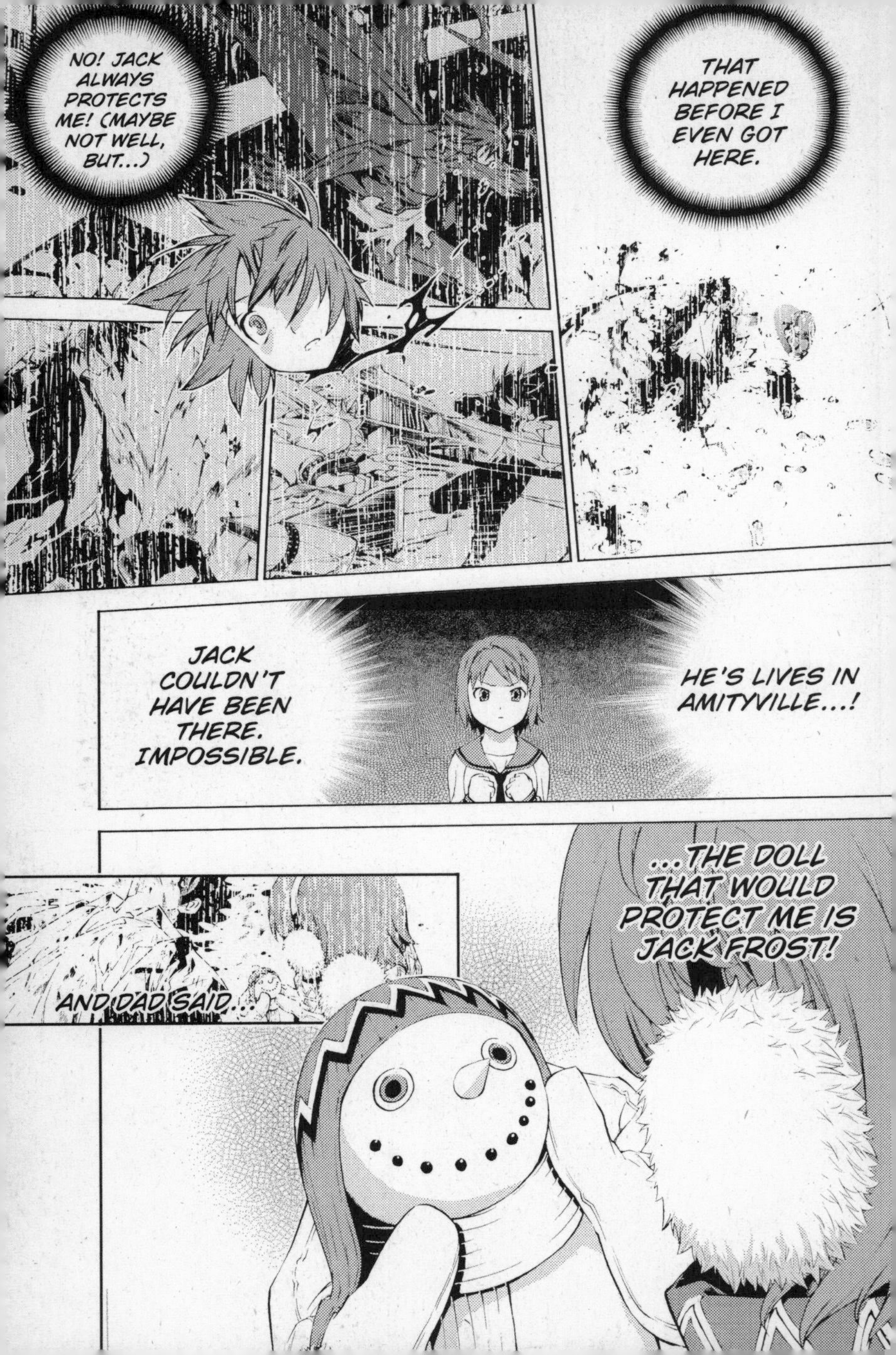
NO! JACK ALWAYS PROTECTS ME! (MAYBE NOT WELL, BUT...)
THAT HAPPENED BEFORE I EVEN GOT HERE.
JACK COULDN'T HAVE BEEN THERE. IMPOSSIBLE.
HE'S LIVES IN AMITYVILLE...!
AND DAD SAID...
...THE DOLL THAT WOULD PROTECT ME IS JACK FROST!

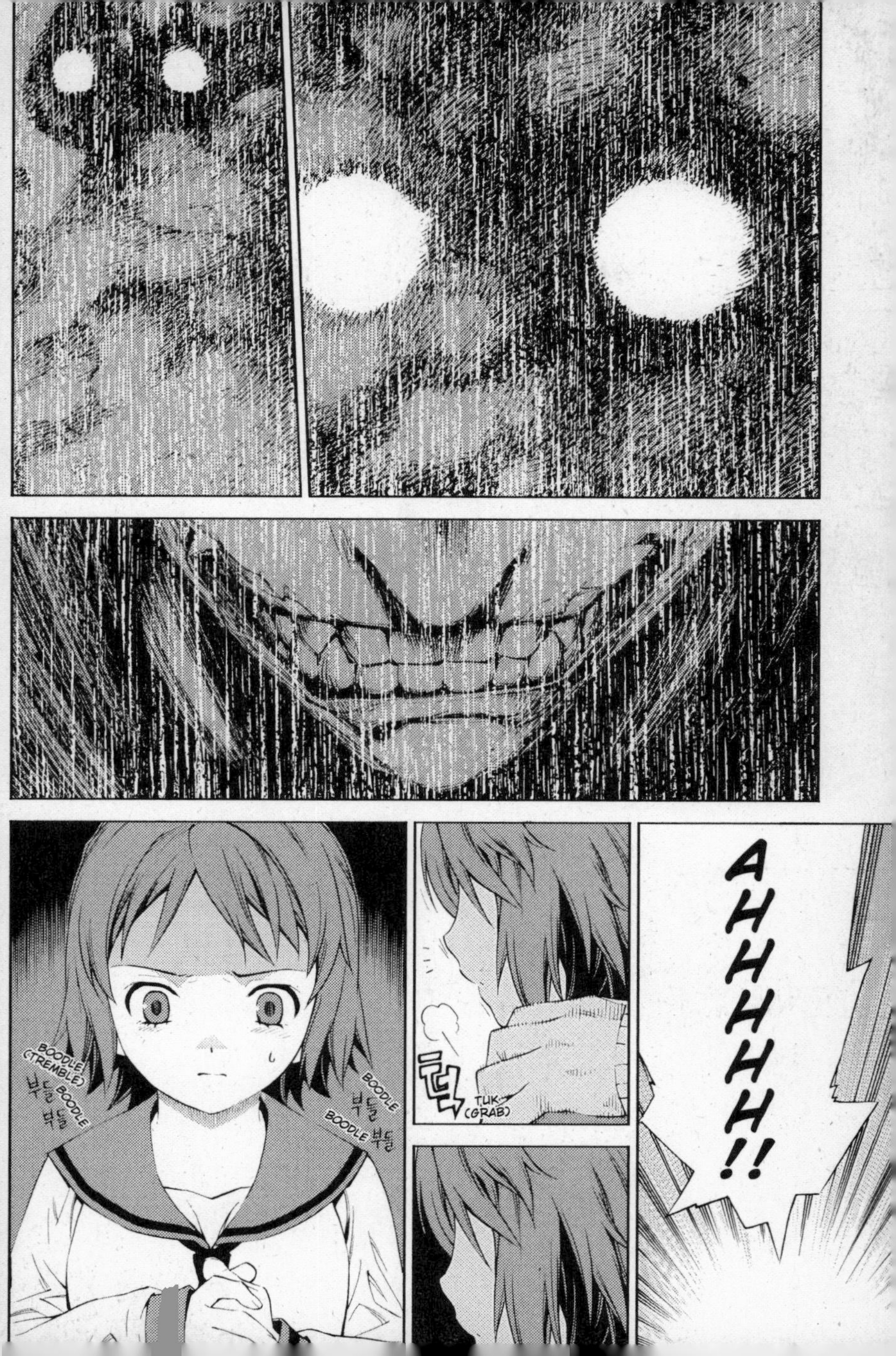
BOODLE (TREMBLE)
부들
BOODLE
부들
BOODLE
부들
BOODLE 부들
턱
TUK (GRAB)
AHHHHHH!!

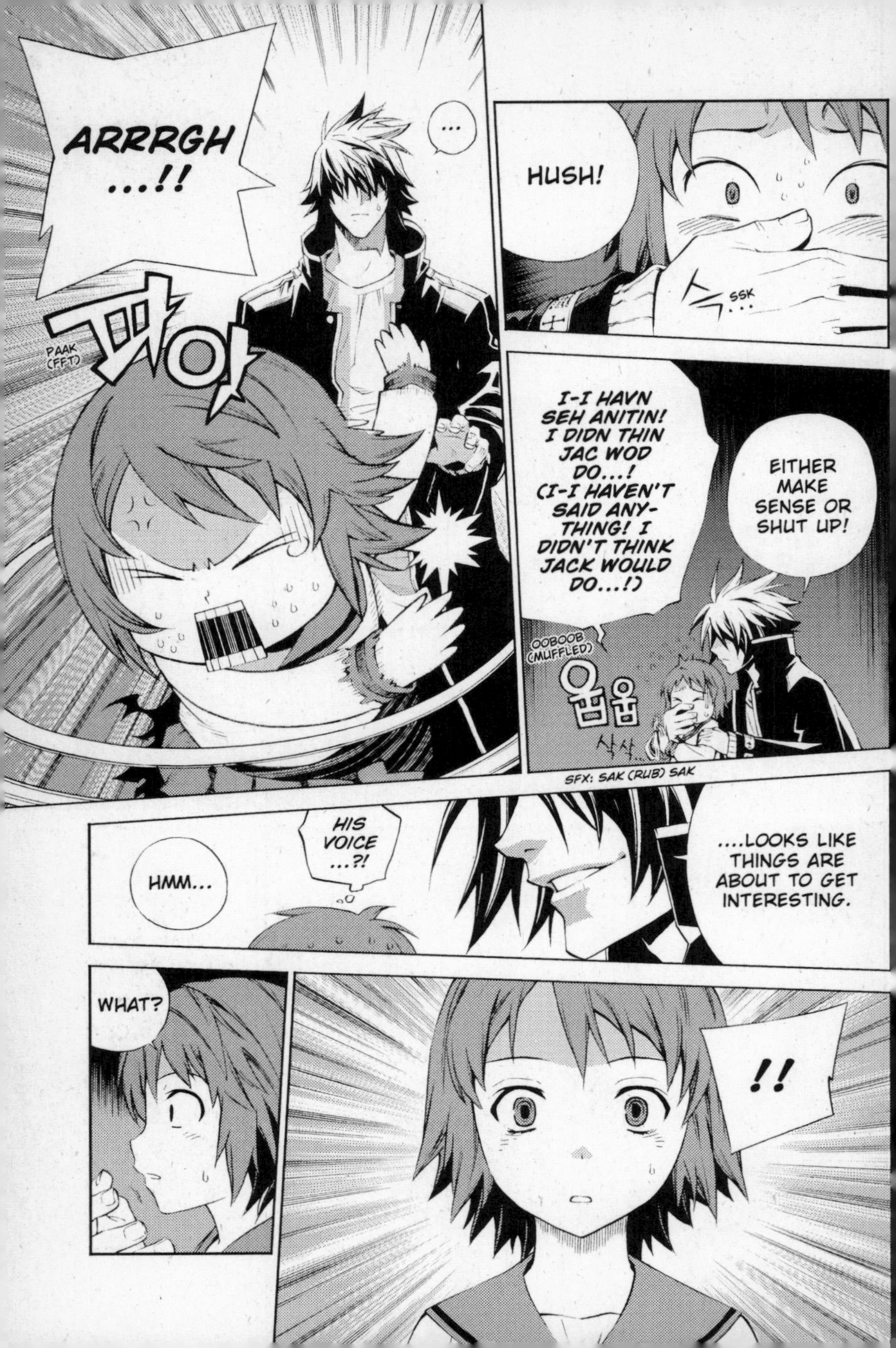
ARRRGH ...!!
...
PAAK (FFT)
HUSH!
SSK...
I-I HAVN SEH ANITIN! I DIDN THIN JAC WOD DO...! (I-I HAVEN'T SAID ANYTHING! I DIDN'T THINK JACK WOULD DO...!)
EITHER MAKE SENSE OR SHUT UP!
OOBOOB (MUFFLED)
SFX: SAK (RUB) SAK
HMM...
HIS VOICE ...?!
....LOOKS LIKE THINGS ARE ABOUT TO GET INTERESTING.
WHAT?
!!

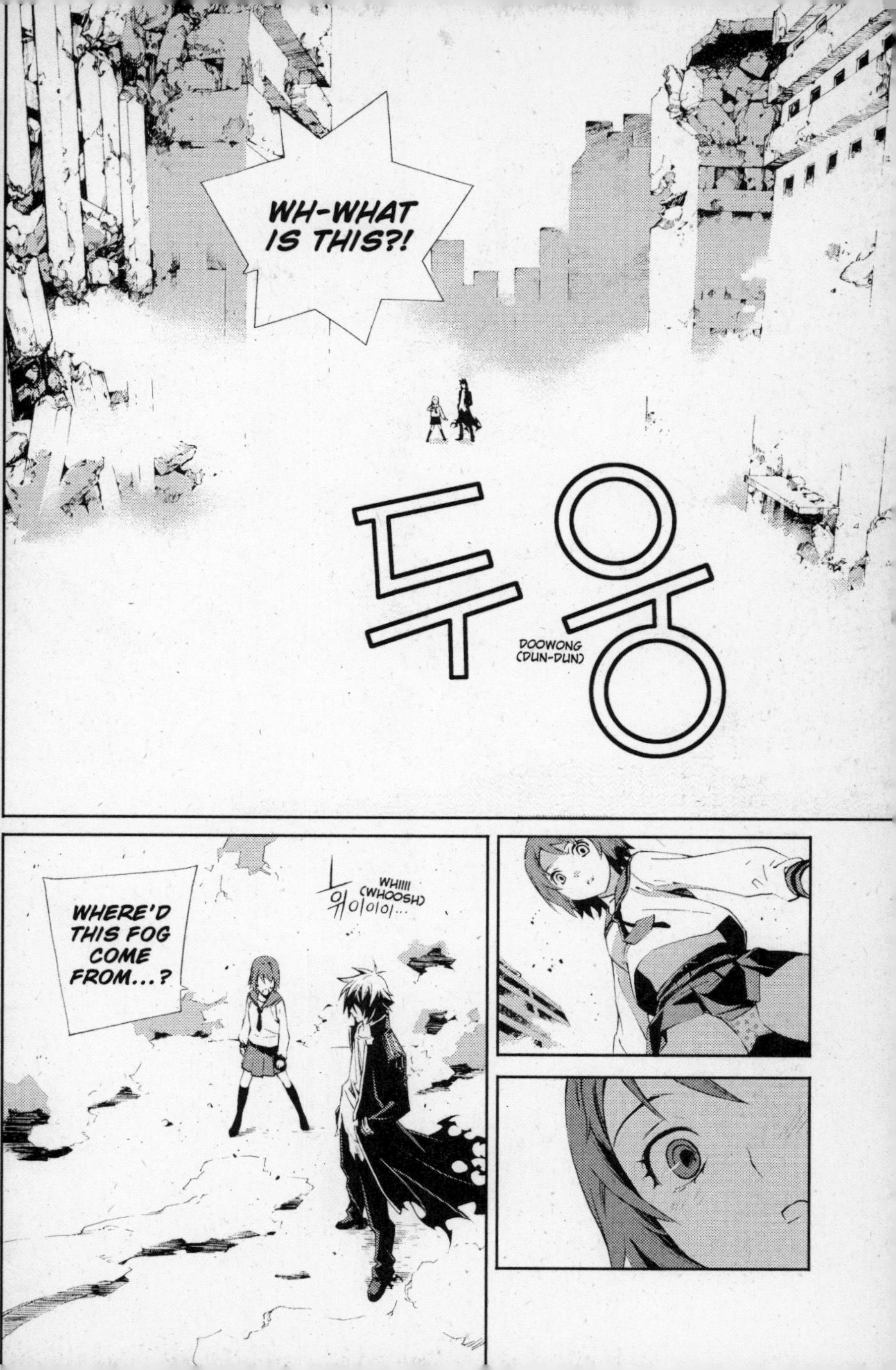
WH-WHAT IS THIS?!
두웅
DOOWONG (DUN-DUN)
WHERE'D THIS FOG COME FROM...?
WHIIII (WHOOSH)

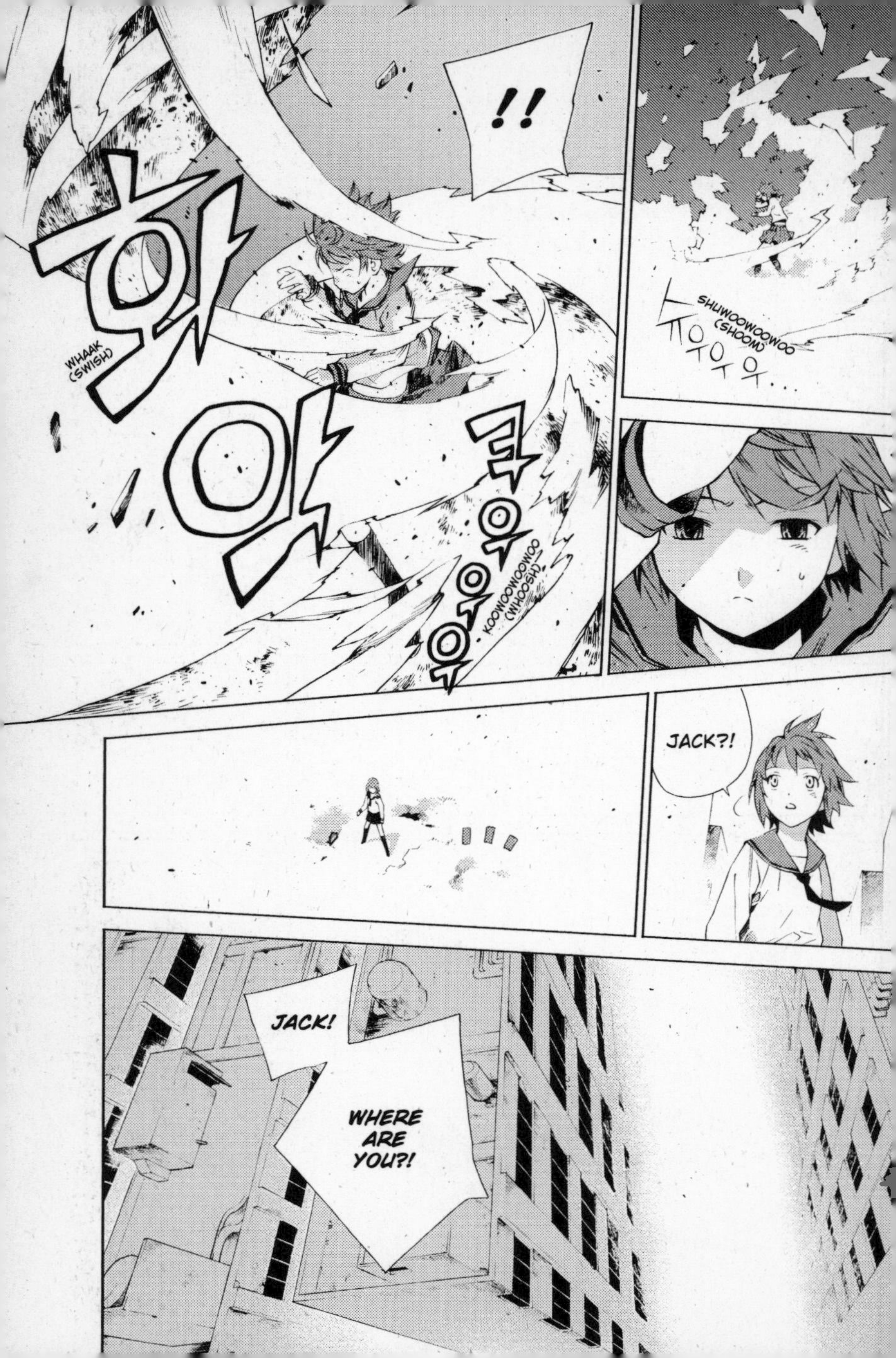
!!
WHAAK (SWISH)
KOOWOOWOOWOO (SHOOM)
SHUWOOWOOWOO (SHOOM)...
JACK?!
JACK!
WHERE ARE YOU?!

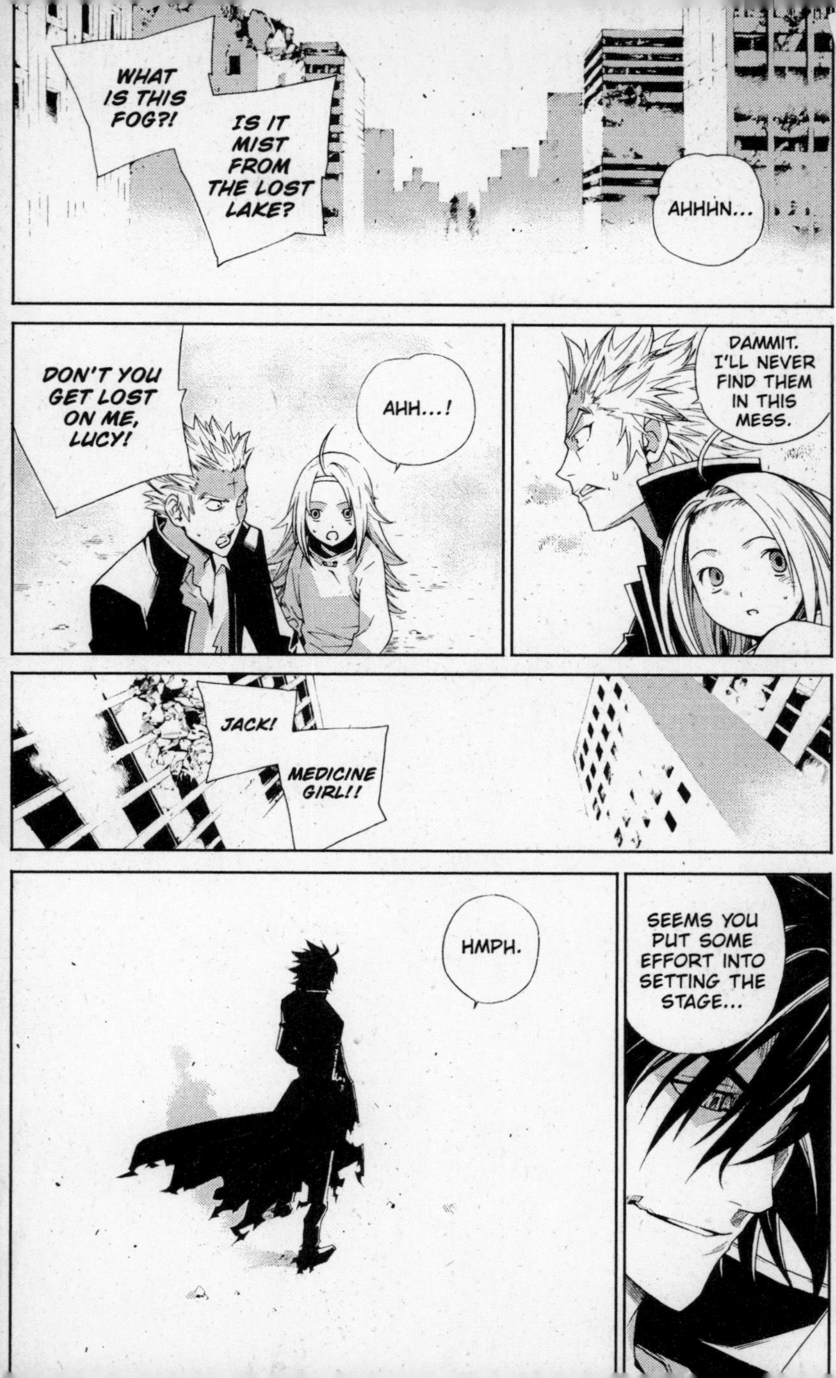
WHAT IS THIS FOG?!
IS IT MIST FROM THE LOST LAKE?
AHHHN...
DON'T YOU GET LOST ON ME, LUCY!
AHH...!
DAMMIT. I'LL NEVER FIND THEM IN THIS MESS.
JACK!
MEDICINE GIRL!!
HMPH.
SEEMS YOU PUT SOME EFFORT INTO SETTING THE STAGE...

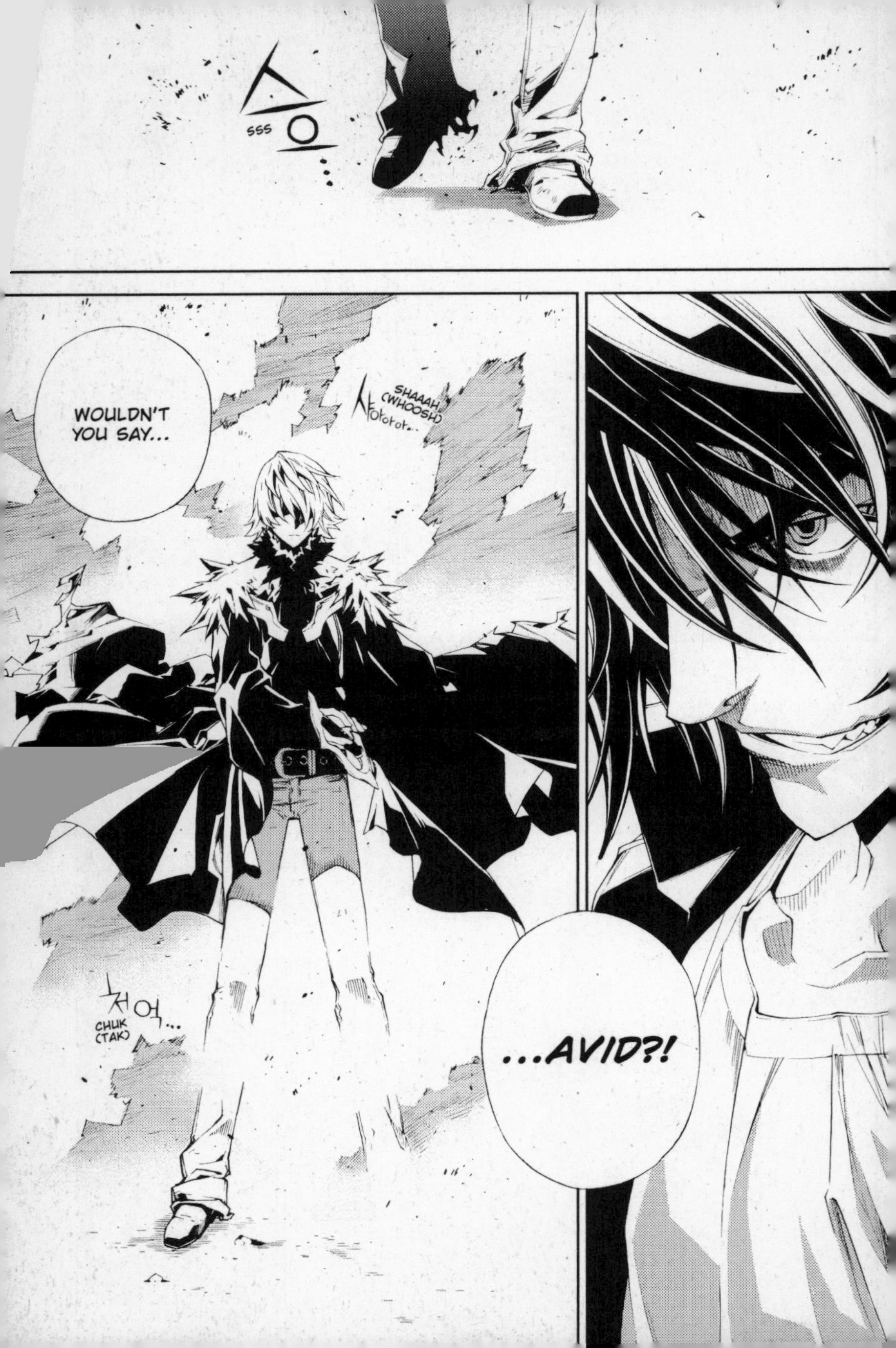
SSS
WOULDN'T YOU SAY...
SHAAAH (WHOOSH)
CHUK (TAK)
...AVID?!

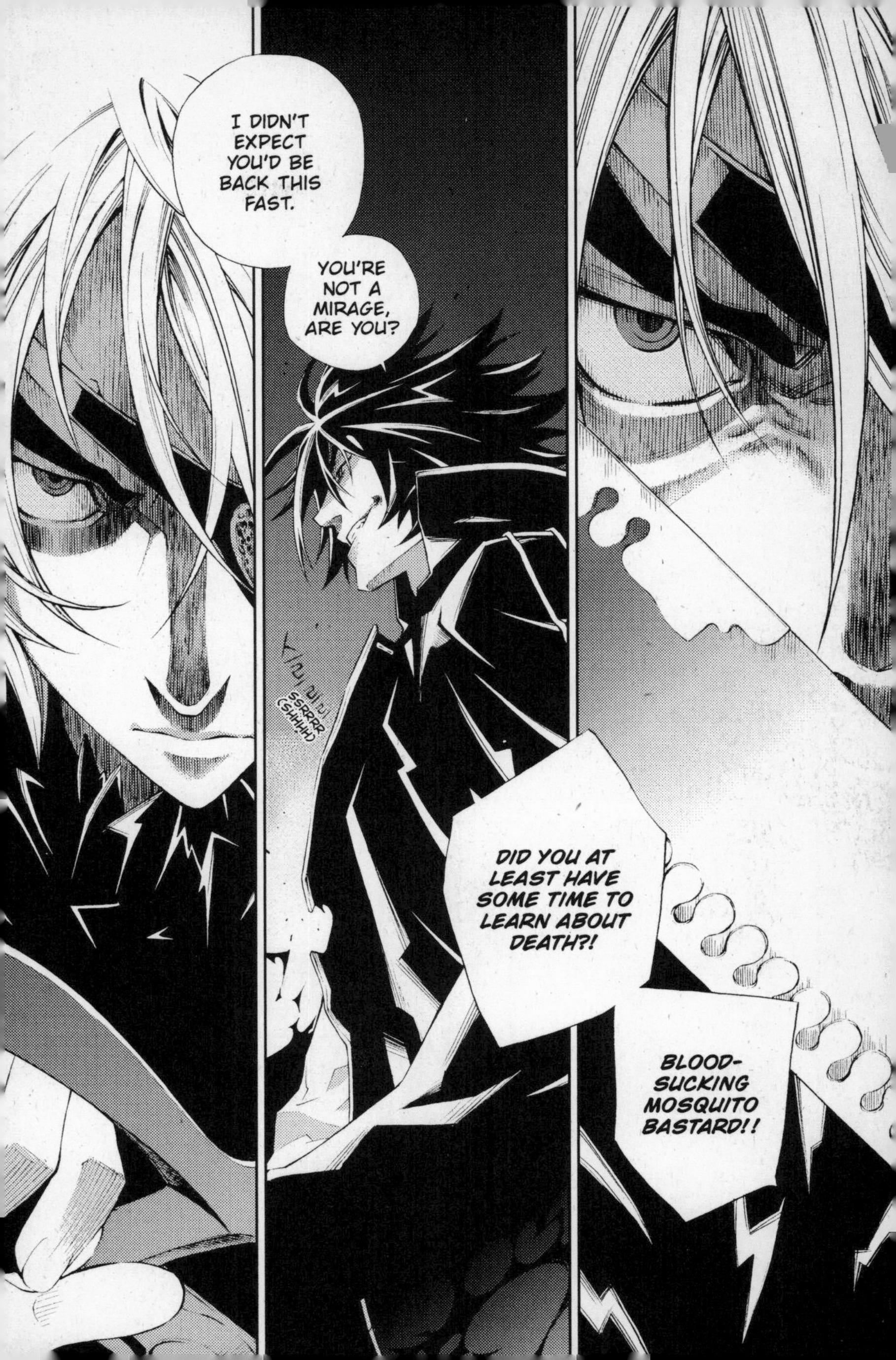
I DIDN'T EXPECT YOU'D BE BACK THIS FAST.
YOU'RE NOT A MIRAGE, ARE YOU?
SSRRRR (SHHHH)
DID YOU AT LEAST HAVE SOME TIME TO LEARN ABOUT DEATH?!
BLOOD-SUCKING MOSQUITO BASTARD!!

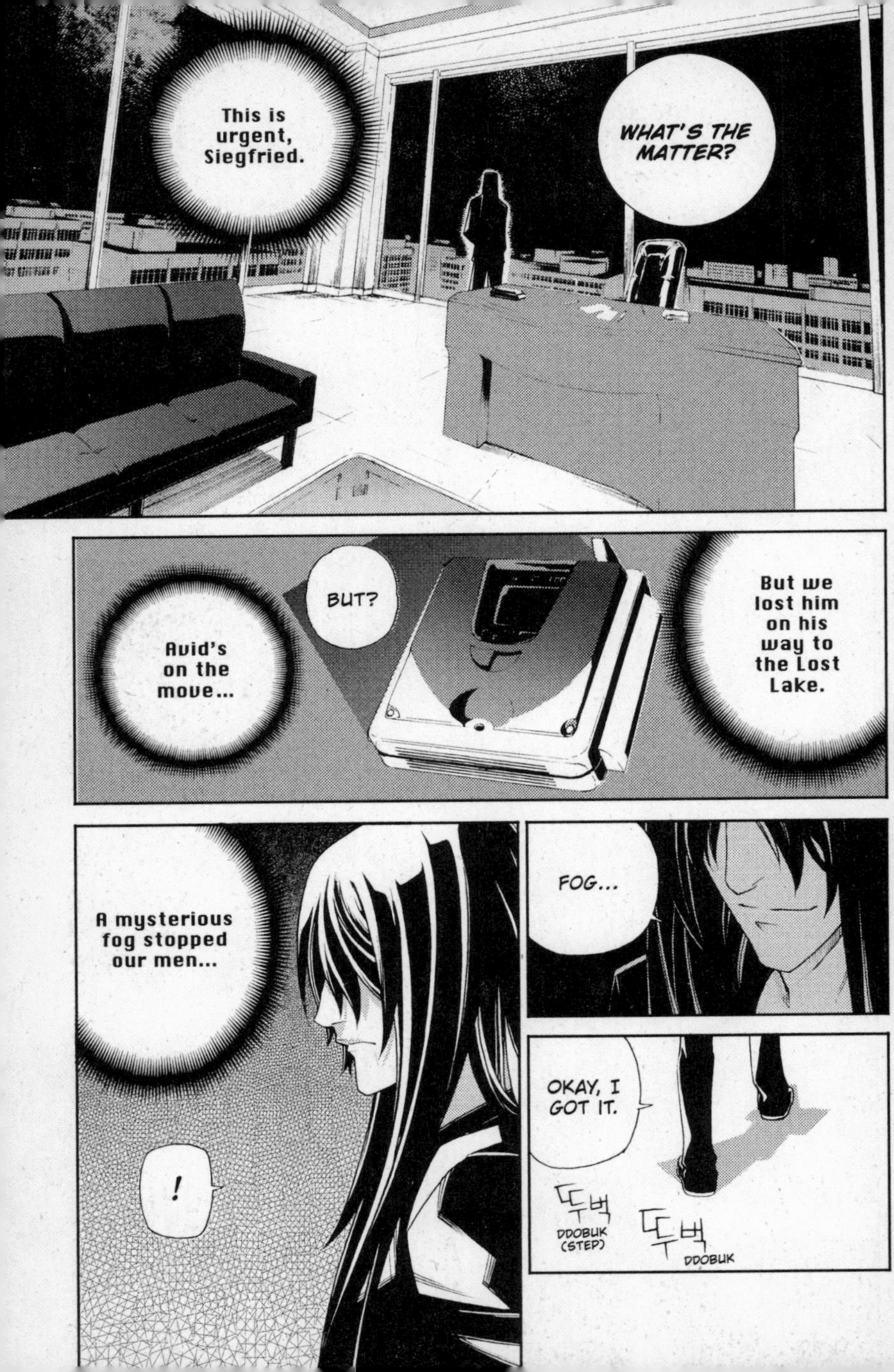
This is urgent, Siegfried.
WHAT'S THE MATTER?
Avid's on the move...
BUT?
But we lost him on his way to the Lost Lake.
A mysterious fog stopped our men...
!
FOG...
OKAY, I GOT IT.
DDOBUK (STEP)
DDOBUK

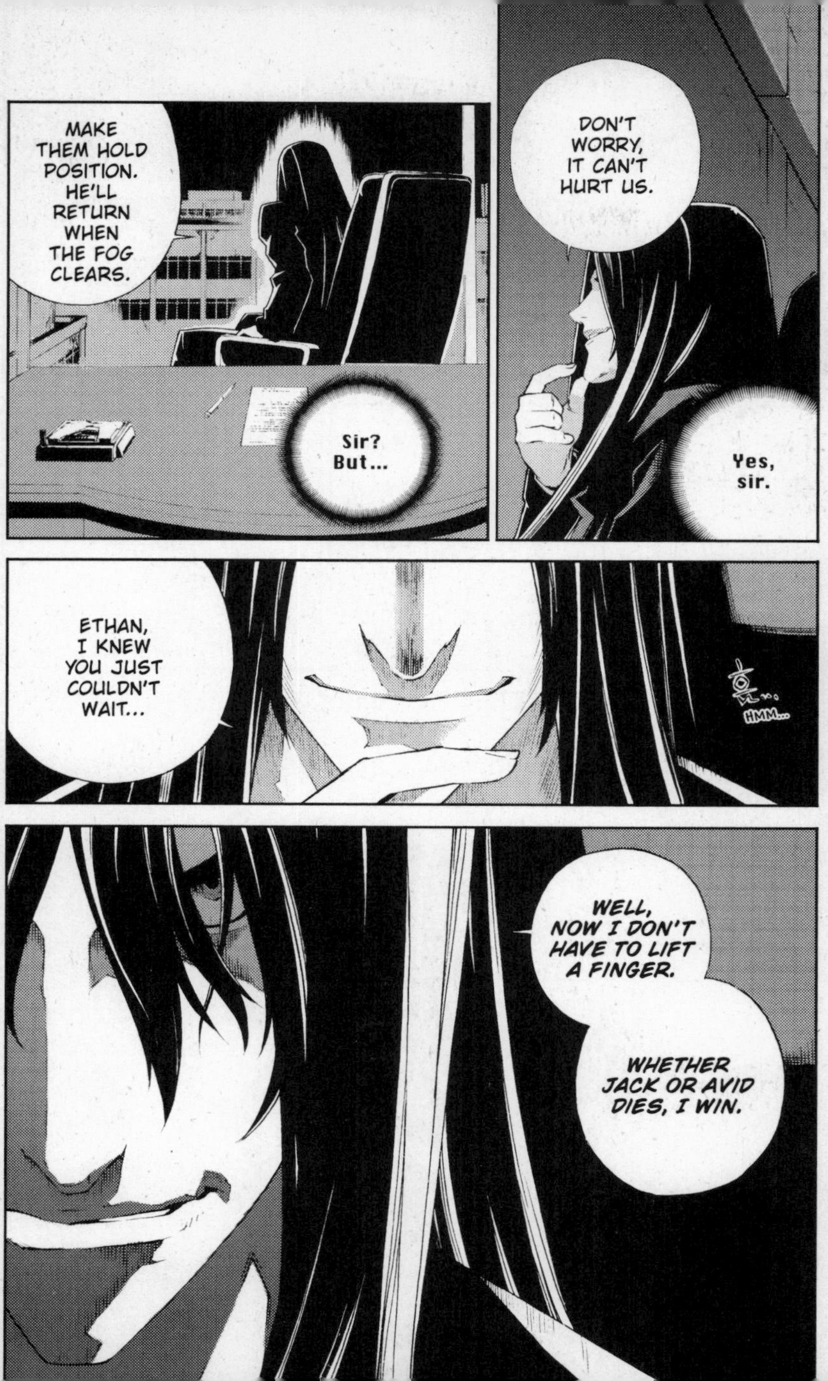
MAKE THEM HOLD POSITION. HE'LL RETURN WHEN THE FOG CLEARS.
Sir? But...
DON'T WORRY, IT CAN'T HURT US.
Yes, sir.
ETHAN, I KNEW YOU JUST COULDN'T WAIT...
HMM...
WELL, NOW I DON'T HAVE TO LIFT A FINGER.
WHETHER JACK OR AVID DIES, I WIN.

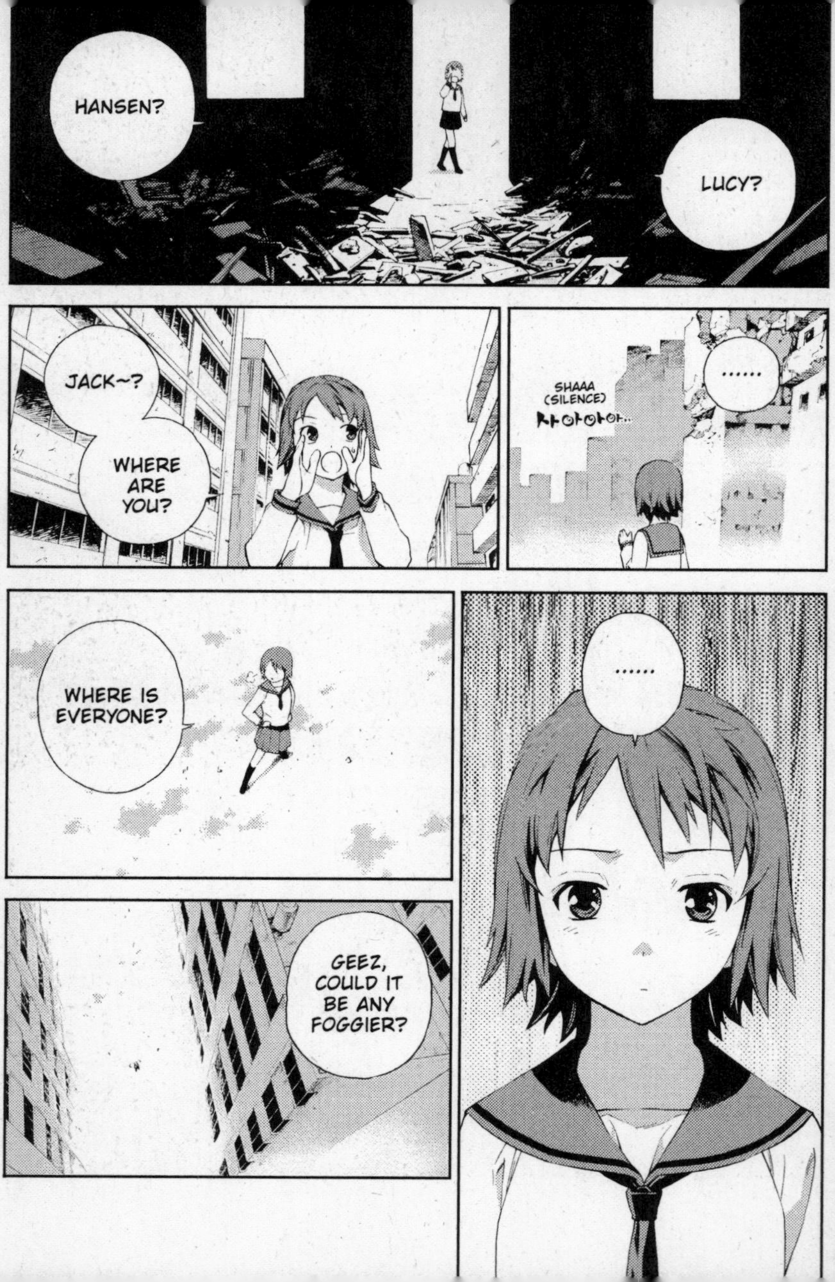
HANSEN?
LUCY?
JACK~?
WHERE ARE YOU?
SHAAA (SILENCE)
자아아아..
......
WHERE IS EVERYONE?
GEEZ, COULD IT BE ANY FOGGIER?
......

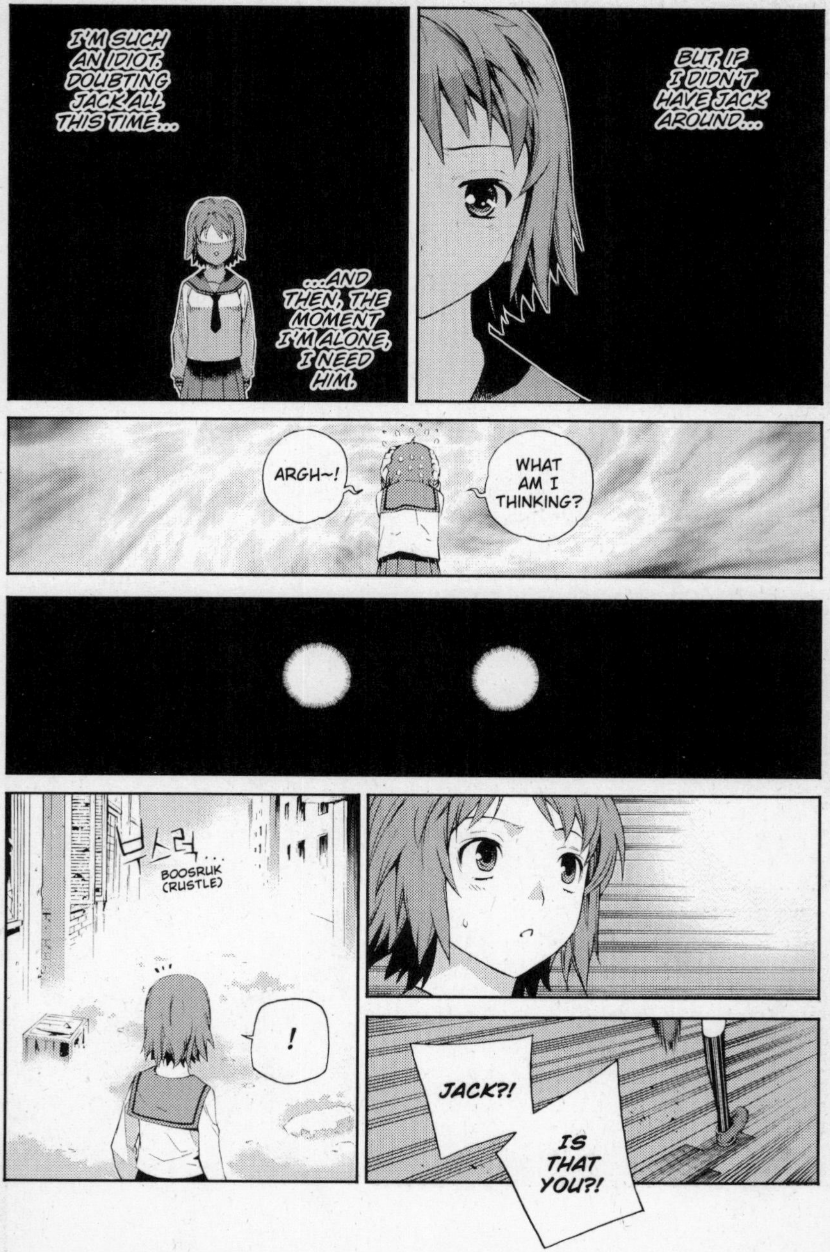
I'M SUCH AN IDIOT. DOUBTING JACK ALL THIS TIME...
...AND THEN, THE MOMENT I'M ALONE, I NEED HIM.
BUT, IF I DIDN'T HAVE JACK AROUND...
ARGH~!
WHAT AM I THINKING?
BOOSRUK (RUSTLE)
!
JACK?!
IS THAT YOU?!

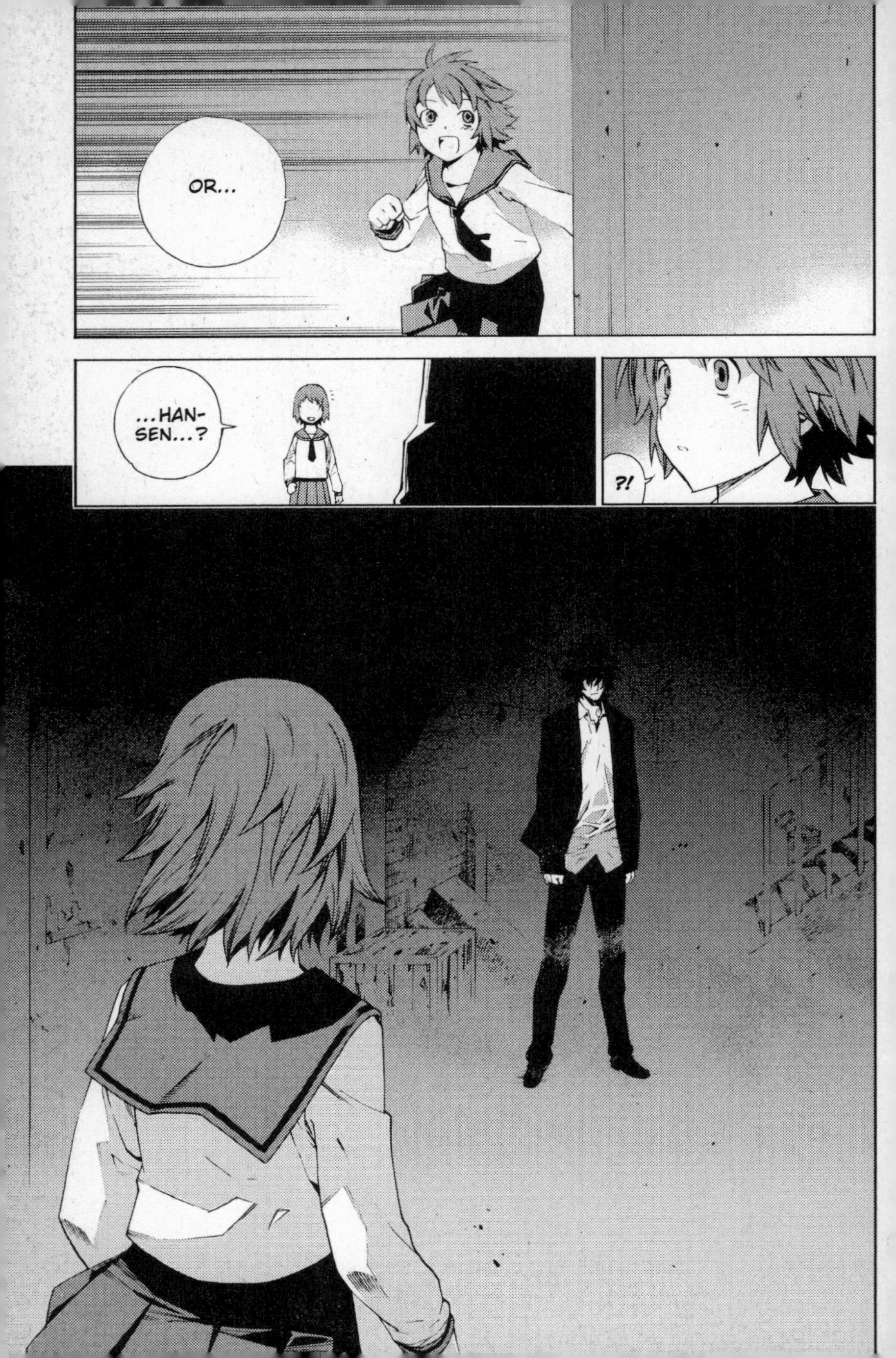
OR...
...HAN-SEN...?
?!

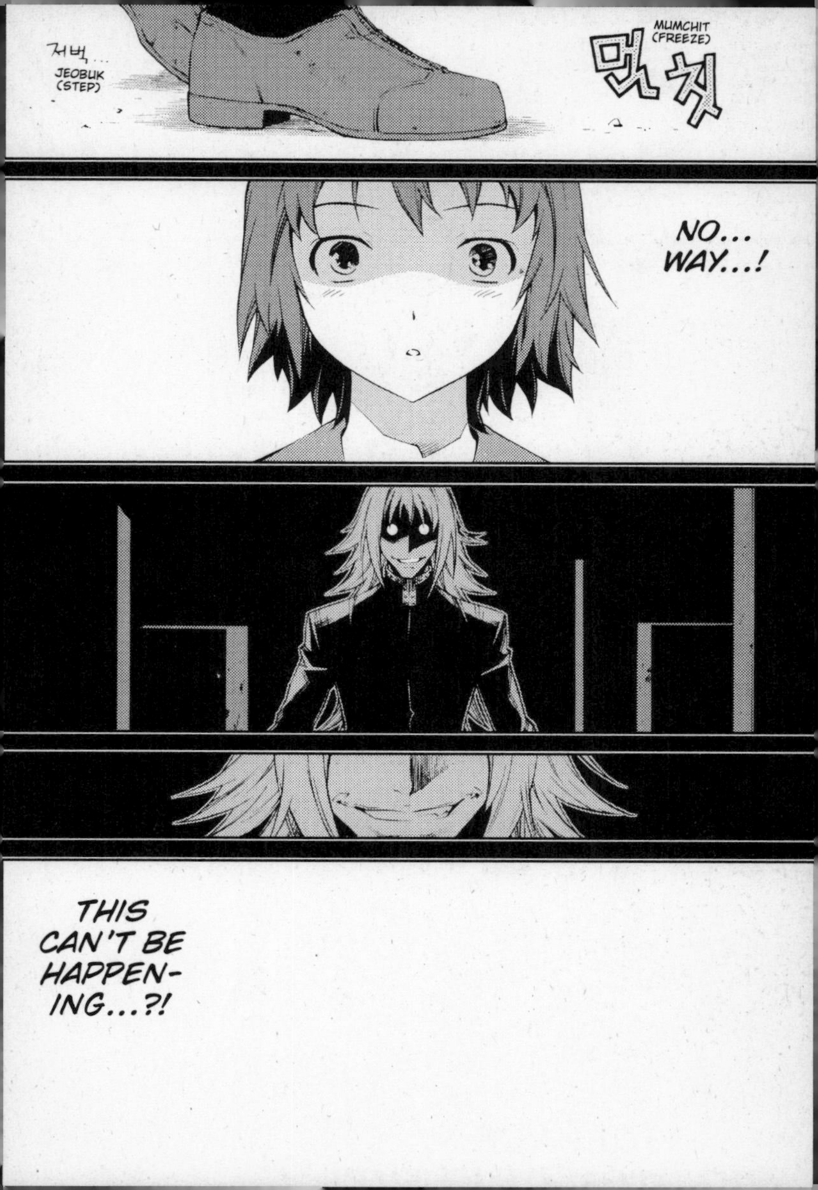
저벅...
JEOBUK (STEP)
멈칫
MUMCHIT (FREEZE)
NO... WAY...!
THIS CAN'T BE HAPPEN-ING...?!

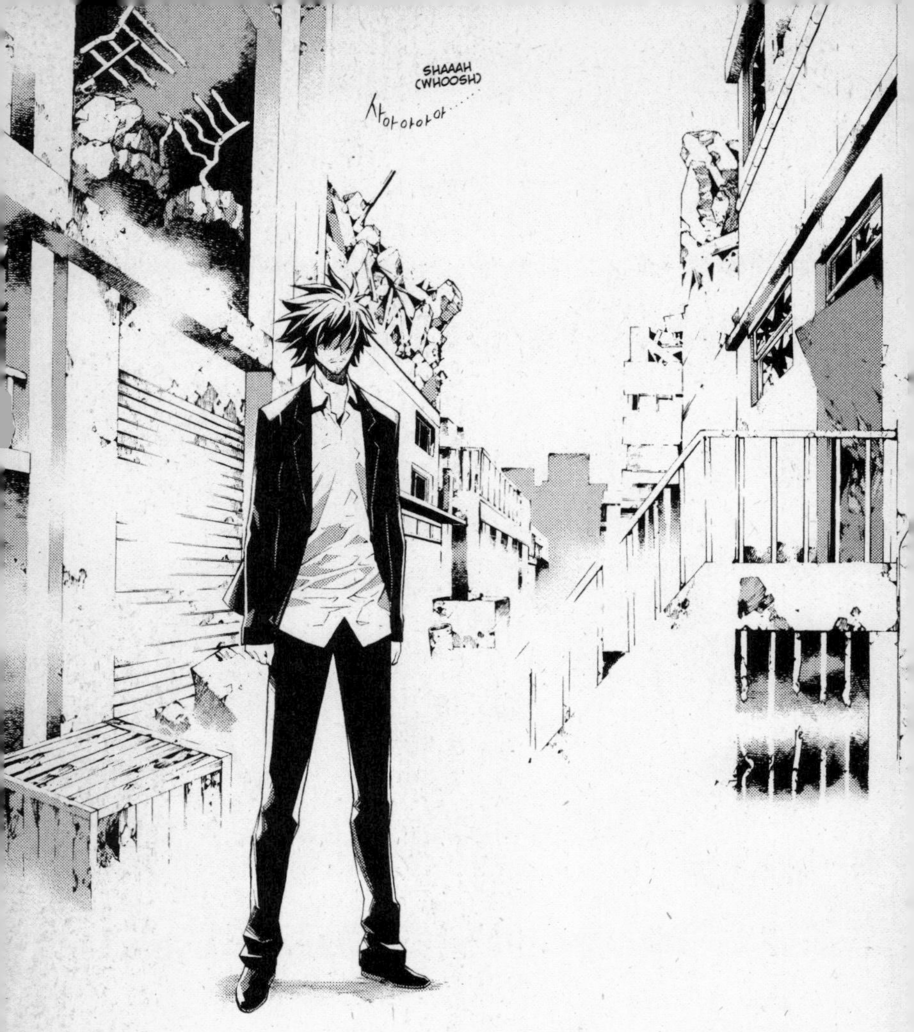
사아아아아……
SHAAAH
(WHOOSH)

VIOLENCE 34.
PHANTOM OF FATHER

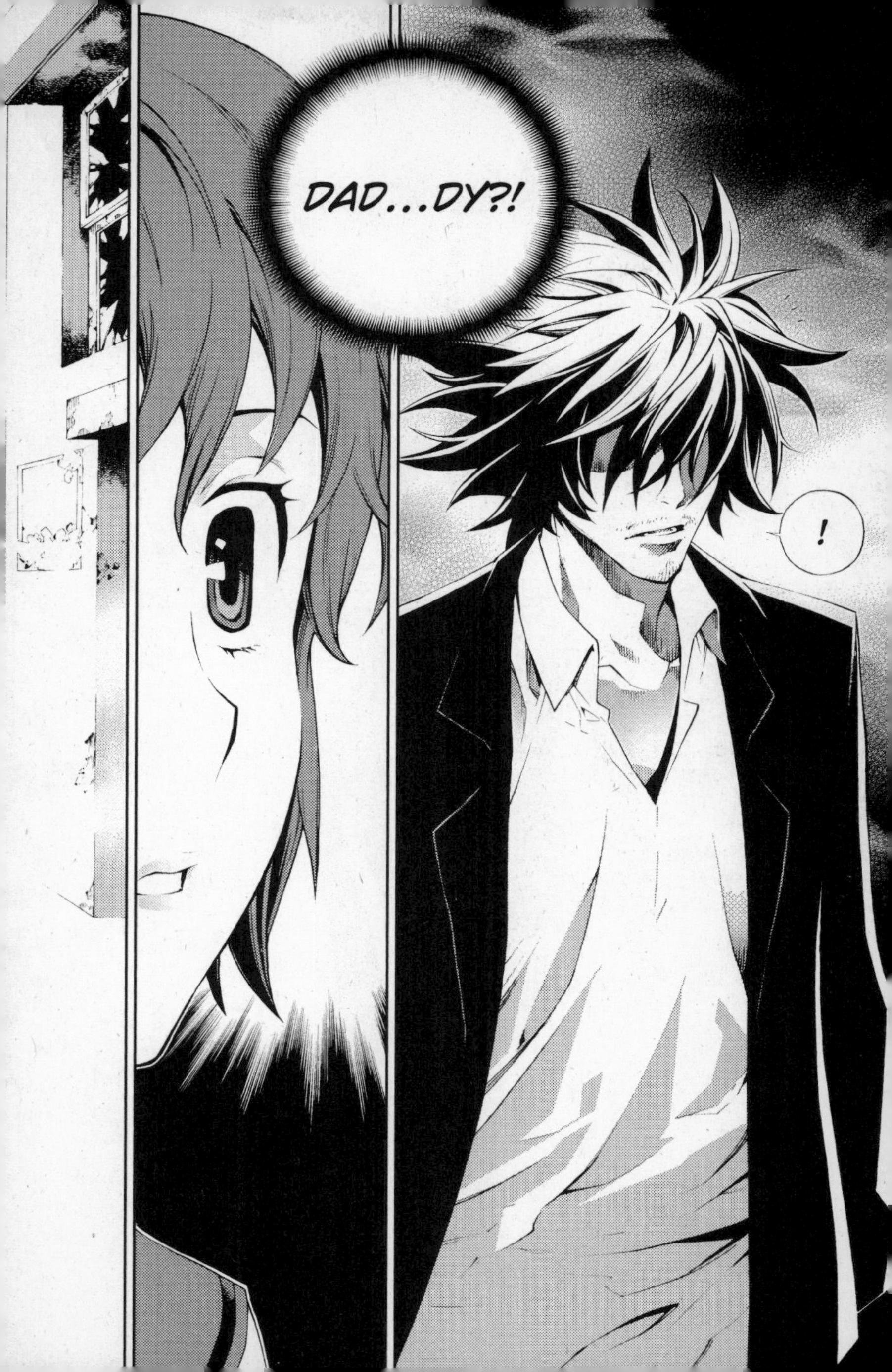
DAD...DY?!
!

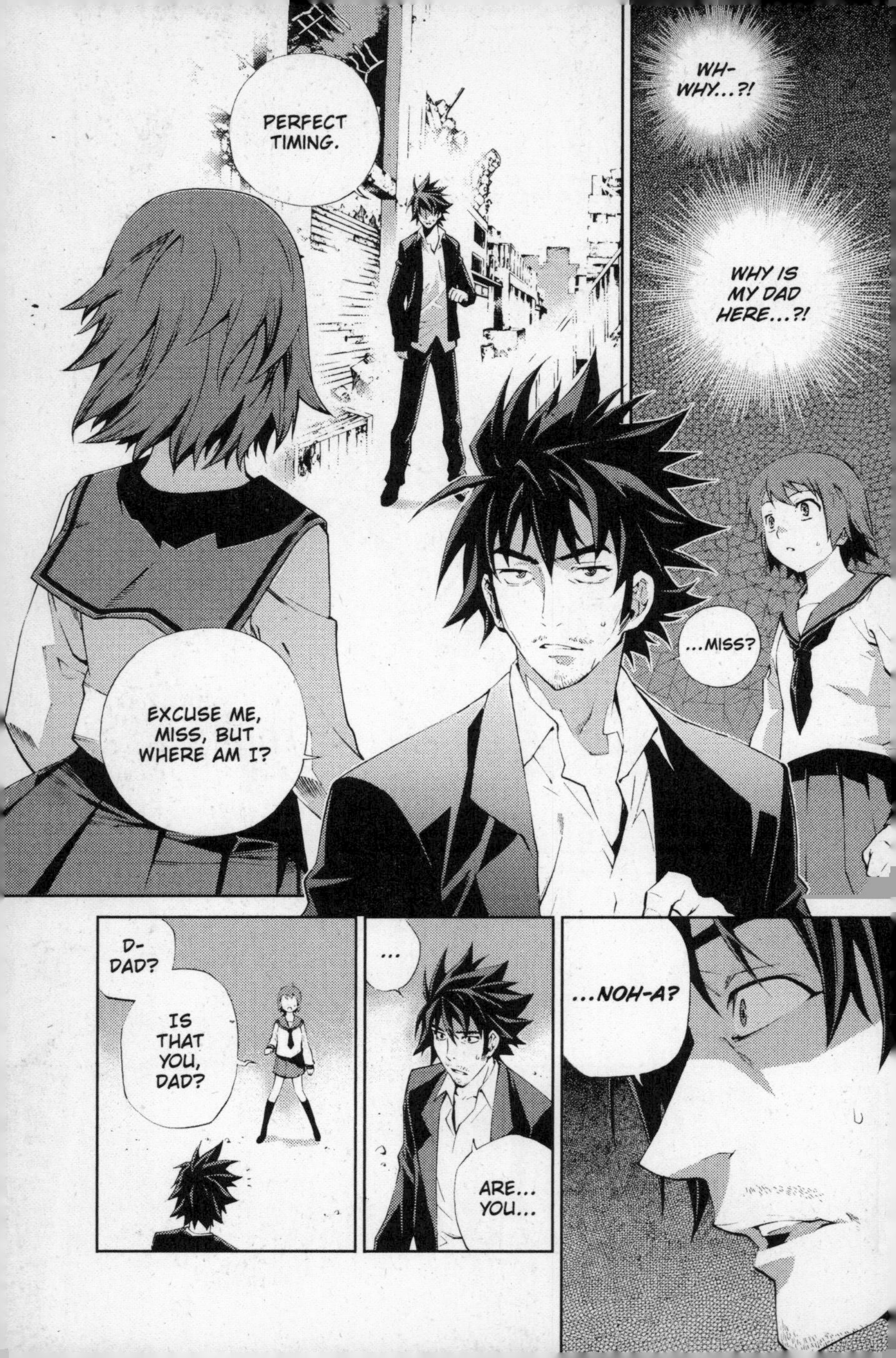
PERFECT TIMING.
EXCUSE ME, MISS, BUT WHERE AM I?
WH- WHY...?!
WHY IS MY DAD HERE...?!
...MISS?
D- DAD?
IS THAT YOU, DAD?
...
ARE... YOU...
...NOH-A?

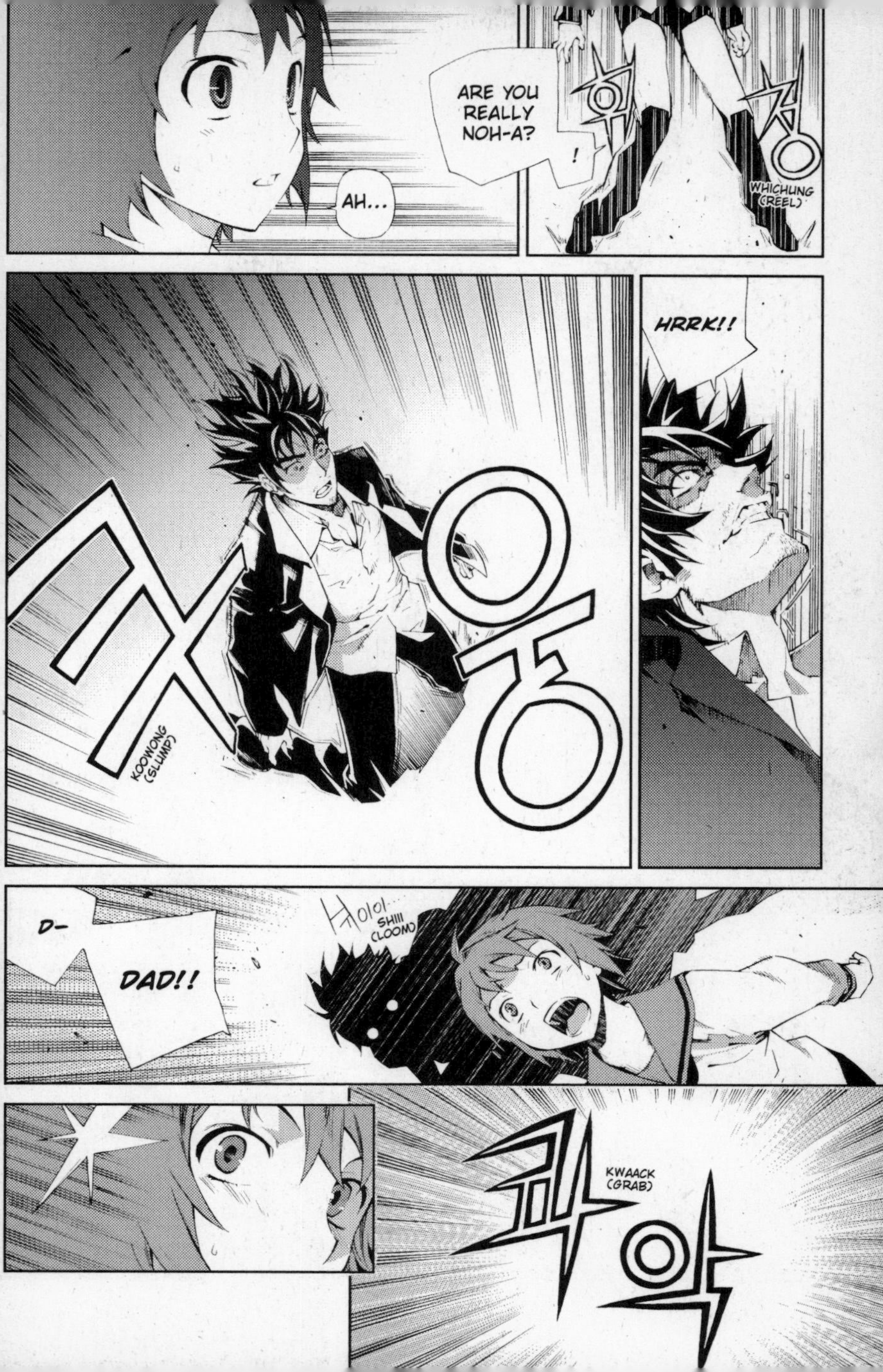
ARE YOU REALLY NOH-A?
AH...
!
WHICHUNG (REEL)
KOOWONG (SLUMP)
HRRK!!
D-
DAD!!
SHIII (LOOM)
KWAACK (GRAB)

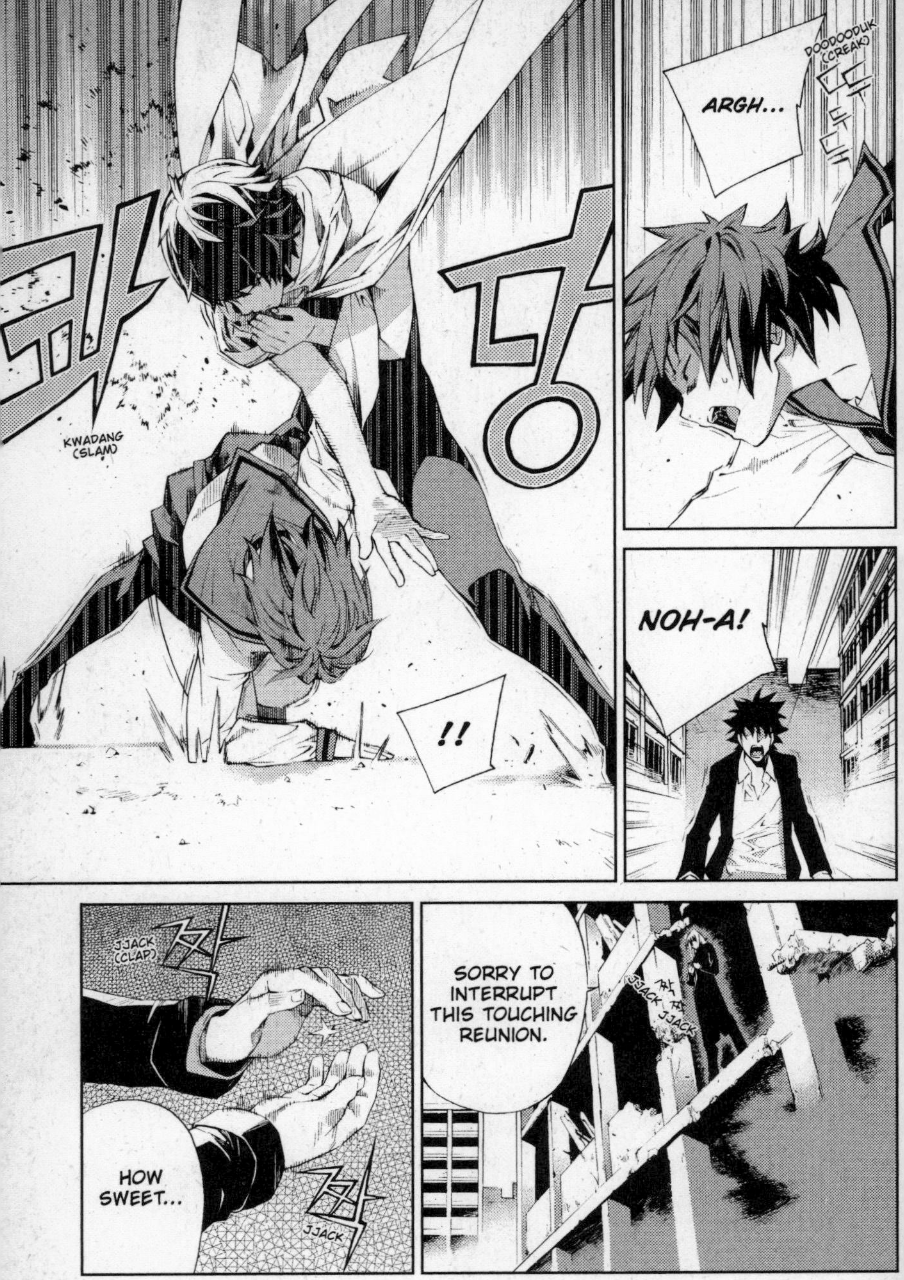
KWADANG (SLAM)
!!
ARGH...
DOODOODUK (CREAK)
NOH-A!
JJACK (CLAP)
HOW SWEET...
JJACK
SORRY TO INTERRUPT THIS TOUCHING REUNION.
JJACK JJACK

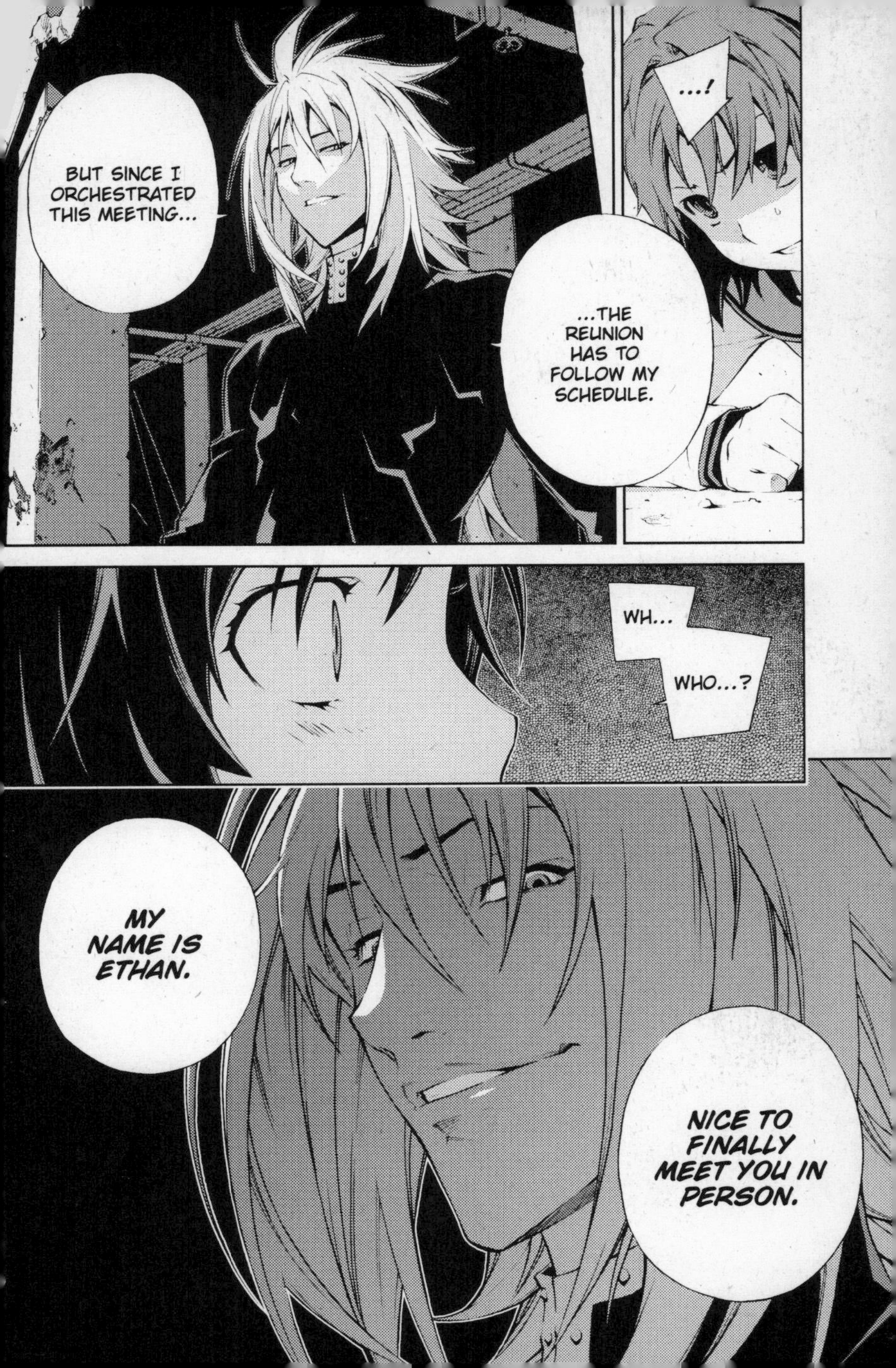

BUT SINCE I ORCHESTRATED THIS MEETING...
...THE REUNION HAS TO FOLLOW MY SCHEDULE.
...!
WH...
WHO...?
MY NAME IS ETHAN.
NICE TO FINALLY MEET YOU IN PERSON.

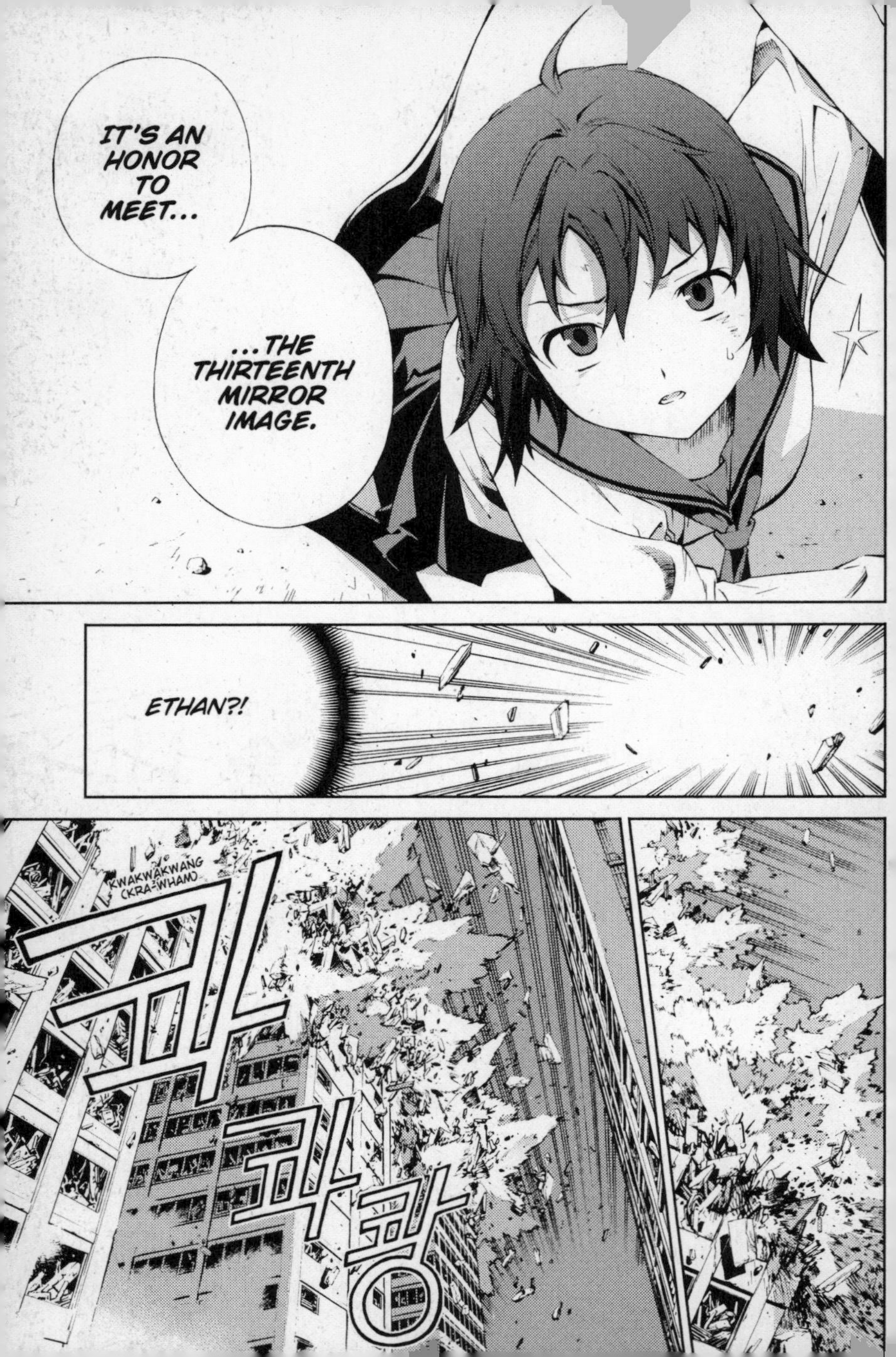
IT'S AN HONOR TO MEET...
...THE THIRTEENTH MIRROR IMAGE.
ETHAN?!
KWAKWAKWANG (KRA-WHAM)

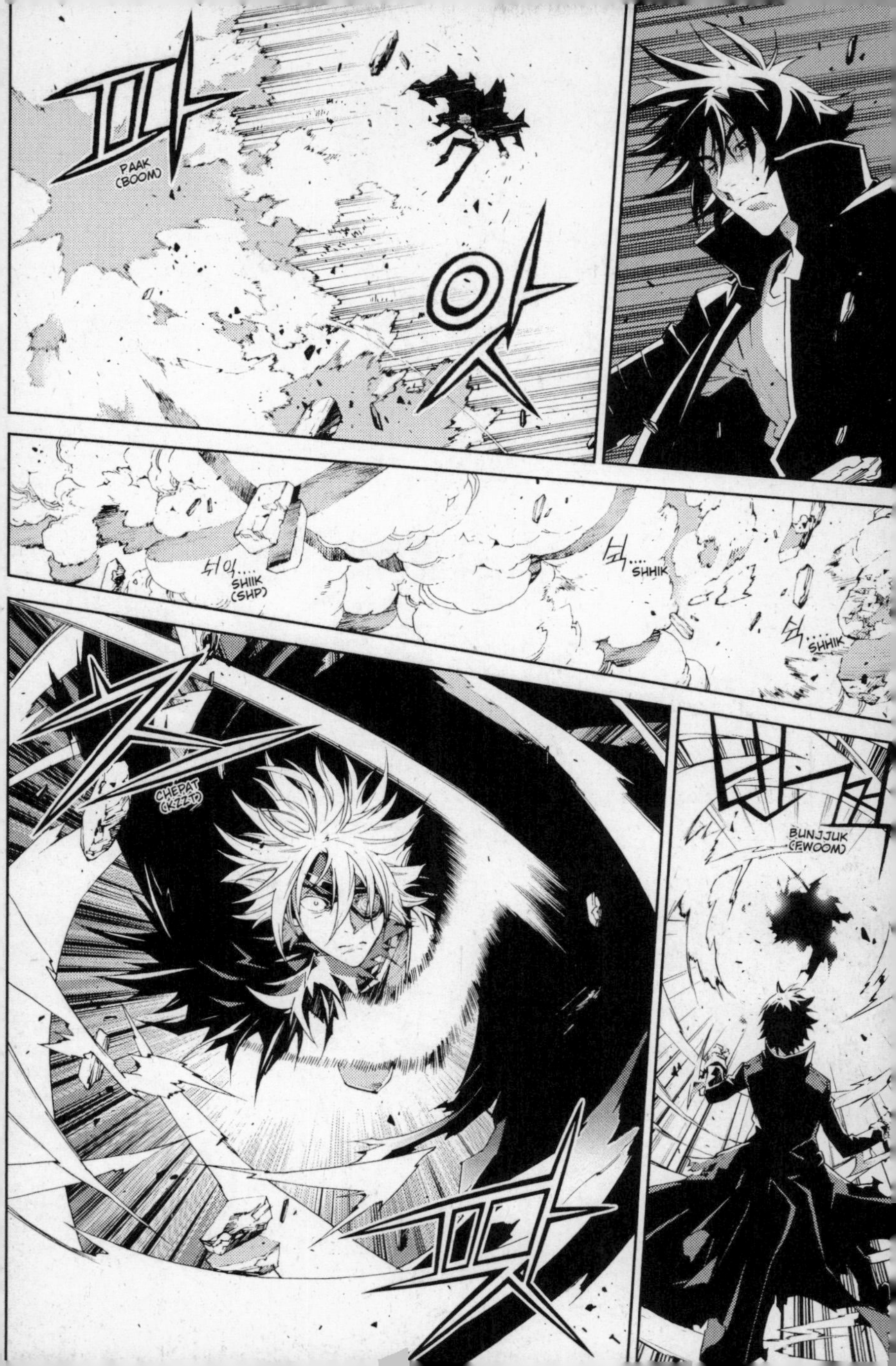
PAAK
(BOOM)
쉬익....
SHIIK
(SHP)
쉭....
SHHIK
쉭....
SHHIK
CHEPAT
(KZZT)
BUNJJUK
(F-WOOM)

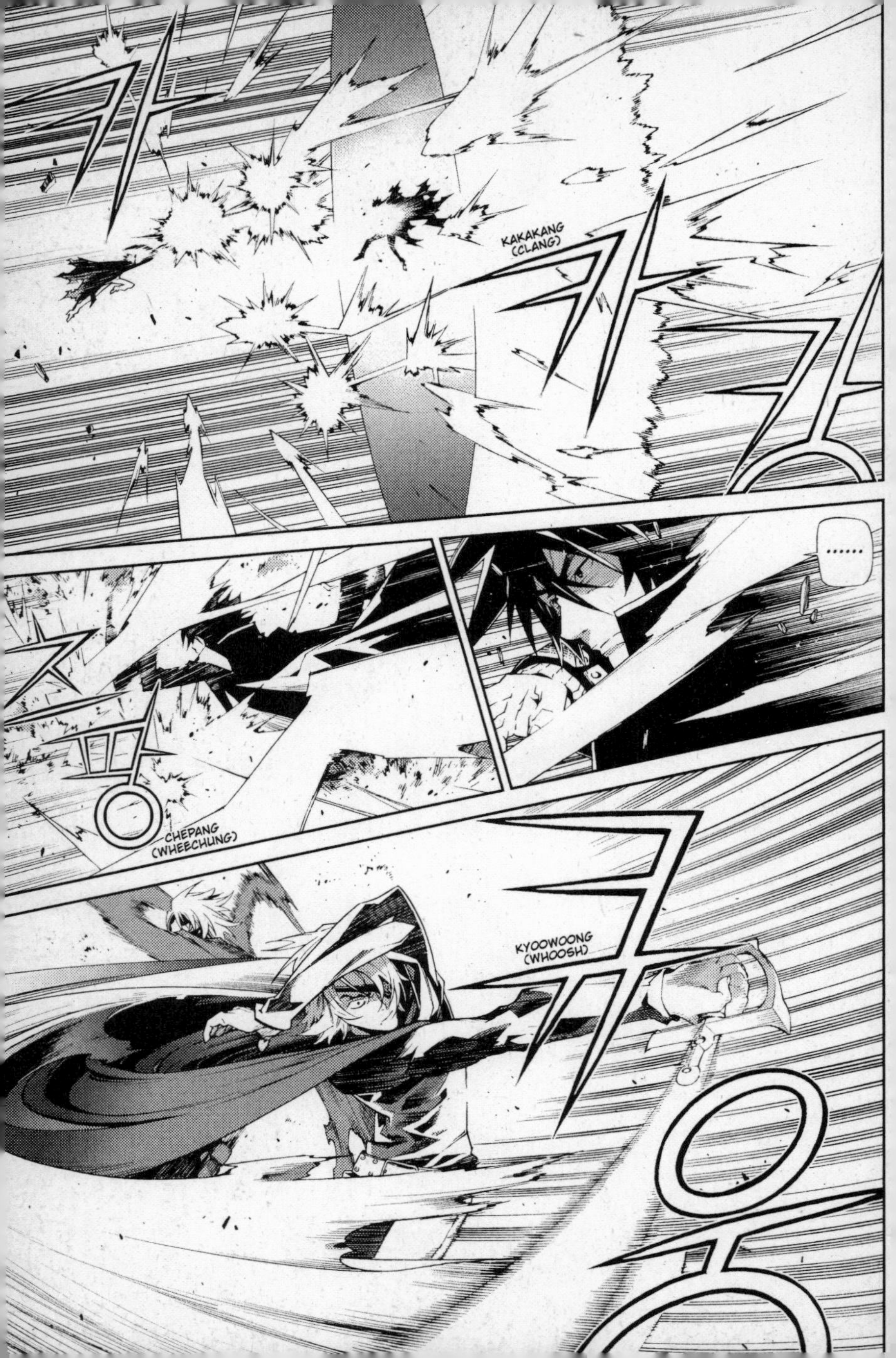
KAKAKANG
(CLANG)
......
CHEPANG
(WHEECHUNG)
KYOOWOONG
(WHOOSH)

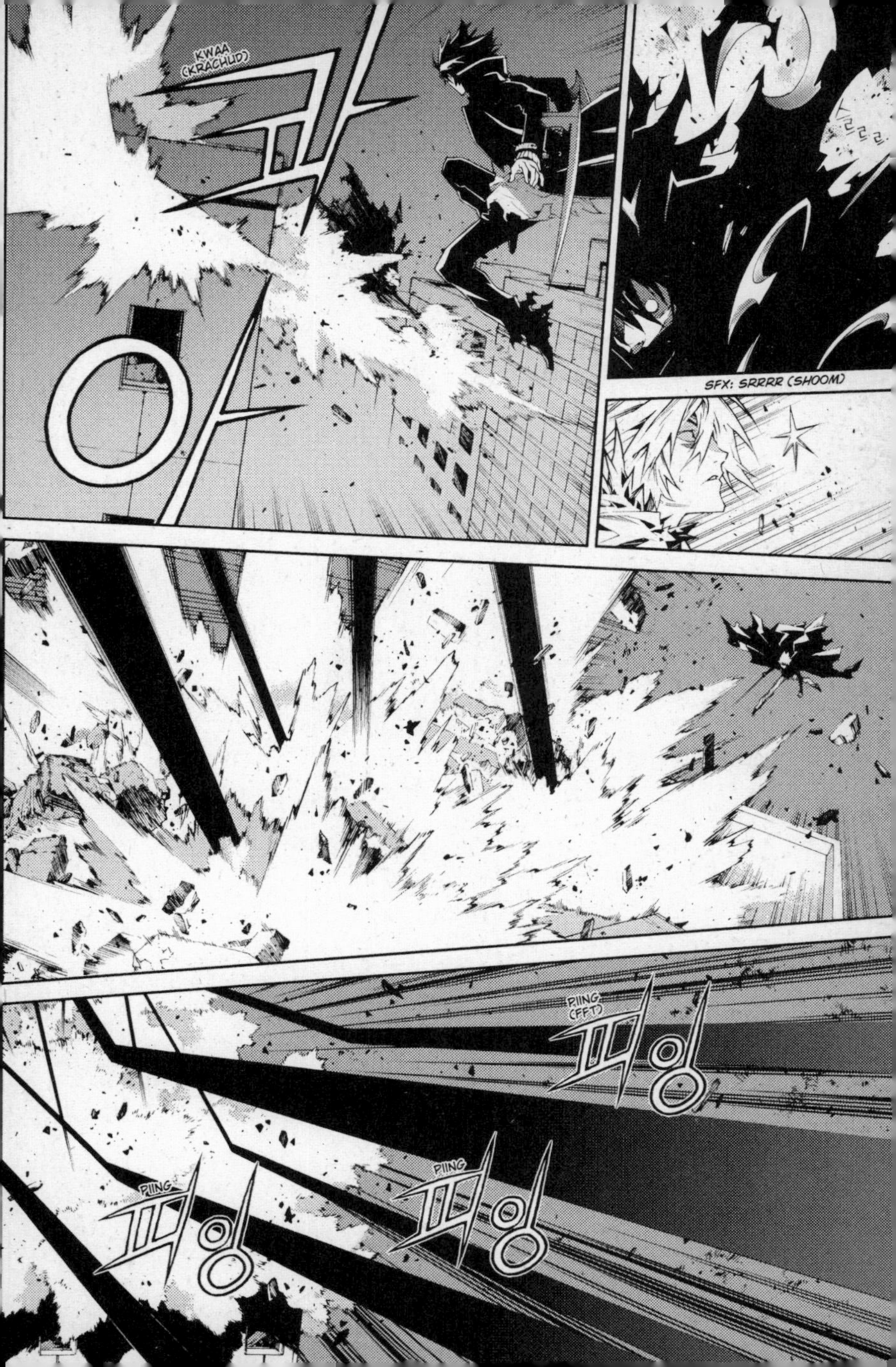
KWAA (KRACHUD)
SFX: SRRRR (SHOOM)
PIING (FFT)
PIING
PIING

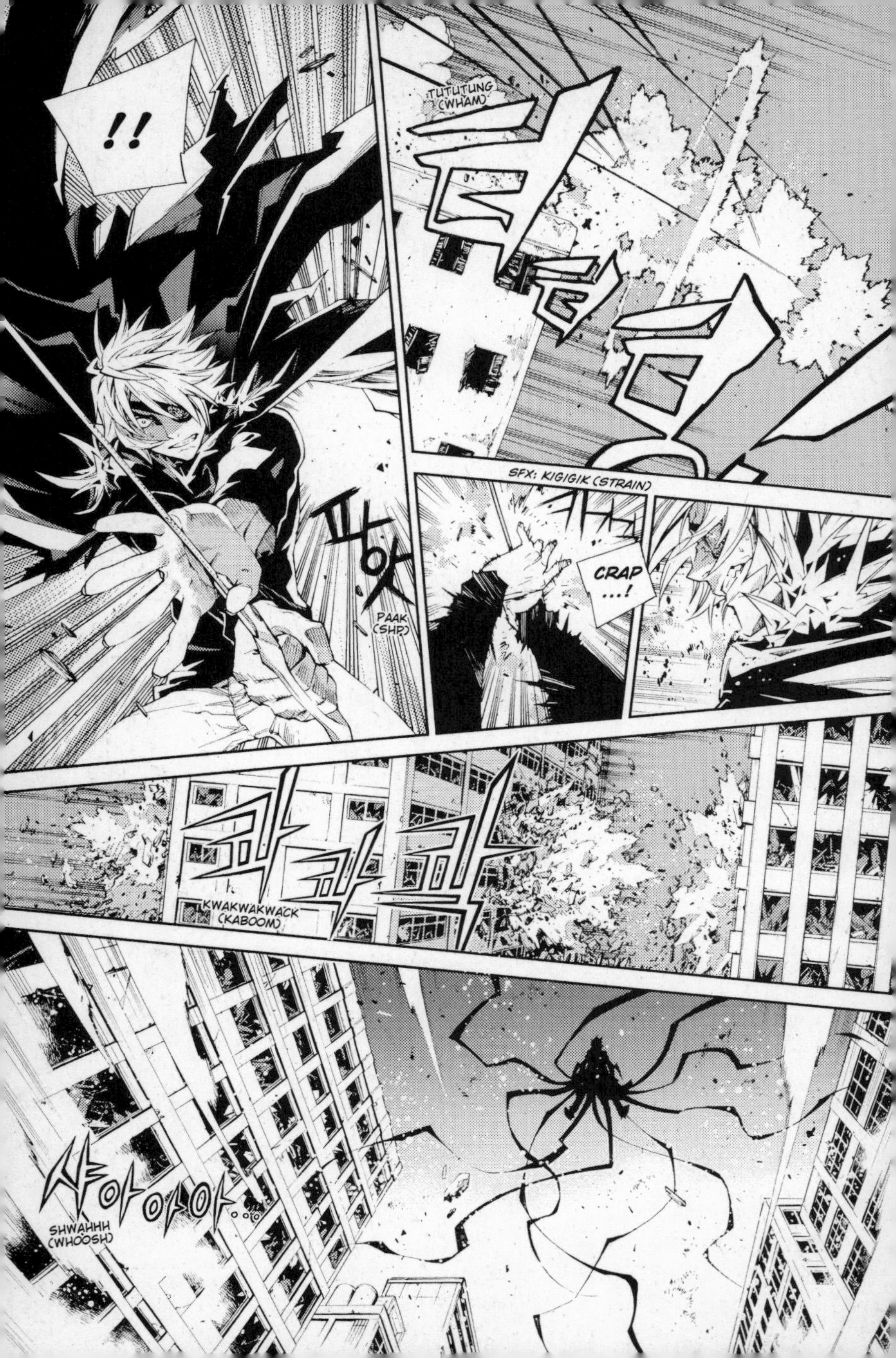
!!
PAAK (SHP)
TUTUTUNG (WHAM)
SFX: KIGIGIK (STRAIN)
CRAP ...!
KWAKWAKWACK (KABOOM)
SHWAHHH (WHOOSH)

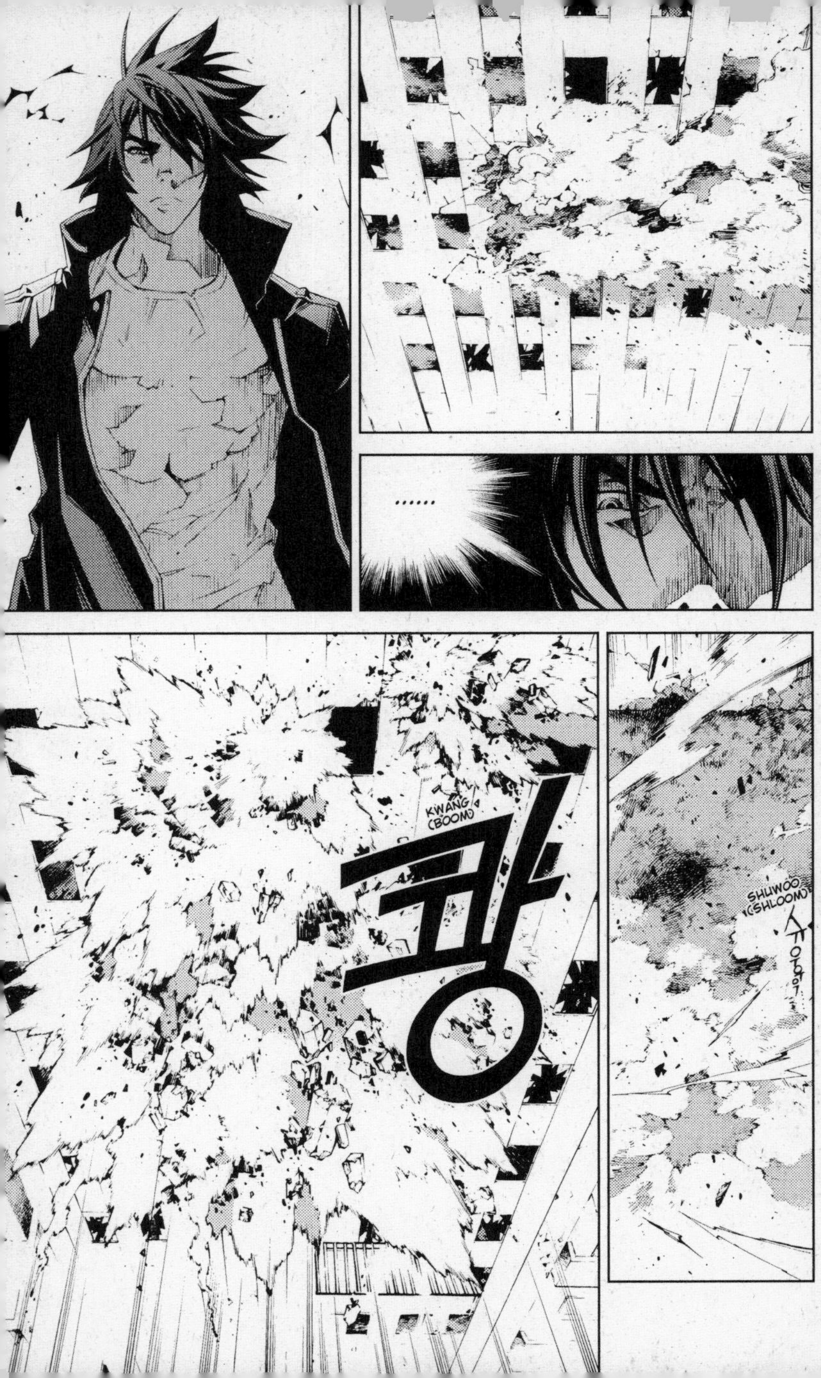
......
KWANG (BOOM)
쾅
SHUWOO (SHLOOM)

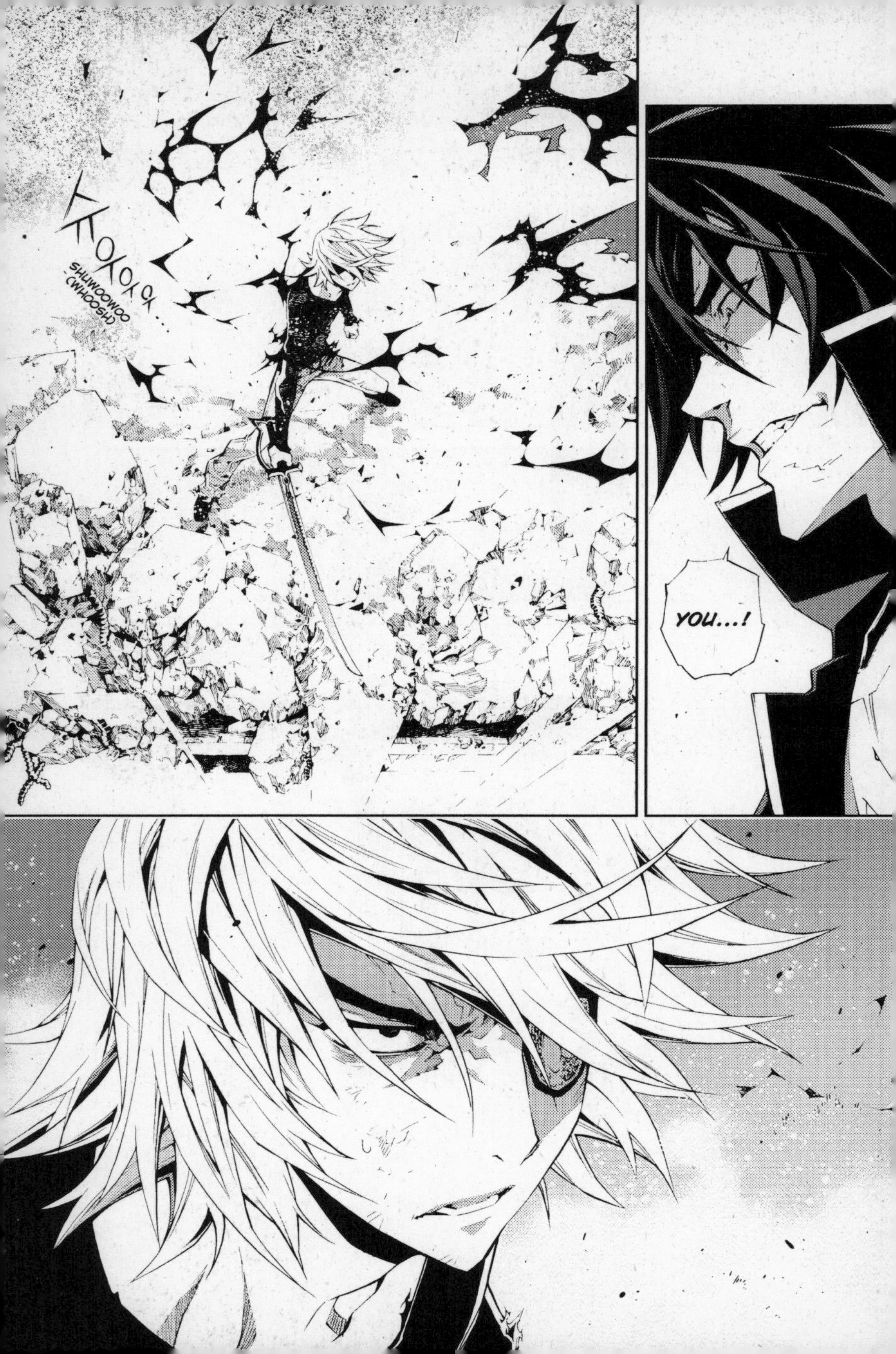
SHUWOOWOO (WHOOSH)
YOU...!

HELMINA.

JACK AND THE MIRROR IMAGE ARE IN TROUBLE.

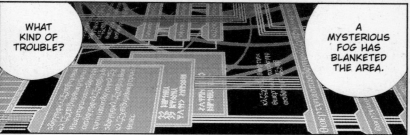

WHAT KIND OF TROUBLE?

A MYSTERIOUS FOG HAS BLANKETED THE AREA.

CONSIDERING THE TEMPERATURE, HUMIDITY, AND PROXIMITY TO THE LAKE...

...THERE'S NO WAY THAT FOG COULD HAVE FORMED NATURALLY.

THERE'S ONLY ONE LOGICAL EXPLANATION...

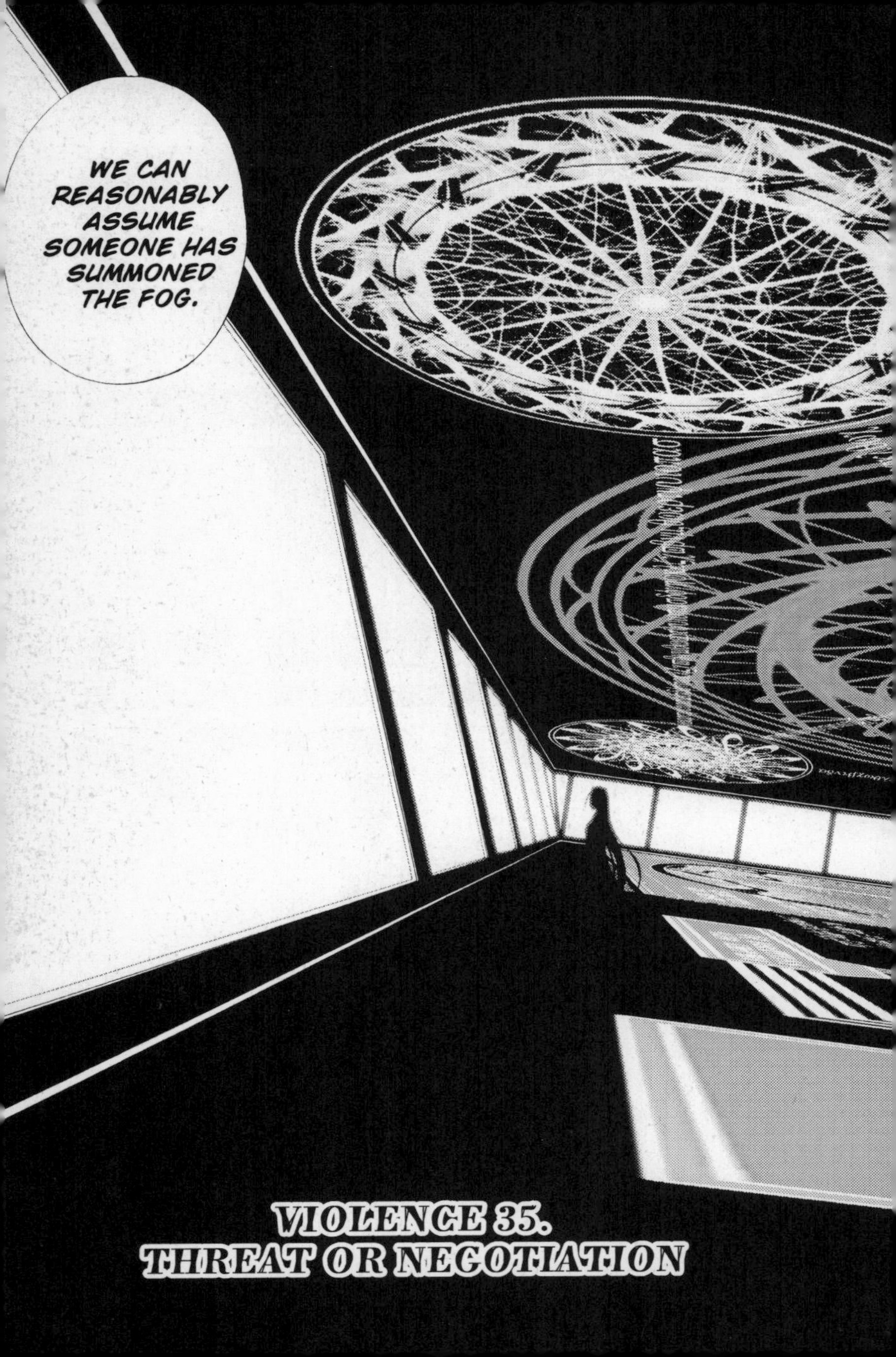
WE CAN REASONABLY ASSUME SOMEONE HAS SUMMONED THE FOG.
VIOLENCE 35.
THREAT OR NEGOTIATION

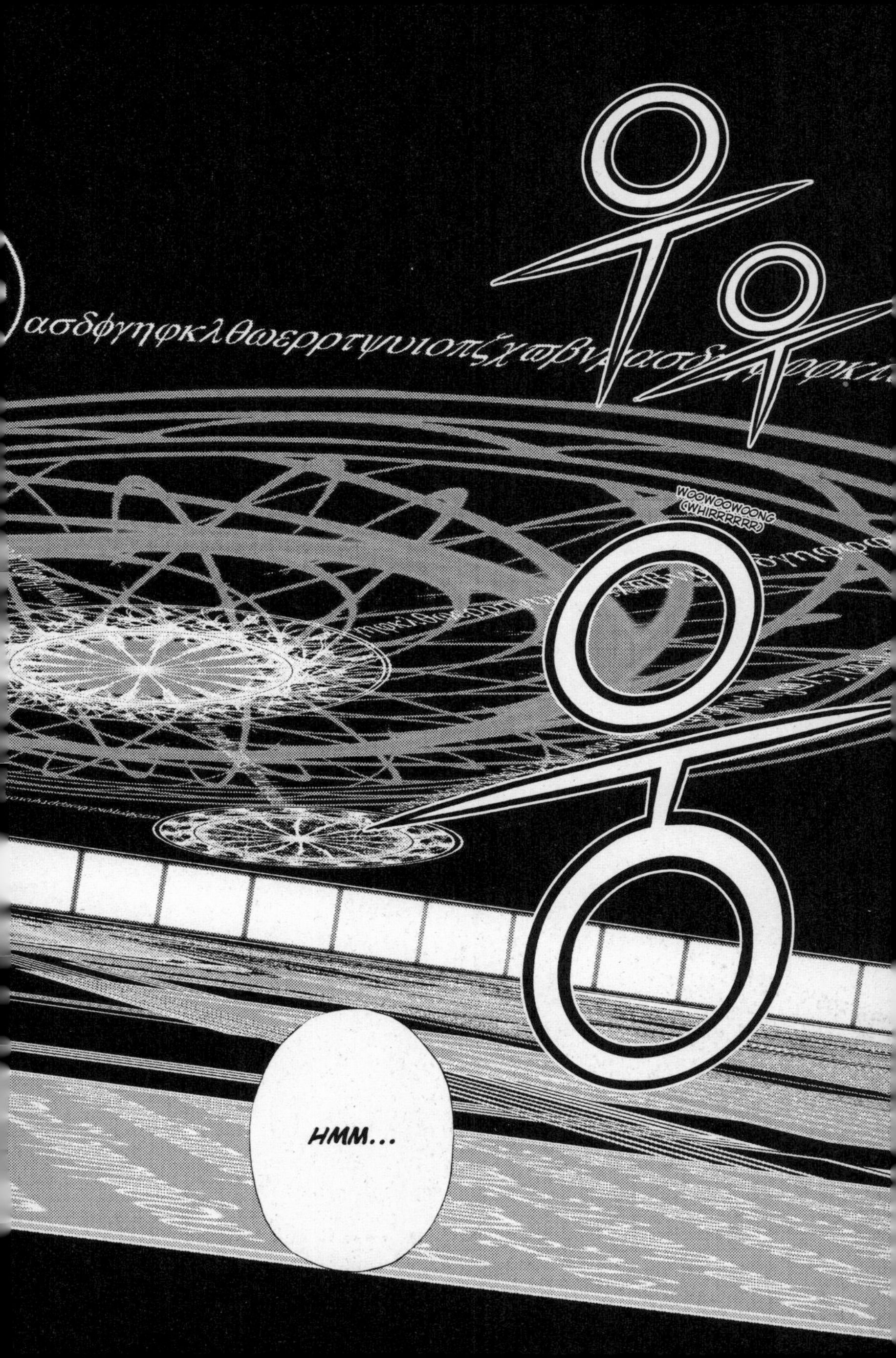
WOOWOOWOONG (WHIRRRRRR)
HMM...

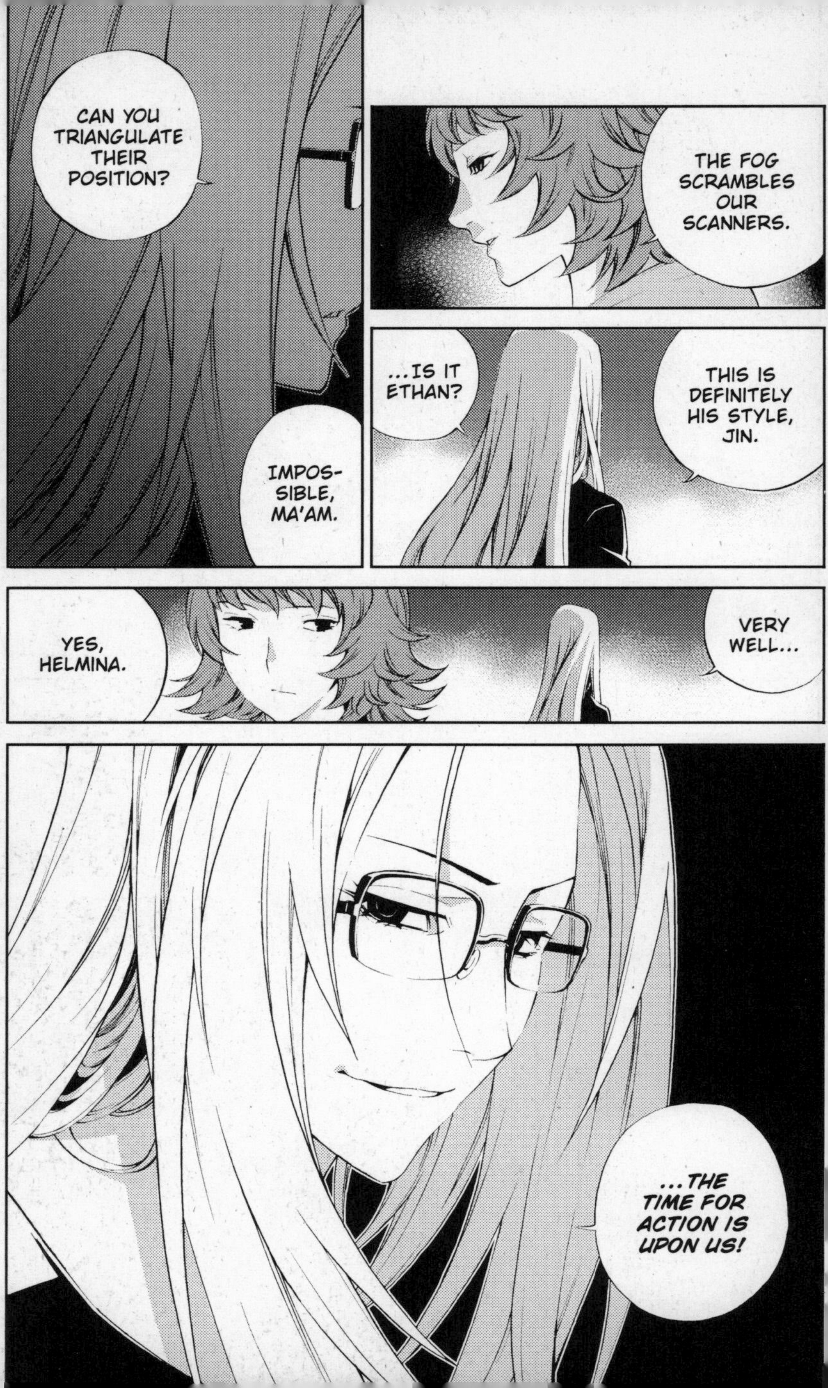
CAN YOU TRIANGULATE THEIR POSITION?
IMPOSSIBLE, MA'AM.
THE FOG SCRAMBLES OUR SCANNERS.
...IS IT ETHAN?
THIS IS DEFINITELY HIS STYLE, JIN.
YES, HELMINA.
VERY WELL...
...THE TIME FOR ACTION IS UPON US!

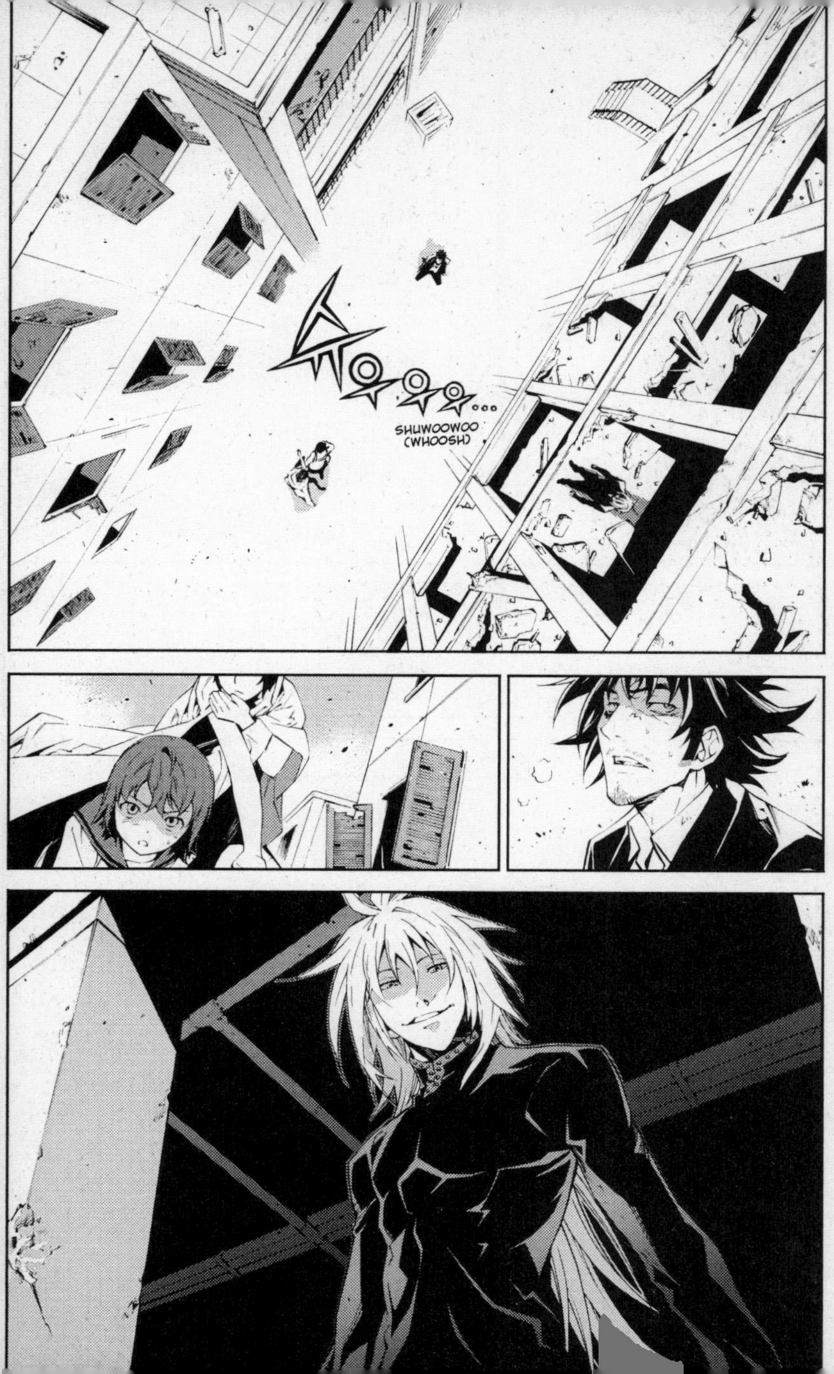
SHUWOOWOO
(WHOOSH)

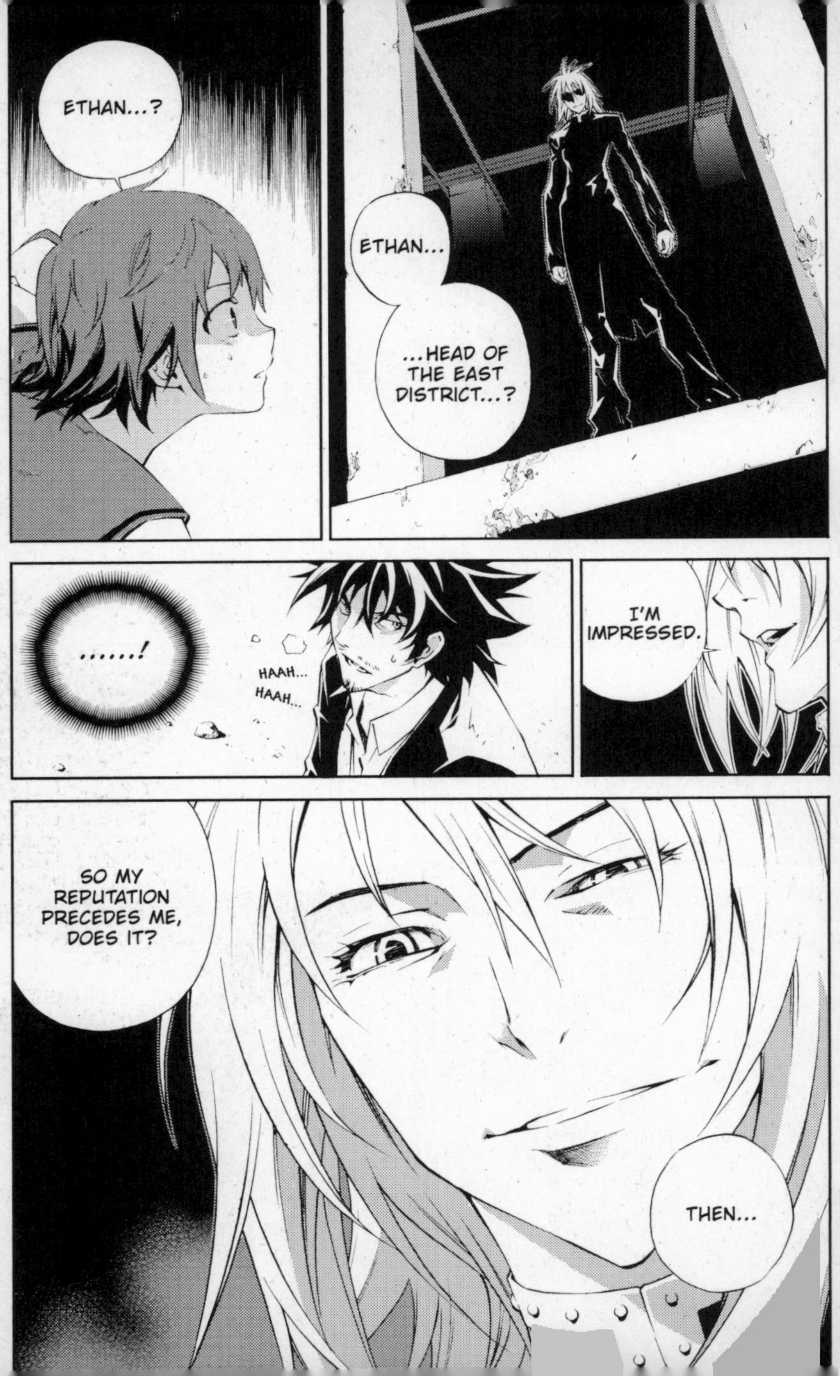
ETHAN...?
ETHAN...
...HEAD OF THE EAST DISTRICT...?
......!
HAAH... HAAH...
I'M IMPRESSED.
SO MY REPUTATION PRECEDES ME, DOES IT?
THEN...

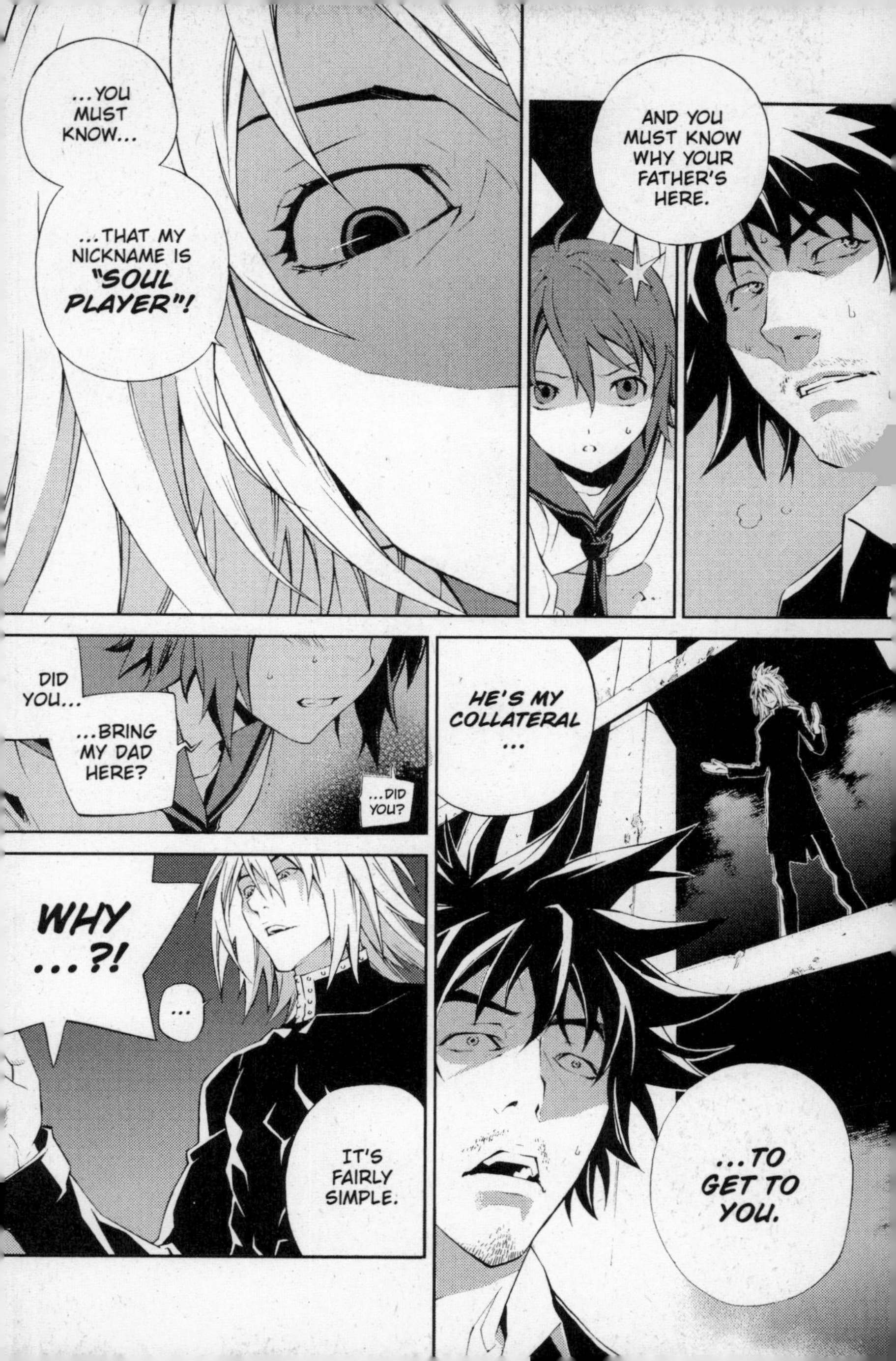
...YOU MUST KNOW...
...THAT MY NICKNAME IS "SOUL PLAYER"!
AND YOU MUST KNOW WHY YOUR FATHER'S HERE.
DID YOU...
...BRING MY DAD HERE?
...DID YOU?
WHY ...?!
...
IT'S FAIRLY SIMPLE.
HE'S MY COLLATERAL ...
...TO GET TO YOU.

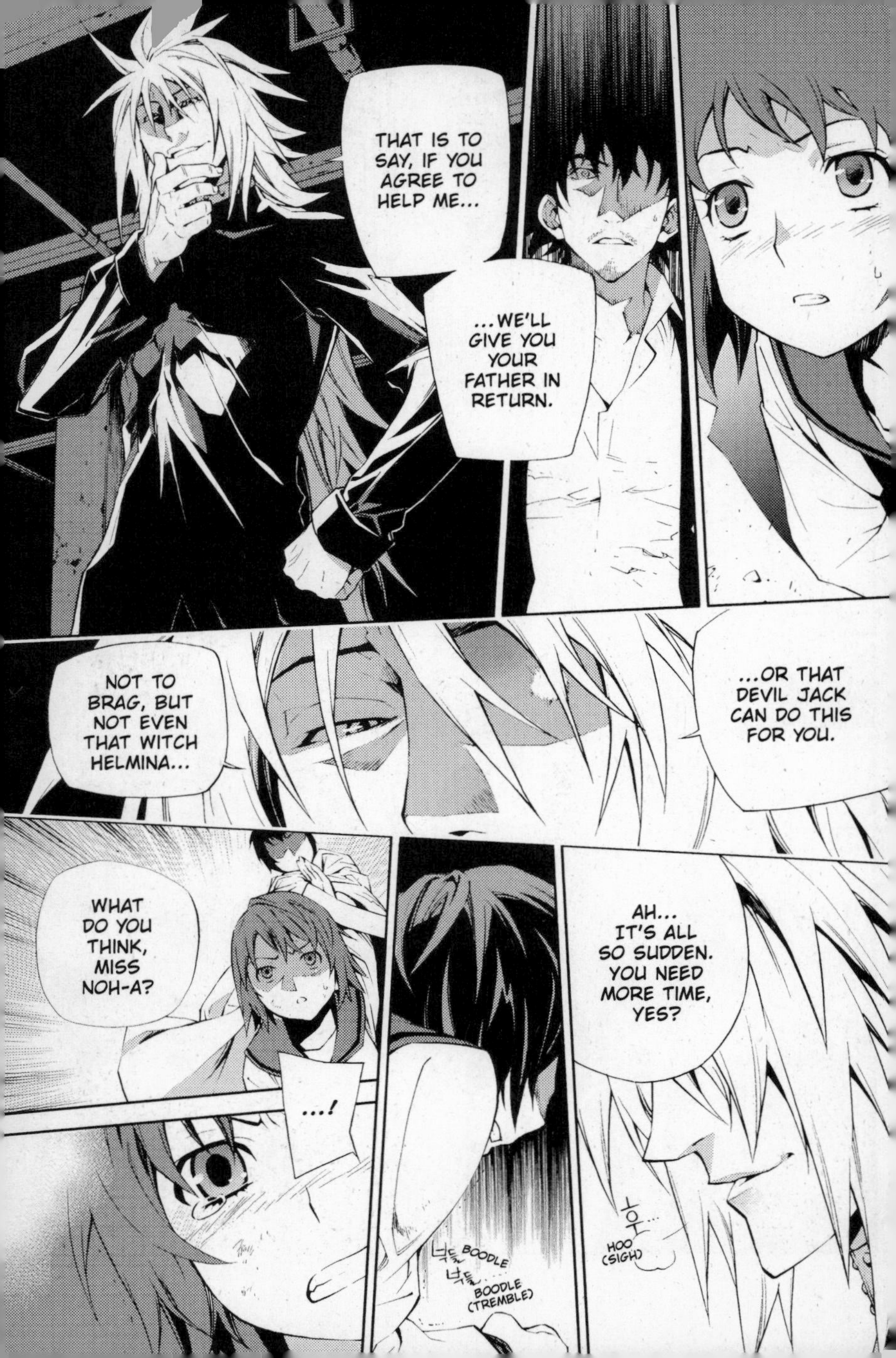
THAT IS TO SAY, IF YOU AGREE TO HELP ME...
...WE'LL GIVE YOU YOUR FATHER IN RETURN.
NOT TO BRAG, BUT NOT EVEN THAT WITCH HELMINA...
...OR THAT DEVIL JACK CAN DO THIS FOR YOU.
WHAT DO YOU THINK, MISS NOH-A?
...!
AH... IT'S ALL SO SUDDEN. YOU NEED MORE TIME, YES?
부들 BOODLE
부들... BOODLE (TREMBLE)
후우... HOO (SIGH)

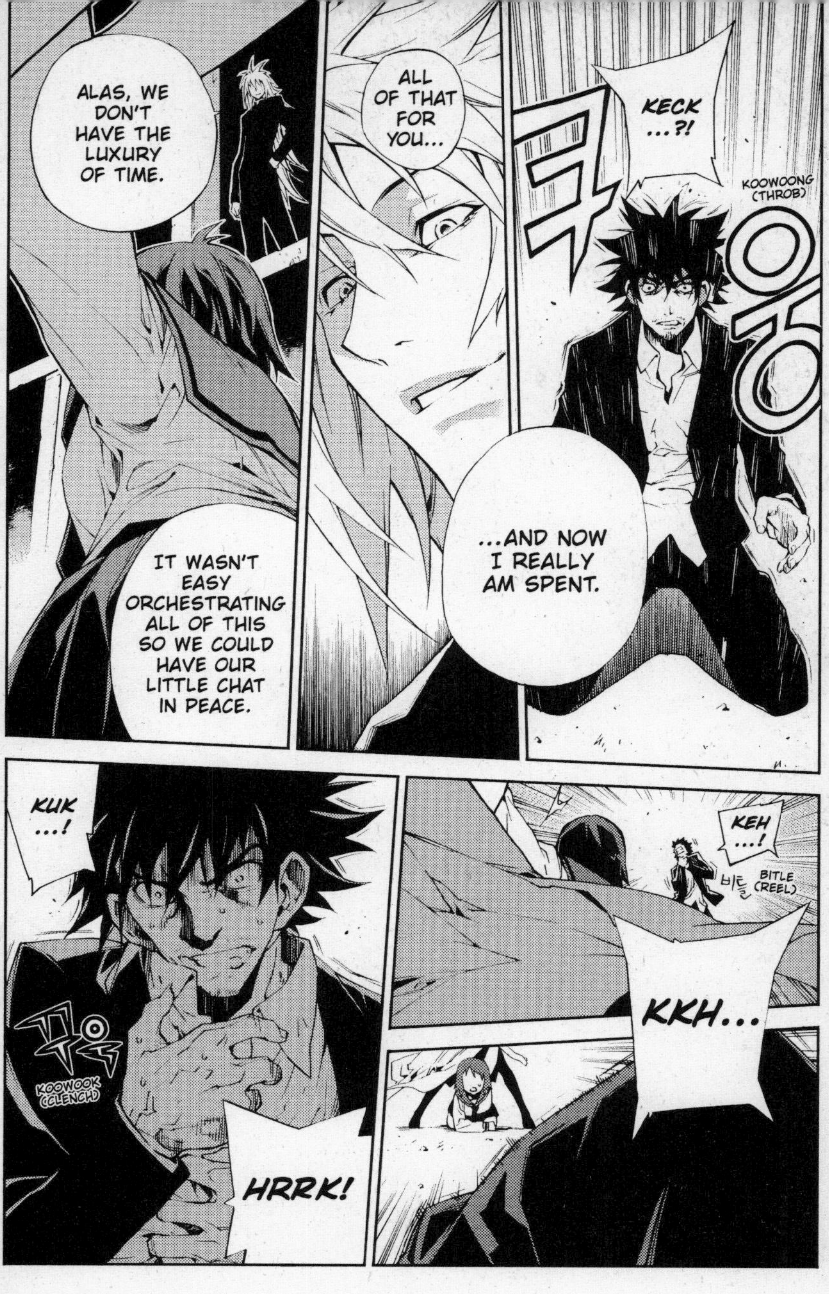
ALAS, WE DON'T HAVE THE LUXURY OF TIME.
IT WASN'T EASY ORCHESTRATING ALL OF THIS SO WE COULD HAVE OUR LITTLE CHAT IN PEACE.
ALL OF THAT FOR YOU...
...AND NOW I REALLY AM SPENT.
KECK ...?!
KOOWOONG (THROB)
KUK ...!
KOOWOOK (CLENCH)
HRRK!
KEH ...!
비틀
BITLE (REEL)
KKH...

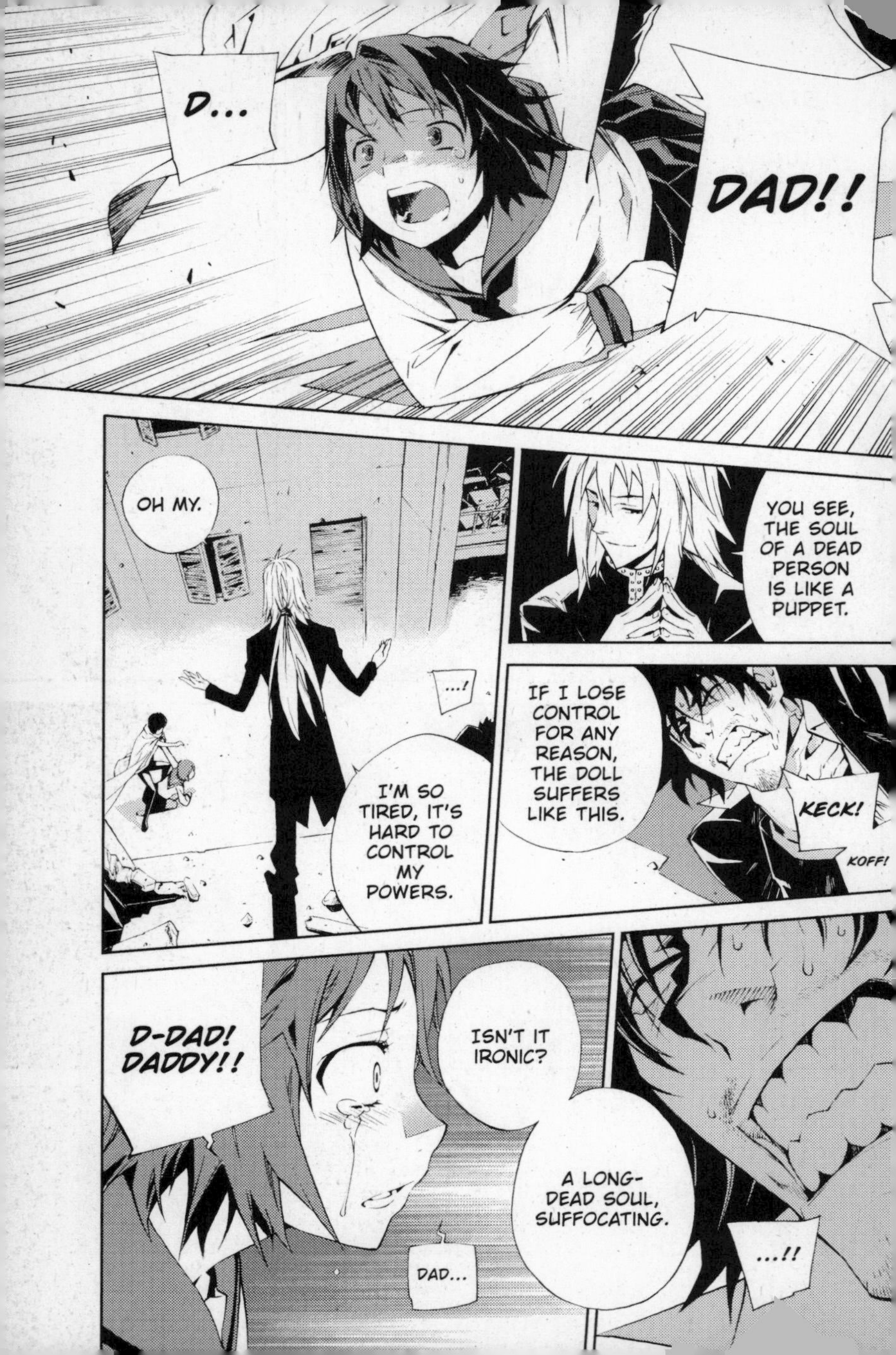
D...
DAD!!
OH MY.
...!
I'M SO TIRED, IT'S HARD TO CONTROL MY POWERS.
YOU SEE, THE SOUL OF A DEAD PERSON IS LIKE A PUPPET.
IF I LOSE CONTROL FOR ANY REASON, THE DOLL SUFFERS LIKE THIS.
KECK!
KOFF!
D-DAD! DADDY!!
ISN'T IT IRONIC?
A LONG-DEAD SOUL, SUFFOCATING.
DAD...
...!!

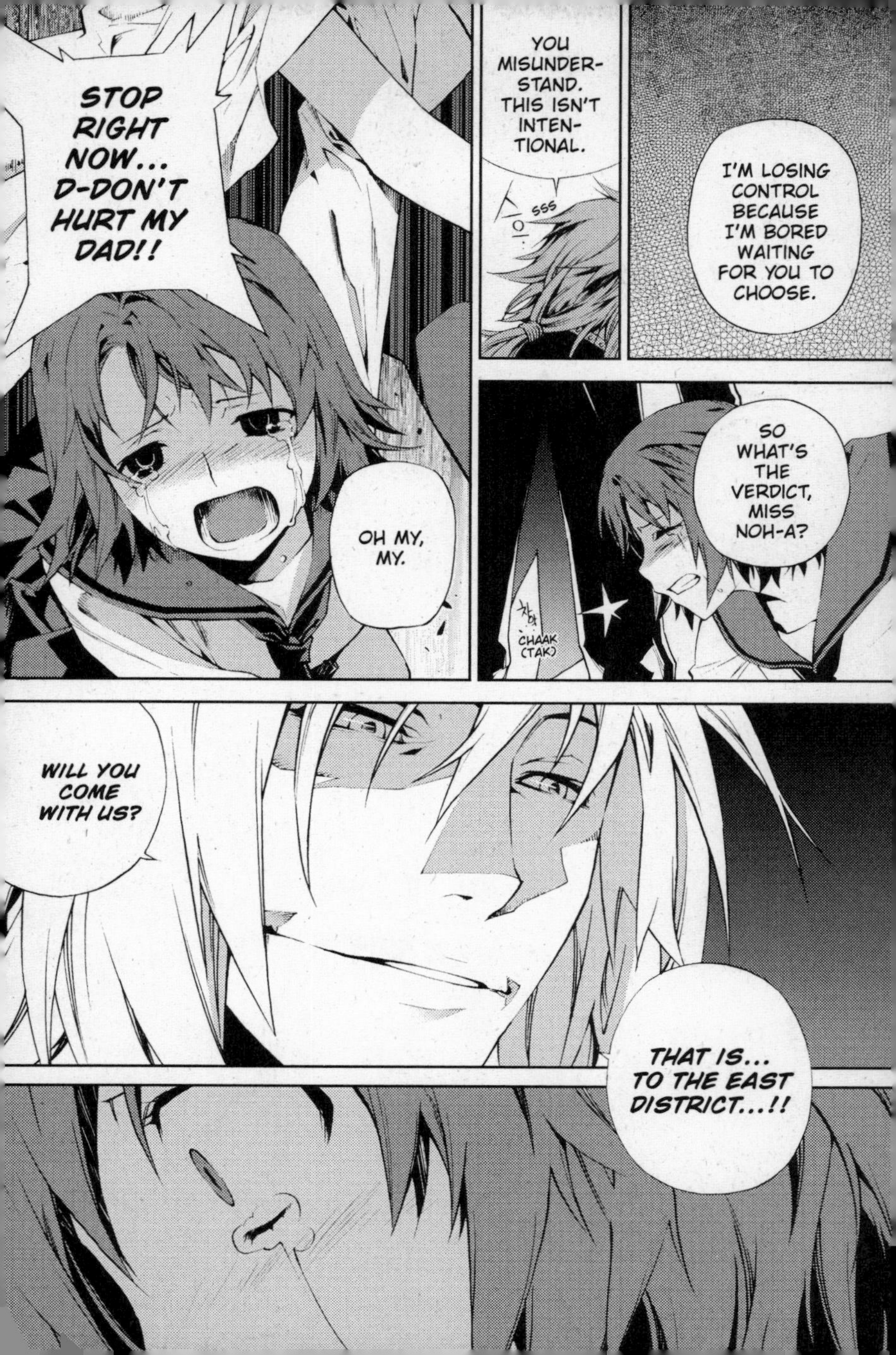
STOP RIGHT NOW... D-DON'T HURT MY DAD!!
OH MY, MY.
YOU MISUNDERSTAND. THIS ISN'T INTENTIONAL.
SSS
I'M LOSING CONTROL BECAUSE I'M BORED WAITING FOR YOU TO CHOOSE.
SO WHAT'S THE VERDICT, MISS NOH-A?
CHAAK (TAK)
WILL YOU COME WITH US?
THAT IS... TO THE EAST DISTRICT...!!

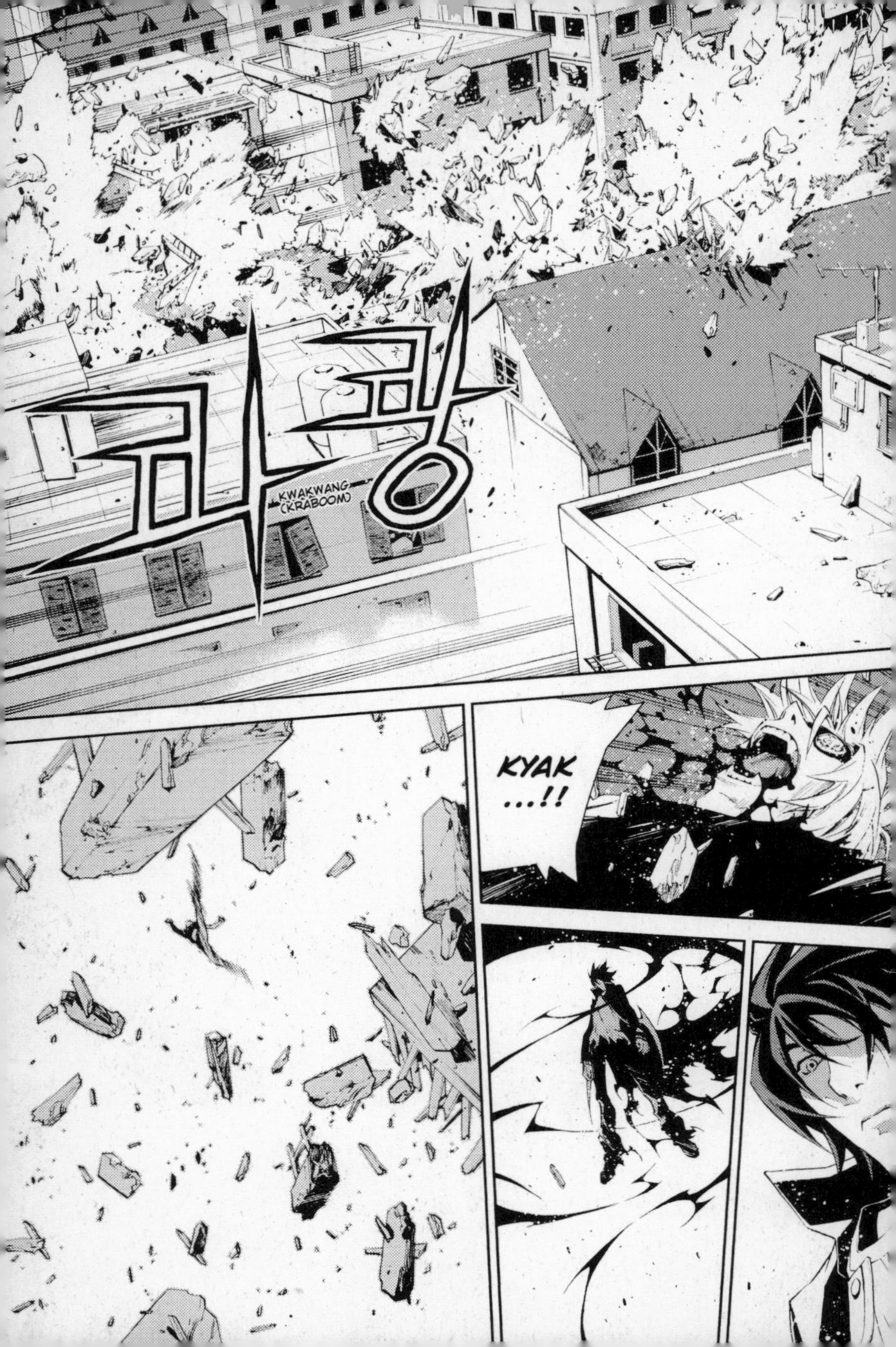
콰광
KWAKWANG (KRABOOM)
KYAK ...!!

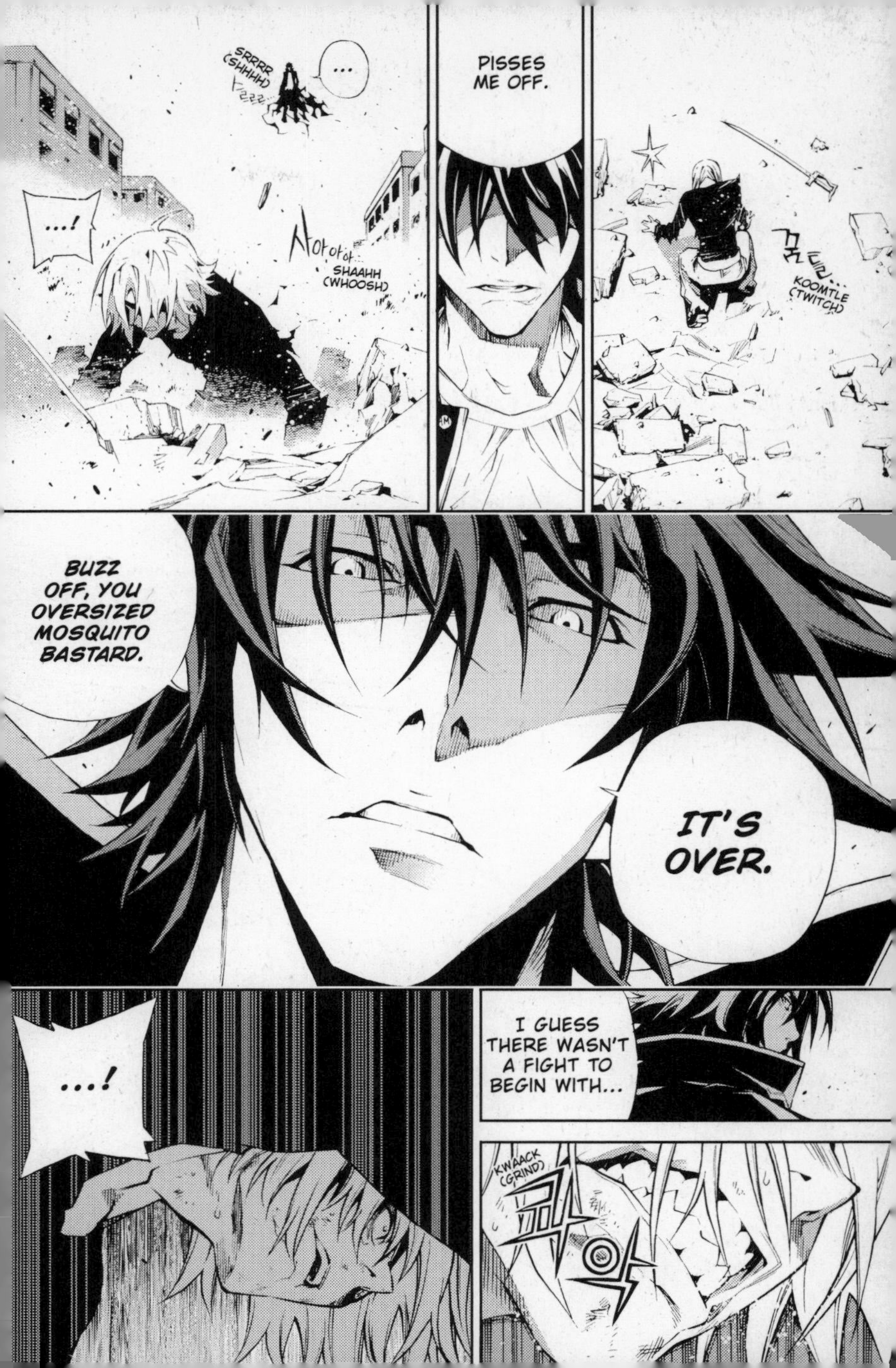

SRRRR (SHHHH)
...
...!
SHAAHH (WHOOSH)
PISSES ME OFF.
KOOMTLE (TWITCH)
BUZZ OFF, YOU OVERSIZED MOSQUITO BASTARD.
IT'S OVER.
...!
I GUESS THERE WASN'T A FIGHT TO BEGIN WITH...
KWAACK (GRIND)

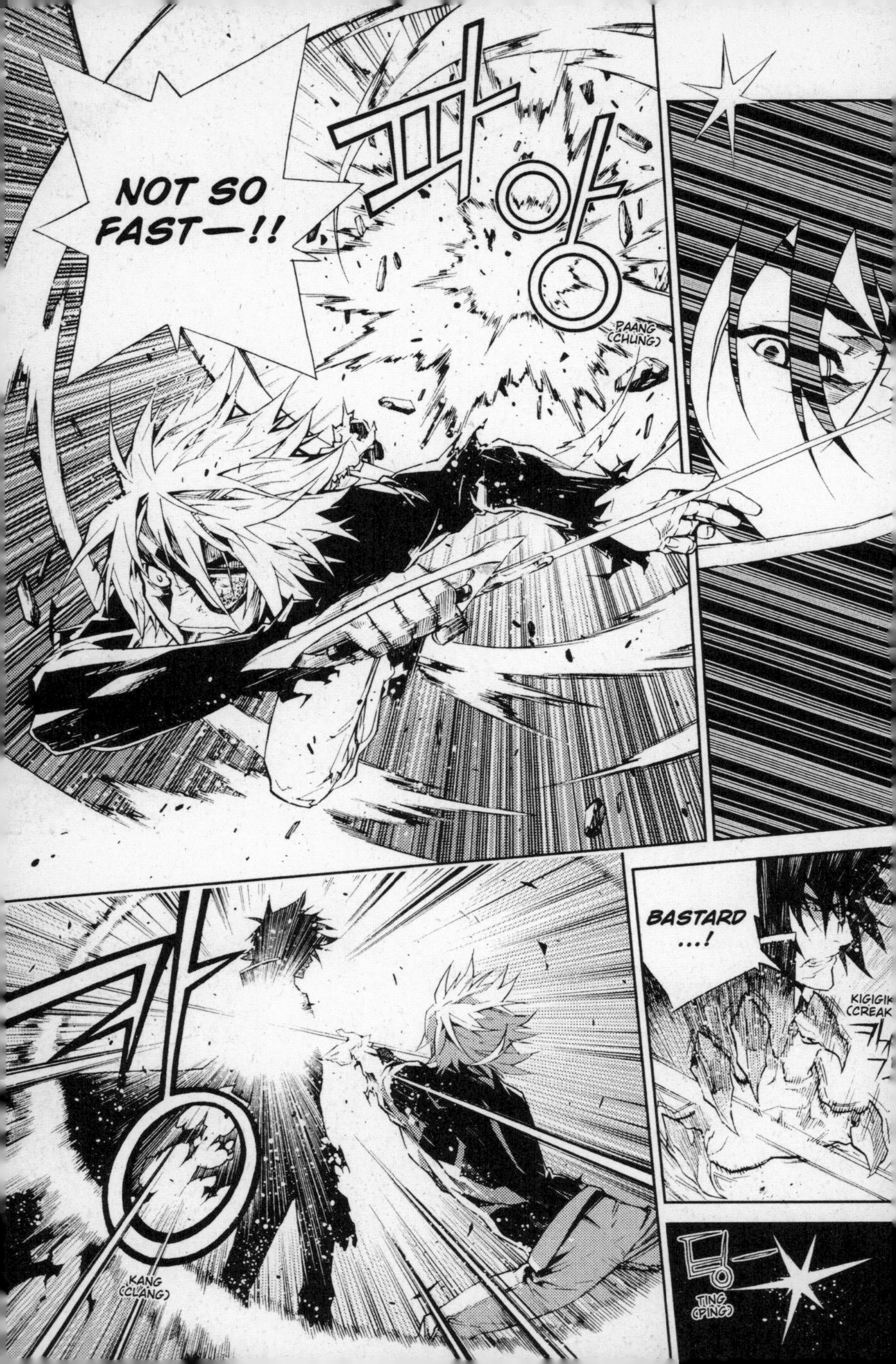
NOT SO FAST—!!
PAANG (CHUNG)
BASTARD ...!
KIGIGIK (CREAK
TING (PING)
KANG (CLANG)

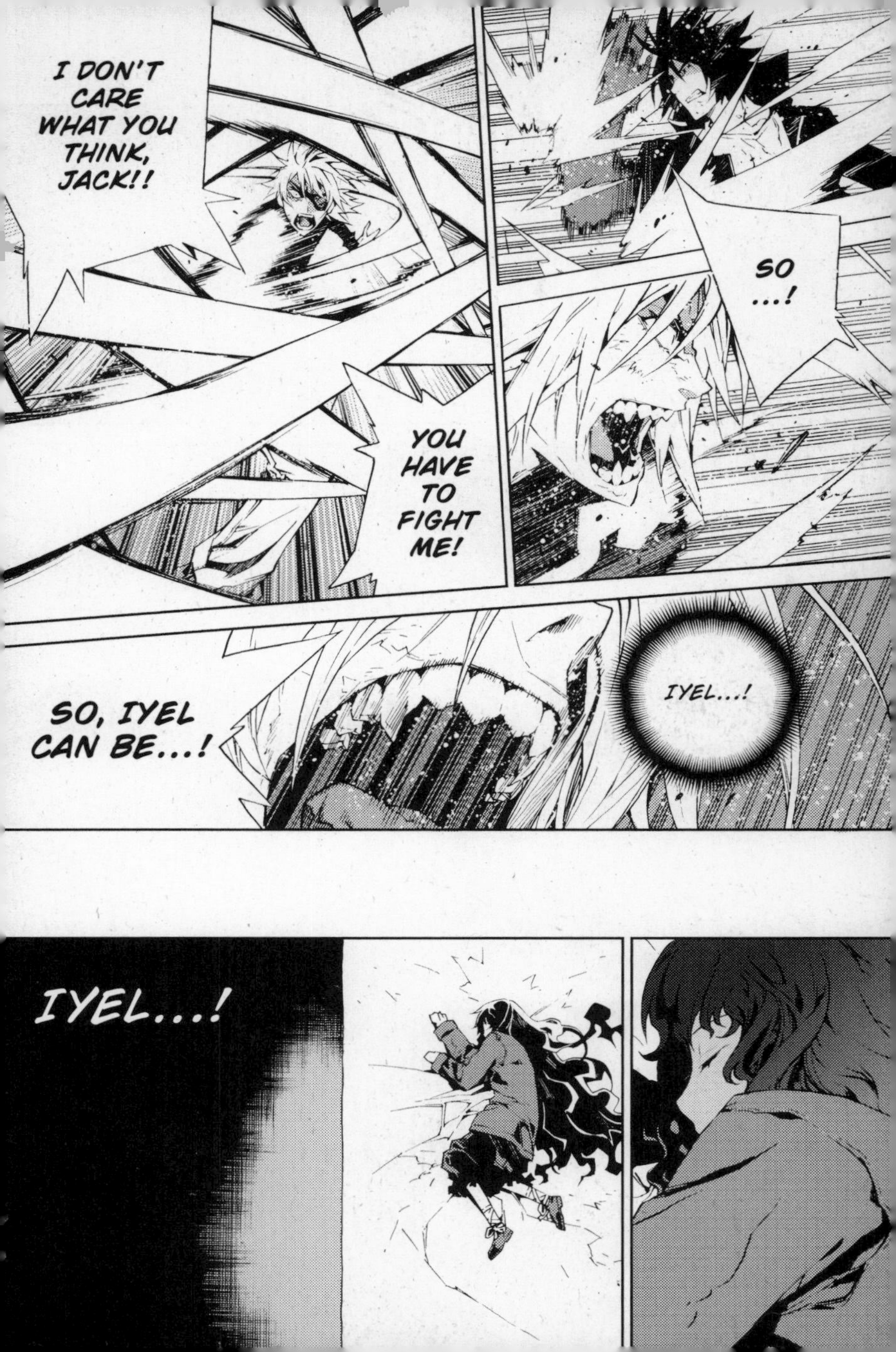

I DON'T CARE WHAT YOU THINK, JACK!!
YOU HAVE TO FIGHT ME!
...
SO ...!
SO, IYEL CAN BE...!
IYEL...!
IYEL...!

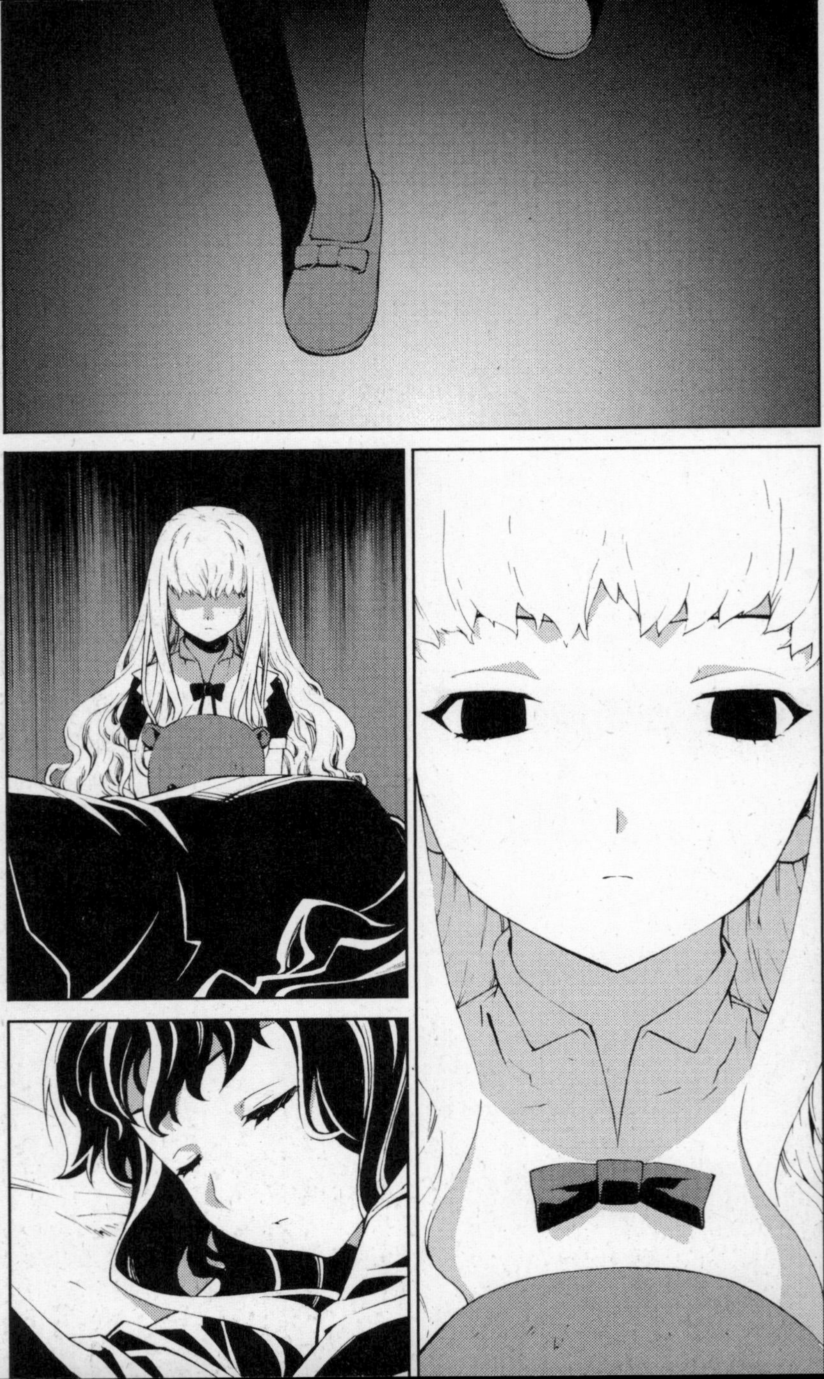

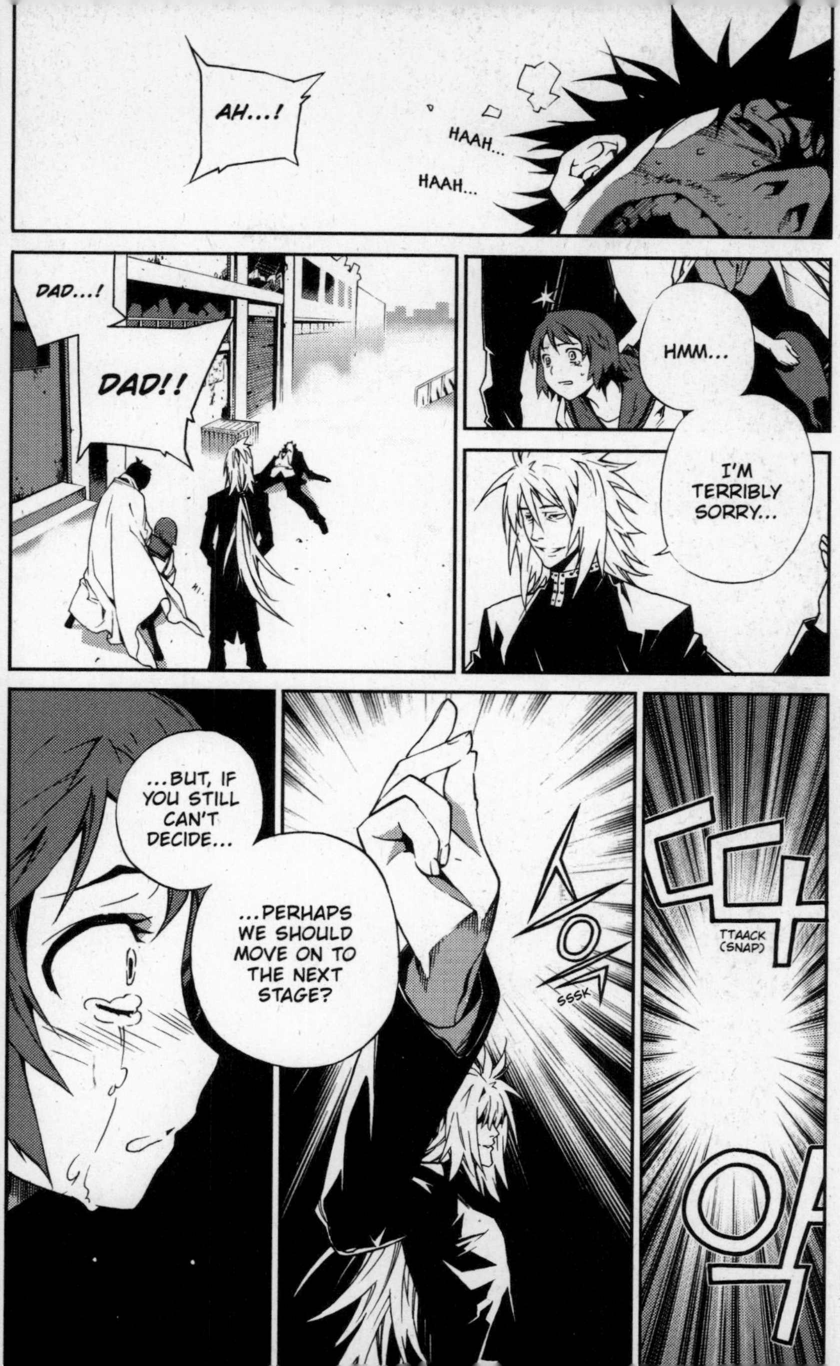
AH...!
HAAH...
HAAH...
DAD...!
DAD!!
HMM...
I'M TERRIBLY SORRY...
...BUT, IF YOU STILL CAN'T DECIDE...
...PERHAPS WE SHOULD MOVE ON TO THE NEXT STAGE?
SSSK
TTAACK (SNAP)

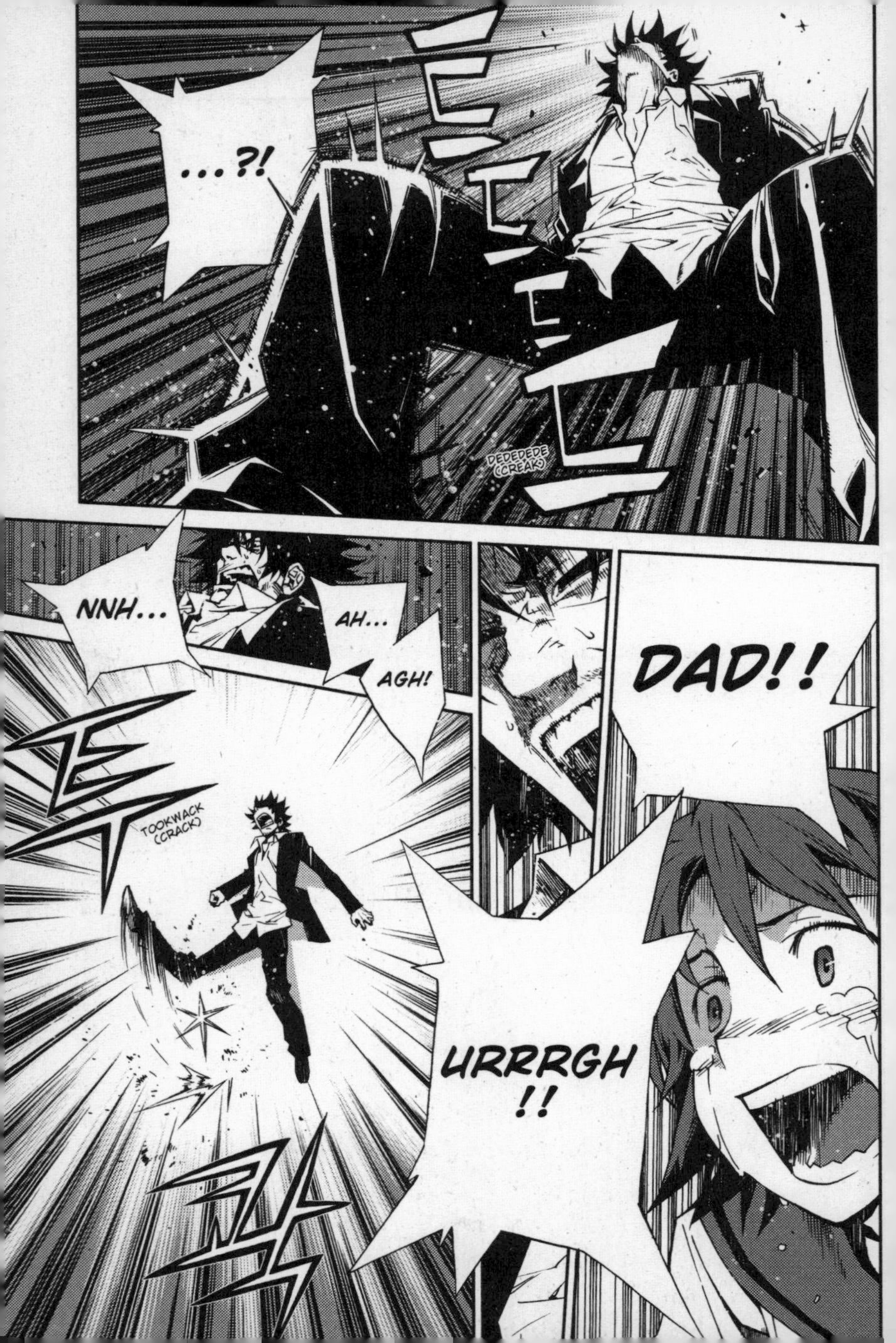
...?!
DEDEDEDE (CREAK)
NNH...
AH...
AGH!
DAD!!
TOOKWACK (CRACK)
URRRGH !!

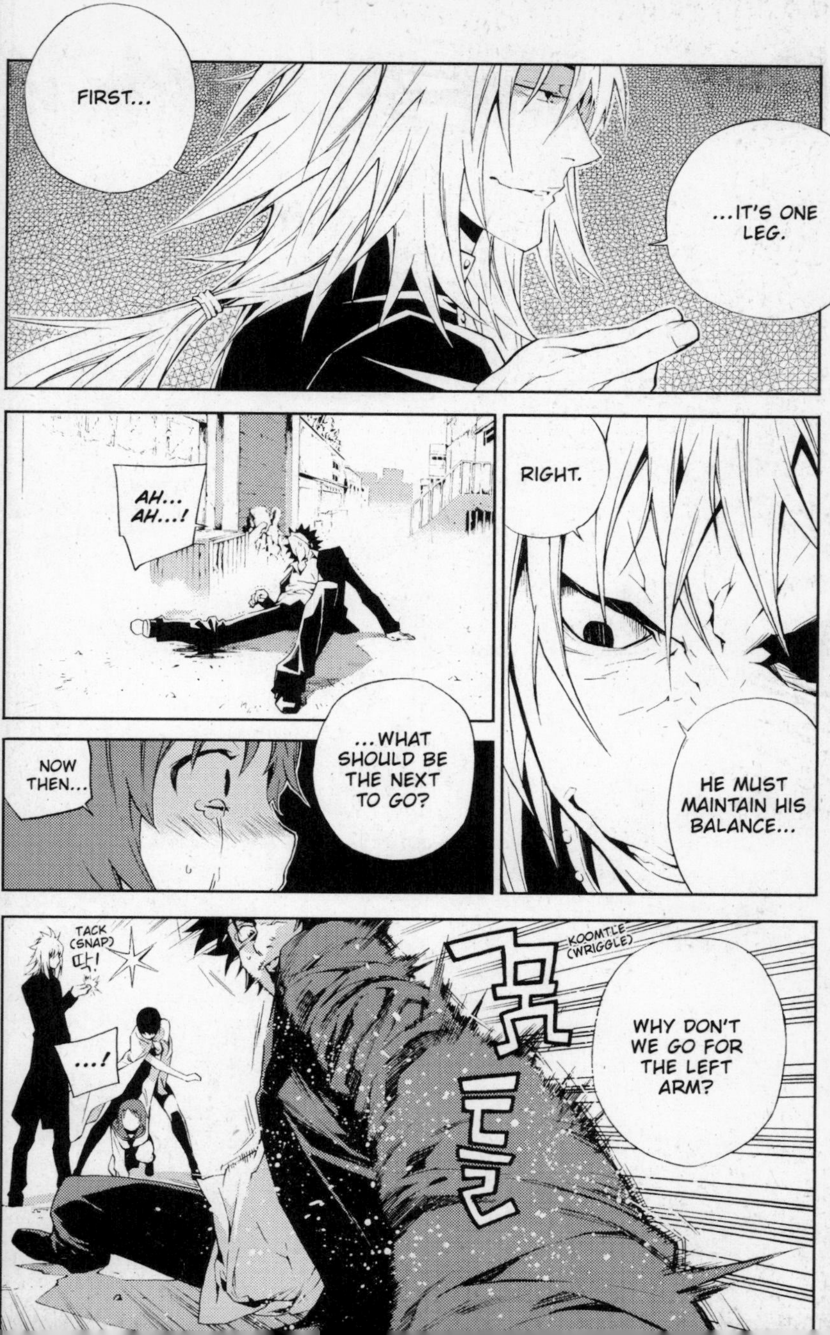
FIRST...
...IT'S ONE LEG.
AH... AH...!
NOW THEN...
...WHAT SHOULD BE THE NEXT TO GO?
RIGHT.
HE MUST MAINTAIN HIS BALANCE...
TACK (SNAP)
딱!
...!
KOOMTLE (WRIGGLE)
꿈틀
WHY DON'T WE GO FOR THE LEFT ARM?

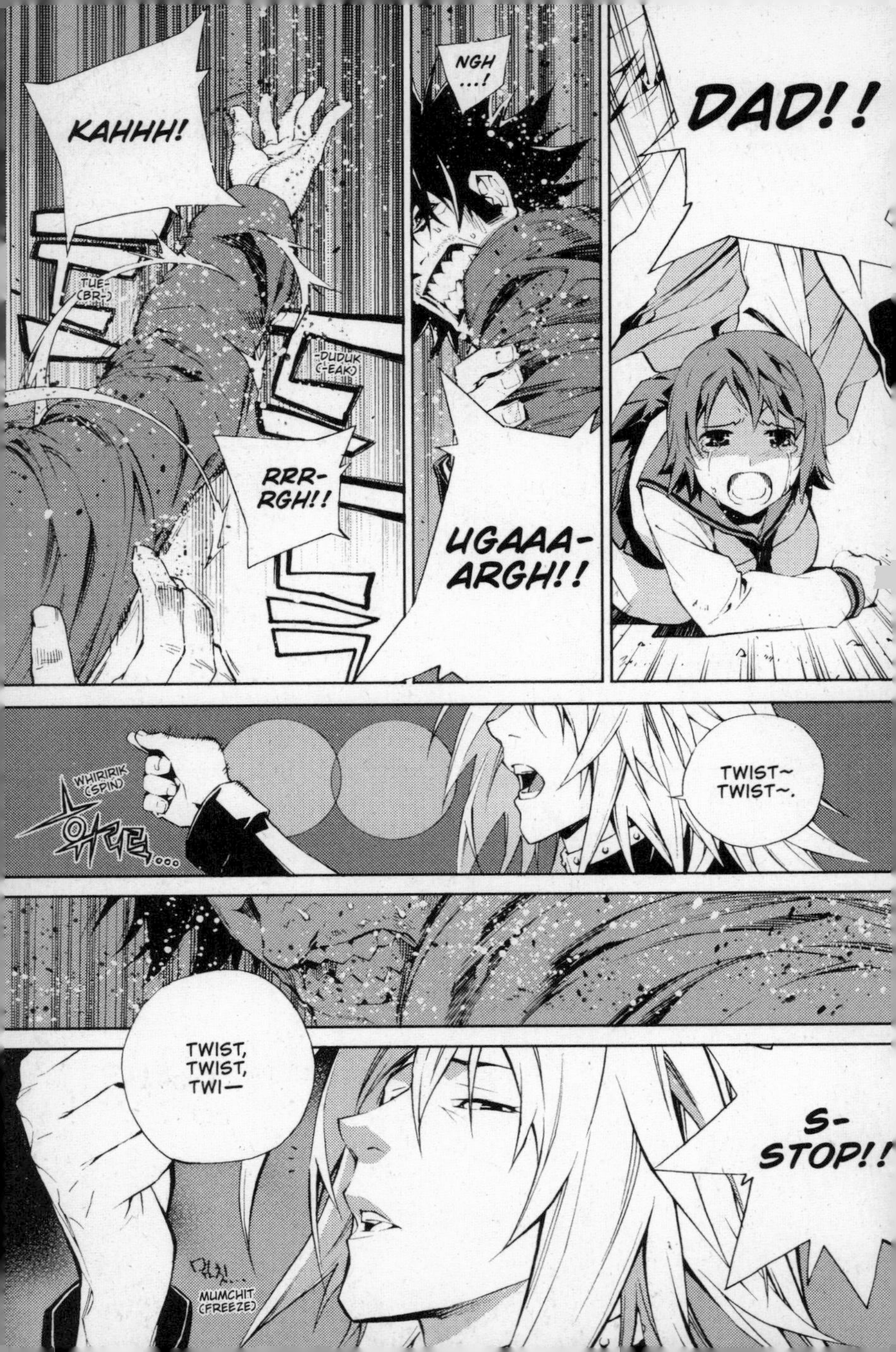
KAHHH!
TUE-
(BR-)
-DUDUK
(-EAK)
RRR-
RGH!!
NGH
...!
UGAAA-
ARGH!!
DAD!!
WHIRIRIK
(SPIN)
TWIST~
TWIST~.
TWIST,
TWIST,
TWI—
MUMCHIT
(FREEZE)
S-
STOP!!

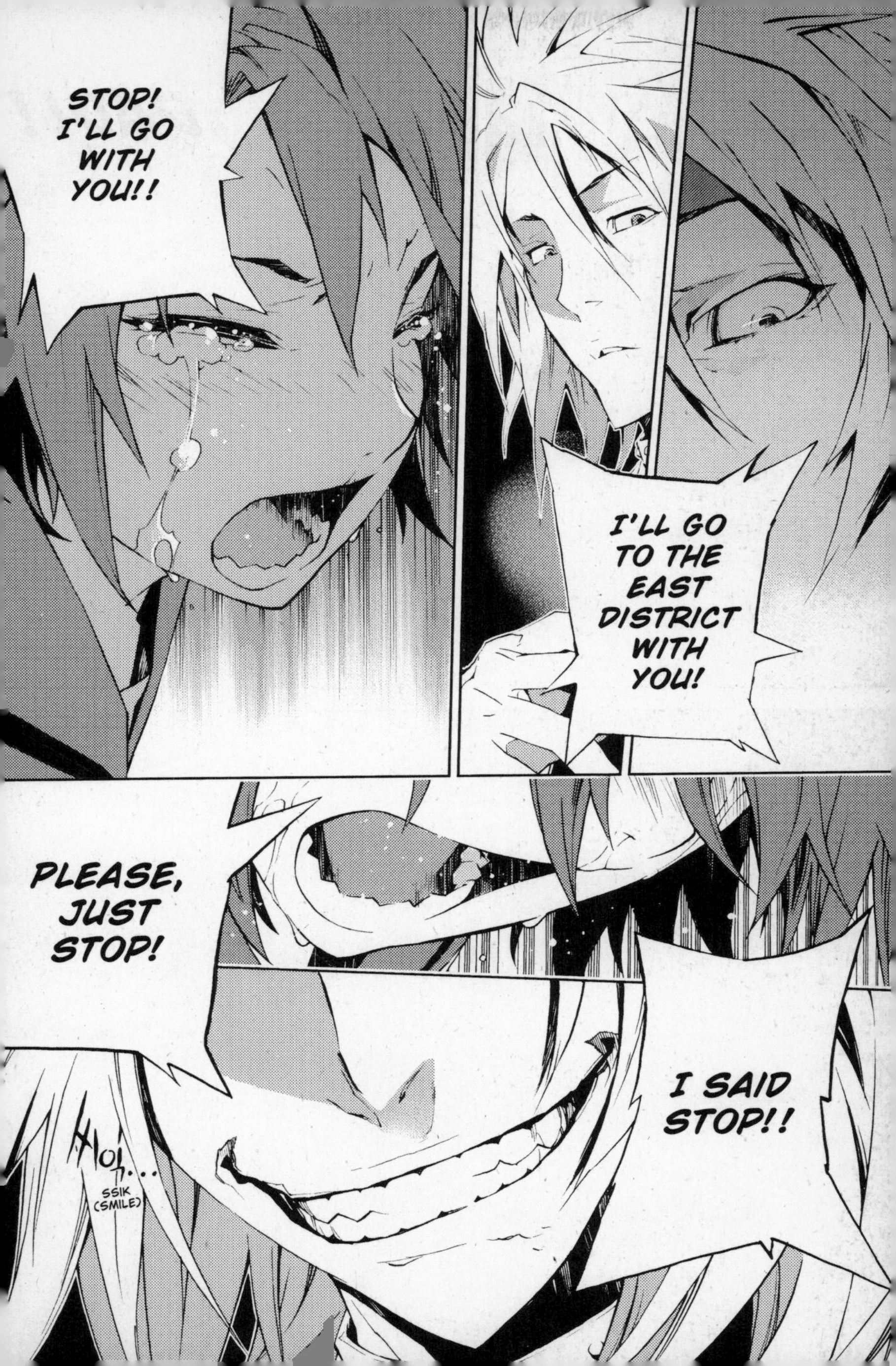
STOP! I'LL GO WITH YOU!!
I'LL GO TO THE EAST DISTRICT WITH YOU!
PLEASE, JUST STOP!
I SAID STOP!!
SSIK (SMILE)

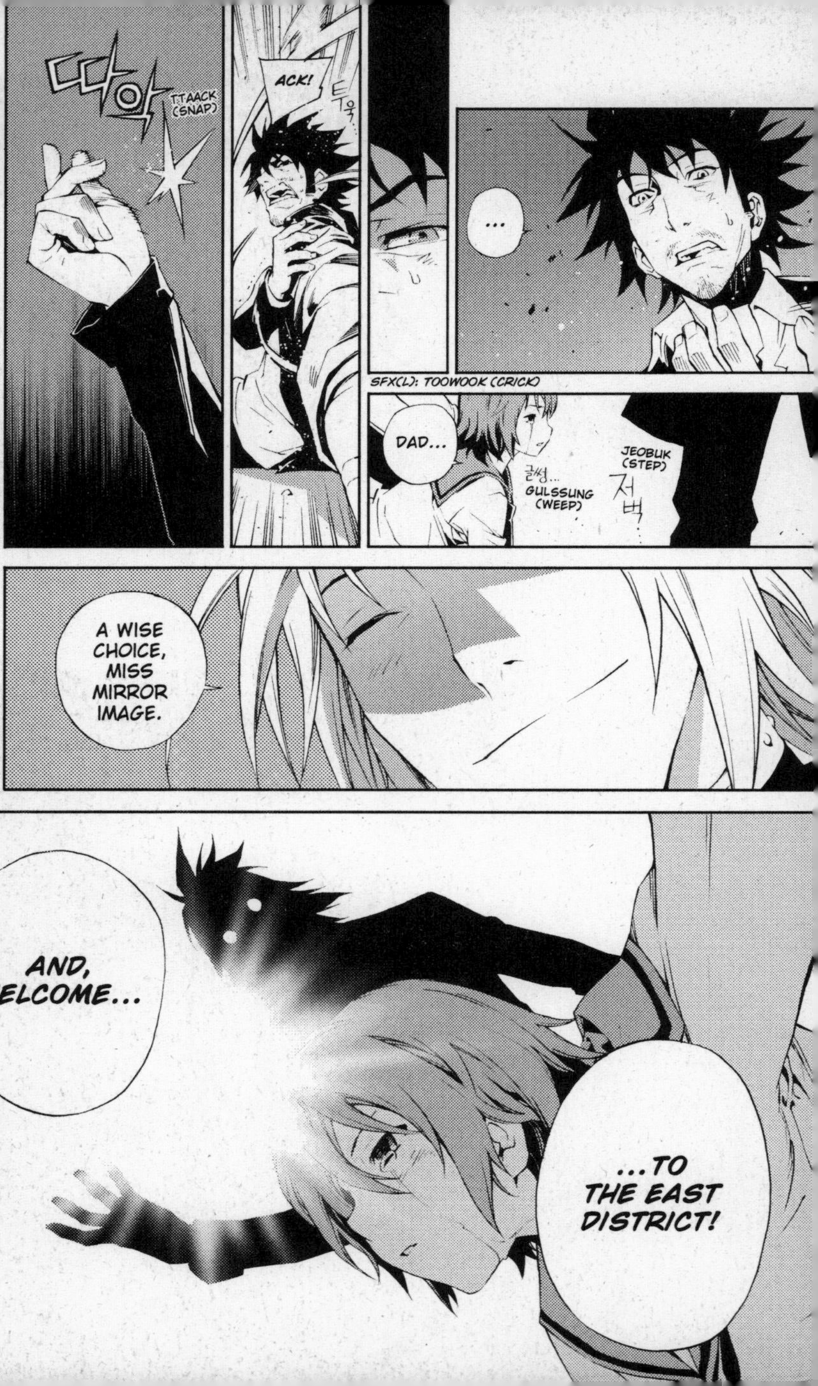

따악
TTAACK (SNAP)
ACK!
투욱...
...
SFX(L): TOOWOOK (CRICK)
DAD...
글썽...
GULSSUNG (WEEP)
JEOBUK (STEP)
저벅...
A WISE CHOICE, MISS MIRROR IMAGE.
AND, WELCOME...
...TO THE EAST DISTRICT!

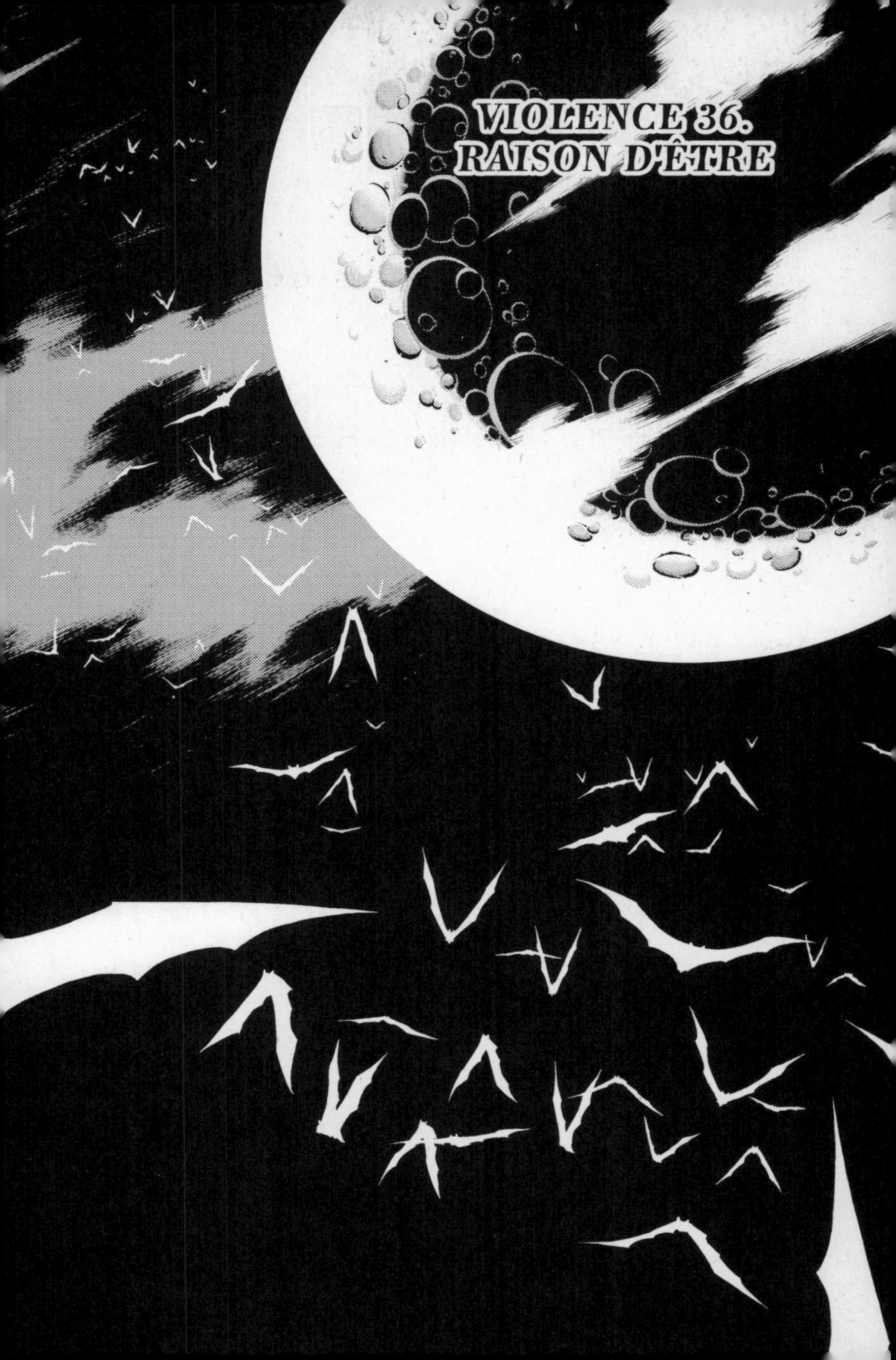
VIOLENCE 36.
RAISON D'ÊTRE

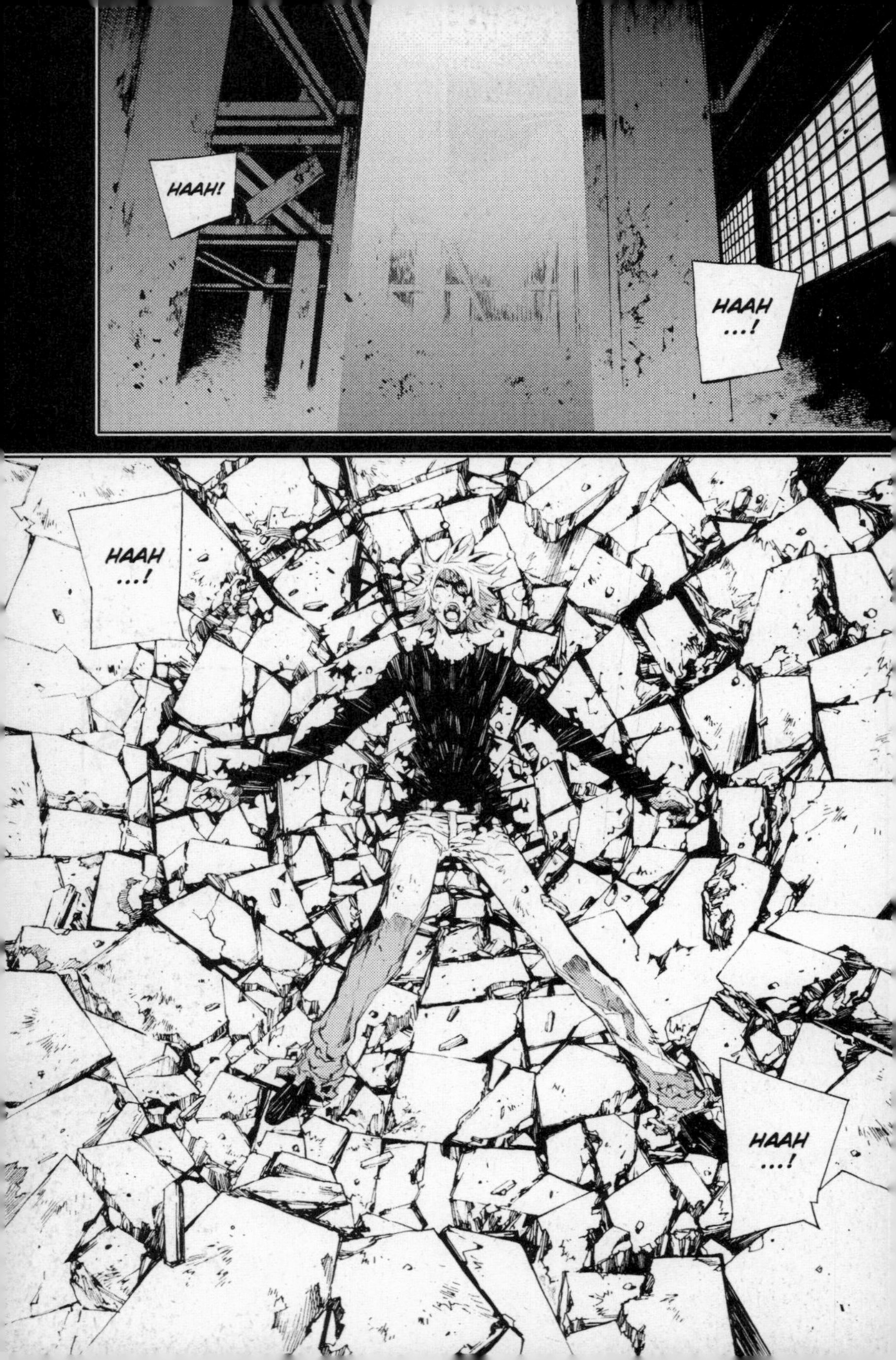
HAAH!
HAAH ...!
HAAH ...!
HAAH ...!

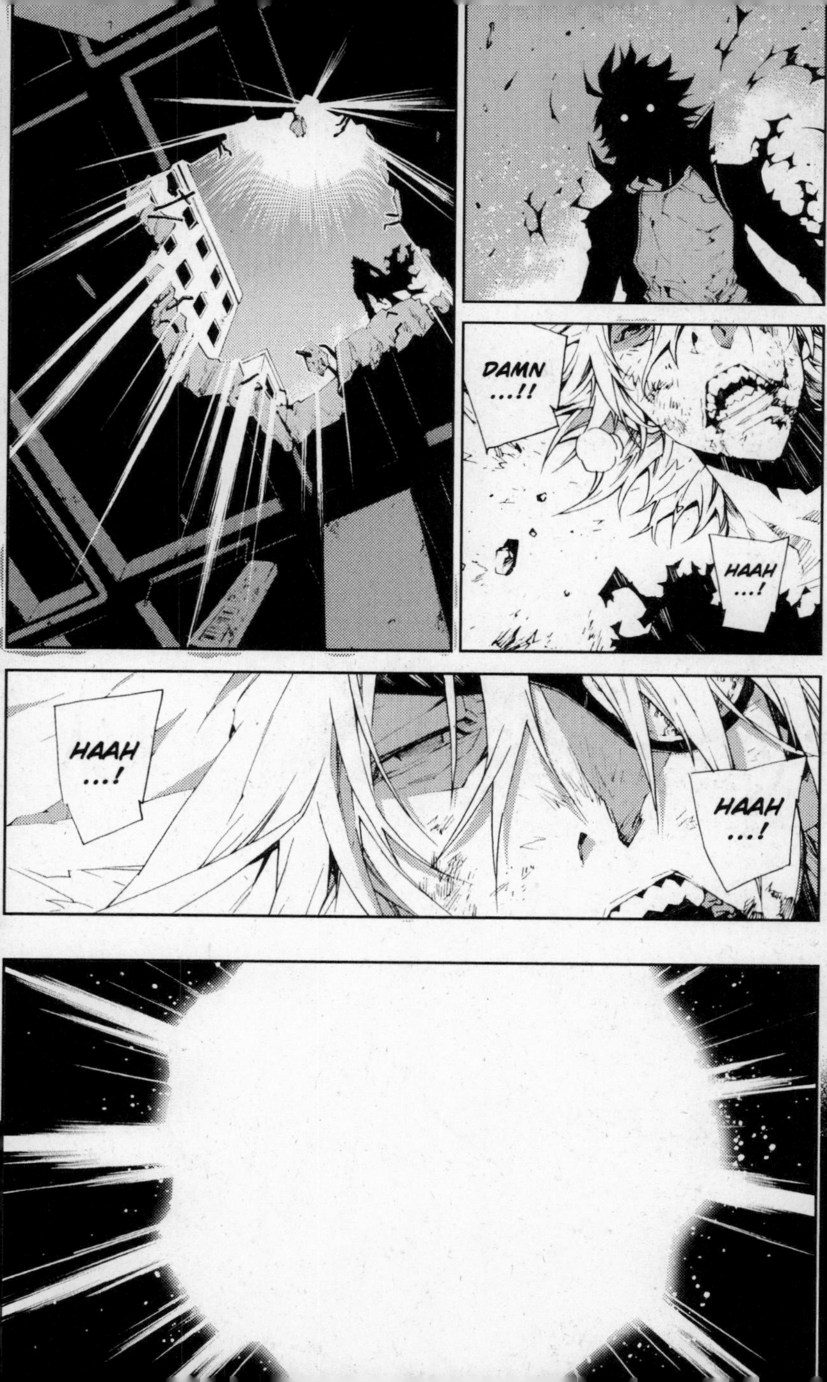
DAMN ...!!
HAAH ...!
HAAH ...!
HAAH ...!

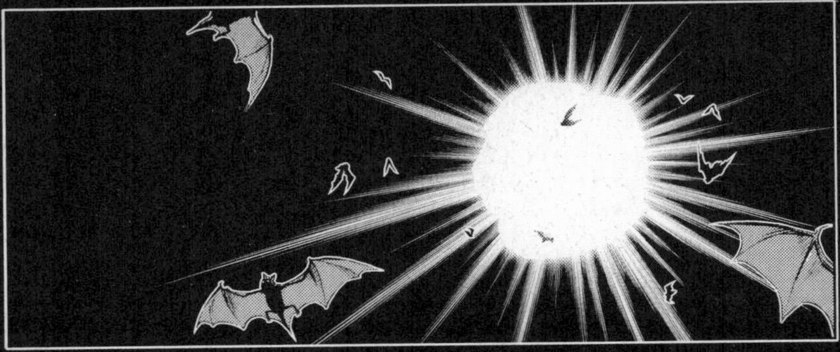

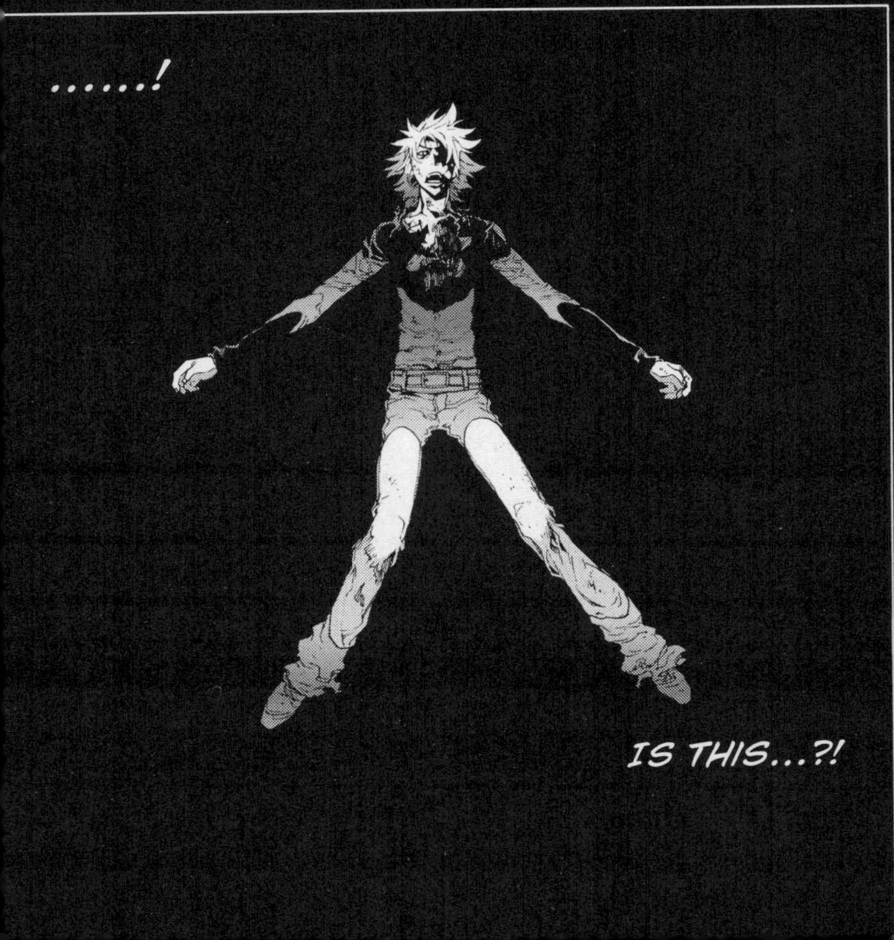
......!
IS THIS...?!

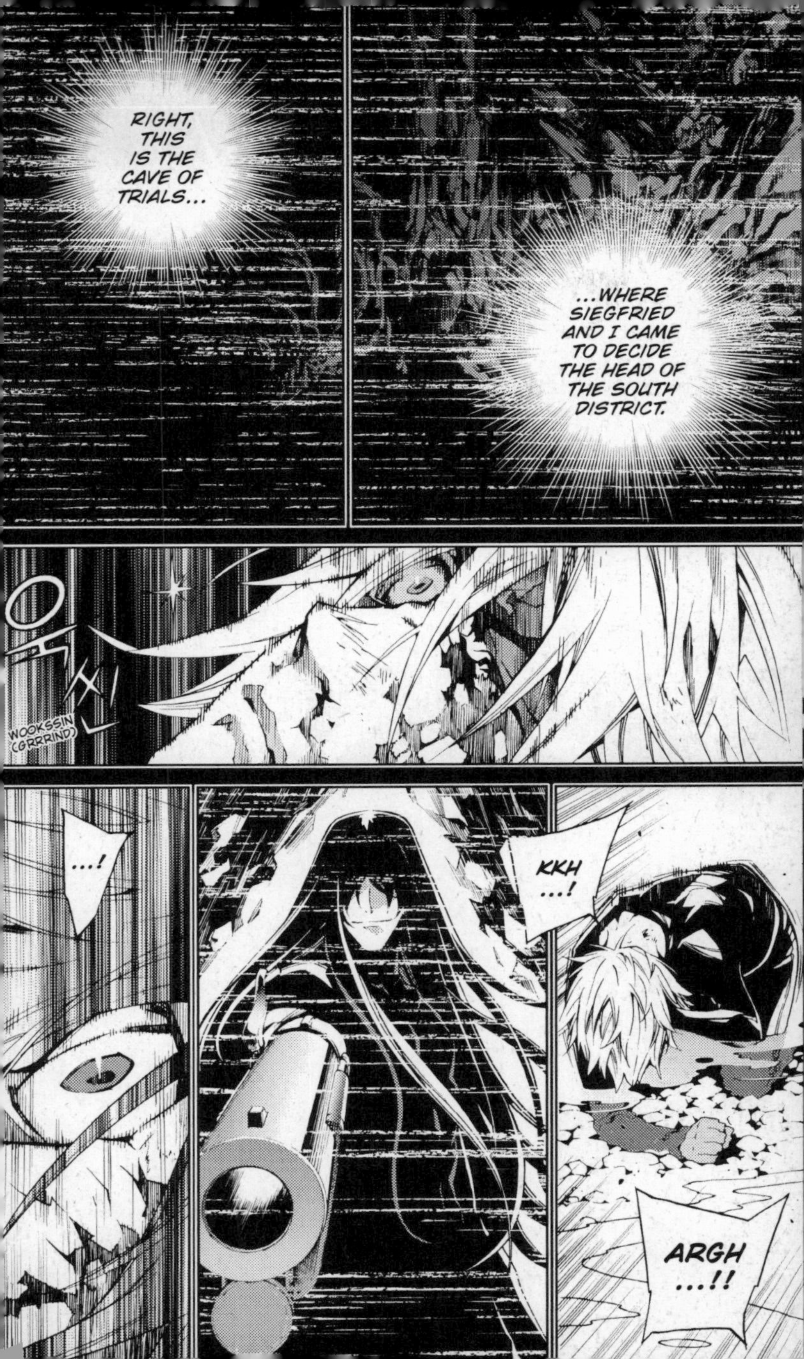
RIGHT, THIS IS THE CAVE OF TRIALS...
...WHERE SIEGFRIED AND I CAME TO DECIDE THE HEAD OF THE SOUTH DISTRICT.
WOOKSSIN (GRRRIND)
...!
KKH ...!
ARGH ...!!

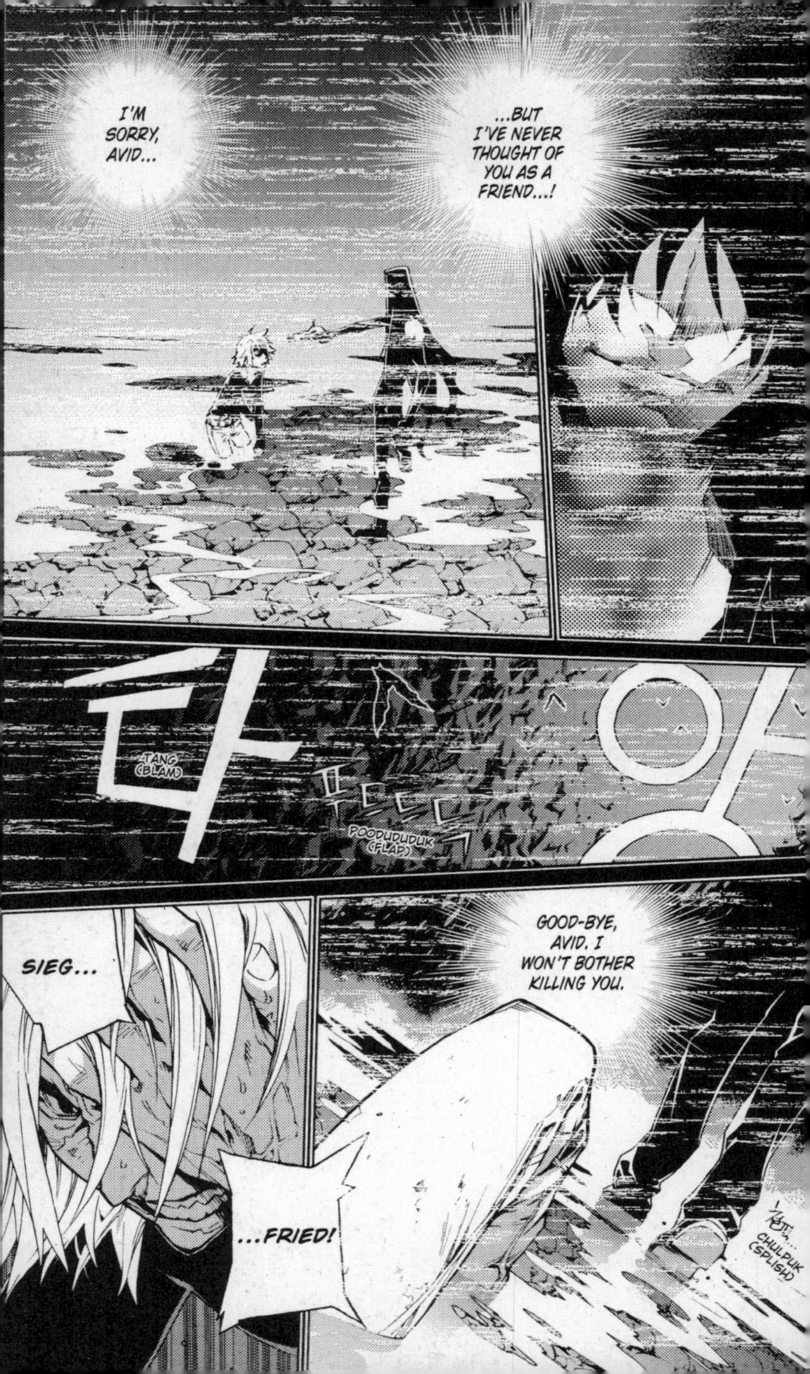
I'M SORRY, AVID...
...BUT I'VE NEVER THOUGHT OF YOU AS A FRIEND...!
TANG (BLAM)
POODUDUDUK (FLAP)
SIEG...
...FRIED!
GOOD-BYE, AVID. I WON'T BOTHER KILLING YOU.
CHULPUK (SPLISH)

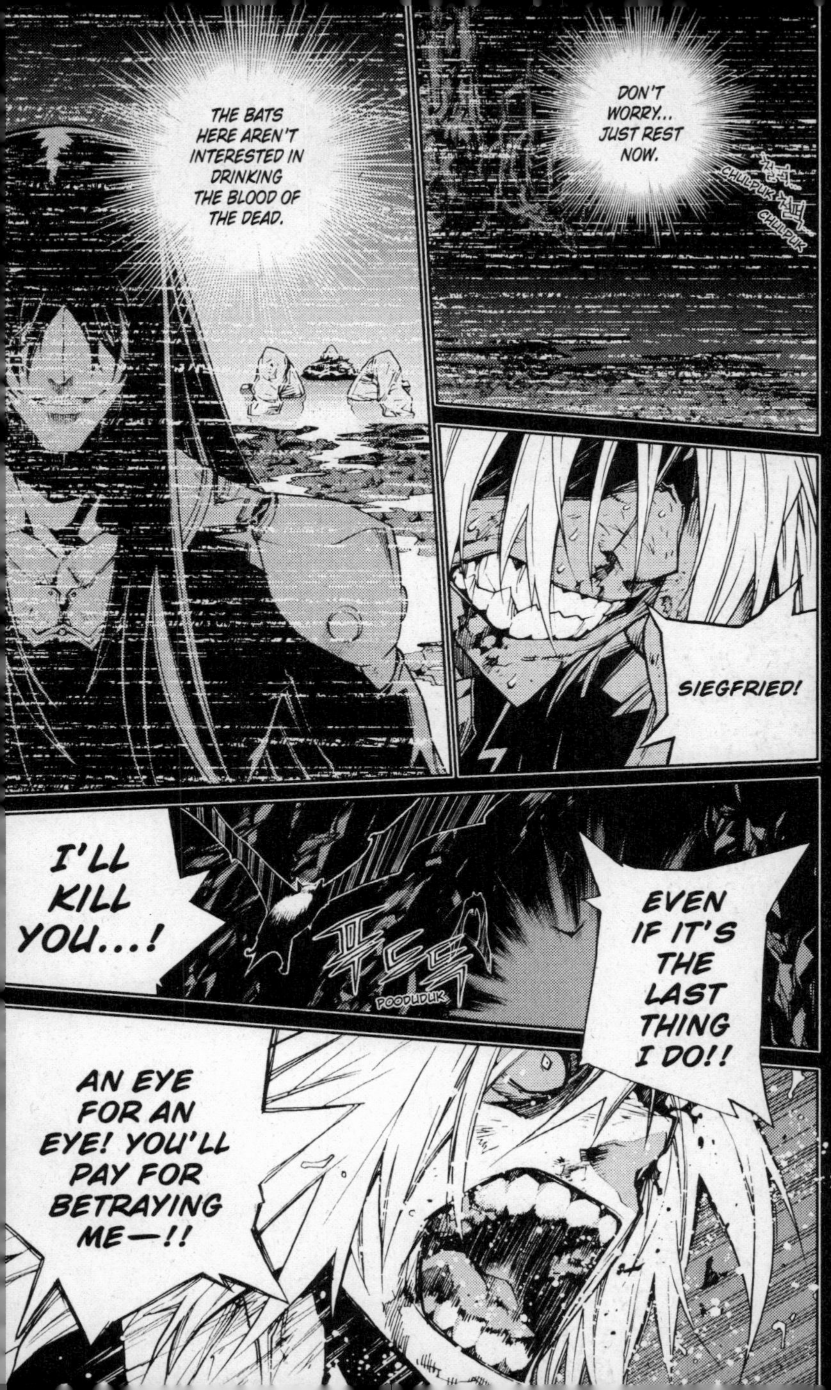
THE BATS HERE AREN'T INTERESTED IN DRINKING THE BLOOD OF THE DEAD.
DON'T WORRY... JUST REST NOW.
CHULPUK
CHULPUK
SIEGFRIED!
I'LL KILL YOU...!
POODUDUK
EVEN IF IT'S THE LAST THING I DO!!
AN EYE FOR AN EYE! YOU'LL PAY FOR BETRAYING ME—!!

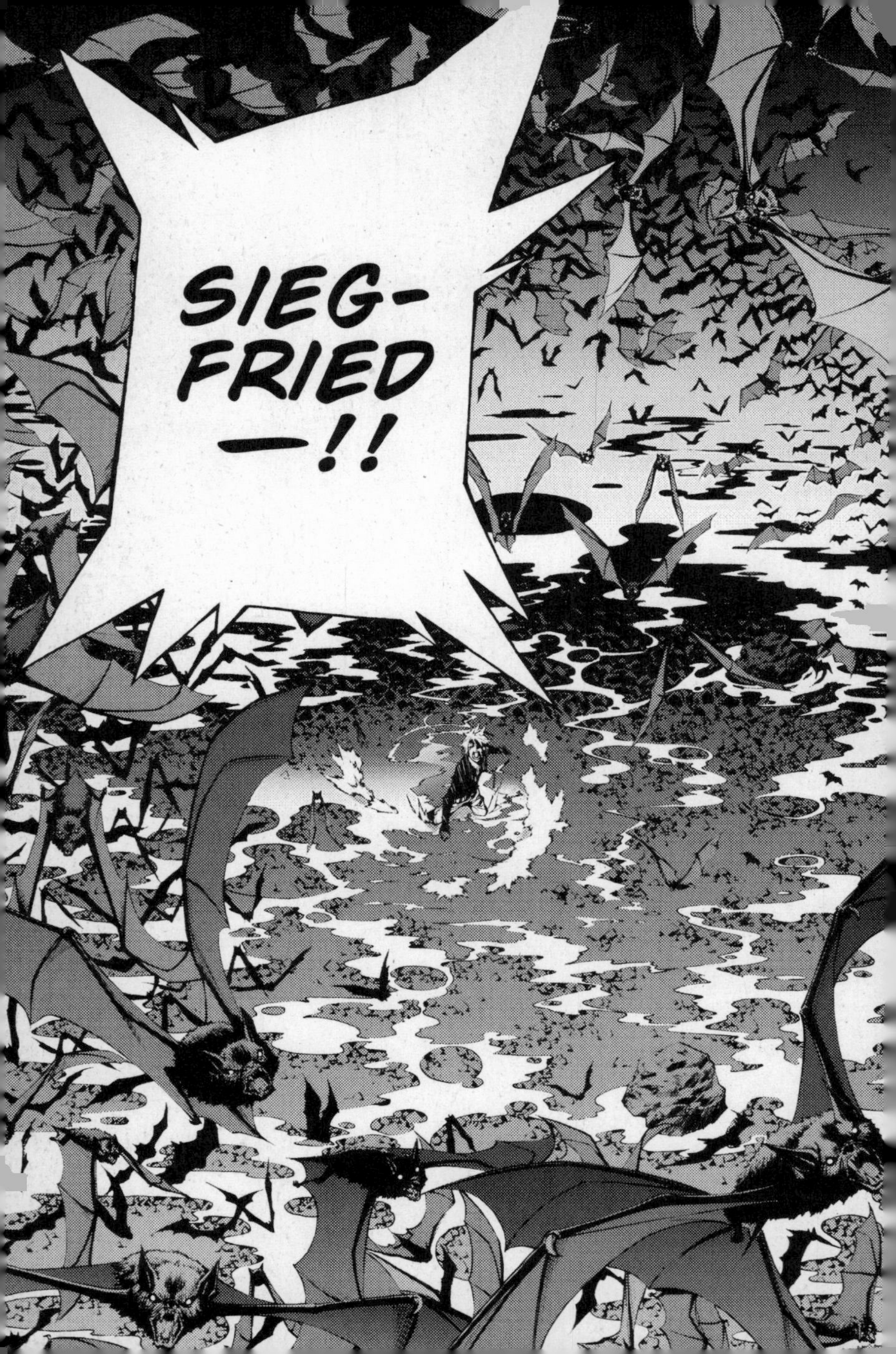
SIEG-
FRIED
—!!

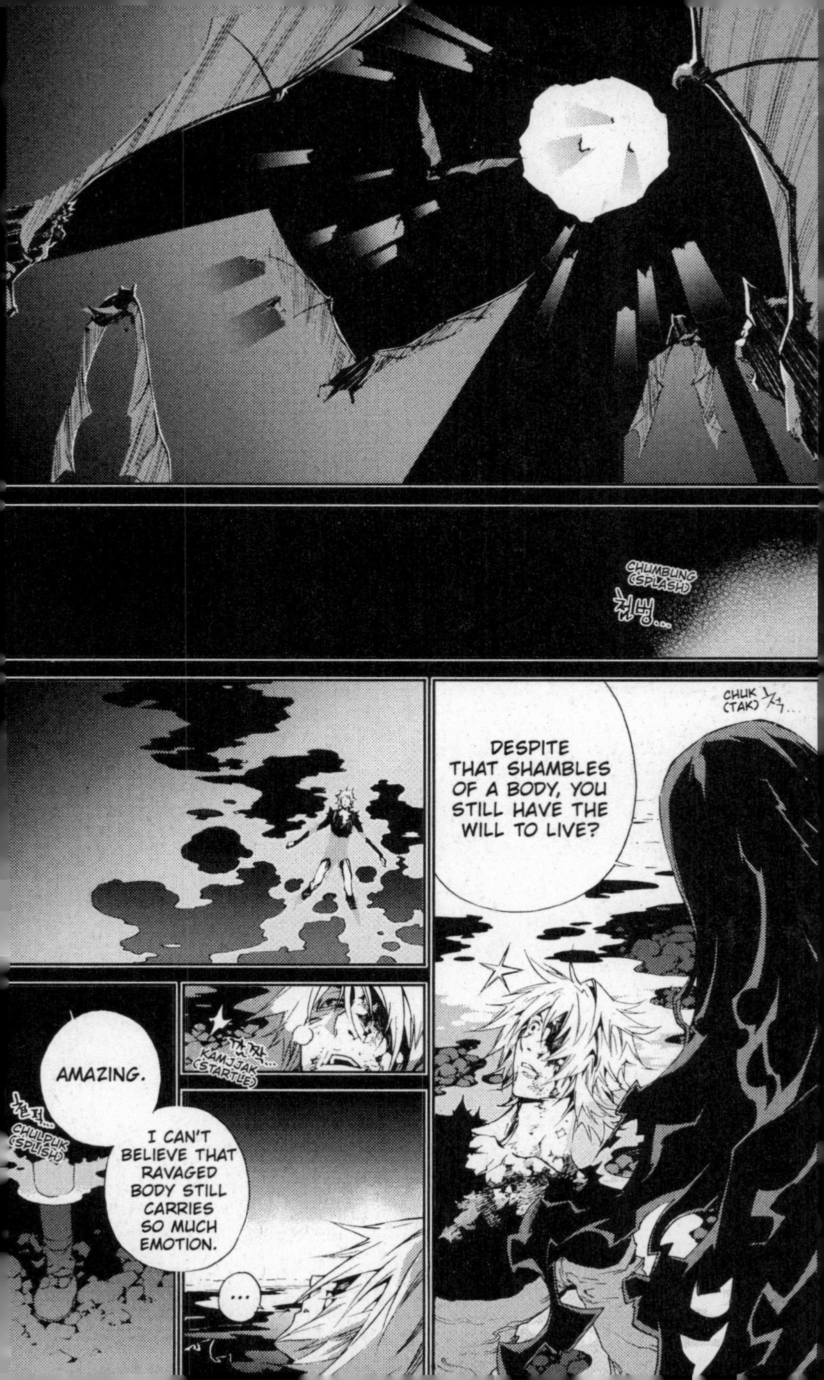
CHUMBUNG (SPLASH)
첨벙...
AMAZING.
철퍽
CHULPUK (SPLISH)
I CAN'T BELIEVE THAT RAVAGED BODY STILL CARRIES SO MUCH EMOTION.
깜짝...
KAMJJAK (STARTLE)
...
CHUK (TAK)
척...
DESPITE THAT SHAMBLES OF A BODY, YOU STILL HAVE THE WILL TO LIVE?

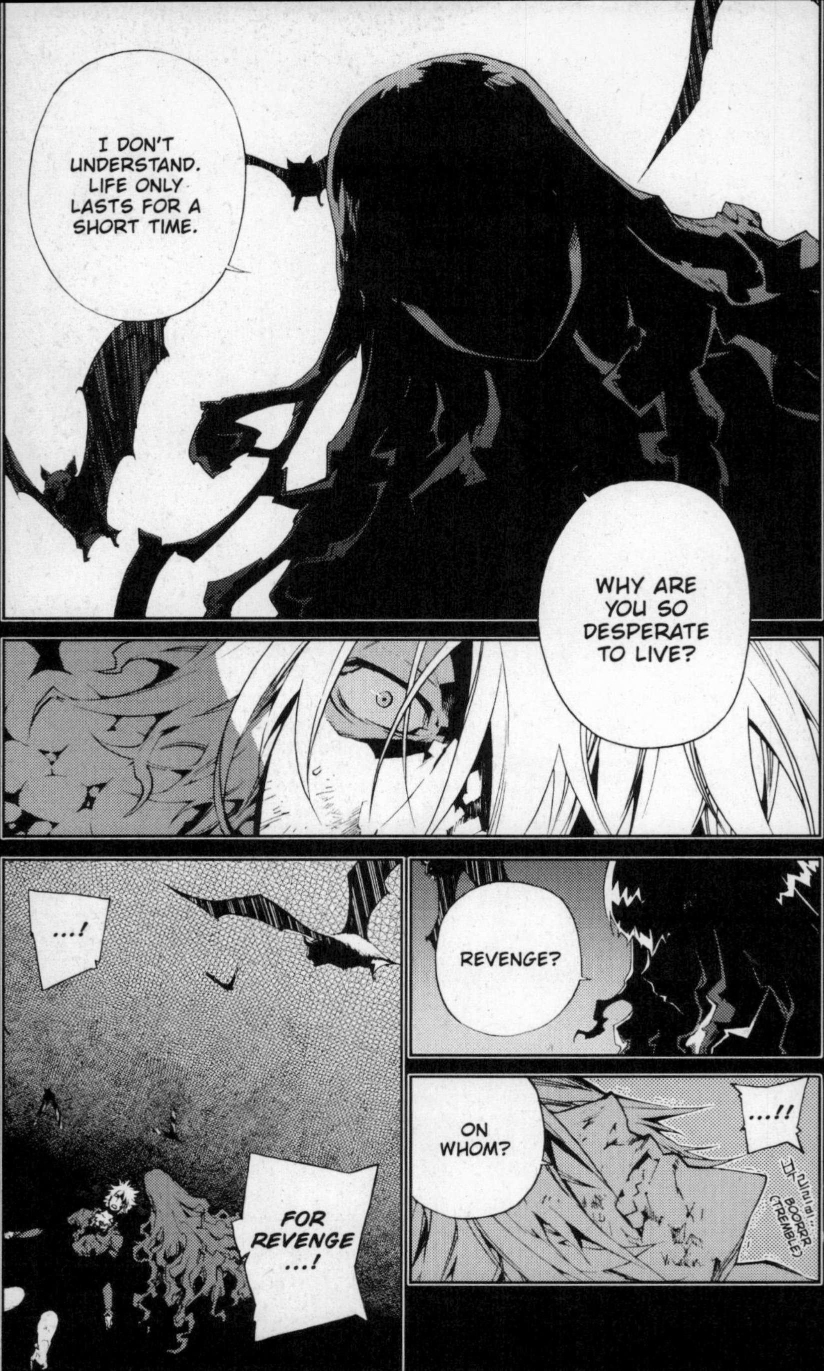
I DON'T UNDERSTAND. LIFE ONLY LASTS FOR A SHORT TIME.
WHY ARE YOU SO DESPERATE TO LIVE?
...!
FOR REVENGE ...!
REVENGE?
ON WHOM?
...!!
BOORRR (TREMBLE)

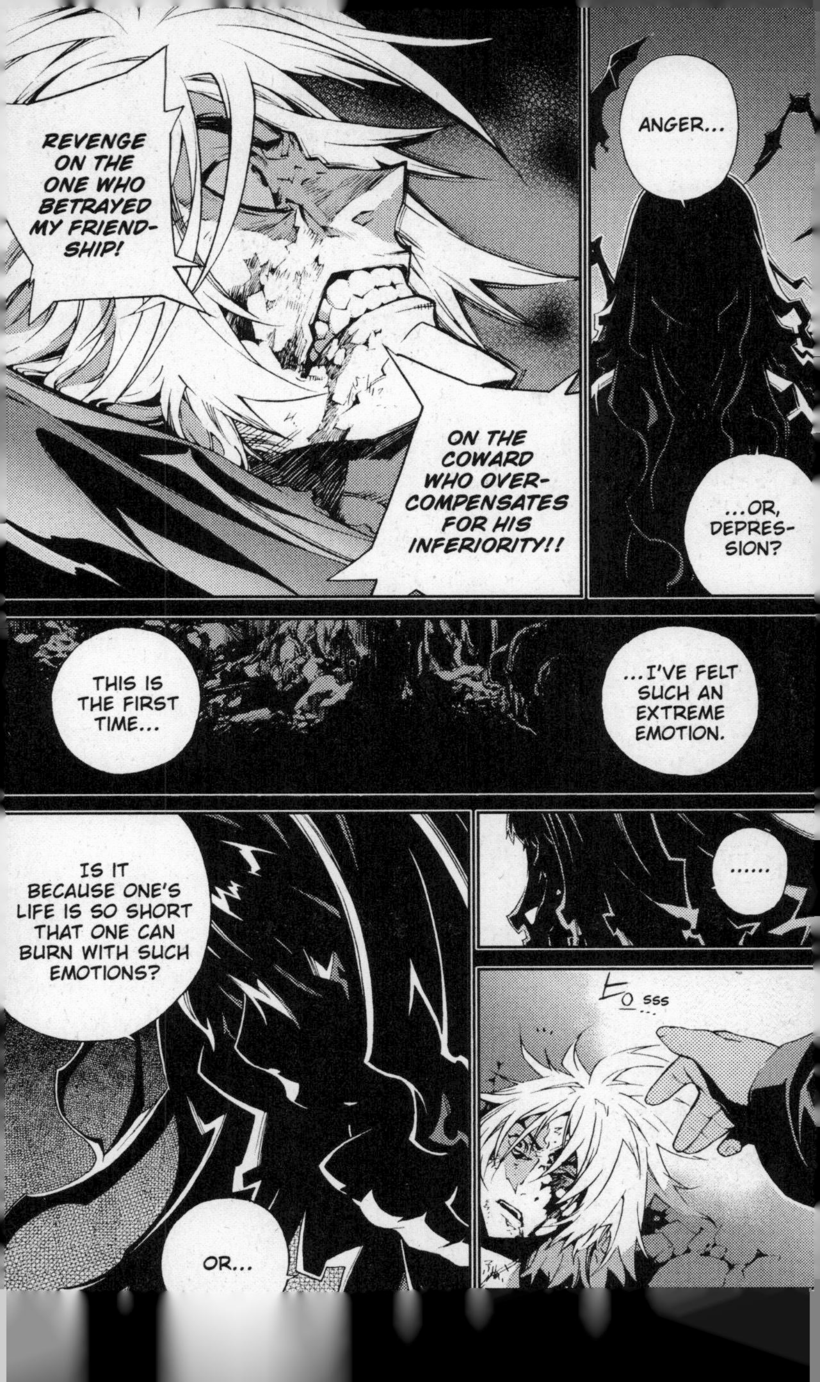
REVENGE ON THE ONE WHO BETRAYED MY FRIENDSHIP!
ON THE COWARD WHO OVERCOMPENSATES FOR HIS INFERIORITY!!
ANGER...
...OR, DEPRESSION?
THIS IS THE FIRST TIME...
...I'VE FELT SUCH AN EXTREME EMOTION.
IS IT BECAUSE ONE'S LIFE IS SO SHORT THAT ONE CAN BURN WITH SUCH EMOTIONS?
OR...
......
SSS...

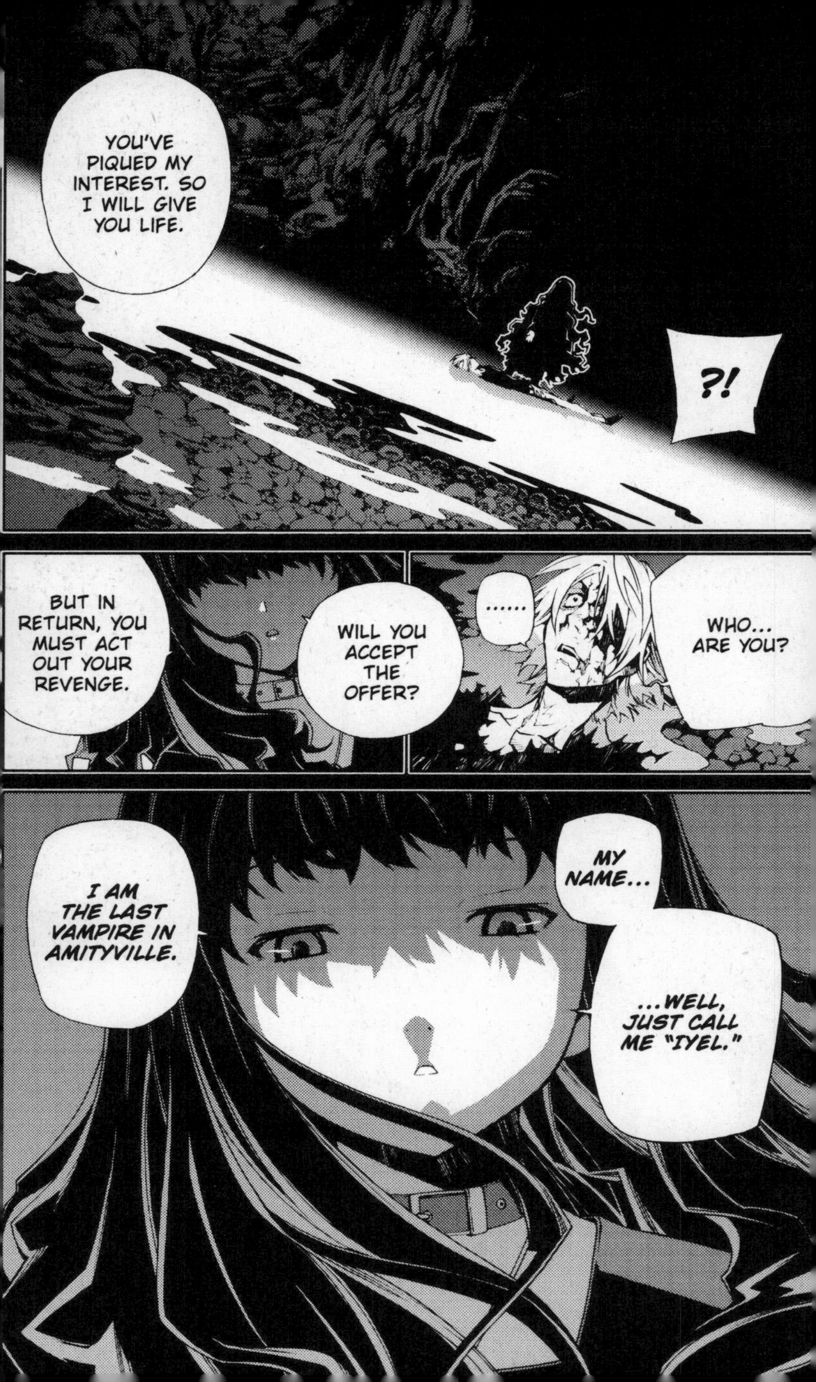
YOU'VE PIQUED MY INTEREST. SO I WILL GIVE YOU LIFE.
?!
BUT IN RETURN, YOU MUST ACT OUT YOUR REVENGE.
WILL YOU ACCEPT THE OFFER?
......
WHO... ARE YOU?
I AM THE LAST VAMPIRE IN AMITYVILLE.
MY NAME...
...WELL, JUST CALL ME "IYEL."

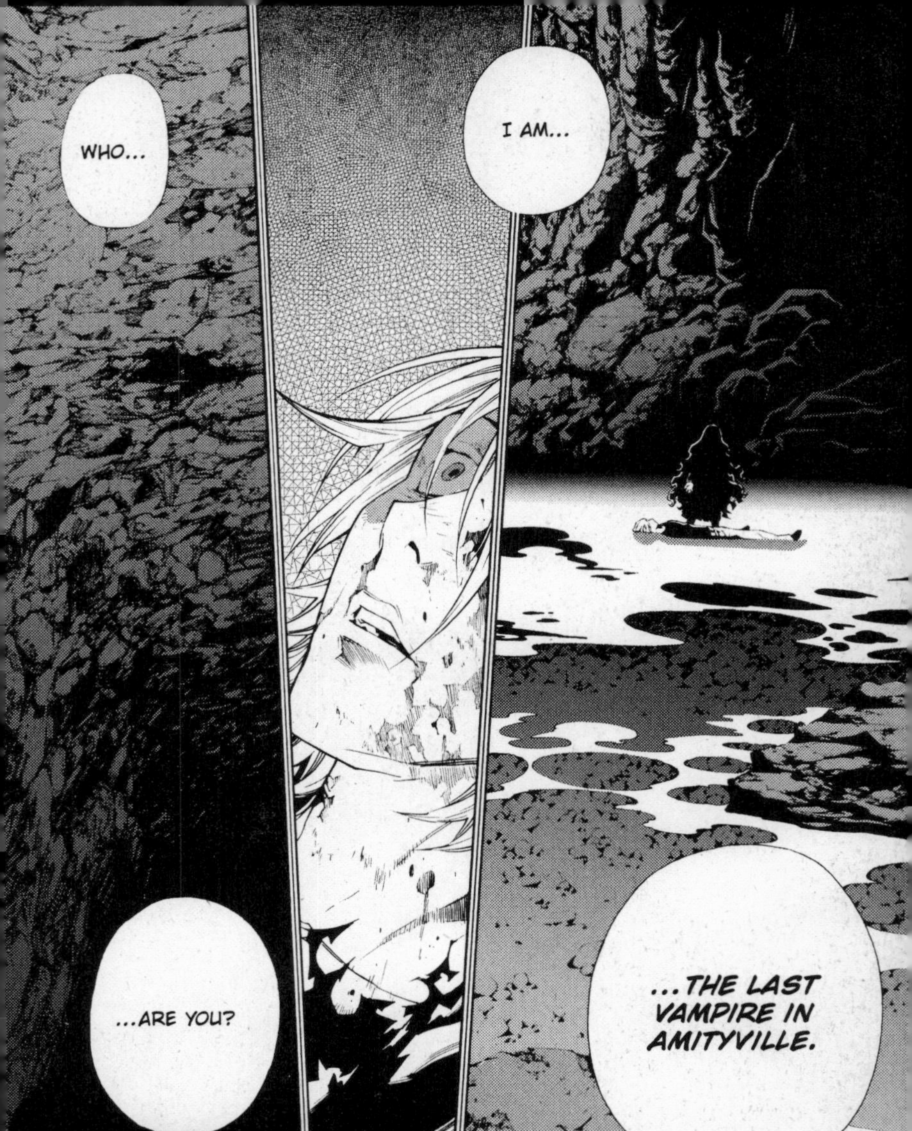
WHO...
...ARE YOU?
I AM...
...THE LAST VAMPIRE IN AMITYVILLE.

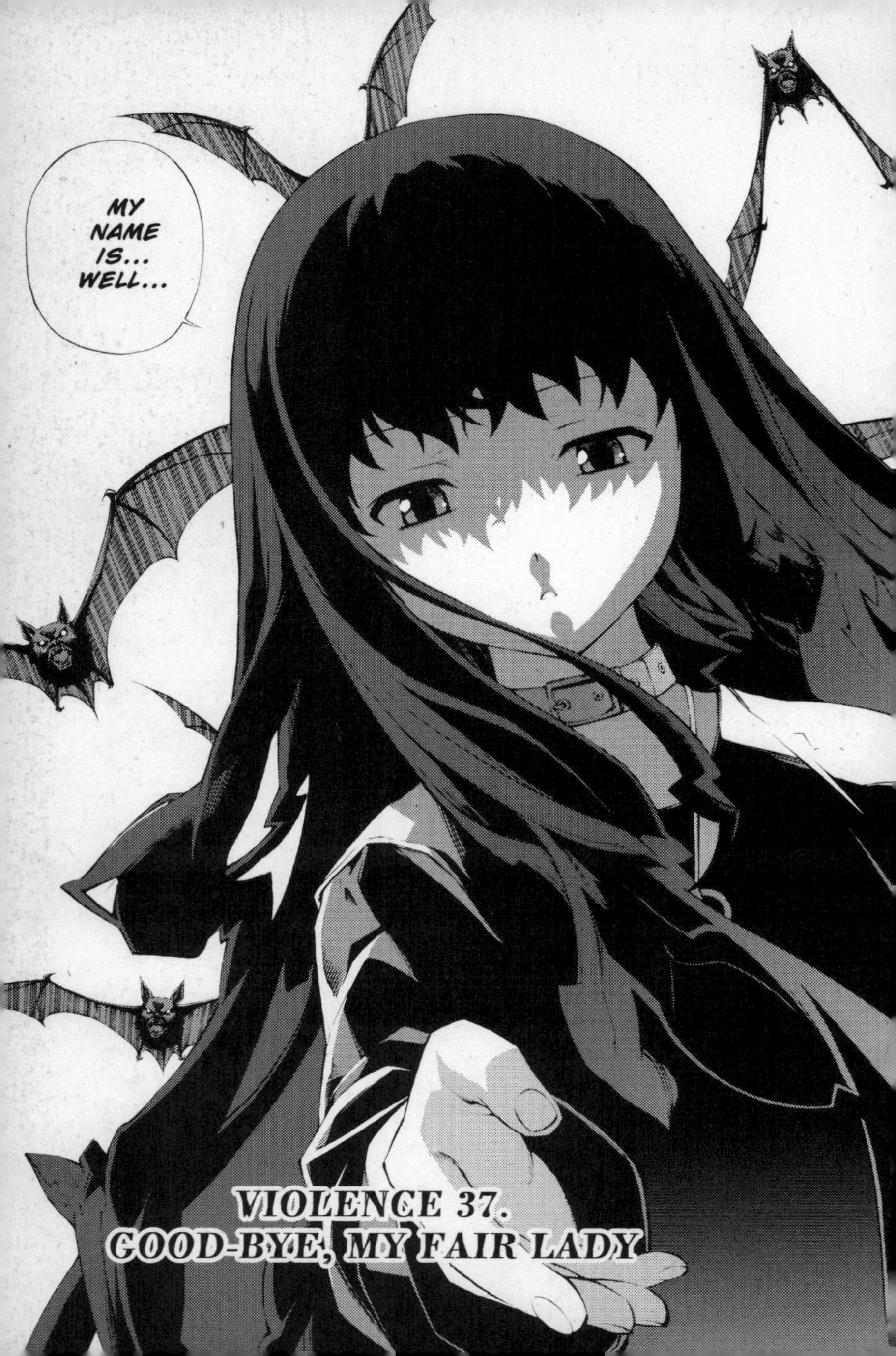
MY NAME IS... WELL...
VIOLENCE 37.
GOOD-BYE, MY FAIR LADY

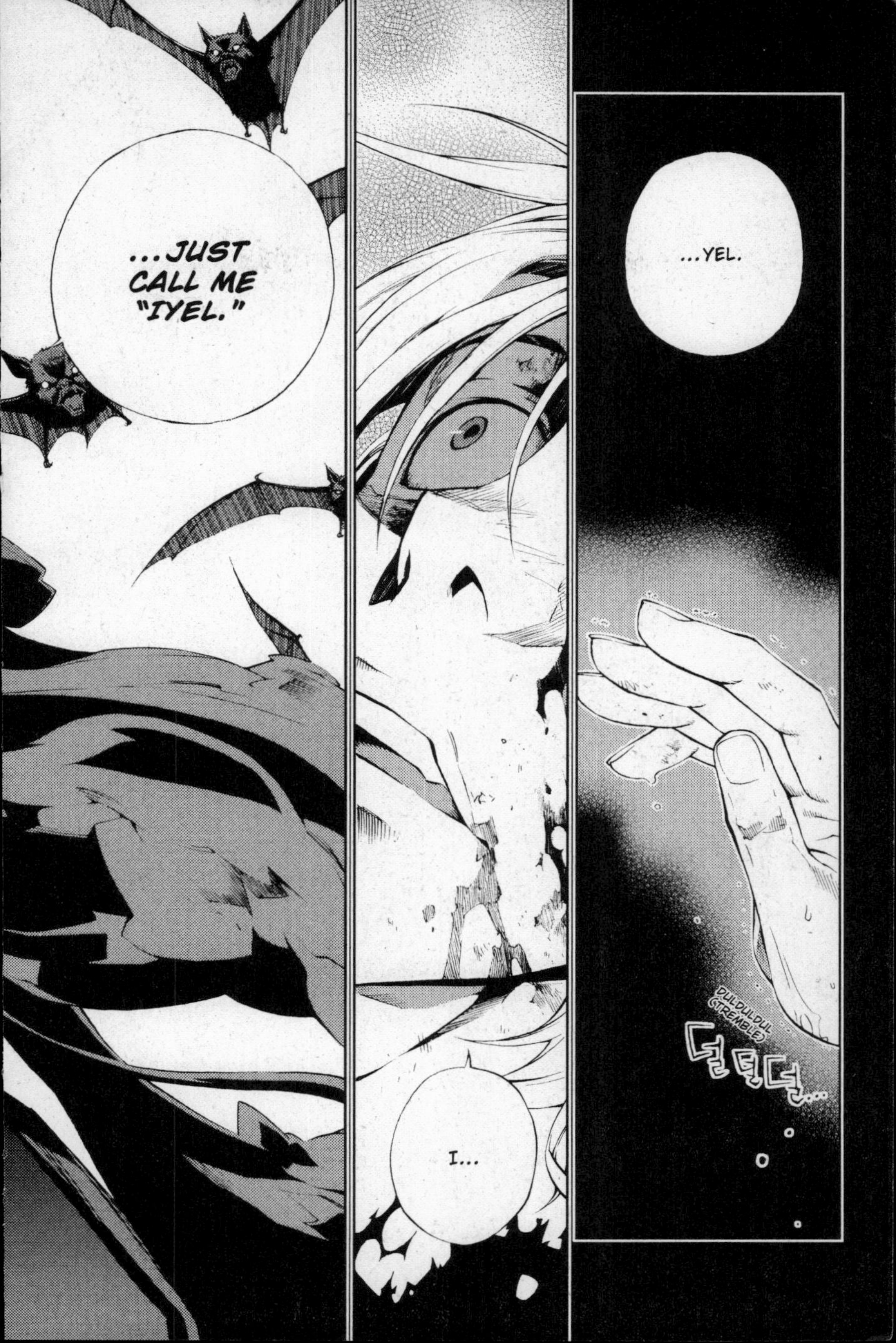
...JUST CALL ME "IYEL."
I...
...YEL.
DULDULDUL (TREMBLE)
덜덜덜...

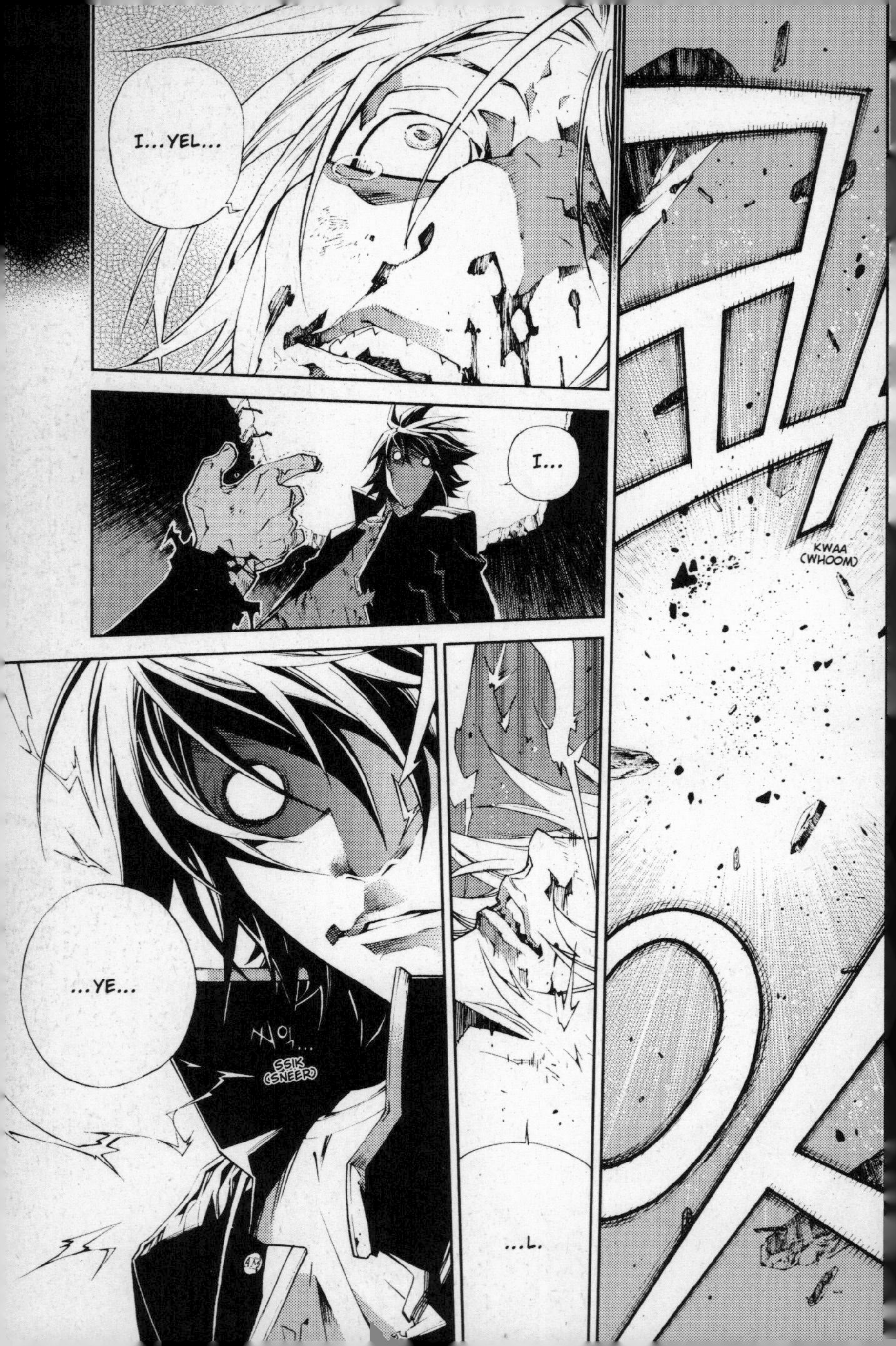
I...YEL...
I...
...YE...
씨익...
SSIK (SNEER)
...L.
KWAA (WHOOM)

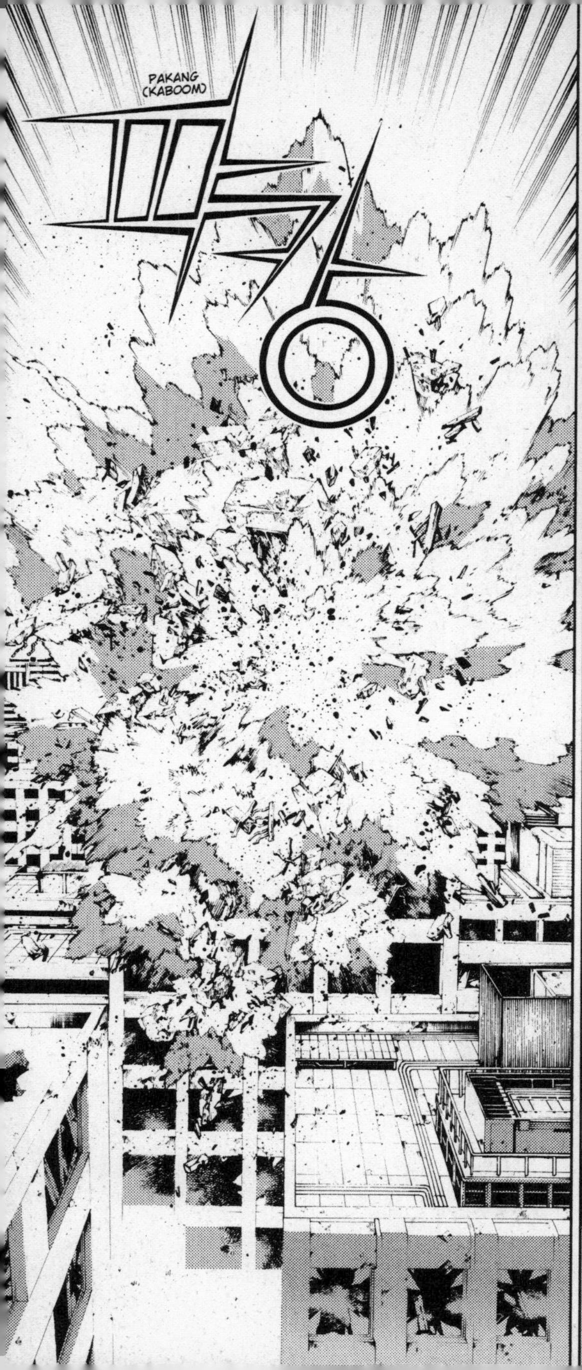
파캉
PAKANG (KABOOM)
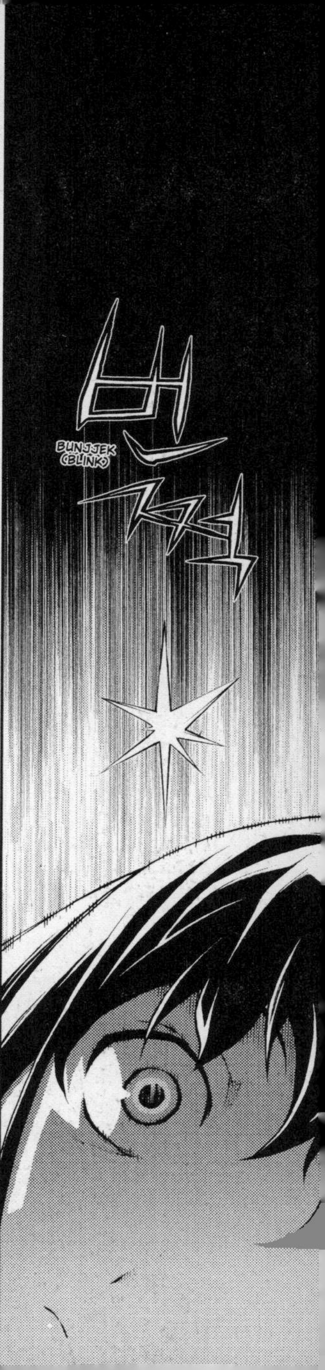
번쩍
BUNJJEK (BLINK)

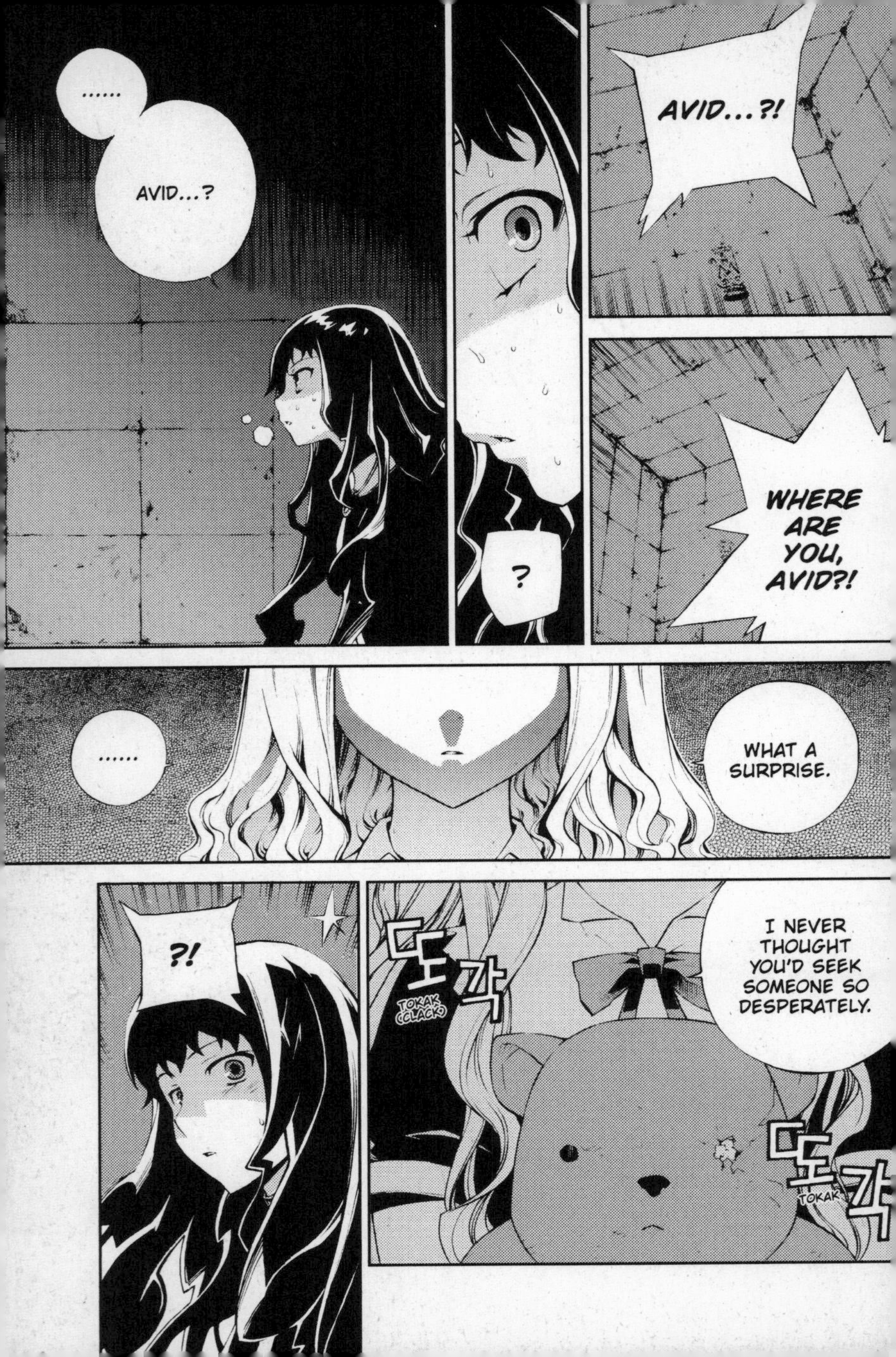
......
AVID...?
?
AVID...?!
WHERE ARE YOU, AVID?!
......
WHAT A SURPRISE.
?!
또각
TOKAK (CLACK)
I NEVER THOUGHT YOU'D SEEK SOMEONE SO DESPERATELY.
또각
TOKAK

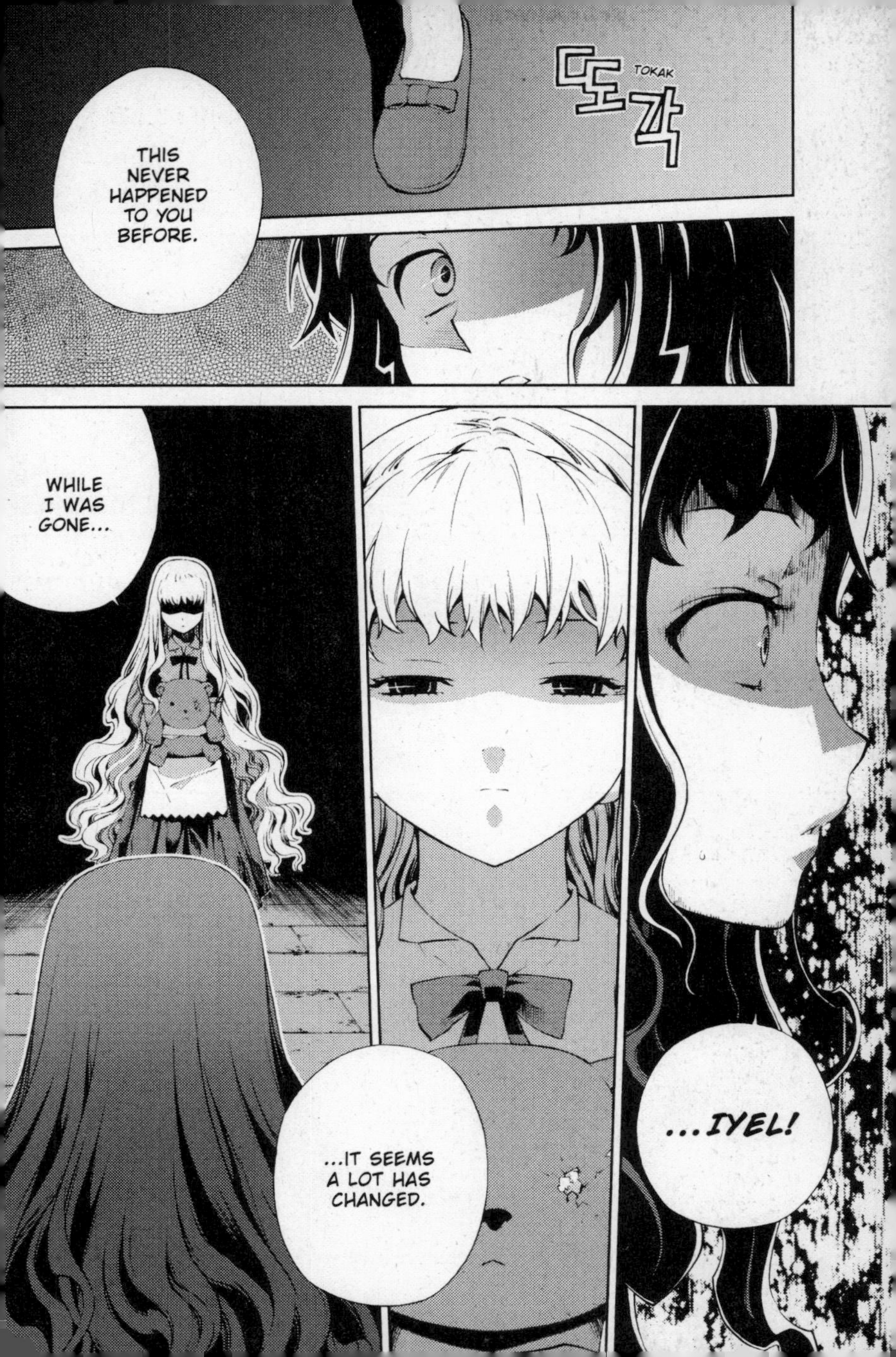
THIS NEVER HAPPENED TO YOU BEFORE.
TOKAK
WHILE I WAS GONE...
...IT SEEMS A LOT HAS CHANGED.
...IYEL!

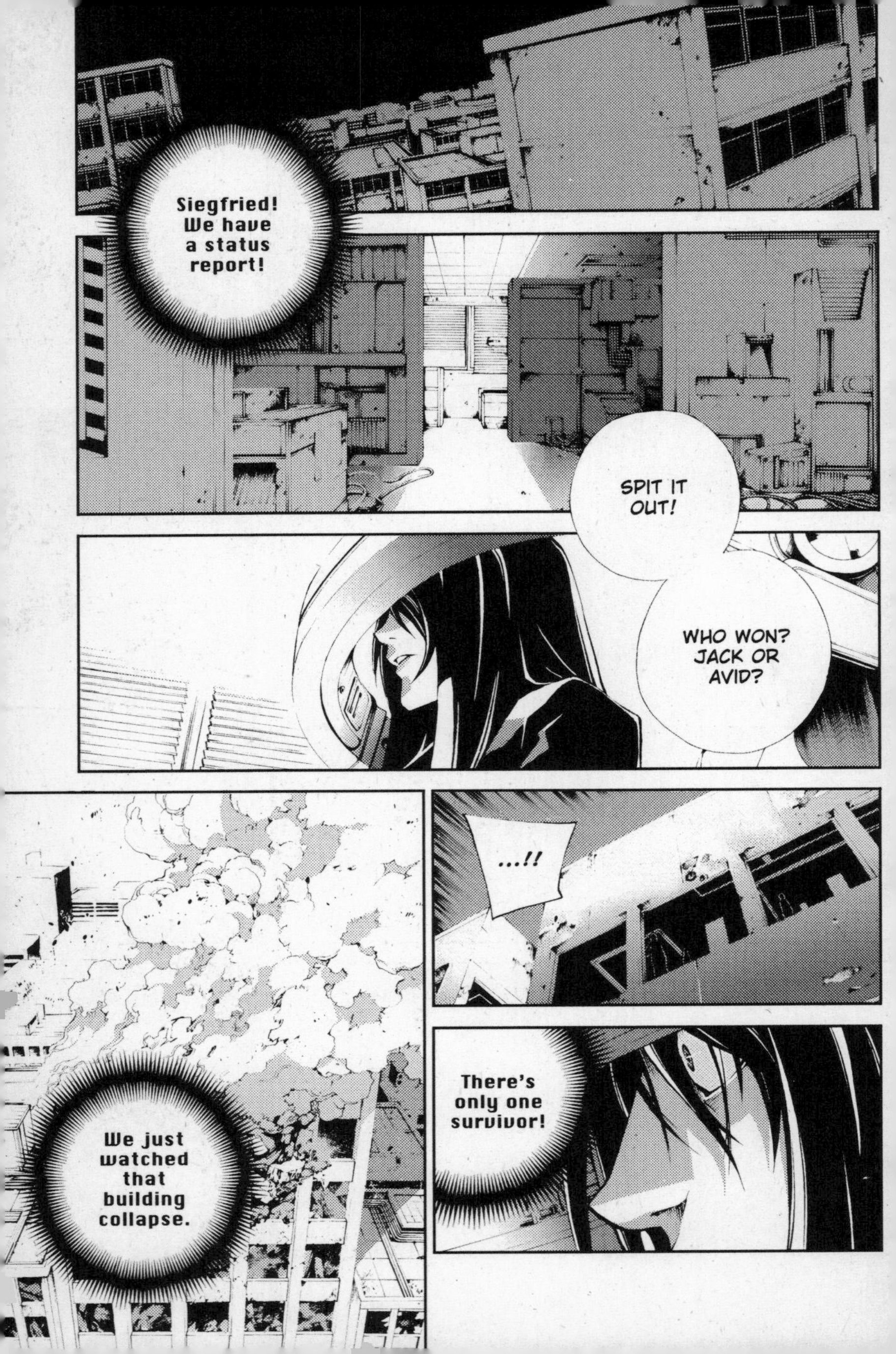
Siegfried! We have a status report!
SPIT IT OUT!
WHO WON? JACK OR AVID?
We just watched that building collapse.
...!!
There's only one survivor!

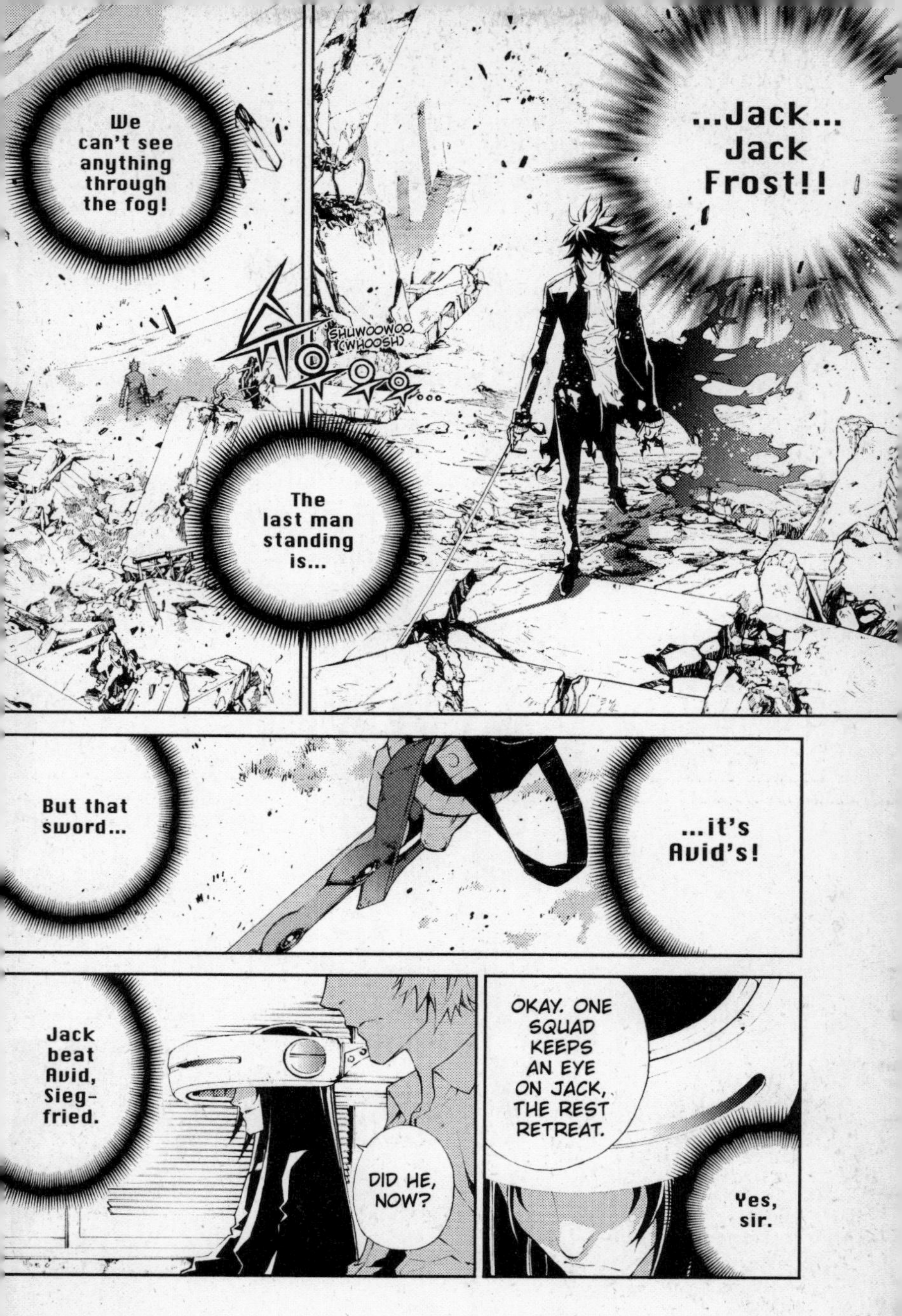

We can't see anything through the fog!
SHUWOOWOO (WHOOSH)
...Jack... Jack Frost!!
The last man standing is...
But that sword...
...it's Avid's!
Jack beat Avid, Sieg-fried.
DID HE, NOW?
OKAY. ONE SQUAD KEEPS AN EYE ON JACK, THE REST RETREAT.
Yes, sir.

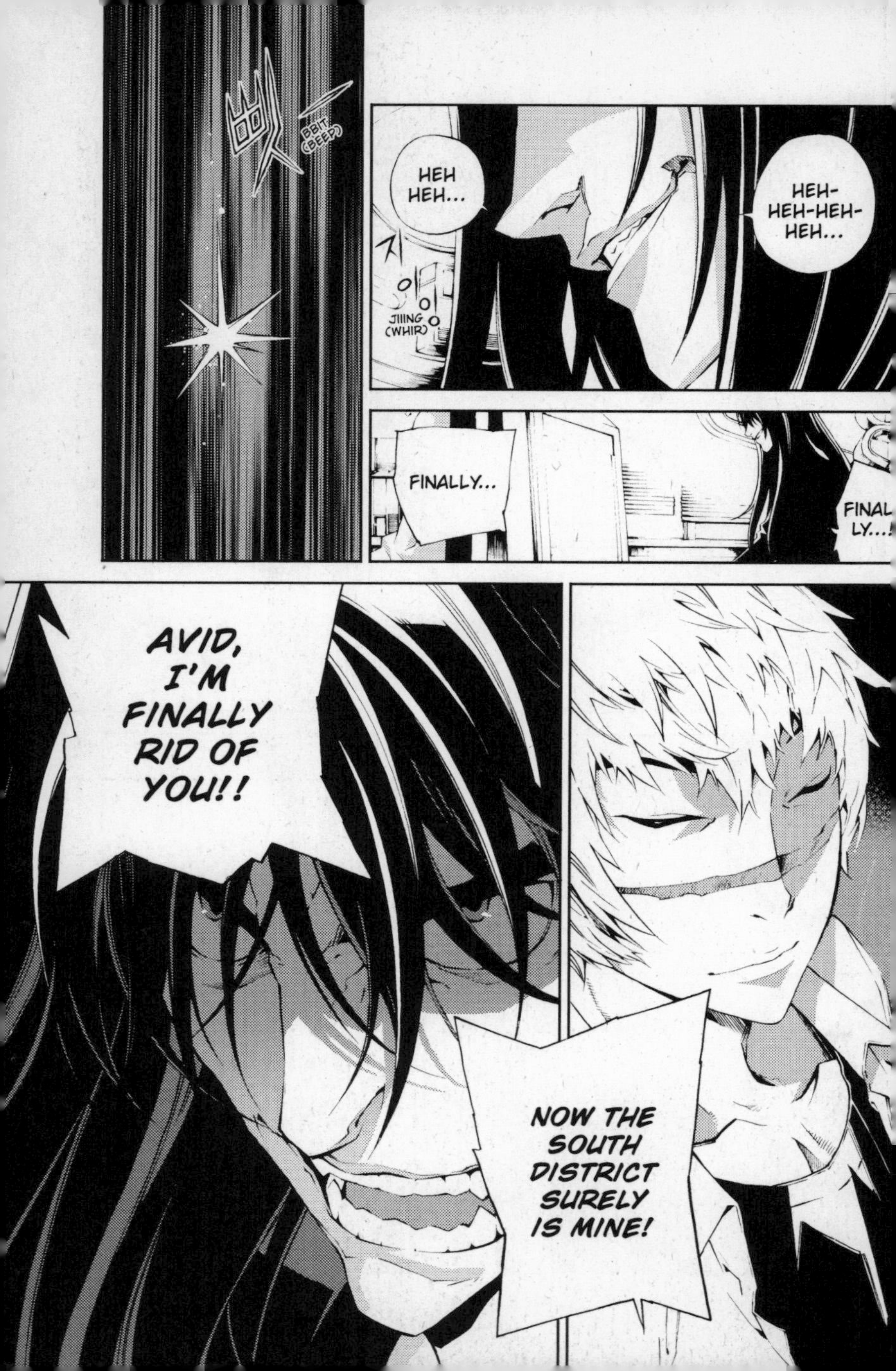
BBIT (BEEP)
HEH HEH...
JIING (WHIR)
HEH-HEH-HEH-HEH...
FINALLY...
FINALLY...
AVID, I'M FINALLY RID OF YOU!!
NOW THE SOUTH DISTRICT SURELY IS MINE!

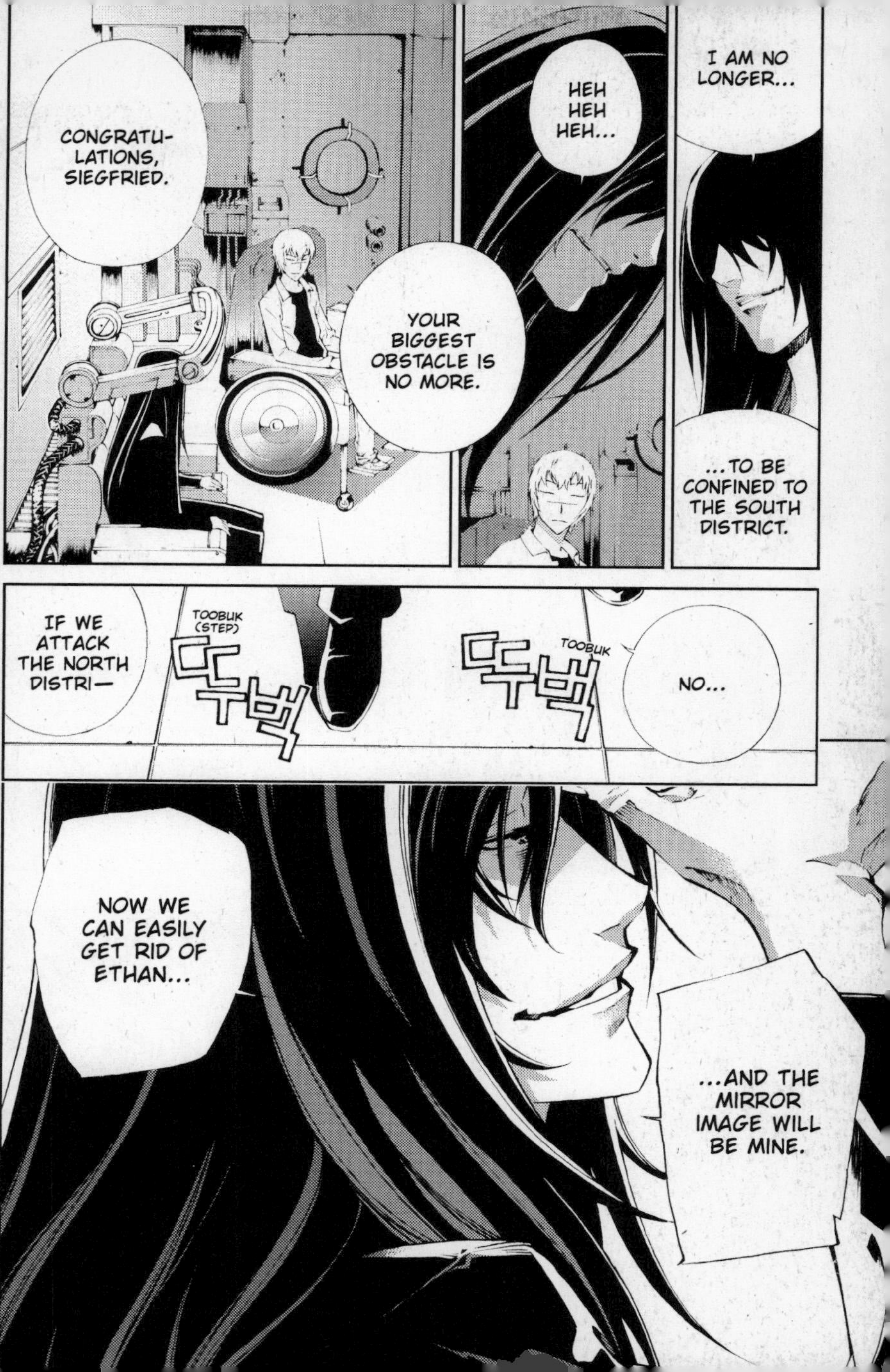
CONGRATU-LATIONS, SIEGFRIED.
YOUR BIGGEST OBSTACLE IS NO MORE.
HEH HEH HEH...
I AM NO LONGER...
...TO BE CONFINED TO THE SOUTH DISTRICT.
IF WE ATTACK THE NORTH DISTRI—
TOOBUK (STEP)
뚜벅
뚜벅
TOOBUK
NO...
NOW WE CAN EASILY GET RID OF ETHAN...
...AND THE MIRROR IMAGE WILL BE MINE.

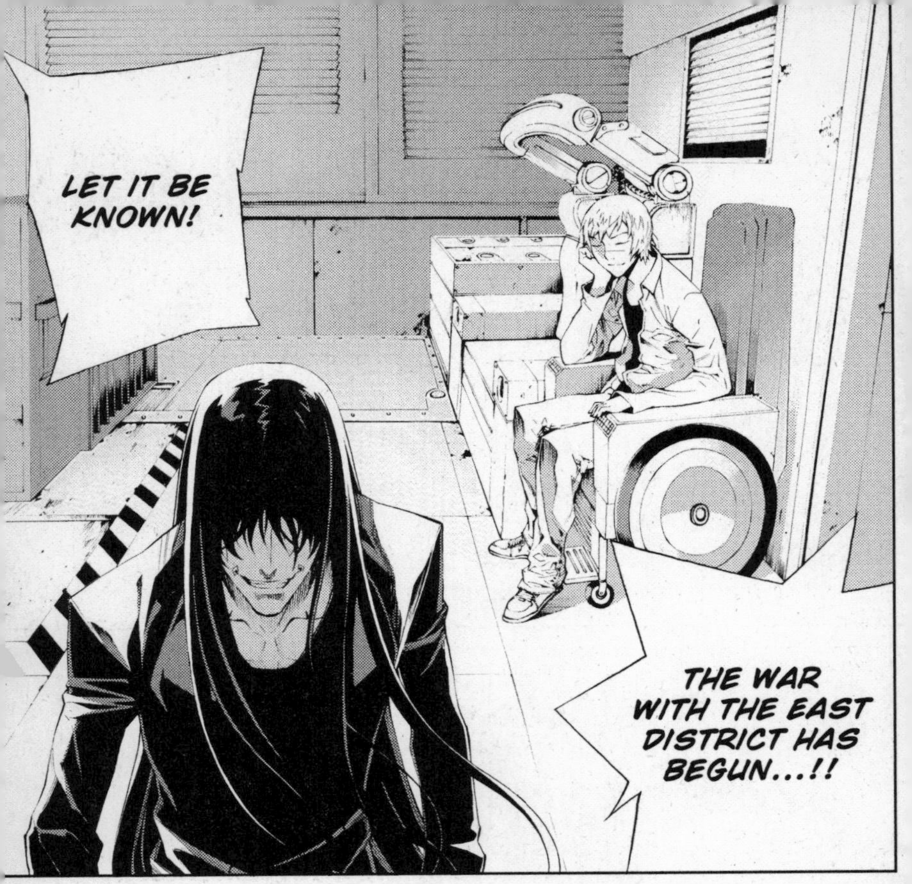
LET IT BE KNOWN!
THE WAR WITH THE EAST DISTRICT HAS BEGUN...!!
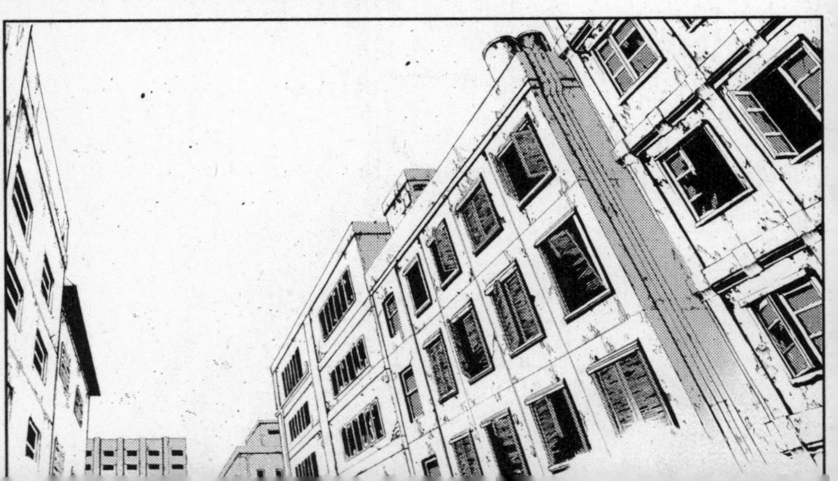

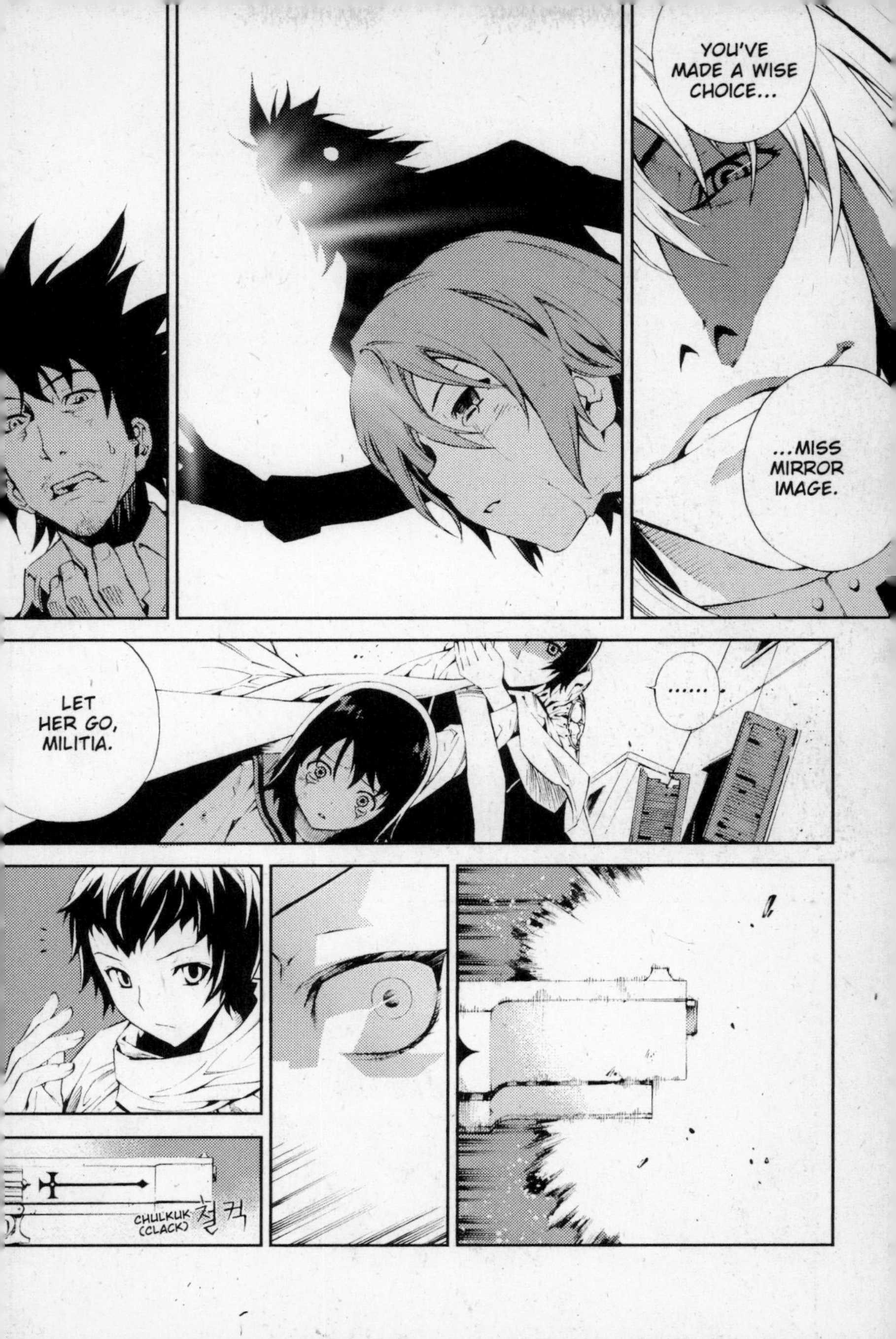

YOU'VE MADE A WISE CHOICE...
...MISS MIRROR IMAGE.
LET HER GO, MILITIA.
......
CHULKUK (CLACK) 철컥

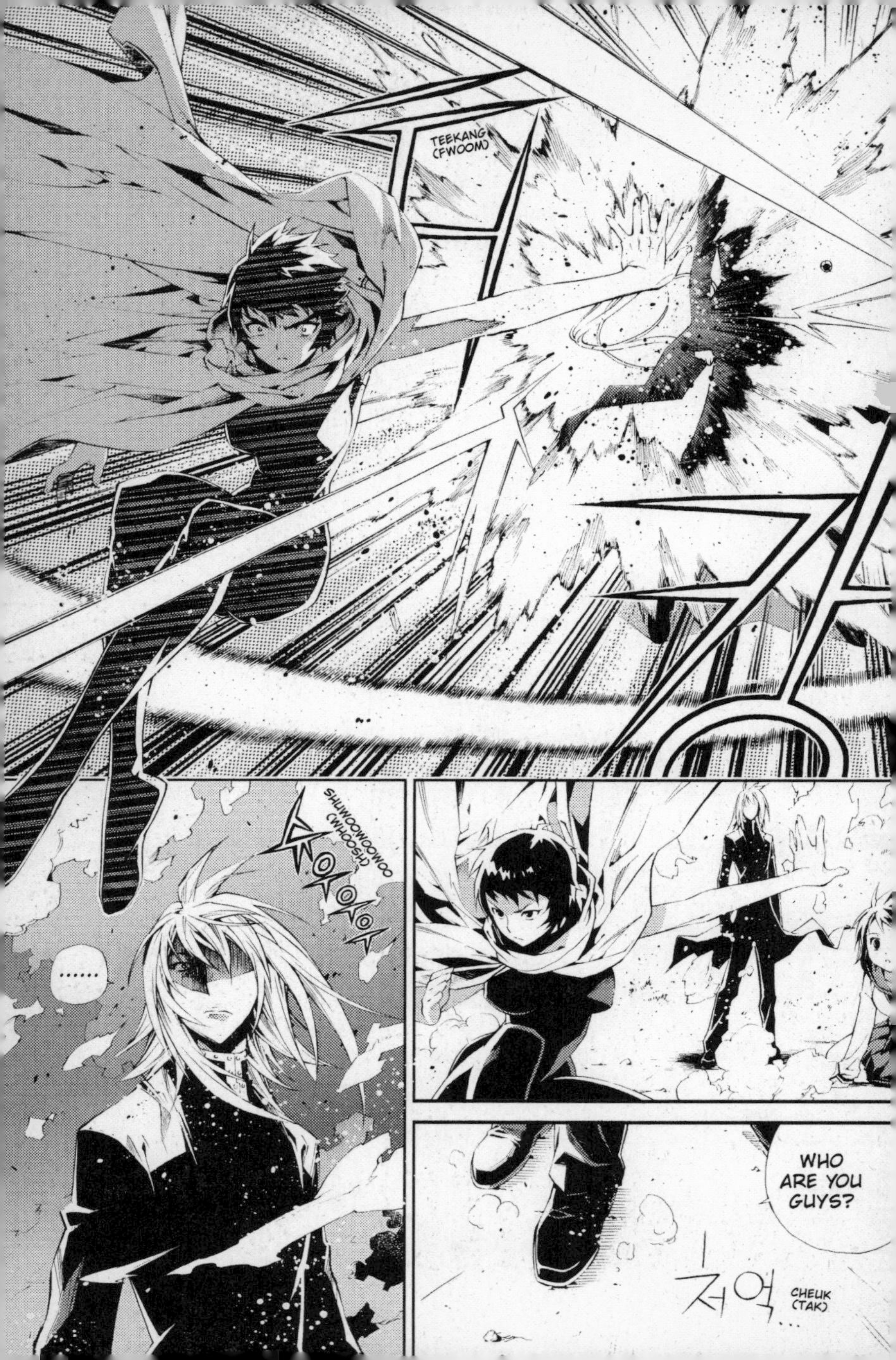
TEEKANG
(FWOOM)
SHUWOOWOOWOO
(WHOOSH)
......
WHO ARE YOU GUYS?
처억...
CHEUK
(TAK)

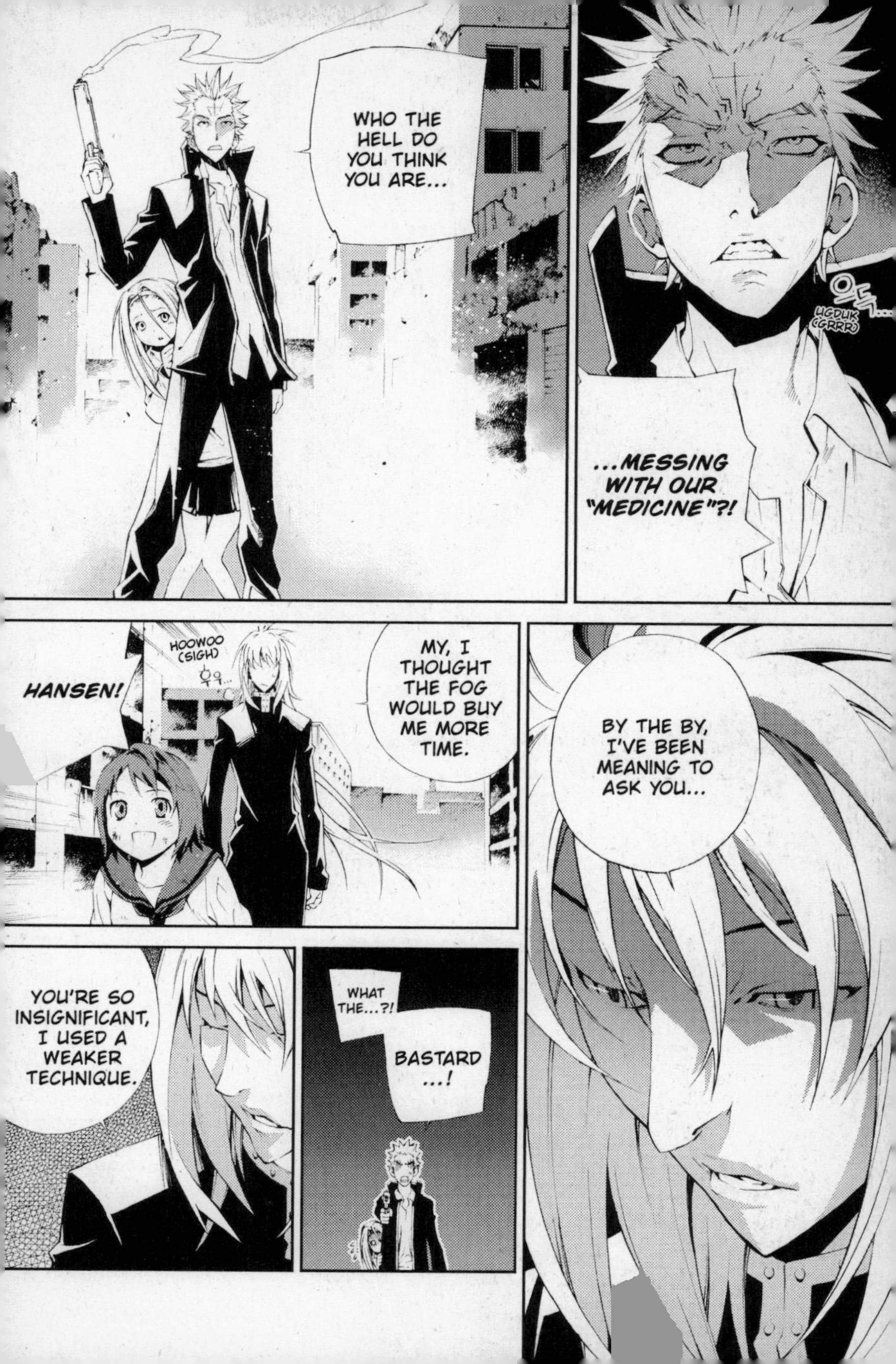

WHO THE HELL DO YOU THINK YOU ARE...
으득...
UGDUK (GRRR)
...MESSING WITH OUR "MEDICINE"?!
HANSEN!
후우...
HOOWOO (SIGH)
MY, I THOUGHT THE FOG WOULD BUY ME MORE TIME.
YOU'RE SO INSIGNIFICANT, I USED A WEAKER TECHNIQUE.
WHAT THE...?!
BASTARD ...!
BY THE BY, I'VE BEEN MEANING TO ASK YOU...

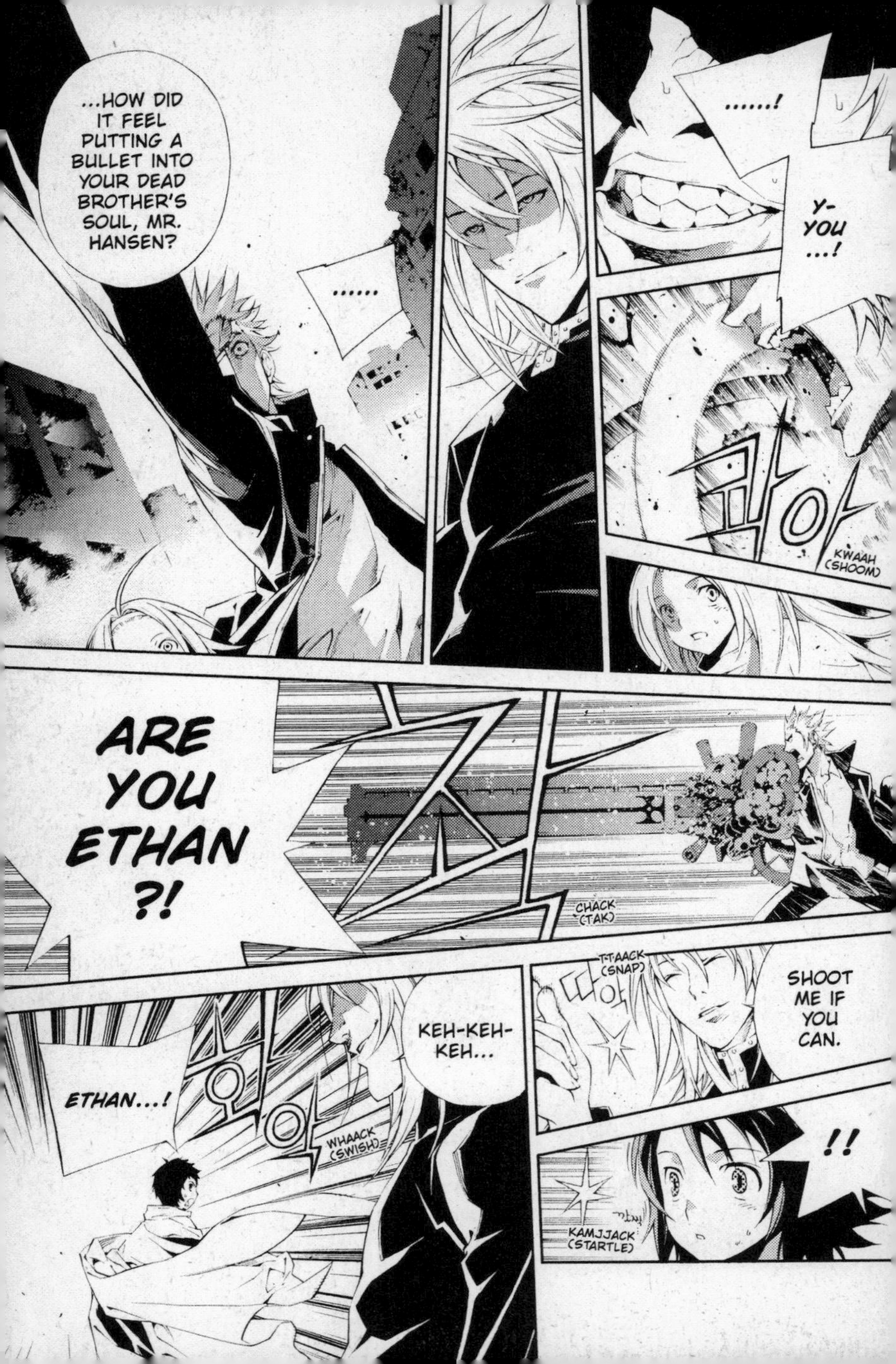
...HOW DID IT FEEL PUTTING A BULLET INTO YOUR DEAD BROTHER'S SOUL, MR. HANSEN?
......
......!
Y-YOU ...!
KWAAH (SHOOM)
ARE YOU ETHAN ?!
CHACK (TAK)
ETHAN...!
KEH-KEH-KEH...
WHAACK (SWISH)
T-TAACK (SNAP)
SHOOT ME IF YOU CAN.
!!
KAMJJACK (STARTLE)

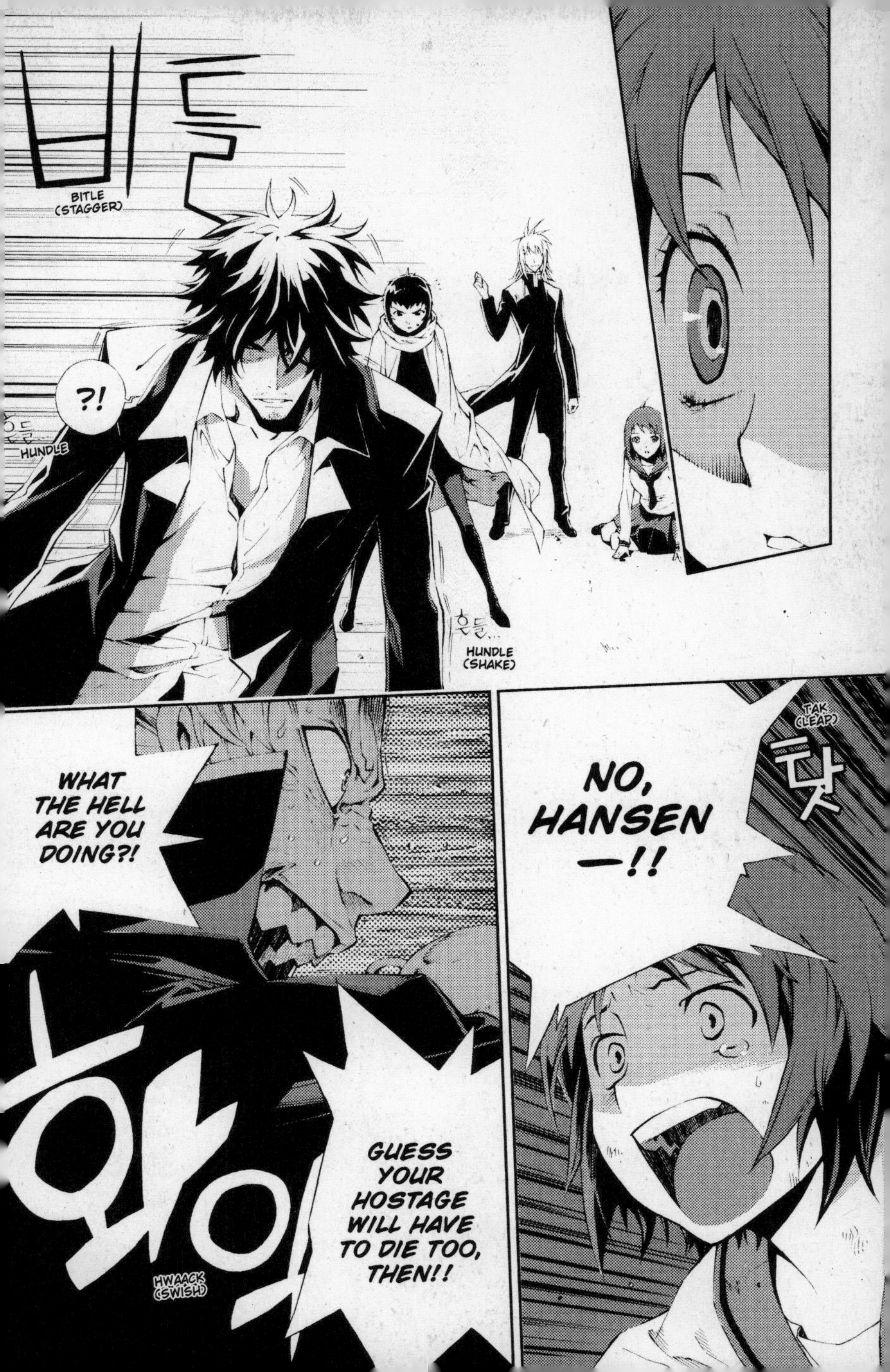
비틀
BITLE (STAGGER)
?!
흔들
HUNDLE
흔들...
HUNDLE (SHAKE)
WHAT THE HELL ARE YOU DOING?!
화악
HWAACK (SWISH)
GUESS YOUR HOSTAGE WILL HAVE TO DIE TOO, THEN!!
NO, HANSEN—!!
탁
TAK (LEAP)

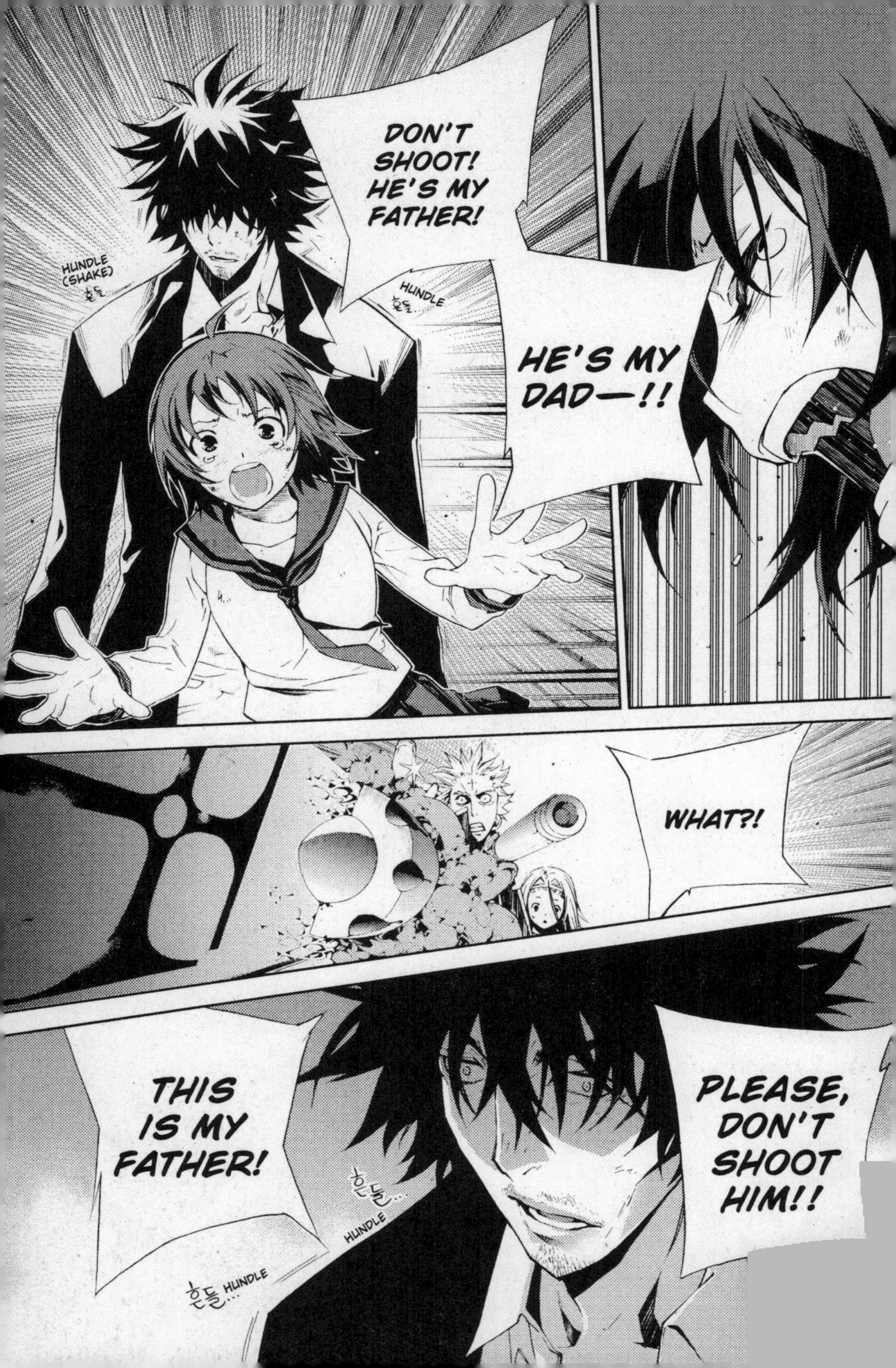
HUNDLE (SHAKE)
흔들
DON'T SHOOT! HE'S MY FATHER!
HUNDLE
흔들...
HE'S MY DAD—!!
WHAT?!
THIS IS MY FATHER!
흔들...
HUNDLE
흔들 HUNDLE...
PLEASE, DON'T SHOOT HIM!!

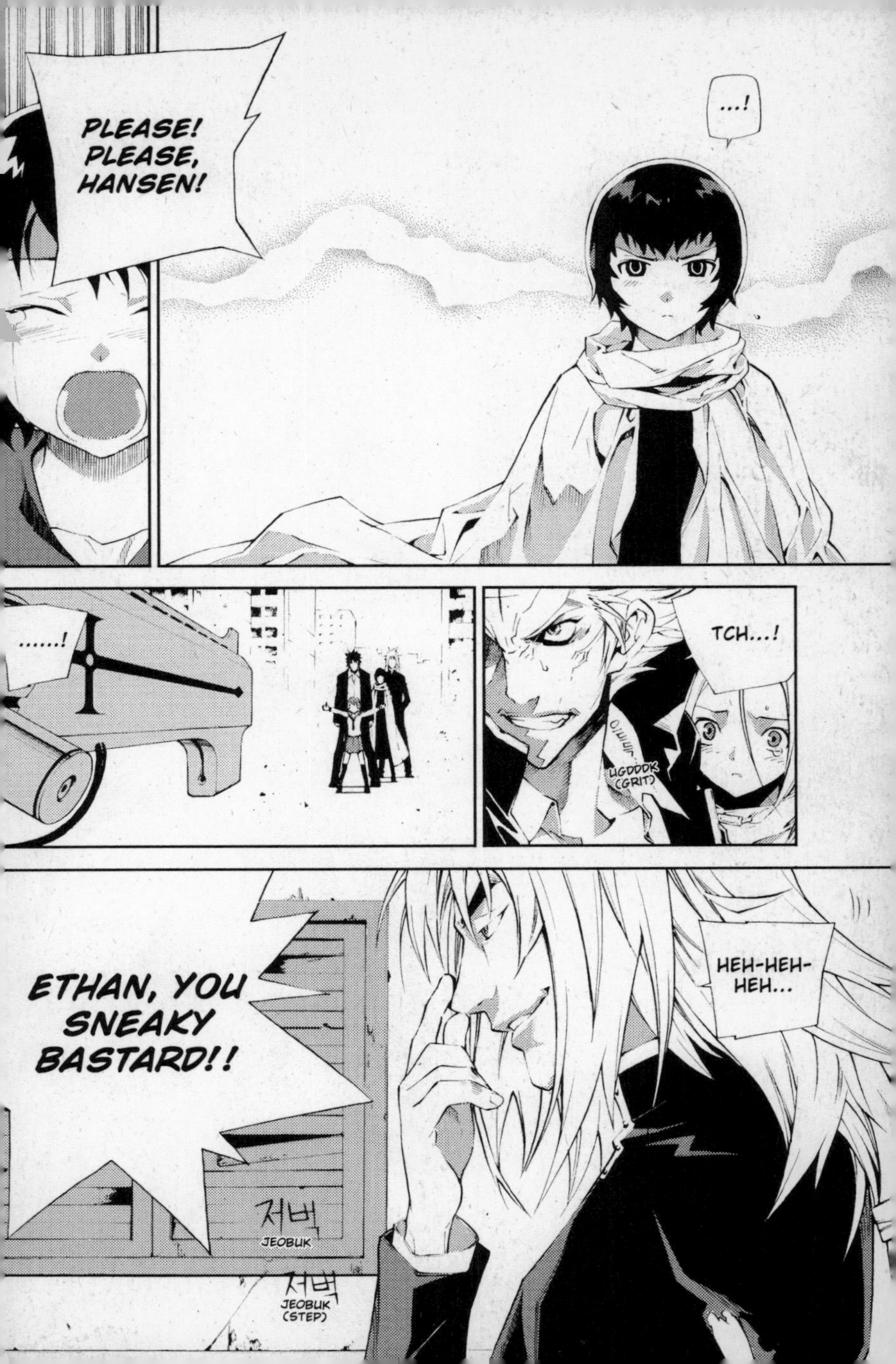
PLEASE! PLEASE, HANSEN!
...!
......!
TCH...!
이이익
UGDDDK (GRIT)
ETHAN, YOU SNEAKY BASTARD!!
HEH-HEH-HEH...
저벅
JEOBUK
저벅
JEOBUK (STEP)

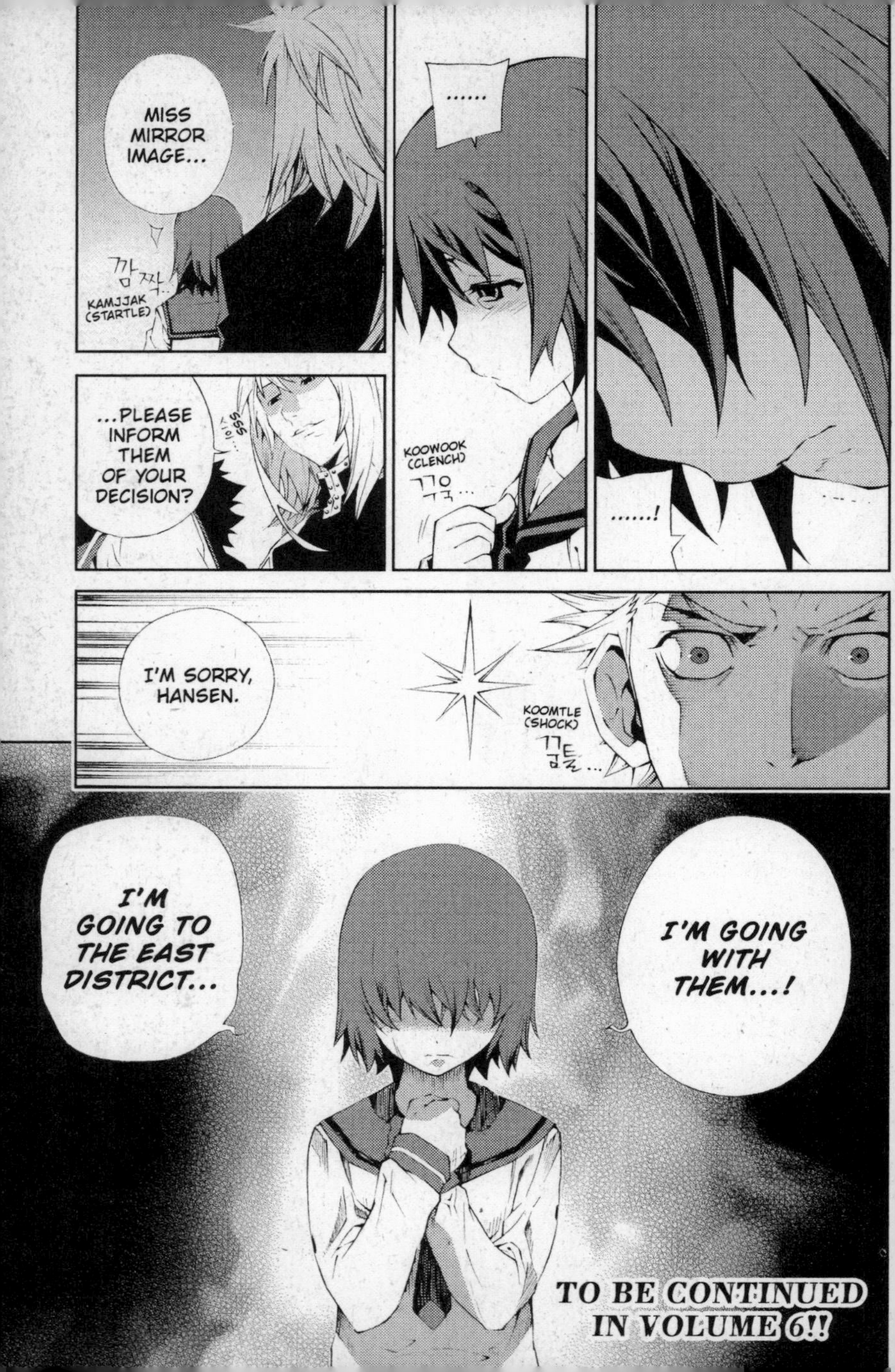
MISS MIRROR IMAGE...
깜짝..
KAMJJAK (STARTLE)
...PLEASE INFORM THEM OF YOUR DECISION?
SSS...
......
KOOWOOK (CLENCH)
꾸욱...
......!
I'M SORRY, HANSEN.
KOOMTLE (SHOCK)
꿈틀...
I'M GOING TO THE EAST DISTRICT...
I'M GOING WITH THEM...!
TO BE CONTINUED IN VOLUME 6!!

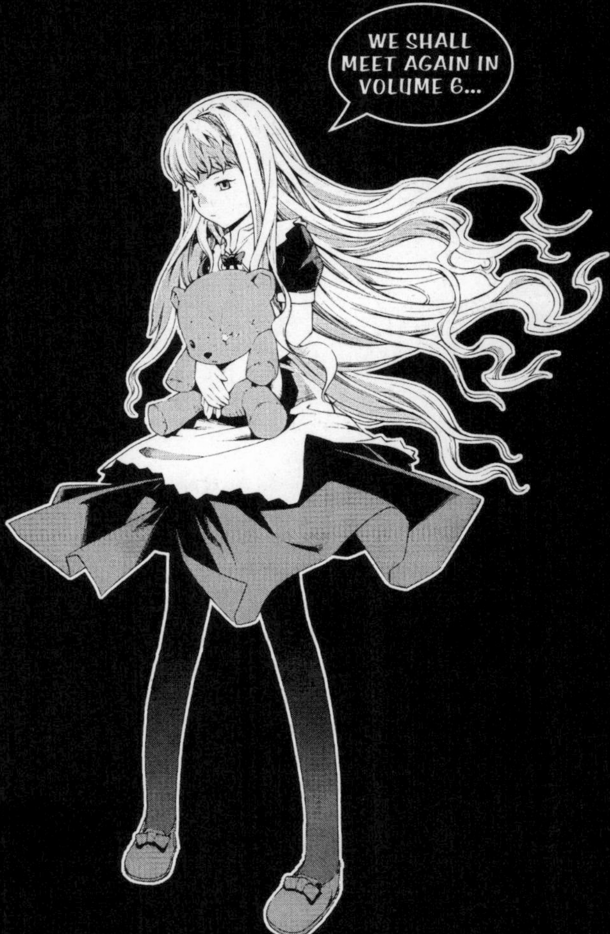
WE SHALL MEET AGAIN IN VOLUME 6...

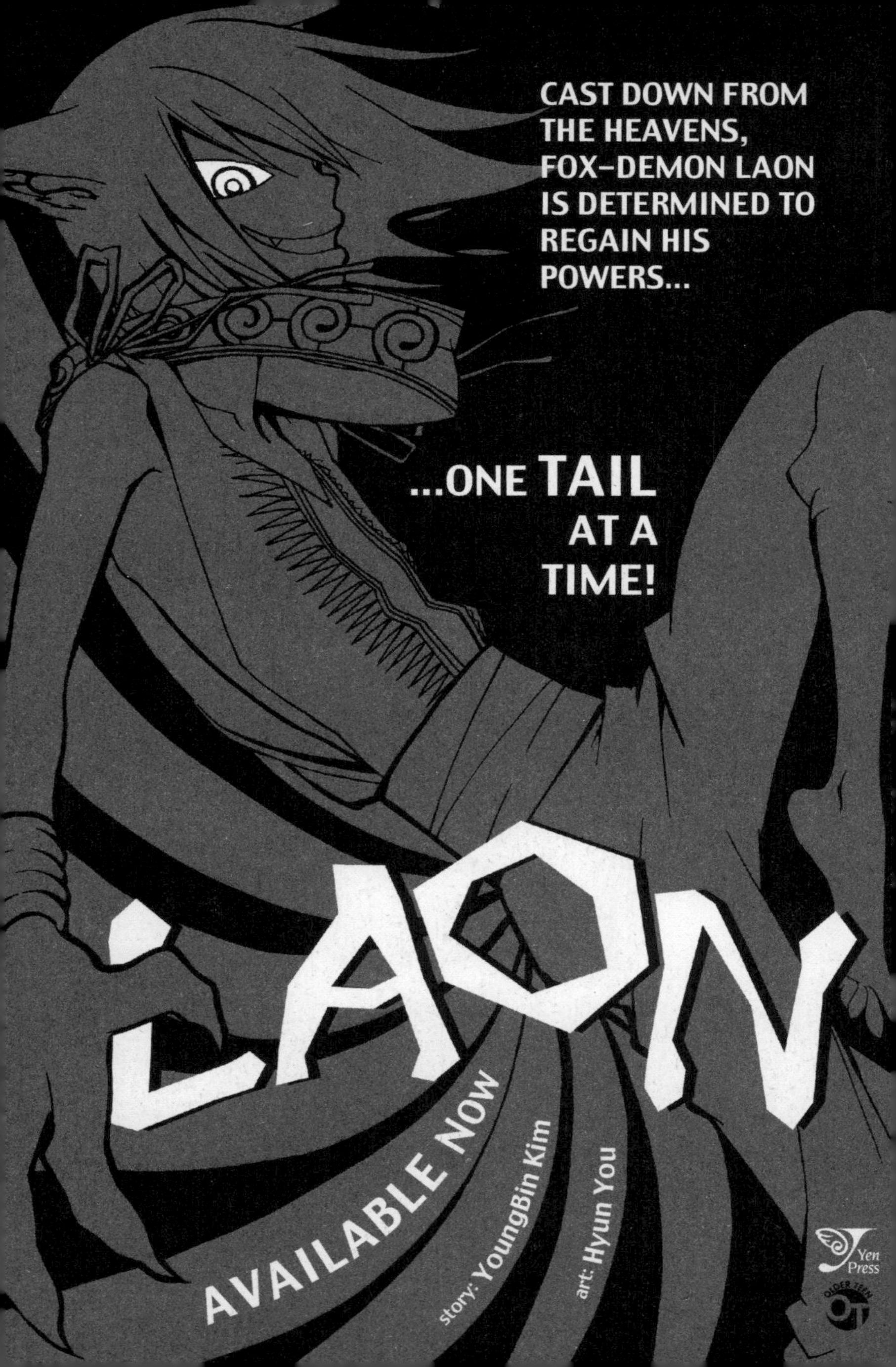
CAST DOWN FROM THE HEAVENS, FOX-DEMON LAON IS DETERMINED TO REGAIN HIS POWERS...
...ONE TAIL AT A TIME!
LAON
AVAILABLE NOW
story: YoungBin Kim
art: Hyun You
Yen Press
OLDER TEEN
OT

DEALING WITH THE DEAD IS EVEN WORSE THAN DEALING WITH THE DEVIL!

ZOMBIE-LOAN

BY PEACH-PIT

JACK FROST ⑤

JINHO KO

Translation: JiEun Park
English Adaptation: Arthur Dela Cruz

Lettering: Jose Macasocol, Jr.

Jack Frost Vol. 5 © 2009 JinHo Ko. All rights reserved. First published in Korea in 2009 by Haksan Publishing Co., Ltd. English translation rights in U.S.A., Canada, UK, and Republic of Ireland arranged with Haksan Publishing Co., Ltd.

English translation © 2011 Hachette Book Group, Inc.

Yen Press
Hachette Book Group
237 Park Avenue, New York, NY 10017

www.HachetteBookGroup.com
www.YenPress.com

Yen Press is an imprint of Hachette Book Group, Inc.
The Yen Press name and logo are trademarks of Hachette Book Group, Inc.

First Yen Press Edition: April 2011

ISBN: 978-0-316-12675-5

10 9 8 7 6 5 4 3 2 1

BVG

Printed in the United States of America